PRAISE FOR *CULTURE A*
IN FINANCIAL SERVIC

'A highly useful travelogue written by acclaimed experts in an easy-going manner that nevertheless serves to deepen awareness and understanding. After a survey of concepts and how conduct regulation is evolving, *Culture Audit in Financial Services* opens a window on using behavioural science to frame "better questions" and introduces straightforwardly the benefits of some advanced technology. These elements weave together to explain where thought leadership has been and points to areas for further exploration including purpose, individual character development and the excitement that awaits firms that are not quite prepared for their first earnest discussion of culture with a regulator.'
Ted MacDonald, Technical Specialist, Wholesale Banking Supervision, UK Financial Conduct Authority

'Regulators have recognized that workplace culture is vital to any financial firm giving the best of itself to its customers and other stakeholders. This can only occur in a climate in which every employee feels safe to ask better questions, to challenge assumptions and to explore possibilities. I have been very encouraged to see the term "psychological safety" widely taken up by the world's financial conduct regulators and it's great to see this book's expert team urging firms, in clear terms, to take the message to heart. A firm that puts these ideas into practice may become the most socially beneficial version of itself, securing its social license to operate to the benefit of all stakeholders.'
Professor Amy Edmondson, Harvard Business School and author of *The Fearless Organization*

'Roger Miles has brought together a stellar group of experts in conduct risk and fashioned a unique resource for the financial services industry and beyond. The authors and Dr Miles himself have been there, done that and have the T-shirt when it comes to conduct risk management. Oozing with practical wisdom, this book brings concepts from psychology and behavioural science to a financial services audience, to help address the seemingly intractable challenge of workplace misconduct. Culture change programmes fail at least as often as they succeed, but *Culture Audit in Financial Services* contains many insights that will enhance the chances of success.

'As a business school professor teaching post-experience, post-graduate programmes, I'm often looking for material that is evidence-based but accessible; that avoids bland motherhood statements and excites interests; that presents solutions that are seen as feasible and not utopian. This book has all those qualities and I expect it will help the industry chart a new course, consistent with its recent aspirations. A must-have for financial services leaders and regulators, and those who aspire to such roles.'
Elizabeth Sheedy, Professor of Risk Governance, Macquarie University

'*Culture Audit in Financial Services* fills a welcome gap between procedural "how to" manuals, which can be dull and conceptually empty, and academic research, which is often brilliant but difficult to translate into real organizational programmes and initiatives. This book takes many of the best ideas out there from behavioural science, then sets them within a framework with action points, making it genuinely useful for practitioners. The lively writing and provocative examples really help overcome the difficulty of making culture a practical consideration for companies without losing important nuances. This work deserves to make a big positive impact.'
Alison Taylor, Executive Director, Ethical Systems and Professor, NYU Stern School of Business

'Just what the finance industry wants, and more importantly, what it needs. A definitive "how to" guide to understanding your firm's culture, its strengths and weaknesses and, most importantly, how to systematically and thoroughly set about improving it throughout your workforce and firm. It is packed with helpful real-life anecdotes from finance experts, academics' and regulators' perspectives, helpful history, insightful psychology and pithy illustrations of key points. A clear-sighted, up-to-the-minute view on progress made and what's left to do. This will long be seen as the magnum opus on this critical topic – and it is compelling reading at that. If the industry follows even half of the good advice here it will be in a much better place a few years from now.'
Sean Carney, COO/CFO, Telemos Capital

'What a timely book! Plenty here to interest financial services regulation practitioners. It seems extraordinary that we are still talking about culture, more than 12 years after the global financial crisis exposed such huge problems in financial institutions. With great clarity, the authors have explained why these problems persist and if this book can help to improve culture then they've done a fine job.

'*Culture Audit in Financial Services* contains a wealth of knowledge including a topical chapter on the behavioural science techniques that supervisors have adapted in recent years. A vast amount of research and analysis from leading industry thinkers has clearly gone on behind the scenes to enlighten the reader, yet the authors keep the tone straight-talking, lucidly unpacking complex and technical topics without compromising the quality of the analysis. For those whose interest is piqued, a list of further reading is provided in the appendix and there's a properly helpful glossary. *Culture Audit* is very likely to achieve its aim of starting a wider conversation about conduct and culture across the regulated financial sector and beyond.'
Alexander Robson, Managing Editor, Thomson Reuters Regulatory Intelligence

'I really like the multiple author approach, and what a list of co-authors! There's huge value in just being able to read insights from this remarkable group of people all in one place. Their different perspectives throughout, and their evident sense of fun, make *Culture Audit in Financial Services* engaging and thought-provoking. A set of "Interlude" stories also brings the theory to life, such as the hugely enjoyable account of how a central bank supervisor went on to "rebrand" an investment bank's compliance department as behaviour-aware – a mindset shift that would benefit many firms.

'*Culture Audit*'s view of the genesis of conduct regulation, and robust predictions for its future, ground our understanding of why it is now so vital for firms to focus on culture and behaviour. The book is always engaging – as if the reader is enjoying a chat with the authors – and thankfully avoids getting bogged down in regulatory small print. With so much still to be done to improve financial sector culture, this is a book which really will spark timely conversations in firms: around purpose, psychological safety, diversity and inclusion. These are vital foundations for any firm to set out, then act on to start a lasting culture change. *Culture Audit* jump-starts these conversations in a friendly, understandable way. It's a great addition to the discourse.'
Olivia Fahy, Head of Culture, TCC Group and Culture Team Lead, Supervision, UK Financial Conduct Authority 2016–21

'This masterful book gives the reader an easy lens to get familiar with the latest thought and regulatory agenda for supervising financial firms' conduct and culture.

'Following the global financial crash and numerous scandals such as LIBOR rigging and mis-selling, we have seen a shift from a consumer protection regime based on disclosure towards a new focus on the root cause of misconduct: firms' culture. *Culture Audit in Financial Services* answers many questions that will be on the minds of firms' executives and compliance professionals, as well as regulators. Uniquely, this book addresses head-on the controversial topic of how people opt for different roles at different career stages, moving between regulatory agencies and commercial roles. This brings a fresh perspective so we can reflect in a new way on how regulators and firms interact.

'A summary condensed from years of research, empirical experience, hundreds of real life talks and sharing by firms' executives, this book is a joy to read for its clear display of theory and its practical action points. Dr Miles is a fascinating guide as he unlocks a door to the secrets of human minds, group dynamics and applying behavioural science to financial services. With an impressive group of colleagues, he addresses the big questions: What is culture and conduct? Why do regulators care about culture and conduct, as opposed to codified laws and regulations? And more importantly: What shall we (the firms) do in response to the call? Arguing for a clear difference between conventional audit and culture assessment, it rightly also questions even whether the term *culture audit* is broad enough to yield the "better questions" that firms now need to ask themselves.'

Davis Tsui, JD, CPA, Insurance Conduct Supervisor, Hong Kong Insurance Authority and former Treasury Markets Association Secretariat, Hong Kong Monetary Authority

'There's something about the variety of expert content, the demonstration of behavioural science in action, and the evident humour peppered throughout, that makes this book a page-turner. *Culture Audit in Financial Services* is a terrific book and really valuable for the industry, locally and internationally. At a practical level the layout is accessible and simple, while challenging the reader to engage. Themes and concepts, highlighted at the start of each chapter, alert us to what lies ahead. The case studies help everyone to put learnings into context.

'At the heart of this book is the complexity and contradiction of what it means to be human. It is the authors' generosity that both inculcates a sense of responsibility in the reader and also opens up a wealth of education and experience which will help our industry to help itself. Self-regulation has an important part to play but as the book underlines, values drive from the bottom up as well as the top down; improvement isn't just about "tone at the top". To develop the virtuous circle needed, firms must define purpose and culture, measure and monitor them, to prevent systemic hijacking of their good intentions and the good choices they want to make.

'Consistent with what we're advocating, *Culture Audit* urges all firms' staff to "tell the story" of their experiences without fear of adverse consequence. We are now in an environment where employees join organizations not for just what they do but how they do it. A range of initiatives including culture assessments and ethical awareness through "bankers' oath" programmes are recalibrating the sector's moral compass. Decision-making is always buffeted by behavioural biases and knowing how to mitigate these is key. The tricky part is engendering the desire to mitigate. *Culture Audit* gently but firmly instils this, sparking the intrinsic motivation that firms need to achieve it.'
Cris Parker, Head of The Ethics Alliance, The Ethics Centre and Director, The Banking and Finance Oath

'An all-round excellent reading experience: crisply written, with sharp graphics and pithy fact boxes. *Culture Audit in Financial Services* is packed with clear, current and bright insight – no less than we'd expect from the world-leading practitioner experts behind it. Even more impressively, they address it all in a way that's engaging, easily readable and (who'd have expected this?) frequently entertaining. Every regulated finance professional with any leadership responsibilities should read this book.'
Robert Ellison, Co-Founder, Finance Unlocked

'I have found myself dipping into *Culture Audit in Financial Services* regularly, whenever specific culture and conduct issues have surfaced in the news and markets – which now seems to be every day. This book is a friendly source of help in better understanding core concepts such as how "Thinking, Fast and Slow" applies to conduct reporting and it has nudged me to revisit key original research sources. Part of what makes *Culture Audit* such a good read is its distinctive look at both sides of the fence, asking how regulators themselves seek to frame the conduct challenges that they ask firms to address.

'Answering public concern for financial service providers to give a better account of themselves, this book helps practitioners to understand how to focus efforts and resources to better engage with regulatory and public scrutiny. It also makes bravura use of the vast skillset of its expert contributors while maintaining a welcome underlying sense of humour. They unwrap

complex academic insights, then slot these smoothly into practical approaches to getting a better grip on culture. The reader is left with a clear and holistic view of what culture and conduct really mean for day-to-day working, adding business value and resilience for any financial services firm.'
Simon Collins, Managing Director, Financial Services Advisory, Konexo UK–Eversheds Sutherland

'It isn't very often that I would recommend to my book club what appears from the title to be an academic read – but this one breaks the mould. The team of writers has delivered an insightful and practical book that manages to be both strategic and operational as needed, as well as often letting the reader pause to reflect and consider how this all supports their own personal development. The "story" interludes bring the chapters together in that really useful, involving way that storytelling has, by leading the reader towards understanding and applying the concepts in real life. A thoroughly worthwhile read.'
Ann McFadyen, Director, UK Finance

'If you're a senior manager or board member, don't be surprised if a regulator asks in your next regulatory interview whether you've read this book. Its authors have finally put to rest the myth that culture and conduct are too challenging to assess or audit.

'In fact, for anyone looking for a go-to read on culture and conduct, you've found it! This is the A–Z guide to how your leadership team can deliver better customer outcomes and greater profits, all while once and for all demonstrating to the regulator how your firm robustly identifies and rates culture and conduct.'
Philip Allen, Head of Learning, PIMFA

'A fascinating and gripping read through an oft-quoted subject that for many had always felt nebulous. Packed with information and insights, it's a real must-read for anyone in financial services who wants to get their head around culture, cultural change and purpose in a practical way. What I love about projects Roger Miles is involved in is their great readability and insightful "aha moment" tips that make such a substantial difference. It's all about knowing where to tap the widget; this marvellous collection of authors certainly understands and clarifies the subject better than I have seen previously elsewhere. I dare you to read this book and then say you found no important practical, business-changing takeaways that you could start using tomorrow.'

Judy Delaforce, Chief Executive, BP&E Global Ltd and formerly UK Financial Services Authority

'So many books have only one idea; this one has many from Roger Miles and his co-authors. It's a broadly useful book with all kinds of lessons for all kinds of practitioners. As well as efficiently tapping into key high-level research findings, readers will discover how in practice to match culture and conduct principles with the needs of their organization's stakeholders – including regulators, of course. The UK and international context is thoroughly current and well evidenced with real life examples, a full glossary and plentiful references – everything you need is in one place. A thoroughly worthwhile read!'

Bryan Foss, serial iNED, Council member, Financial Reporting Council and Co-Founder, The Risk Coalition

'An enjoyably readable and informative guide to how the scrutiny of culture in financial services is evolving, with clear links between the scholarly and the practical, thanks to an impressive array of expert but plain-speaking authors. Making "better culture", fast, is becoming not only a regulatory but also a commercial imperative. *Culture Audit in Financial Services* will become the go-to playbook for how to analyse what actually happens in your firm, then to use what actually works to measure and improve its culture. Surely a must-read, not just for the whole C-suite but for anyone in financial services involved in improving culture – and isn't that everyone?'

Russell Hornsby-Clifton, private bank CEO, barrister and former UK regulator

'Financial services boards: ignore this book at your peril. I started reading *Culture Audit in Financial Services* and quickly found myself engrossed in it. It is an honest, in-depth and pragmatic tour of insights by serious experts who wear their learning lightly, much to the reader's benefit. Though there is deeply informed thinking, the book affably welcomes newcomers to the table so that all can reflect on why and how firms must develop "cultural capital". This is not just to meet increased regulatory oversight but, more importantly, the new social contract.

'Dr Miles and a hugely respected expert team provide a wonderfully comprehensive and high-level primer. (Given the quality of the authors, their reading list of personal favourites at the end is to die for!) The results gives the industry a powerful jolt to "stir the pot", to shift the dial on culture and conduct. Throughout the book, there is plenty of material for conduct and other senior managers to take on board, to work with the tools they find most useful.

'Despite all the evidence that firms need to raise the bar – and how their businesses will benefit from this – until now, too many senior managers have tiptoed around culture: they still don't "get it", or see it as a hassle or an abstraction. Now that we have *Culture Audit* to join the dots clearly between human factors and risk governance, more senior executives should be persuaded to start giving culture the attention it deserves.'
Peter Neville Lewis CMIRM, Director, The Risk Coalition

'Congratulations to Roger Miles and such a distinguished team; this guidebook is a genuine breakthrough. As well as being outstandingly well researched, and remarkably timely, it is also an enjoyable and fascinating read – a great "picker-upper" that rewards us with something thoughtful on each fresh visit. *Culture Audit in Financial Services* helpfully distils the complexities of behavioural and cognitive science into an easy-to-understand framework for auditing, analysing and understanding the key human and systemic drivers that underlie errant or maladaptive cultures in financial services. The learning, analytical techniques and case examples suggest a series of approaches and tools for practical reporting on culture.

'Any firm that is serious about engendering responsive operational change – whether this is subtle or a complete paradigm shift – will need to grapple with how to make it happen in practice. This book addresses the "how to" factor candidly and with a smile. It becomes clear how every organization can benefit from starting a conversation around attitudes to reputational risk and how employees and stakeholders respond to change – vitally important in the financial sector where change is highly dynamic and where the environment at large delivers shock impacts in many forms.

'Beyond finance, this guidebook is truly universal in its structure, opening up a friendly conversation with a wider audience: anyone who is looking to comprehend, set in context, and shape behaviour – whether in dealings with a regulator or with their peers in a sector's regulated community.'
Chris Stears, Solicitor and Founding Director, CCP Research (Cambridge University and City University)

'An excellent resource for anyone looking to understand culture assessment, *Culture Audit in Financial Services* provides good practical advice and an

evidence-based approach to reporting on culture. While it focuses on financial services (a heavily regulated sector context), directors and business professionals in many sectors can usefully apply these insights. With case studies and practical tools, this is a must-read to deepen your knowledge of the practice of culture audit and the business value gained by "asking better questions".'
Jean-Philippe Perraud, Director, NEDonBoard and Chair, Institute of Board Members

'Good governance is the art of constructing a well-functioning system from those imperfect components we call "people". Where in the past analysis has focused on business models and operating models, it's clear we must now look to the third defining aspect of any organization: its culture. A firm's culture is seen in how its people behave; the financial industry's history of bad behaviour now makes its management of culture a matter of intense regulatory focus. However, it is still difficult to find rigorous and actionable advice to improve a firm's poor culture.

'What a pleasant surprise and an education, then, to read *Culture Audit in Financial Services* – a likeable but also technically sharp analysis of financial industry culture from the viewpoint of an accomplished analyst of human risk. In conversations with a group of renowned practitioners and conduct regulators, Dr Roger Miles guides us gently through just what we need to know about the psychology, social science (and even neurophysics) of how a firm's culture emerges, grounding it all with absorbing real-world examples, anecdotes and case notes on how to make things better. I highly recommend this book to anyone in the financial sector who is looking for an accessible text that will help them raise their governance skills to the next level.'
Paul Kennedy PhD, Chief Risk Officer, international investment bank and Honorary Fellow, Macquarie University

'I love this book – many sections are nothing less than compelling reading – addressing a very interesting topic that reaches well beyond the financial services sector. *Culture Audit in Financial Services* deserves to be on every change leader's bookshelf, and not just those in financial firms whose backdrop and specific cultural challenges it focuses on. This book includes compelling models, case studies, key questions and insights that every leader, irrespective of where they operate, should consider moving forward. The pandemic has changed and will continue to change the way that every organization operates, sharply increasing the importance of considering its

culture and its links to those associated behaviours that are at the heart of how businesses operate. Calling in a pragmatic way for organizational development and change, *Culture Audit* provides fresh perspectives about how to make those vital changes stick in the future.'
Dave Millner, Author and Founder and Consulting Partner, @HRCurator

'I am absolutely a fan of this book! It's a tour-de-force on how to embed the right company culture in a way that reduces conduct risk and increases organizational resilience. Its practical approaches and tools will be of great use for many regulated firms as well as FinTechs as they increasingly deploy big data, artificial intelligence and deep learning; as well as Big Tech companies. Roger Miles has assembled an international co-author panel of renowned behavioural science practitioners and regulatory thought leaders. The result is a fantastic best practice guide and go-to resource that's my favourite new book on the topic. *Culture Audit in Financial Services* is a must-read for anyone active in managing conduct risk, cultural change or regulatory engagement.'
Markus Krebsz, challenger bank iNED, United Nations Risk Management Expert Group, Co-Founder, Citizen Shareholders and Chair, CISI FinTech Forum

'Regardless of firm size, offering financial services is a complex and people-intensive business – and getting teams aligned on "what good looks like" is no mean feat. In a sector that's increasingly digital yet with divergent rule sets, the ability to manage compliance expectations is fast becoming the critical factor that marks senior managers for success in offering financial products and services across borders. New tooling can help, but firms need more than "just technology" to get established: competitive success is about a firm's people being aligned and duly responsive to local culture and pressures for good conduct and accountability. This means all staff maintaining high situational awareness, with a keen focus on assessing their own firm's culture and how it comes across.

'For anyone nervous about all of that, here comes a book jam-packed with practical insight from Roger Miles and his truly impressive group. "Thought leaders" is a much-overused term but this team is the real deal, giving us the essence of what it takes to get culture right and to demonstrate robustly to external (and internal) stakeholders that you've done so. *Culture Audit in Financial Services* is a must-have on any financial practitioner's bookshelf for the next three to five years ahead, as the answer to "what's your culture?" becomes a regular part of every provider's report card.'
PJ Di Giammarino, CEO, JWG Group and Member, ISO (International Organization for Standardization)

'This is a thoughtful yet straight-talking work that will prove invaluable to any firm that makes good use of it. Noting how pandemic has changed the frame of the debate, Roger Miles and colleagues set out a clear case for improving business culture. With simple examples, they show how to identify and assess key human behavioural factors that influence both the working environment and business decision-making processes. Using case studies consistently to illustrate how to apply the learning in practice, they build the reader's understanding of the role of culture across all levels of a business.

'Some people will buy this book as a "how to" guide on dealing with the regulator, which it certainly covers. Many more, hopefully, will also use it to go deeper: Dr Miles talks about a "wider purpose" as a firm learns to see itself in the greater context of society, appreciating the moral and ethical concerns of a new generation, upon whose view of "acceptable and expected behaviour" every firm's future success depends.'
Jon Dear, Head of Learning, Finance and Leasing Association

'An impressive work, *Culture Audit in Financial Services* provides a compelling insight into the importance of behavioural science and people analytics to measuring organizational culture. It focuses on the practical aspect of culture audit using clear frameworks, methodologies, risk analysis, evolution path and, critically, how to deliver the exceptional actionable business insights critical for a rapidly changing world.'
David Green, Managing Partner, Insight222 and co-author of *Excellence in People Analytics*

Culture Audit in Financial Services

Reporting on behaviour to conduct regulators

Roger Miles

KoganPage

First published in Great Britain and the United States in 2021 by Kogan Page Limited

2nd Floor, 45 Gee Street
London
EC1V 3RS
United Kingdom
www.koganpage.com

122 W 27th St, 10th Floor
New York, NY 10001
USA

4737/23 Ansari Road
Daryaganj
New Delhi 110002
India

Kogan Page books are printed on paper from sustainable forests.

ISBNs

Hardback   978 1 78966 777 6
Paperback   978 1 78966 775 2
Ebook   978 1 78966 776 9

British Library Cataloguing-in-Publication Data

A CIP record for this book is available from the British Library.

Library of Congress Cataloging-in-Publication Data

Names: Miles, Roger (Roger T.), author.
Title: Culture audit in financial services : reporting on behaviour to
   conduct regulators / Roger Miles.
Description: New York, NY : Kogan Page, 2021. | Includes bibliographical
   references and index.
Identifiers: LCCN 2021010403 (print) | LCCN 2021010404 (ebook) | ISBN
   9781789667752 (paperback) | ISBN 9781789667776 (hardback) | ISBN
   9781789667769 (ebook)
Subjects: LCSH: Financial services industry. | Corporate culture–Auditing.
   | Organizational behavior–Auditing. | Employee attitude surveys.
Classification: LCC HG173 .M6248 2021 (print) | LCC HG173 (ebook) | DDC
   332.1068/3–dc23
LC record available at https://lccn.loc.gov/2021010403
LC ebook record available at https://lccn.loc.gov/2021010404

Typeset by Integra Software Services, Pondicherry
Print production managed by Jellyfish
Printed and bound by CPI Group (UK) Ltd, Croydon, CR0 4YY

for Deirdra

CONTENTS

03 The house is on fire: How regulators' own research has pointed to 'culture reset' 34

Cosette Reczek

04 What's the big idea? (1): How conduct regulators use behavioural science 58

Roger Miles

INTERLUDE 1

From poacher to gamekeeper to poacher… to scientist: A supervisor's tale 85

Christian Hunt

05 What's the big idea? (2): Regulators' challenge to firms: framing 'purposeful culture' 99

Cosette Reczek and Roger Miles

06 A 'behaviour-at-risk' agenda emerges: Questioning purpose, lost trust and cultural coercion 130

Stephen J Scott, Roger Miles and Mirea Raaijmakers

07 The new mindset and language of culture: Assessing financial and non-financial conduct 154

Hani Nabeel and Roger Miles

INTERLUDE 3

A sector-wide group seeks culture 'tells': (Observing indications of good and poor conduct) 305

Julie Ampadu

13 Putting respected research tools to work, example 1: Tools for cultural transformation: Barrett Analytics 315

Ruth Steinholtz

ABOUT THE AUTHORS

Roger Miles researches behavioural risk, regulatory design, and why control systems fail, counselling boards on risk governance, management of uncertainty and human risk factors. He delivers bespoke small-group risk workshops for leaders in business, government, NGOs, professional firms and industry bodies.

He began his business career as a (frankly not very good) auditor with a London-headquartered Big Four accounting firm. He found his business feet as a partner in a global investor relations consultancy, advising major US and EU public companies on market events and value protection. He was then invited to lead financial sector dialogues with Westminster and Brussels, later to advise HM Government on risk communications. Mid-career, he escaped all that to complete an observational research PhD on banks' rule-gaming of capital controls, in which he predicted the coming of 'the behavioural approach to regulation' as a remedy for this. After the global financial crisis in 2008, the arrival of the Conduct control regime vindicated his research prediction, leading to various calls to re-engage with the City.

Roger leads teaching faculties for financial sector Conduct and Culture Academies in the UK, EU and Asia-Pacific. He is Conduct lead for the Finance Unlocked global learning series and a visiting lecturer on risk perception and communication at the Universities of London (Imperial College and Cass Business School), Cambridge, and UK Defence Academy where he has also been an examiner for MBA and MSc (Risk) courses. He co-edits the encyclopaedia of psychological terms for the LSE's annual *Behavioral Economics Guide* and is a long-term contributing editor at Thomson Reuters Regulatory Intelligence. His serial commentaries on risk culture and his research on behaviour in financial-sector boardrooms are published by Reuters, Risk Books, the *Financial Times*, Berkeley Research, and Board Matters (BP&E Global). Also published by Kogan Page is his popular handbook *Conduct Risk Management: A behavioural approach*.

Christopher Hodges is Professor of Justice Systems and Head of the Swiss Re Research Programme on Civil Justice Systems at the Centre for Socio-Legal Studies, Oxford; a Supernumerary Fellow of Wolfson College, Oxford; and a

Fellow of the European Law Institute. He is co-founder of the International Network for Delivery of Regulation (INDR) and advises governments, regulators and businesses on regulation and dispute resolution systems across the globe. He has been Erasmus Professor of the Fundamentals of Private Law at Erasmus University, Rotterdam and has held visiting Chairs at the China University of Political Science and Law, Beijing, Leuven University and ANU Canberra. He has chaired committees in the pharmaceutical, pharmacy, medical device, and property sectors. Before becoming an academic, he spent 25 years as a corporate lawyer based in the City of London.

Recent books include *Regulatory Delivery* (with Graham Russell, 2019); *Delivering Dispute Resolution: A Holistic Review of Models in England & Wales* (2019); *Ethical Business Practice and Regulation* (with Ruth Steinholtz); *Law and Corporate Behaviour* (2015); *Redress Schemes for Personal Injuries* (with Sonia Macleod, 2017); *Delivering Collective Redress: New technologies* (with Stefan Voet, 2018); *Consumer ADR in Europe* (with Iris Benöhr and Naomi Creutzfeldt, 2012) and *The Costs and Funding of Litigation* (with Stefan Vogenauer and Magdalena Tulibacka, 2010).

Julie Ampadu is an experienced compliance practitioner and leads the Working Group on Culture for the Association of Professional Compliance Consultants (APCC). She is owner/director of Chameleon Compliance Ltd and Business Chameleon Ltd, offering regulatory compliance support, regulatory compliance training and executive coaching for senior managers of firms authorized and regulated by the FCA, or for those seeking authorization.

She is Deputy Chair of the APCC, a former regional Chair of the Personal Finance Society and Committee member for the Chartered Insurance Institute. Julie has worked with an extensive range of clients, from sole traders to high street banks, in a wide variety of UK Financial Conduct Authority (FCA) regulatory areas and is regularly invited as an expert contributor to conferences and publications throughout the UK.

Julie's focus is supporting firms not only to understand FCA rules, but to recognize that adhering to FCA rules does not necessarily make an authorized firm compliant. Examining culture and behaviours throughout the business, she supports firms to question their own mindset of what it means to be an authorized and regulated firm in the UK today. On this basis, beyond traditional compliance support her expertise is focused on governance, culture, diversity and inclusion, as well as training and competence and the personal development of senior managers.

Elizabeth Arzadon is a psychologist and Managing Director of Kiel Advisory Group. She is a recognized global expert on the topic of cultural risk, pioneering the use of behavioural science in the auditing of culture and its impact on conduct, governance and risk management outcomes within the financial sector.

Elizabeth first started examining culture as a driver of performance in 2000 as an organizational specialist at McKinsey & Company. Following the global financial crisis in 2008, she turned her attention (along with many others) to risk and conduct. Working in corporate and advisory roles, she set her sights on solving a challenge faced by many internal audit functions: how to assess culture in an evidence-based way. Leading behavioural risk audit programmes in a range of global banks, Elizabeth developed tangible, real-world insight into the systemic drivers of behaviour within the financial sector.

This systemic lens led Elizabeth into the world of regulation. As a special adviser to the Australian Prudential Regulatory Authority (APRA) she developed and piloted the regulator's approach to evaluating culture, devising a new methodology for supervisory reviews of risk culture, and enhanced the agency's capability on the issue of culture. She worked closely with peer regulators around the world, taking a key role in drafting global regulation forum the Financial Stability Board's institutional toolkit for mitigating cultural drivers of misconduct. During this period she was also a leading member of the prudential inquiry into the Commonwealth Bank of Australia.

Elizabeth now aims to strengthen cultural drivers of sustainable performance by working across the entire system, with institutions, regulators, boards and professional bodies globally. In particular, her firm is passionate about bringing behavioural science and transparency to the challenge of culture and its impact on corporate behaviour.

Christian Hunt is the founder of Human Risk, a training and consulting firm that specializes in 'bringing behavioural science to ethics and compliance'. He works with companies and individuals to design and implement compliance programmes that are more effective as a result of being designed to operate with, rather than against, the grain of human thinking.

He began his career in the business consulting division of Arthur Andersen, qualifying as a Chartered Accountant while working on projects ranging from advising the UK gas regulator on pre-payment tariffs (the first of many forays into regulation) to the matching of dormant accounts in Swiss banks with Holocaust victims.

A move into investment banking led to him being asked to run the newly established Office of the Chairman of Deutsche Bank, London. A two-year secondment at the UK takeover regulator ended just as the 2008 global financial crisis was starting. It was hardly the best timing for a return to frontline banking, so he joined a family office with a focus on private equity and hedge funds.

What followed was a career-defining decision that sowed the seeds for Human Risk, which is explored in a case example on pages 85–97 of this book. That decision was to take up an invitation to lead supervision at one of the newly formed financial services regulators, before – perhaps inevitably – crossing the divide to become a compliance officer.

He is a regular writer, presenter and producer of online Human Risk-related content.

Hani Nabeel is the Chief Behavioural Scientist at iPsychTec, a world-leading people analytics and behavioural science company. He is the architect and founder of CultureScope, an award-winning and groundbreaking behavioural analytics platform for scientifically measuring and embedding an organization's desired culture using predictive analytics and actionable insights. His work combines the best elements of scientific and applied research with a focus on organizational culture by providing groundbreaking diagnostics, delivering advanced predictive analytics and producing actionable business insights to help organizations achieve sustainable competitive advantage. In 2017, CultureScope won the Wharton People Analytics Award, the only non-US company to ever achieve this. Hani recently deployed behavioural analytics as the first line of defence against financial crime for a global bank across 71 countries.

Hani has over 20 years of experience delivering leadership and talent management consulting services as well as quantitative behavioural research. Hani also has an MSc in Occupational Psychology, an MSc in Advanced Research Methods, a BSc in Physics and holds a commercial pilot licence.

He is a regular guest at organizational culture and data analytics events such as the Wharton and Tucana People Analytics conferences. Hani is also a frequent contributor to the UK Finance Academy and Forums and has written articles on culture for the *Business Times, Executive Grapevine, Disrupt HR, HR Director* and *HR Zone.* Hani is a lecturer and a talent development consultant for a number of corporate universities.

Mirea Raaijmakers is Global Head of Behavioural Risk Management at ING and previously led the Dutch central bank (DNB)'s supervision programme for Governance, Behaviour and Culture. At DNB she was the main architect of a national and subsequently global initiative to bring financial regulation into the 'behavioural era', as lead author of the hugely influential guidance for regulators, *Supervision of Behaviour and Culture: Foundations, practice and future developments* (2015).

She was the first psychologist ever appointed by a central bank to use her specific skillset in supervision. Globally, DNB's *Supervision of Behaviour and Culture* is perhaps the most highly regarded post-financial crisis innovation in supervision. Next to the design and development of this new type of supervision, Mirea has always been in the lead of executing behaviour and culture inspections; she understands from the inside why and how this innovation works.

Prior to DNB she worked as an organizational consultant at consultancy firms as well as the Dutch Tax and Customs Administration.

Mirea's work is deeply grounded in observational understanding and influencing the behaviour of individuals, groups and organizations, especially during complex and large-scale changes. An experienced leader, both at the highest levels in the banking industry and as a thought leader in behaviour and culture supervision, she continues to run sector-level initiatives for large-scale change, organizational development, leadership development, and behavioural change.

A graduate of Harvard Business School, Mirea also holds an MSc in Psychology and PhD in Behavioural Science from the University of Groningen.

Cosette Reczek has worked in banking for over 25 years in capital markets, divisional and Group roles at J.P. Morgan, Citibank, Deutsche Bank, RBS, PWC, Barclays, and HSBC.

At HSBC, she facilitated Group-wide evolution of the scheme of delegation and governance committee best practices. She was the inaugural Group Head of Organization Design & Human Capital Analytics and was accountable for forming and leading the Senior Manager & Certification Regime (SM&CR) management office, working with boards and staff to implement conduct, certification and senior manager requirements and guidelines.

In 2016 Cosette founded Permuto Consulting to advise on board effectiveness, organizational design, and culture and conduct including training and SM&CR.

In 2018 she was appointed Chief Executive Officer of Conduct Academy, which delivers culture and conduct training for boards, executive committees and front-office supervisors. Cosette now maintains a portfolio career focused on governance, culture, conduct, and risk management.

Stephen J Scott is Founder and CEO at Starling, a globally recognized pioneer in the RegTech space. Starling's Predictive Behavioral Analytics platform allows firms to measure and mitigate culture- and conduct-related risks, and to identify opportunities for performance improvement across business lines and functions.

Stephen spent a 25-year career in risk management and corporate intelligence, serving clients when they were: entering new markets, ventures, or commercial relationships; conducting pre-investment due diligence or testing an investment thesis; carrying out investigations into fraud or corruption; pursuing redress through litigation, arbitration, or government inquiry; and when seeking to advance their interests before government and regulatory agencies.

He has led successful investigative inquiries in over 50 countries, and has lived and worked in New York, Washington, London, Frankfurt, Madrid and Shanghai.

Stephen holds degrees from Cornell University, the London School of Economics, the Columbia Graduate School of Business and the London Business School.

Ruth Steinholtz assists, cajoles and supports organizations creating effective ethical cultures based on values and the principles of behavioural science. She founded AretéWork in 2011 for this purpose. She uses the Barrett cultural values assessment analytics whenever possible to provide management with a realistic view of their culture(s) to enable them to use resources wisely and to the best effect.

A corporate lawyer in her first career, Ruth was General Counsel and head of Ethics and Compliance at petrochemical company Borealis AG before deciding to devote herself to values-based ethics. Her career has led her from San Francisco to Italy, Egypt, Spain, Denmark and Austria and despite her accent, London has long been her home. At Borealis she created the concept of ethics ambassadors: networks of employees who assist in nurturing values, ethical decision-making and other aspects of an organization's ethics and compliance infrastructure. Ruth's mission is to fight corruption by changing attitudes and practices relating to regulation and compliance.

Ruth is co-author with Professor Christopher Hodges of *Ethical Business Practice and Regulation: A behavioural and values-based approach to compliance and enforcement.* Her other publications include the Institute of Business Ethics' *Good Practice Guides to Ethics Ambassadors* (2010) and *Performance Management for an Ethical Culture* (2014). She is a member of the UNODC E4J panel of experts on Ethics and Integrity and advisor to the Anti-Corruption panel. Ruth is a certified Barrett Values Analytics consultant, a trained mediator and has an Advanced Practitioner Diploma in Executive Coaching from the UK Academy of Executive Coaching. She is a frequent speaker globally on topics related to values and ethics.

Rachel Wolcott is Senior Editor, risk and compliance for Thomson Reuters Regulatory Intelligence. With unequalled high-level direct contacts with the world's investment banking officials, investors, regulators, consultants and technical innovators, she has more than 20 years' experience covering banking and financial markets in New York and London, writing on everything from private banking and capital markets to derivatives, cybercrime, FinTech and RegTech.

Rachel's current role follows a series of distinguished editorial positions, as former European Editor of *Risk Magazine*, at *Euromoney* magazine and at *Institutional Investor*. In these roles she had a front-row seat to some of the worst banking misconduct perpetrated in the name of risk management and financial engineering.

She is a Master's graduate of New York University and holds a Bachelor of the Arts degree from Reed College in Portland, Oregon.

FOREWORD

Culture and conduct need to be taken seriously, as they are critical to successful financial firms and resilient financial systems, and hence to the success of effective regulatory systems. But we need to apply the knowledge we have properly and convert it into effective action.

Finance as a sector is a late arrival to the Conduct and Culture debate but it has spread quickly. Many other businesses, professions and regulatory systems have understood the ideas and invested greater effort in applying them. There are two major drivers to this profound change and why it has transformed some sectors more quickly than others. The first is whether the findings of behavioural science have been heard and applied. Some of the findings are challenging since they point to changes that may be difficult to make or might be seen as likely to hurt. Second, the basic desire of populations for fairness is a voice that is increasingly insistent and needs to be listened to.

The public's sense of natural justice and perception of institutional injustice have been sorely tested by two events in particular. In the aftermath of the 2008 global financial crisis, governments were seen to have used taxpayer funds to bail out failing banks; then in 2020–21 the stresses of the global Covid-19 outbreak exposed many institutions (government, science, healthcare, finance) to a critical public reappraisal.

On a longer-term view it is apparent that the shock waves, both from new behavioural insights and institutions failing under stress, have penetrated more quickly in some sectors than others. The most receptive areas traditionally were those where safety is key (aviation, nuclear); systems are evolving at speed (AI, online harms); where an industry is simply more open to this type of innovative thinking (some parts of food, healthcare and technology); or where public or existential pressure is effective (global sustainability, corporate governance). In contrast, some sectors have been less inclined to listen because they retain strong entrenched interests – and the levels of remuneration in financial services are certainly one barrier to change.

The financial crisis of 2008 highlighted why corporate culture matters to people 'on the street'; and the financial sector started to recognize their social concerns as valid. That is good news. However, few institutions have taken these lessons to heart and invested the time and effort to get it right.

The bad news is that there are sectors – including finance, as will be seen in this book – where we have allowed too much entrenched resistance to keep us from responding effectively. There have been practical excuses for inaction: But how do we affect culture? Can we really measure culture? Isn't culture irrelevant unless we can measure it? Isn't it enough to have 'tone from the top'? Isn't it enough to have the latest governance structures? Or to have laid claim publicly to some broad social purpose? Don't all financial people behave with integrity? Isn't having a code of ethics enough? Surely we don't need to change the whole system or the way the industry works? Don't profits trickle down to alleviate poverty, so pursuit of profits is good?

The deep disconnect here is ultimately between what human beings know to be right and the way we *think* we need to do things in order to be success-ful. Ultimately, it's about how we behave in capitalist markets. The orthodoxy was always about maximizing individualism, profits, shareholder value, and competition. This has led to increasing inequality and people have rightly objected to the outcomes and hence questioned the way we do things. A disillusioned public now looks for evidential proof that financial firms and the people who work in them actually behave according to the values regarded as fair by most people. Not by insiders. In other words, it's about ethical behaviour, driven by positive values. All the time. Consistently.

It's not a question of whether the bank manager smiles and gives you a cup of tea. It's whether they provide supportive and objectively fair assis-tance that is relevant to you – not PPI or putting your small family business into rapacious intensive care. Businesses ruled by econometrics seemed to have lost the humanity of caring for others, even though a culture of human-ity reaps huge dividends in the long term. As the world starts to rebuild itself in 2021, the new outlook is about interpersonal trust: values, emotion, rela-tionships, caring and social solidarity. Far from being an abstract mystery, a healthy dialogue around purposeful culture and what's good behaviour is or should be an extension of the everyday social relationships we all have. These are the force that constantly reshapes our view of what is 'acceptable and expected' behaviour – a phrase the UK's financial conduct regulator is fond of using.

This isn't a polemical or political statement. A robust, and growing, body of behavioural science shows it to be true. The science challenges *theories* and entrenched ways of doing things. Legal theory and classical economic theory assume that imposing sanctions will affect future behaviour, through deterrence. Most of us, however, have intrinsic motivation. We come to work because we like to do good things, to contribute to society, to engage with colleagues and help others. Having enough money may be the starting point, but it is not the end. Excessive focus on financial reward itself crowds out other important things and the result is an industry that is perceived to focus exclusively on making vast sums of money for itself; meanwhile huge swathes of people on the planet have barely enough to meet their basic needs. This engenders resentment, lowers trust, and threatens the foundation of our society.

The much-trailed 'new' culture audit technique of direct observation/floor-walk, both by regulators and internal audit, is not so new at all, of course. It is a rediscovery of what any good business manager or auditor has always done: walk about and directly observe What Actually Happens. A personal anecdote: when I was a departmental manager in a City law firm in the mid-'90s, the firm paid large sums to a Harvard professor for advice on how we should manage ourselves to achieve (financial) success. The answer was simple: walk the floor, be open and nice to people, be demonstrably fair, build teams that have good social engagement, and manage out people who don't cooperate as team players, however much of a star they might be. Forget working from budgets and billings – success and profits are not objectives but follow good ethical teams. As we found, he was absolutely right (ironically enough, 'on the money').

My initial training was as a scientist and now, as an empirical socio-legal scholar, one automatically follows the evidence. It's a wonderfully liberating experience to be able to ask what the evidence is for doing what we take for granted. You can come up with some really powerful answers, even if implementing them challenges a lot of people who hate losing what they think they have in existing ways of doing things. As Dan Ariely enjoins us, we should be 'relentlessly empirical'.[1] At the macro policy level, the scientific evidence about the need to focus on ethical values is clear. At the micro-operational, managerial and regulatory levels, it is not difficult to find data that shows what sort of culture we have, such as from customer feedback and complaints, anecdotes, and weak signals from multiple frontline (and online) sources. But we have been too driven by theories and risk models, as John Kay and Paul Collier say in powerful recent books.[2] Again other sectors/times have used the 'simple culture' approach to great effect, in preference to paper-based retrospective audit. This raises another point.

The culture audit view moves firms beyond reliance on past operational risk-style controls and 'rear-view mirror' value-at-risk analysis. It looks instead to improve current situational awareness and reflexivity. Some sectors are outstandingly good at this, having learnt from their mistakes – the ways that people deliver safer outcomes in aviation, food and healthcare are inspirational. There is so much good practice to learn from. There are structured techniques such as a Barrett cultural values assessment. There are straightforward changes of habit such as making more time for Management By Wandering About, blame-free open discussions of risk and socializing of problem-solving. The second part of the story, which the financial sector has been slower to grasp, is once the true root causes of a problem are revealed, to deal with them fearlessly.

We know intuitively, as well as through behavioural science, that people may not obey norms intrinsically, but will when they see that most people do. This is where cooperation can break down: the old-fashioned way of achieving compliance and preventing free riders was to use heavy-handed enforcement. The culture approach asks a different question: 'Why would anyone make that mistake, so we can try to prevent it happening again?' That is surely a better way to inform future decisions than 'This person made a mistake and we will blame them'. Learning from root cause analysis, informed by open and fair culture, demonstrably improves performance. We should not need to coerce anyone, as a 21st-century democracy that values human integrity and respecting each other.

And yet... finance has put up a vigorous rear-guard action of arguing that its value to society means that it cannot be touched by the change: it would lose talent; it cannot be allowed to fail, goes the story. Unfortunately for the public interest, for a long time this defence succeeded in deflecting the searchlight of stark reality. It prevented the reform of attitudes to risk, the much-needed socializing of values – of people bringing their 'whole selves' to work, feeling content to raise a problem and to work with others to solve it. Ironically for an industry rooted in one form of risk analysis, its culture of risk aversion needed to be challenged; other sectors have meanwhile moved far ahead in learning from mistakes, in opening themselves up to controlled experimentation. Outside the financial sector, many organizations have a mature view of ethics, values and culture that allows people to try, then fail or succeed, but learn and improve in either event.

This is serious. It's one thing to mess up customers (especially in large numbers). It's another to mess up the viability of an institution (bank). But it's a whole different level of threat if your collective culture undermines trust in an entire financial and economic system. What is the financial sector selling, if not trust?

Whether based inside or outside the industry, anyone with fresh insights to bring to the table – be they into behaviour, culture, cognition, or whatever field – has a public duty to add these to the call for change. We should bring the best of what we know, applying the best knowledge and wisdom currently available, to change how our institutions function. 'Organizations don't change, people do' said Richard Barrett,[3] and this means that each and every one of us working in financial services must commit to this change. This book invites everyone in the industry to find here and share – and, quite originally, to enjoy as they do so – a wider knowledge of the science, the available assessment tools, the practical issues and the obstacles. This is too important to leave to backroom people. Accordingly, it's great to see here a team of authors with such collective enthusiasm, knowledge, and commitment to share it in plain language.

Despite the work of the world's many conduct regulators, there are few practical guides as to how to assess culture in the specific context of conduct-regulated financial services. The next stage will need businesses and regulators working together to improve culture and conduct. The fact that leading regulators are focusing on culture and culture audits will in itself create improvements as people focus more on managing what they have now measured. There is more to do here, and this book is a major contribution to that effort. Whoever gets it right on the business side should do very well commercially. The lesson is to be ahead of what you are forced to do in showing that your organization Does The Right Thing.

The context has been made easier by the growing realization by all of us, and especially now by investors, that we face existential challenges (climate change, event extinction of the planet, and unpredictable pandemics) that have provoked real engagement with things that matter, such as through ESG evaluations and the need to demonstrate that our organizations' general social licence is deserved. Corporate behaviour really matters. If we don't support people, small businesses and jobs, it's going to hurt us all. This is more than a marketing attempt to use reputational claims to gain competitive advantage. The reputation needs to be deserved. It's about what we can do to deserve real trust.

This book shows the way forward in science- and evidence-based approaches to monitoring, measuring, and reporting culture. It highlights specific solutions to bridge the gap in understanding and measuring culture, not only for regulatory reporting but more importantly to help businesses grow sustainably, resilient to disruptions, and in line with rising public expectations of exemplary conduct. *Culture Audit in Financial Services* tells firms why and how. Now let's get to it!

Christopher Hodges
Professor of Justice Systems, University of Oxford
Co-Founder, International Network for Delivery of Regulation

Notes

1 Ariely, D (2009) *Predictably Irrational*, 2nd Edition, Harper Collins
2 Collier, P (2019) *The Future of Capitalism: Facing the new anxieties*, Harper; Collier, P and Kay, J (2020) *Greed is Dead: Politics after individualism*, Allen Lane; Kay, J (with King, M) (2020) *Radical Uncertainty: Decision-making for an unknowable future*, W W Norton
3 Barrett, R (2016) Cultural Transformation vs Change, www.slideshare.net/ ValuesCentre/cultural-transformation-vs-change-richard-barrett (archived at https://perma.cc/6YZF-5M6Z)

ACKNOWLEDGEMENTS

From Roger: To co-authors and to Chris Hodges, boundless thanks and respect. Gatherings round our writers' table, if ever so virtual, have been a constant delight. I'll own any errors of fact or judgement.

To fellow-travellers, for general encouragement; especially Alain Samson, Alex Chesterfield, Ann McFadyen, Bryan Foss, Chris Stears, David Emms, Emma Arnold, Judy Delaforce, Lucy Snowden, Nick West, Olivia Fahy, Patrick Butler, Paul Hodge, Peter Ewing, Philip Allen, Prasad Gollakota, Rob Ellison, Simon Hills, Ted MacDonald, Tony Moroney and Wieke Scholten.

To the many hundreds of research respondents (you know who you are): four years after *Conduct Risk Management: A behavioural approach*, thank you for continuing to take time out from busy boardrooms to answer so many impertinent questions, so frankly.

Special thanks from Ruth to Richard Barrett, for his vision and energy, inspiring people globally to transform culture.

Any questions?

The FCA has announced that an extra question is to be added to the Five Conduct Questions. In the absence of any detail as we go to press, and rather than resorting to a cumbersome formula such as 'the Five (or Six) Conduct Questions', we have simply continued to refer to them as five.

01

A culture quest for 'better behaviour'

ROGER MILES

Introduction

Entering 2021, two events summed up the challenge that this book seeks to answer.

First, the chairman of a high-profile global conference dared me to summarize, in 10 minutes, 'the culture assessment outlook' for the world's financial service firms. Quite an ask, as more usually I'd unpack the topic over 10 hours or even 10 days in business leader workshops and full-time courses. As it turned out, the mental discipline of stripping down this vast field of knowledge to its essential points for practitioners was a great exercise – and one which this book's distinguished co-authors here have joined in, with enthusiasm.

Second, self-assessing his leadership through five years of culture initiatives for the UK conduct regulator, outgoing head of supervision Jonathan Davidson congratulated firms for their progress on cultural engagement and for their positive service response to the challenges of Covid-19. The pandemic crisis had shown that 'the financial services sector can be trusted to fulfil its purpose of providing support to consumers and small businesses and keeping the economy going'; firms had become 'part of the solution, rather than the problem'.[1] But I thought 'Really, have they?'

For sure, myriad firms in the UK and around the world rose magnificently to the challenge of maintaining service against strong headwinds. Yet on the wider question of achieving durable, deep change in culture, on an objective assessment it's far from proven that conduct regulators' latest global mission to promote 'purposeful culture' is succeeding. Away from public platforms, regulators themselves strike a more cautious tone. Mixed messaging may partly explain why so many firms haven't yet taken the long view of culture. More meaningful and effortful work – including honest corporate self-examination – is required to achieve real cultural transformation in financial services.

Culture post-Covid: regulators' frank views[2]

Regulators' response to the financial services workplace's rapid and unprecedented conversion to remote working during the Covid-19 pandemic, itself illustrates how much culture and conduct work remains to be done. Enforcers had to realign their own work programmes and redeploy staff to meet the many prudential and conduct risks the crisis created seemingly overnight.

Would working from home without supervision – the first line of defence – increase market abuse and improper information sharing? Would firms' outward-facing employees – traders, front office, customer service – conduct themselves 'exemplarily' or otherwise? Whilst there has been a 'vital' focus on healthy cultures to 'get everyone through times of uncertainty', unfortunately remote working has affected conduct and culture in some unwelcome ways. Employees inevitably behave differently when out of their controlled office environment; home working brings its own stresses and can all too easily fragment collective culture. Where many firms hopefully assumed that remote working could be 'business as usual', in practice for some it dissolved organizational cohesion and entrenched teams' tendency to silo working – whilst in some cases, ignoring vital issues of anxiety and emotional pressure.

In its own bitterly perverse way, Covid-19 proved that active engagement with culture and conduct matters. As vaccines, new therapies, and the prospect of collective recovery emerge, the agenda is now for firms to show they have realized for themselves that a 'healthy culture' is the key to producing sustainable long-term business value.

Regulating using behavioural science: influence above enforcement

The oncoming 'culture assessment' approach is driven by regulators' realization that a pure enforcement approach – punishing wrongdoers – has never fully gained traction. As we'll see during this book, fines and other punishments are still regarded in certain quarters as a 'friction cost of doing business', rather than any kind of deterrent. Culture audit approaches the challenge of wrongdoing differently, applying behavioural insight to understand the human motivations behind decisions and actions, then looking to establish conduct frameworks that encourage 'virtuous circles' of firm-wide good behaviour to create desired outcomes.

Though firms already have a regulated duty to identify and report on their 'conduct risk', the frame of reference for this has moved on from traditional operational risk metrics and compliance, to include other disciplines in the business – notably Legal, Human Resources, Governance and Risk. With fresh 'eyes on', conduct-based culture audits offer a new opportunity to develop business value, growth and resilience. Yet many businesses remain unsure how to begin, whilst regulators remain – for reasons we'll see – coy about specifying any reporting formats or indicators. Several major financial brands have made early efforts to bridge this gap by up-skilling themselves, including hiring behavioural scientists. This is great news for graduate psychologists, behavioural economists and political scientists who can now look forward to developing exciting careers in the financial sector.

As we'll also see, financial services face a long-term crisis of public trust following a seemingly endless series of misconduct scandals. Regulators have responded to such control failures by redoubling their behavioural research efforts, homing in on 'purposeful culture' and urging firms to better express their positive contribution to the wider good of society. Firms passively concede this is a fair approach in theory – why wouldn't they? – but are either frustrated by or indifferent to the lack of a generally agreed reporting methodology to deliver it in practice. For example, how should firms and regulators identify (measure, manage) which 'people risks' are the most effective to focus on? Agreed, the old value-at-risk (VaR) controls weren't quite up to it; also human-factor risk (conduct, culture) is a broadly useful field for supervisors to look in, to prevent abuses. Not yet generally agreed, though, is a common framework for assessing the new 'behaviour-at-risk' (BaR).

Shortfall in public trust drives regulatory culture change

Research into how people respond to events of crisis has noted that at the moment when hazard strikes – be it market crash, tsunami, product failure, or pandemic – it imposes an 'abrupt and brutal audit'[3] of the credibility and workings of all kinds of infrastructures. It tests the legitimacy of institutions' claims to be able to manage risks on the public's behalf.

Following 2008's financial crisis, regulations and controls were themselves part of the problem – and still are, as we'll see. Mostly they're designed to work best when the domain they seek to control is stable, not stressed. Controls that work fine during a 'steady state' unfortunately then have a way of failing under the stress of crisis. Indeed, the control design assumption itself fails. Granted, the financial firms must do supervisory 'stress testing' to make sure that they can continue to function when, for example, markets' credit sources run dry. But this doesn't (yet) test what happens when *public trust* dries up. (By the way also, the stress tests aren't applied to regulators' framing of their own rules; we'll be exploring such 'failures of metacognition' shortly.)

Testing what's 'legitimate', on both sides

It follows that a big piece that's still missing from the culture picture is an assessment of *regulatory legitimacy*. In plainer terms, how far do the public trust – or mistrust – that the system will protect them? Partly to answer that concern, in 2020 the UK regulator's researchers alerted firms frankly to how hard culture assessment might be, especially if they hadn't given it any thought before.[4] Culture is going to be assessed because it is 'now widely recognized' that a firm's culture is a reliable predictor for 'organizational success or failure'.[5] Conduct regulators see firms' past misdeeds – such as rule-gaming, falsifying reports, accounting fraud, abuse of staff, or heedlessly putting citizens at risk – as 'rooted in culture'.

During the first wave of the Conduct regime (2013–20), prosecutions swiftly followed from new types of research and audit insight, invoking science reports about harmful mindsets and behaviours and (non-specifically) exhorting firms to measure culture, identify patterns of harmful behaviour and engage with wider societal concerns. With 2021's advent of culture assessment, culture-conscious working is becoming central to good governance, supporting emerging dialogue on 'non-financial (mis)conduct'; overtly rating positive human-risk indicators such as psychological safety, diversity and inclusion; and aligning these with existing discourses on environmental, social and governance indicators (ESG).

Why we're here, any of us: discovering purpose and culture

There's now a unifying call to improve the 'conduct conversation' with provider firms, a theme that runs through the rest of this book. In the four years since publishing *Conduct Risk Management: A behavioural approach* (2017), I've continued working closely with many financial firms, industry groups and regulators across several conduct regulatory jurisdictions, to start and encourage these conversations.

Regulators have meanwhile been absorbing more of the latest research findings from behavioural science; it has been a privilege to discuss these in experimental spaces, to co-produce and to share the most useful research insights with practitioners. For this book's panel of authors, such work draws us closer together professionally. The book you're now reading is a happy result of our great collective curiosity, our amicable sharing of insights, and our enthusiasm to gather every voice around the table to help create better ways forward for the industry.

WELCOME, NEW DISCIPLINES!

This book's authors represent these specialist disciplines, and more: behavioural science, economics and law; political science; cognitive psychology; linguistic and narrative analysis; and control design. We welcome you as a 'behaviour-at-risk' fellow traveller from whatever field of practice. With this book in your hands, and an inclusive view of all relevant thinking, there's a brighter future for financial services.

At that proverbial table, the main topic of conversation now has moved on beyond simply how to define 'conduct risk'. As foreseen through my behavioural lens in the 2017 book, the focal point of industry attention on our collective 'behaviour-at-risk' is now set to become who and what is 'socially useful', answering increasingly strident public concerns. This sharply rising but weakly predictable 'vox populi risk' may in time hugely disrupt patterns of service in our sector. Challenger providers have been quick to learn how to convert public frustration into sales of more user-friendly, fresh-faced products and services. The global financial crisis of 2008 lit a long fuse of public discontent, whilst social stresses accelerating during 2020 (and not just Covid-related) prompted more citizens than ever to take to the streets to express their concerns over the 'legitimacy' of many kinds of institutions. It now seems incredible, yet at the turn of 2017 we hadn't even heard of #metoo, #extinctionrebellion, Greta Thunberg, or Zoom; the public's greatest anxieties over epidemic illness still centred on SARS and Ebola; social critiques of institutional governance, such as #blacklivesmatter, #glassdoor, and #stakeholdercapitalism were still vying for mainstream awareness; Brits had only just voted for Brexit; and the Trump presidency had barely started.

Tumultuous 2020 taught us to revise assumptions of all sizes: Why commute to an office? Why are life-saving care workers so poorly rewarded? Do we trust institutions' 'expert' briefings? And why does market economics continue to super-reward a few, whilst harming so many ordinary lives?

Small wonder then that corporate purpose, and the culture behind it, has leapt to the top of the risk governance agenda. The industry needed to 'get things right, compared to the past',[6] now more than ever, to better explain its value to a sceptical and exhausted public.

The financial services workforce is also, largely, of 'the public' mind. Staff's belief systems are now post-millennial, meaning – again as we'll see shortly – that they typically see ethical purpose as a precondition of a job; it's now as vital as, or more vital than, mere financial reward.

Meanwhile customers, investors and the public want to see financial firms present solid evidence of 'purposeful culture', not as 'just a slogan on a brochure'[7] but by giving direct and authentic answers to public questions. Starting with: What steps are we taking to transform the way our firm converses with the rest of the world? How are we doing at moving beyond the stance of simply being a profit-seeking enterprise, towards being a fully stakeholder-aware, socially useful service?[8]

My goodness. What should we do about all that, in practice? Let's find out.

Chapter previews

From financial services' existential conduct crisis there has burst an explosion of output – white papers, research, blogs, speeches, books – from regulators, academics, business leaders and advisory firms, on the topics of corporate purpose, social psychology in organizations, culture assessment, change management, cognitive science and regulatory design. Some of these published pieces are excellent, in each of those specific fields; the authors of this book share our personal favourites (with our comments as to why) in a Recommended Reading list on page 379).

Yet few resources weave together all these topics. As at time of writing, none gathers them together in plain language for the general reader as this book aims to do.

To be clear, what we're presenting here can't be, in a couple of hundred pages, an exhaustive technical guide to conduct and culture regulation and practice. Nor is it a legal manual; there will never be a shortage of those. Thankfully for your ease of reading, this is none of the above. It *is*, though, a thought-provoking tour and starter guide if you're looking to square up to the challenge of culture assessment. It's an access point to help start the conduct and culture conversation in your firm, so you can make that dialogue inclusively inviting, diversely thoughtful, easily accessible and even – whisper it – popular with everyone. That's how I like to work; because this approach works.

On a note of due humility from your editor, much of this book's co-authors' work is already unimprovable. I'm thinking here of our globally esteemed colleague Mirea Raaijmakers, whose authoritative work *Supervision of Behaviour and Culture* is, without dispute, the world's best guide to the regulator's conception of the topic. Of other colleagues at the writers' table, Chris Hodges and Ruth Steinholtz, whose epic 30-year research has led to their producing the definitive critique of regulatory engagement in every sector that matters, *Ethical Business Practice and Regulation*. Of Hani Nabeel, whose advancement of the quant science of behaviour and culture assessment has won him major academic prizes. Of Rachel Wolcott, whose 'front-row access' to global financial scandals, and published body of keenly observed, clear-sighted regulatory critiques is peerless, extending over 20 years. Of Cosette Reczek, a driving force behind the first worldwide Conduct Academy, conduct risk leader and consultant for numerous megabanks. Of Stephen Scott, the intelligence analysts' favourite intelligence analyst, whose comprehensive insights keep him on the speed-dial list of central bank leaders the world over. Of Elizabeth Arzadon – where to start? For her country's regulator she published a trenchant assessment of an entire sector's conduct failures and is now, as we go to press, co-producing the global internal audit profession's pathfinder guide to culture audit. Of Christian Hunt, who, not content with leading the behavioural charge for the UK's prudential supervisor, is now transforming the entire commercial world's engagement with human-risk literacy, reconceiving controls with a revolutionary rethink of compliance design. As is, elsewhere on the professional landscape, Julie Ampadu, who's teaching compliance practitioners to question their own long-held assumptions. Not forgetting a head of conduct in one of the UK's major high street banks, who (anonymously) has kindly shared a case study of the bank's programme of culture reappraisal.

With friends like these... conversation around our table is never dull, even when (as currently) the table is virtual. What, then, do we have to share with you? Here's a drone-eye overview.

Under the introduction in each of the following chapters you'll find a handy summary of its core topics and concepts. Within each chapter you'll find several boxes which help understanding of key terms and offer examples of concepts discussed. At three points between chapters we share first-person case examples of how individuals, as regulators and/or within financial firms and practitioner groups, have worked to grasp the nettle of culture assessment. These open windows onto often lively views of 'what actually happens' as people and organizations wrestle with questions of culture. So, on with the core content:

In Chapter 2, I'll whisk you through a recap of 'how we got to where we are today' in conduct regulation, identify regulators' collective longer-term agenda, and point to which regulators are pushing hardest to develop and implement culture assessments.

In Chapter 3, star conduct regulation analyst Cosette Reczek demystifies the research programmes that regulators are running, that inform their approach to developing culture assessment. She compares regulator-sponsored and private-sector research initiatives, contrasts these with their apparent failure to stop a long history of misconduct events, and suggests that last-generation accountability regimes for senior managers are already overdue a major upgrade to improve awareness of culture factors.

Chapter 4 unpacks the first resulting set of regulatory 'big ideas', setting out in plain terms the essentials of behavioural science that you'll need to know before embarking on a culture audit programme. We'll look at human risk factors in play, such as how our brains interject biases that disrupt decisions, and how there's a positive side to the science that helps us promote previously overlooked brain-based business assets such as psychological safety and cognitive diversity.

Then there's the first of three point-of-view interludes where we share practice-based material – though that description hardly does justice to this episode. Christian Hunt tells his extraordinary story of both prosecuting and remediating a major misconduct incident, seeing at first hand and from both 'sides of the fence' the challenge of regulatory design. His narrative is frank, fast-paced, full of humanity and a refreshing intellectual humility. It's rare that the rest of us outside the 'fence' get to see the other side's experience so clearly. As in all three 'interlude' sections in this book, tapping into such real-life experiences is a great talking point, to help get your colleagues started discussing what good conduct and culture means to them in practice, as a prelude to a culture assessment. This is ultimately what you're looking for (as is any conduct regulator): getting going with a conduct conversation that everyone enjoys continuing spontaneously, because they want to engage constructively in it.

In Chapter 5, we're back into the second set of 'big ideas', as Cosette and I forensically examine what's meant by 'purposeful culture'. We look at both the regulator's own sense of purpose, and two healthy-culture essentials that they'd like to see evident in every firm. You'll need to consider these as you frame your first draft response to the core culture assessment question: 'Why are we here?' Along the way, we note the history of industrial-scale abuses and failed previous attempts at conduct control, which made it so important that the new regulation needed to work differently and better – if indeed it does, yet, as Rachel Wolcott will assess a little later.

For Chapter 6 we're in the distinguished company of Stephen Scott and Mirea Raaijmakers, looking at the evolution of 'behaviour-at-risk' – starting with how ancient human tribal evolution contributed to this. We'll see how culture assessment has itself evolved as a response to a wider social movement that, uniquely, is backed both by regulators and institutional investors. Is reformed governance up to the task of managing human factor risk, to give a proper answer to the general public's 'vox populi risk' challenge to our industry? Are firms sufficiently aware of how the tensions between 'in-groups' and 'out-groups' quietly shred leaders' attempts at risk control? Read this chapter, play with some of its models of evolution, socializing of risk and 'coercive competition', and decide for yourself.

In Chapter 7, with eminent behavioural data scientist Hani Nabeel we uncap an analytic 'culture lens' that contrasts individual employees' viewpoints with the collective, observed values of the firm, to reveal where we should look to identify unhealthy tensions between the two, and how to intervene to overcome them. Hani approaches quant analysis of cultural engagement and transformation in a practical way that delivers valuable action points. By identifying and measuring the right indicators, he shows us how it's perfectly possible to build a firm-wide mindset that acts to reduce misconduct in all its forms, overcomes the 'bystander problem' and builds resilient value by encouraging 'speak-up' constructive criticism. We include a case example of how this technique has worked in practice to transform a global bank's business resilience.

Elizabeth Arzadon is in a very exclusive club: qualified behavioural analysts who have both published world-leading culture assessments on behalf of a national regulator, and now lead the current practice of culture audit within financial firms. (Two other members of this club, Mirea Raaijmakers and Alexandra Chesterfield, have of course also had a hand in the creation of this book.) Elizabeth joins me in Chapter 8 to explain critical differences between conventional audit practice and the new approach to culture assessment. How can and should internal auditors transform their professional knowledge and toolkits to support this innovation, and thrive commercially by using it? In what ways can controls that are currently unfit for this purpose be adapted to it and improved? Building on our encounter with behavioural science in Chapter 4, Elizabeth identifies how the science shapes the practice of the new audit techniques, and examines the most useful of these.

Continuing into Chapter 9, Elizabeth and I approach the thorny topic of how to create 'better MI' – the new indicators that firms will need to report adequately on culture. Pausing to identify six systemic reasons why poor cultures have persisted for so long, we show which current MI isn't fit for the task for culture assessment, why that is, and what firms need to do practically about this. Having made this big conceptual leap forward, we start to look at some real indicators and practical approaches to the design of culture reporting.

The detail of this is in Chapter 10, where, having started with a crash revision course on some abstract concepts that regulators say you *should* measure, I guide us towards some much more practical ways to question and frame your 'purposeful culture'. After touring a few influential framings of purpose, motivation and culture templates, there's a robust 'dashboard' concept that you're unlikely to have seen published anywhere else before, and a toolkit that gets you quickly from abstract 'culture paradigms' into practical sets of 'better questions'. There are some direct answers to the question, 'what's the MI we need?' The regulator's own pro-forma questions turn out to have practical design value – after we rephrase them. I also identify here some much more effective questions, including previously unpublished ones that the regulators secretly have. You'll soon see how to present better answers to these, once you understand what's really at stake, as when you're designing your firm's own culture assessment.

Following Chapter 10, there's a second interlude as we join a UK high street bank, in a case example review of its experience in producing a prototype culture self-assessment. There's a frank appraisal of lessons learnt, as well as benefits of the exercise.

In the first of two tour-de-force critiques, in Chapter 11 Rachel Wolcott brings her famously forensic laser focus to bear on regulators' varied interventions as they attempt to remedy the sector's 'culture problem'. Contrasting three jurisdictions' distinctive experiences of attempted conduct control – in the UK, the United States and the Netherlands – she highlights a continuing gap between the promises of many well-intended interventions and the reality of a continuing slow pace of cultural change. With five case examples, and insights into related topics (discover new forms of 'nonfinancial misconduct', 'sludging', and more), it's a turbulent ride through recent history. So into Chapter 12, in which Rachel interrogates a range of potential modern tools for culture assessment, interviewing their creators. There's a nod to the much-feared regulatory 'floor-walk test', then a frank analysis of a central conundrum that firms face, but haven't yet properly resolved. It's this: all of the following techniques are already being used for prototype conduct and/ or culture assessments, but which ones work and which ones really don't?: workforce surveillance technology, market research techniques, employee surveys, regulatory surveillance, behaviour-predictive analytics, language analysis. An early clue: at least two of these techniques are useless and one of them is actually dangerously divisive. To find out which are the duds, and which are the *best* – those sought-after 'silver bullet' analytics – you'll need to read this excellent chapter.

There's then the third of our interludes, in which compliance maven Julie Ampadu reveals her profession's previously unpublished insights into the 'tells' that internal auditors look for, as signs of healthy and unhealthy culture in a firm. There are some reassuring, worrisome and occasionally startling findings on 'what works' in first-person observational audit of culture.

The final two substantive chapters are detailed case examples of practically applied culture evaluation tools; their distinctive insights and value to better understanding human risk and intervening to transform firm-wide culture. In Chapter 13, Ruth Steinholtz applies the Barrett Model of cultural values assessment, setting out tools for culture transformation, identifying the benefits of cultural health (alignment) and risks inherent in 'cultural entropy'. She rationalizes the appeal of this model to regulators, with reassurance that culture indicators are valid; and for corporate boards who may be understandably cautious of any disruption that a culture initiative might create, a well-designed culture analytic such as this brings positive change by creating a 'common language' with which to openly discuss positives and the overcoming of limitations. Ruth presents case studies of two financial services groups, showing how they benefited from using this approach.

In Chapter 14, Hani Nabeel demonstrates how applying the CultureScope 'combined analytic' to culture change programmes can ensure delivery of measurably better culture, pleasing regulators, staff, leaders and business owners alike. Revealing a selection of the model's (normally hidden) 'behavioural dimensions', he steps through the practical method, how to prevent culture programme failure and ensure that leaders remain on-side. He shows how to assess how far your staff are in a state to respond positively to the 'ask' of culture change, and reveals a set of assessed outcomes following a culture change intervention. Finally, Hani argues cogently for a more enlightened 'persuasive design' approach to ensure maximum engagement of all involved, with a case study showing the value of this in practice.

Chapter 15 looks ahead, reflects on the book's core content, and offers fresh practical tips to set you on your way in the task of creating or improving your firm's culture audit approach.

The end of the beginning

Naturally, with a lack of unified methods, there has been frustration – among regulators, practitioners, politicians and the public – at our industry's lack of substantive progress to date. The absence of globally agreed, industry-standard tools and metrics for culture and conduct risk needn't be a barrier to making a purposeful start on answering the regulator's challenge of culture assessment. Whether at first your efforts are designed to inform internal governance process, to stand ready to report to regulators, or to evidence success to interested stakeholders, the rest of this book offers a bridge across the knowledge gap. Join us on the other side!

Notes

1 Jonathan Davidson, FCA Executive Director of Supervision (2020) The Business of Social Purpose, speech to Culture and Conduct Forum of the Financial Services Industry, 26 November
2 FCA Culture supervisors (2020) Private briefing to SMCR and Conduct programme leaders, 29 April, attended by the author

3 Lagadec, P (1993) *Preventing Chaos in a Crisis*, McGraw-Hill

4 FCA Insight (2020) Measuring corporate culture: a warning, 18 March, https://www.fca.org.uk/insight/ (archived at https://perma.cc/5L83-2AZB)

5 FCA Insight (2020) Measuring corporate culture: a warning, 18 March, https://www.fca.org.uk/insight/ (archived at https://perma.cc/5L83-2AZB)

6 Chris Woolard, FCA Interim Chief Executive (2020) Evolution of a New Model for Financial Regulation, speech to International Financial Services Forum, 21 September fca.org.uk/news/speeches/evolution-new-model-financial-regulation-uk (archived at https://perma.cc/FL8U-9Q9P)

7 Marc Teasdale, FCA Director of Wholesale Supervision (2020) A regulatory perspective: the drivers of culture and the role of purpose and governance, speech to The Investment Association, 17 September, fca.org.uk/news/speeches/regulatory-perspective-drivers-culture-and-role-purpose-and-governance (archived at https://perma.cc/RG9R-YDN6)

8 See eg Davidson, as above; and US Business Roundtable (2020) Statement on the Purpose of a Corporation, s3.amazonaws.com/brt.org/BRT-StatementonthePurposeofaCorporationOctober2020.pdf (archived at https://perma.cc/QCA4-PA6S)

02

How regulators' 'behavioural approach' went global – with culture its latest focus

ROGER MILES

Introduction: exploring why and how financial regulators want to check on conduct and culture

In this chapter we'll start by looking at 'Conduct 1.01', some basics of conduct regulation: why we have it, where it came from – the political and popular impulses for it – and the regulators' belief system which drives it. We will identify the three main elements of a conduct regulators' behavioural lens – how they look at all our industry's activities – then offer a quick preliminary working definition of culture and conduct. Towards the end of the chapter we'll look at why and in what forms conduct regulation and culture supervision have exploded around the world. This includes a handy tour of places where regulators are pushing hardest for 'culture audits' in which firms show how they're connecting purpose to governance and risk-taking to a sense of social responsibility.

The chapter first briefly recaps material I've explored at greater length in *Conduct Risk Management: A behavioural approach* (Kogan Page, 2017). Then it brings up to date the background to the regulatory 'culture agenda', which has largely arisen since publishing *Conduct Risk Management*.

THEMES AND CONCEPTS IN THIS CHAPTER

behavioural lens – cognitive biases – cognitive diversity – 'compliant' as 'unchallenging' – conduct and culture – conduct-based supervision – Covid-19 pandemic – culture as capital – dominant individual – environmental, social and governance (ESG) reporting – extension of regulatory powers – FinTechs and RegTechs – 'floor-walk test' – global financial crash – governance – intervention policy – leadership character assessment – personal accountability – preventing harms – promoting challenge – psychological safety – psychology of sales practices – public responsibility – regulatory agenda to transform culture – regulatory supervision of culture – social goods – social licence – speak-up – starting the firm's conduct and culture conversation – systemic misconduct – the 'normal people' – the 'new MI' (management information) – unconscious bias – value-at-risk vs behaviour-at-risk – 'what does good behaviour look like?' – working conduct-aware

What is conduct regulation?

Conduct regulation is a term used loosely to describe any set of financial market rules that tell practitioner firms what is 'expected and acceptable behaviour'.[1] These behaviour-based rules differ from conventional financial regulation. Where the old type of regulation tended to examine the legal structures of financial product contracts and/or value-at-risk, the new rules address how people interact in financial trading spaces – in particular how salespeople interact with customers or clients.

CUSTOMER/CLIENT

During this book, we often use 'customer' and 'client' more or less interchangeably. If you have clients rather than customers, or vice versa, please do apply whichever term you prefer, as we go along.

Conduct rules essentially tell people in financial firms to behave themselves well, in ways such as:

- taking personal and public **responsibility** for their actions;
- actively making sure that no one causes any **harm** to customers;

- making sure all staff feel comfortable to **challenge** (question) anyone in the firm they see behaving badly towards colleagues or customers;

- under **culture audit,** reflecting on why they're in business; the broader **purpose** of the firm and how this benefits anyone beyond just making a profit for its owners.

As we'll see in Chapters 5 and 10, various conduct regulators around the world apply these broad tenets in more detail in the form of local rules, questions and tests. Although those tests and questions vary between different jurisdictions, as we'll also see, the gist of them is similar wherever there is a conduct regulator. Here's why:

Conduct regulators freely share research, information and case studies between each other. They also share motivation, driven by a sense of the common 'social purposes' of aiming to protect citizens' financial security and maintain stable markets. Both those impulses are a regulatory reflex response to three dismal experiences across the world's financial markets (detailed in Chapter 11), summarized here:

- In 2008, a global financial crisis (GFC): following a catastrophic 'credit crunch', sovereign governments were forced to use taxpayer and central bank funding to cover the debts of failed financial firms.

- Throughout the 2010s, a series of major financial scandals continued, even after post-GFC regulatory reforms. Firms mis-sold products, traded on privileged information, and 'rigged' market pricing systems (reference rates and benchmarks).

- In 2020, the event of the Covid-19 pandemic triggered waves of local and regional economic shocks, with regional recessions enduring into 2021.

Each of these crises contributed to a broader global pattern. Economic hardship, together with a growing sense that big institutions in general couldn't be trusted, have hardened public opinion against financial firms and the regulatory agencies and governments who supervise them. 'Normal people' (see box) sensed that governance has failed to protect ordinary citizens' interests. Conduct regulation and its latest incarnation, 'culture assessment', is a major tool of policy response to counter persistent popular anxiety over these three catastrophes. Let's explore this.

THE NORMAL PEOPLE

In culture audit, behavioural scientists may describe anyone who isn't a business leader, risk analyst or scientist as 'the normal people'. Whilst it's a bit of a science-nerdy in-joke about corporate titans and behavioural scientists not being 'normal', frankly it also sounds snooty. So we'll generally avoid using that phrase in this book, instead talking about 'public opinion' and 'vox populi risk'. As we'll see in Chapters 5 and 10, taking these views into account is a vital part of any culture audit's check on a firm's 'social licence'.

Where does conduct regulation come from?

Before conduct regulation started, financial regulators had tended to focus on elements of market risk such as the soundness of legal contracts and trading systems, and the pricing of risk, rather than practitioner behaviour. After the 2008 GFC, governments realized that much of the failed regulation had over-relied on purely financial indicators such as credit quality (inflated by over-friendly rating agencies) and value-at-risk (VaR) models. There was a realization that only looking at the monetary value of financial contracts doesn't give a broad view of everything that's going on in a market; a 'financial lens' doesn't focus on how salespeople are really treating – and mistreating – their customers.

For example: our industry stands accused of wilfully making the workings of many financial products opaque. When a customer says they're perfectly happy with a product they've just bought, it may be quite the wrong financial contract for them, sold to them by a salesperson who has exploited the average retail customer's limited financial literacy.

Accepting that purely financial risk-based regulation was failing, in the early 2010s governments in major financial centres launched a new style of regulator using a 'behavioural lens' to focus on how *people* interact. By 2020, this approach became common, with the focus of regulatory assessments shifting from collective contract value-at-risk towards individual conduct of practitioners in financial firms (known as 'behaviour-at-risk'). The UK's new (2013) regulator was branded a Financial Conduct Authority (FCA), clearly signalling by that word 'conduct' that its primary business is observing how practitioners behave. For reasons we'll now explore, conduct regulation took off quickly; the FCA is just one among dozens of conduct regulators around the world, covering virtually all major financial market jurisdictions. There are more than 50 conduct regulators in securities markets alone,[2] whilst more than 10 of the world's central banks now use conduct assessment tools to supervise commercial banking.

These regulators share several common motivations and points of focus, explored in more detail in Chapter 4. As a summary introduction: conduct regulators look to prevent harm to retail customers from abusive practices such as hidden penalties in products, rewarding staff for mis-selling, and dishonest marketing that uses only partial information. These regulators also share an interest in using modern behavioural science to identify human-risk factors that drive misconduct: the cognitive psychology and motivation in individuals and financial workplace groups that lead to abuses happening. Some abuses result from unchecked human-animal instincts (cognitive biases) that disrupt rational decision-making – more on the science of this also in Chapter 4. By the way, that science is itself fascinating, as well as fun to learn about; pragmatically also, knowing more about it helps us to cope with life in general, besides regulated financial work.

Why it's useful to know about the 'conduct agenda'

The rapid worldwide spread of conduct-based regulation is readily explained.

The first conduct regulators soon earned the approval of their Treasury ministry sponsors by raising record levels of fines against financial firms – triggering some alarm in those firms, even as the fines swelled government coffers. By the mid-2010s, regulators and central banks in the world's main financial market centres had reached consensus that conduct regulation was the way forward.

Besides its public revenue-generating potential, conduct regulation has a broad appeal beyond simply its government sponsors: by inquiring into the *personal* behaviour of financial market practitioners, its enforcers answer the deep, twin public demands for financial firms to both 'explain them-selves better' and put a human face on the abstract complexities of the GFC. One latest method of enforcement, in countries including the UK, Singapore, Hong Kong and Australia, is for a conduct case officer to come and visit you unexpectedly at your desk (or virtual desk) in your firm, where they'll ask you personally about your understanding of what conduct regulation means to you in your day-to-day work. That may sound weirdly personal and even alarming, especially if you've not encountered it before.

Yet this new 'floor-walk' approach to assessing firms' conduct and culture is becoming the norm. We must learn not just to live with it but to engage with enthusiasm; not only because it's what regulators expect, but because it's actually good for business and morale if we can get a good 'conduct conversation' started *before* the regulator comes to call.

Getting that part right needn't be difficult – but start now. Set about the task sympathetically, gently removing any background noise of vague threats and/or jargon from legal and compliance people. In case you've never thought about having a 'conduct conversation' among the team around the desk (or on conference call) before, that's okay: this book will help lead you through it. Although you'll need to know what *type* of questions the regulator will ask you, unlike old-school pre-GFC regulation, this is not as simple as answering a standard set of questions. As we'll see in Chapter 10 on Better Questions, it requires gentle practice to adopt a more thoughtful, less prescriptive approach to regulatory reporting. By the way, this approach also helps to build resilient business, to retain your best staff, and to grow capital value.

Can't we just have simple answers to the obvious questions about 'behavioural' rules?

Senior people arriving at my conduct workshops tend to ask two questions.

First: 'What does good behaviour look like?' By which they really mean: Can you just give me a checklist of 10 things I should do now, that will keep the conduct regulator away from my firm? To which the answer is: Actually no, it doesn't work like that. On the other hand, give us a couple of hours together, as you read the book you're now holding, and you will learn how to think more constructively about the question. You will then be able to work out for yourself not only the right answers, but also how to ask better questions in the first place, so as to produce more useful information about the state of your firm's behaviour and culture, with clear action points to fix any problems.

The second question is: 'Where and how do we find the new measures and sources of information we need to report to the regulator on our conduct and culture?' (the so-called 'new MI' (management information)). They ask this because, beyond just setting out a basic framework of who's responsible for which control functions, the regulator rather leaves the rest of it to you.

That's deliberate, of course: regulators want firms to think for themselves about how best to act responsibly, and to work out for themselves what a fair customer outcome looks like. The 'thinking about it' bit is the whole point. As with the Better Questions approach, which we'll see in Chapter 10 and elsewhere, this book will steer you through the steps needed.

What does a conduct regulator's 'behavioural lens' focus on?

This is such a big topic that there's a whole book about it, as perhaps I've already mentioned.[3]

We've come a long way and all learned a lot since the first wave of conduct regulators launched in the early 2010s. It has become clear that most conduct regulators' outlook is informed by three points of view, or 'lenses' if you prefer. Again, let's introduce these here in summary form, as they're expanded throughout the rest of this book.

Social licence

This jargon phrase embraces fundamental questions of purpose such as: What is each of us *doing* here, from senior managers all the way down, to make sure everyone gets fairly treated? And what is our firm doing in the wider world, other than just enriching its owners and employees? Or asking the same question in negative form: If your firm were no longer here, would anybody miss you? This is a powerful way to get firms to reconsider how (or even whether) they contribute anything to 'social goods', not just to staff pay packets and taxes. Some conduct regulators explicitly factor 'social licence' into their intervention policy (see Table 2.1).

Why people do what they do

Studying human behaviour, not just through formal behavioural science but also informally by gathering a mass of anecdotes from all sorts of sources. Scientific research on cognitive biases is part of this, for sure (when, why and how is our rational decision-making hijacked by our intuitive, animal brain? More on this in Chapter 4). But how about other knowledge sources too, such as ombudsmen's casebooks, activity in consumer online groups and chat rooms, media documentaries, AI-based language analysis, web-crawling,

TABLE 2.1   How likely is the conduct regulator to intervene?

	Regulator is _less_ likely to intervene when...	Regulator _more_ likely to intervene when...
Who is harmed (by price discrimination)?	Product's consumers are wealthier – eg time poor, cash rich	Consumers who might be deemed vulnerable (low income, old age, cognitive impairment, etc)
How much are these persons harmed?	Probability difference between consumer segments is minimal, immaterial to harmed segment	Significant profitability differences; significantly harms those affected
How many people harmed?	Small minority affected	Significant numbers of product's consumers affected
How are firms discriminating on price?	Transparent; consumers can easily challenge/switch	Hidden; hard to identify, challenge or switch
How essential is the product or service?	Product is considered non-essential (though desired by some)	Essential product/service (eg current account, motor insurance)
Do people generally view the pricing practice as (socially) unfair/ egregious?	Little public concern expressed about practices; firm behaviour widely accepted	Persistent and broad-based concern expressed; firm behaviour publicly described as poor conduct

SOURCE Miles-UK Finance, from FCA: _Price Discrimination in Financial Services_ briefing, July 2018

and 'trust rating' portals? The new regulators have boundless appetite for any new research insights into what drives human behaviour (see box below). As a practitioner, you'll need to get up to speed on understanding at least the science basics, so we can keep up with this part of the conversation.

TWO BEHAVIOURAL SCIENCE EXPERIMENTS BY CONDUCT REGULATORS

Alexandra Chesterfield is Head of Behavioural Risk in a major banking group; for more than three years from 2016 to 2019 she ran major behavioural experiments for the UK's conduct regulator (FCA). Here she debriefs on two examples of her experimental work with FCA and Fairbanking Foundation:[4]

Experiment 1: How to encourage bank customers to pay off more than the 'minimum amount due' on their monthly credit card bill:

- 'We wanted to see if removing the minimum payment would cause people to pay more than the minimum, in practice, so could we replicate outside the lab an effect we'd found in initial testing.

- We used a randomized control trial with two outcome measures: primary, to see where people are choosing to pay more than the minimum; and secondary, in the longer term, did that therefore mean that people paid more of their debt down?

- We found in our interventions that removing the minimum payment results in a large positive initial effect on payment choices. Though we were probably more interested in impacting overall levels of debt.

- Our initial intervention had some success, though [unexpectedly] discouraged some people from setting up direct debit payments, which led to a small increase in arrears.'

Experiment 2: How to reduce customers' costs of bank overdraft usage:

- 'UK unarranged overdrafts are (2018) very costly. We wanted to know, as it's really costly, why are people doing it? If overdraft is sometimes a mistake, the policy challenge was, how can we help people avoid [big charges] for unintentionally borrowing what are often quite small amounts?

- We found that auto-enrolling customers into a text message (SMS) 'overdraft alert' scheme reduces charges across all groups – really good news – but...

- Mostly the alert reduced charges for 'rarely overdrawn' users; the heaviest overdraft users still incurred a majority of charges even after automatic [message scheme] enrolment.

- We found that for the most vulnerable overdraft users it's not an 'attention problem' but a financial liquidity problem – [suggesting] another policy lever would need to be used.'

The FCA now (2020–) also uses behaviourally aware 'Product Fairness Test' designs, such as this one, to assess whether any planned new consumer market offering will decently engage with real-world customer behaviour.

FIGURE 2.1   FCA 'Product Fairness Test' prototype

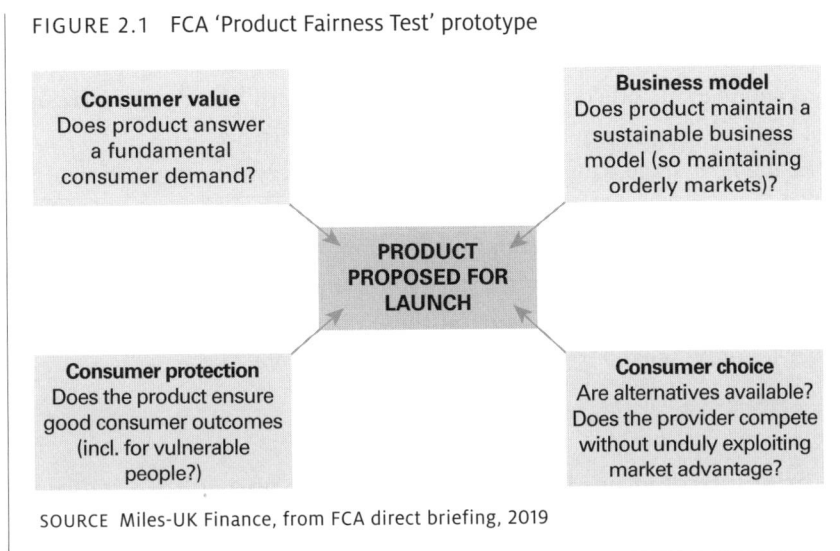

Consumer value
Does product answer
a fundamental
consumer demand?

Business model
Does product maintain a
sustainable business
model (so maintaining
orderly markets)?

**PRODUCT
PROPOSED FOR
LAUNCH**

Consumer protection
Does the product ensure
good consumer outcomes
(incl. for vulnerable
people?)

Consumer choice
Are alternatives available?
Does the provider compete
without unduly exploiting
market advantage?

SOURCE   Miles-UK Finance, from FCA direct briefing, 2019

Strength of character

... especially in business leaders. This touches on lots of indicators that we'll look closer at later, such as that the firm's people willingly take responsibility. That they:

- show moral courage, overcoming 'bystanding' and groupthink;
- welcome others' views and constructive challenges, encouraging hands-up challenge questions by making workspaces psychologically safe and cognitively diverse, and by showing intellectual humility;
- stamp out cynical attitudes and abuses of power;
- look to prevent asymmetries between the firm and its customers: any imbalance of information, knowledge, competence or control.

So... what do we need to know, to start with?

As a regulated financial practitioner, before you launch into the finer points of culture auditing it's useful to have some awareness to be able to 'work conduct-aware'. There will be plenty more detail on the practice of culture assessment in other chapters, as we identify your responsibilities as the regulator defines them; then some elementary (and perhaps enjoyable) behavioural science. This will include basics of how we perceive risk and how biases knock decisions and markets off course. You'll also need to learn how to give a *credible* (not just self-serving) report on your personal competence.

At the next stage, you should prepare to get everyone in your firm – not just the senior managers – ready and able to talk unselfconsciously about what they themselves do to support a healthy workplace culture. It is useful to have a sense of context for the questions the regulator will ask you. Once you better understand the direction these questions are coming from, it's easier to know what a 'right answer' feels and sounds like.

A brief introductory World Tour of conduct and culture regimes

As we've just seen, the new regulators are not only interested in legal certainties such as the legally defensible value in a contract you may have traded. They really want to know how closely you pay attention to, and engage with, what the wider world thinks of you. After wave after wave of scandals, how firms respond to public opinion – and answer public accusations of collective wrongdoing – is of some relevance.

The behavioural lens is now being applied not only to financial firms in the consumer markets, but also in wholesale and capital markets, asset management and business-to-business broking. Whilst regulators dedicated to these individual markets at a national level are busily developing new frameworks for conduct and culture, so too is a powerful cadre of supranational organizations; some regulatory agencies, some professional bodies, some practitioner-sponsored groups.

For example, a global coordinating regulatory group, the International Organization of Securities Commissions (IOSCO), published a worldwide study of how their member agencies are locally using a behavioural lens to protect customers against harms from misconduct.[5] The report identified financial securities regulators around the world already applying behavioural science to customer protection, noting nearly 30 of them – even before counting regulators of any other types of financial market, or central banks.

On which note, as of 2021 more than 10 of the world's major central banks explicitly support 'conduct and culture-based supervision'. Conduct-based regulation is popular with central bankers and their government sponsors for exactly the same reasons that securities and insurance regulators like it, namely that the public (ie voters) welcome the regime's apparent promise to hold individual industry leaders (so-called 'fat cats') to account; and revenue raised through fines offsets regulatory running costs. Besides, public prosecutors see 'direct-to-individual' enforcement as a faster-acting, more satisfying intervention than cumbersome, old-style collective actions against faceless corporates and product classes. A public prosecutor can't help being attracted to a regulatory regime that allows them in effect to say to a firm's senior leaders, in person, 'see you in court' on suspicion of misconduct, without having to build a complex technical product-based case against the firm as a whole.

In short, it's not hard to see how all of this plays well with voters who had lost faith in governments and regulators as a result of the GFC, or the subsequent scandals, or the Covid-19 recession. It is helpful here to highlight some of the regulatory rising stars of the new 'conduct and culture agenda', so that you know who is setting the (furious) pace of development.

World Tour (2): the direction of travel – themes and tools, local and global

Throughout this book we are not aiming to offer an exhaustive, academically rigorous analysis of the field, but rather a general orientation through a series of highlights that pick out significant trends and key examples. These are selected to help inform your deeper understanding of significant developments in the regulation and practice of conduct and culture reporting.

For example: conduct regulation tends to spread from one part of the financial sector across others – so-called 'extension of regulatory powers' or, if you see this more cynically, 'regulatory creep'. In the case of the UK, the conduct regulator started by supervising banks through the Senior Managers and Certification Regime (SMCR) introduced in 2016, then extended this mode of supervision to include first insurers in 2018, then during 2019–20 asset managers, and finally most other kinds of financial business including brokers, credit and car finance providers, inter-market broker-dealers, 'FinTechs' (financial technology product providers or suppliers) and any other forms of retail product sales not previously covered. As the remit spreads across subsectors, so too does the range of tools the regulator uses: again in the UK, this entailed conduct assessments starting in 2016, culture assessments ('culture audit') in 2021, and reputational risk assessments from 2022.

At the same time, the modern conduct regulator looks to add continuously to their stock of ideas and experimental tools as informed by the latest developments in human behavioural research. Thus since 2013 we have seen conduct regulators adopting first the language and techniques from 'nudge economics', then the cognitive psychology analysis of biases, 'rule-gaming' and lying. More recently, there have been forays into newer branches of behavioural science: as of the start of 2021, these include current regulator-sponsored studies on psychological safety, cognitive diversity, reflexivity, unconscious (anti-diversity) bias, motivated reasoning, leadership character assessment, and active open-mindedness.

There are also regulator-sponsored experiments with the theory and practical use of new supervisory tools such as machine learning, AI language analytics, pattern analysis of social media transactions, and machine-readable regulations. All of these will be unpacked in plain language later in this book, by the way (see Chapter 12). We should look forward positively to many more such experiments – maybe even learn to love them as a normal feature of the new regulatory landscape.

Just as conduct rules spread from one subsector to another, so too do they migrate from one jurisdiction to another as regulators copy techniques and learn from each other's experiences. In this broader sweep of conduct regulation around the world, certain trends common to all the regulatory agencies are worth watching.[6] It's not a coincidence that the first of these trends happens to be the theme of the book you're holding:

- Supervisors focusing on **culture**: Regulators are looking at how firms move beyond vague 'good intentions' around conduct, to define a clear sense of purpose and put this into practice. What is the culture that promotes good conduct? How is it assessed, audited and reported? How are firms connecting culture reform with improved risk management outcomes?

- Furthering the use of **behavioural science** to explain why what happens, happens. For example, What can the science teach us about how best to drive healthy culture and exemplary conduct, and how do these improve firm performance and deliver the best possible customer outcomes?

- Regulators and advisory bodies are **collaborating across borders**, with all kinds of sector-wide and supranational groups getting aboard the conduct train. They include IOSCO, as mentioned above; also the Financial Markets Standards Board (FMSB, focusing on foreign exchange markets), the Institute of Internal Auditors (IIA) and the Financial Reporting Council (FRC), looking at reporting practices; the Basel Committee of the Bank for International Settlements (BIS), linking culture and reputational risk to capital adequacy; the Global Financial Innovation Network (GFIN) promoting 'reg tech'; and the Operational Risk Exchange (ORX), publishing data on risk management failures. All are sharing best-practice and worst-practice case examples and lessons learned, many with a view to more assertive intervention against poor workplace cultures.

- Regulators collectively want to press firms to work harder to identify and report on the **gaps** between current and desired culture; the need to promote 'speaking up' under better conditions of psychological safety; and the need for peer review and benchmarking, both against local competitor firms and globally against others' conduct (and misconduct) records.

- Regulators expect technology ('**reg tech**') to play an increasingly key part in this, as they promote a 'roadmap' for industry adoption of reg tech tools and initiatives. British and Hong Kong regulators have both talked of pushing diagnostics for conduct and culture 'upstream', intervening earlier to find and fix rotten cultures. The Hong Kong regulator aspires to support a new reg tech 'ecosystem'.

Conduct or culture, or what?

This is probably a good point for us to start to consider what's meant by the intertwined concepts of conduct and culture, so that we can separate them meaningfully. To begin with, let's keep it simple.

Conduct – what you do, or just did – is down to the individual. But of course your conduct in general – how you behave in a given situation – while it may have underlying patterns, is also highly responsive to the particular situation you're in at any given moment. Big influences on your conduct are, unsurprisingly: hierarchy and your social status in the group you're in; wanting to conform with norms of 'the way we do things around here'; concern not to be cast as the 'outsider' and so ostracized by a tightly knit group, and so on. The point is, it's what individuals do, whether out of personal habit, coercion, being in an overconfident group, or whatever. Unlike...

Culture – itself 'the way we do things around here', in one definition – is confusingly seen by some commentators as the product of conduct, whilst others see culture as the driver of conduct. To me, this 'direction of drive' argument is no more useful than the medieval theologians arguing about how many angels fit on the head of a pin. The evident truth is that conduct and culture interact; each has an effect on the other. We see this all the time in practice.

For example, it's very likely that an organization with a dominant and entrenched culture of, say, managers bullying subordinates, will quickly squash a newly arrived individual's behavioural traits into a more compliant (here meaning 'unchallenging') shape. Yet this driver effect can also, of course, work the other way round – indeed, there are some notorious examples of how a dominant individual can enter an organization and bend its culture into a whole new shape. Two cases that spring to mind – from among many out there – are the arrival of Dick 'The Gorilla' Fuld as CEO of Lehman Brothers, and that firm's subsequent downfall in 2008; and the similarly game-changing effect of Royal Bank of Scotland's appointment of Fred Goodwin as CEO.

The key is to pinpoint the nature of interaction between the individual (conduct/'the person') and the employer organization (culture/'the place'). Where in the organization are the hotspots of positive, or generous, or abusive, or coercive, or defensive behaviour? How do these bend individual incomers' original values and aspirations out of shape? Who, if anyone, cares to identify these and call them out? These are the focal topics of our friend and colleague Hani Nabeel's excellent analytical approach, examined in Chapters 7 and 14.

Conduct, culture and governance

Supervisors are pulling all these initiatives towards the larger domains of corporate governance and stakeholder engagement, with conduct and culture seen as their natural concerns. Governance itself is outgrowing the 'compliance' domain, entering a far broader arena of debate where HR, institutional investors, and environmental and social interests are now converging. Regulators' conversations with industry groups note phrases like 'cultural capital'[7] and that 'a firm's culture is the key driver of their conduct and more general risk management'.[8] The UK's FCA sees its 'coaching' of firms to define clearer purpose as a core element of its mission of 'transforming culture in financial services'.[9] Its series of Culture debate papers[10] promotes a pleasingly plural view of possible ways forward, meaning that whilst there is 'no one correct solution' to reporting on conduct and culture, firms may be left frustrated by a lack of consistent guidance on the best way to set about designing a reporting framework.

From the point of view of audit (the so-called 'third line of defence'), the UK-based Financial Reporting Council and the global Institute of Internal Auditors both want firms' auditors explicitly to link governance practices with audit reporting. This will compel firms formally to 'demonstrate their positive impact' on investors and wider stakeholders, evidencing 'the importance of corporate culture'.[11] A European Commission directive on non-financial reporting is similarly looking to set standards including for diversity, fair treatment of employees, and anti-corruption efforts, as part of a broad initiative for culture reform in 'public interest entities'.[12]

All of which aligns culture reporting within possible future global standards of reporting on environmental, social and governance (ESG) factors. That's of interest not only to regulators but also to institutional investors. As we'll see in Chapter 6, investors and regulators agree that good ESG engagement can strongly predict financial strength and future performance. Though their motives differ, all welcome robust metrics for culture that might help predict disruptive challenges and better govern risk.

Having thus agreed that better reporting is needed, conduct regulators are (as at Q1/2021) promoting the concept of culture audit. It is seen as a means to improve corporate governance, giving supervisors a fresh view of various nests of 'soft risks' that may, in aggregate, produce serious systemic risk. Their ideal is perhaps to identify these predictively, to have *advance* warnings of misconduct; as we'll see in Chapter 12, 'reg tech'-led culture analysis is already assembling the necessary leading indicators.

Developing conduct and culture assessment: global highlights

As trailed earlier in this chapter, it's worth briefly seeing who are the main movers and shakers among the world's conduct regulatory agencies – including conduct, product and prudential supervisors and central banks. Let's briefly introduce here some agencies that lead the world's thinking on culture audit (lots more details in Chapters 10 and 11). Some are regulators, setting principles that others follow. All apply behavioural science to understand how they can better protect customer interests. You may find some of these unfamiliar, possibly even surprising.

The **Dutch central bank** – De Nederlandsche Bank (DNB) announced its 'conduct risk' approach as part of a wider, groundbreaking manifesto on how to supervise financial firms' culture back in 2016.[13] This leadership is partly because the Netherlands has more than 30 years' history of strongly applying behavioural science to the design of all kinds of law making, not only financial regulation, including pioneering a behavioural lens (called 'T11'[14]) back in 1993. DNB's work has a huge and continuing influence on other central banks and regulatory agencies.

In the **United States**, the **New York Federal Reserve** ('NY Fed'). Like DNB, despite being a central bank, NY Fed runs annual conferences promoting reforms to improve culture and behaviour in the financial services sector. At these events, they discuss 'culture as a form of capital'[15] and vocally support DNB's approach to culture supervision.

The **UK's Financial Conduct Authority** pioneered high-level direct engagement with firms it supervised and their stakeholders' conduct in financial services (although Japan, the Netherlands and South Africa had all started their own 'behavioural' approaches to financial regulation before the FCA launched in 2013). As noted above (page 21), the FCA runs its own behavioural economics research programme.

Australia's financial sector avoided the worst consequences of the 2008 financial crash but has since had an unusually turbulent ride, with startling revelations emerging from a 2019 public enquiry into its 'systemic misconduct' throughout the 2010s.[16] Its **Australian Securities and Investments Commission** (ASIC) and **Australian Prudential Regulation Authority** (APRA) were already working conduct-aware during the enquiry period, yet it seems that significant events of misconduct passed unchecked. Australia is pioneering the formulation of 'sharper regulatory teeth', whereby conduct enforcements are fast-tracked towards criminal sanctions, enabling the sending of misbehaving managers straight to prison. APRA says its priority is to transform governance, culture, remuneration and accountability ('GCRA') through more prescriptive and demanding future standards for culture and governance, backed by firmer enforcement including capital charges.

The **Hong Kong Monetary Authority** (HKMA) has trialled culture audit methods with nearly 30 firms. HKMA's report[17] notes some banks engaging external advisers on culture but that most simply solicit staff feedback through surveys and focus groups. HKMA urges use of 'the right tools and technology' so that firms can deliver a 'big picture' analysis, with meaningful culture insights to senior leaders. This would encourage firms to 'assess how close they are to achieving their desired culture' and what forms of intervention can most effectively drive cultural change.

The **Monetary Authority of Singapore** (MAS) focuses on 'nonfinancial risk' after a series of accounting and governance scandals. Its Conduct and Culture Steering Group warns that 'reform of the financial industry – to make it safer and more purposeful – will not be complete until the industry 'gets its culture right'. It aims to promote raised standards for culture and conduct, reflecting an 'era of new social expectation'.

Conclusion

Behaviour-based regulation is here to stay, in the form of conduct and culture assessment, supervision and reporting. This resonates with politicians and citizens who remain deeply distrustful of financial providers, whose past reporting is suspected of being self-serving and disrespecting the public interest. Regulators are energetically gathering new tools to assess firms' culture including, as we'll see (Chapter 12), regulatory technology ('reg tech').

The Covid-19 pandemic has perhaps achieved what a decade of prototype conduct rules couldn't: concerted focus on firms' culture of service delivery. Working from home compromised 'first lines of defence', with patchy management of financial and nonfinancial misconduct risk. Despite and also because of the pandemic, around the world a large number of conduct regulators have been preparing themselves to question directly individuals at all levels in your firm. These 'floor-walk tests' will assuredly ask for your personal take on your firm's culture. Chapter 10 reveals key questions they will ask – and a rote-learned answer will not pass muster.

Absence of proof of misconduct doesn't prove that misconduct is absent. Conduct regulators expect firms to develop leading indicators of misconduct and to intervene earlier to improve unhealthy workplace cultures. Reg tech, tougher live supervision, and rising public expectation all play a part in supporting this.

The time to start a conversation with your colleagues about conduct and culture is *now*. Not only to start thinking about what you should say as a regulator approaches your desk, but to promote pre-emptively a culture of healthy risk taking and problem solving in your firm. Don't leave it until the regulator arrives in the room. Over the next few chapters, we'll see how to get that conversation started.

Notes

1 Financial Conduct Authority (FCA) (2018) Transforming Culture in Financial Services; Discussion Paper 18/2, fca.org.uk/publications/discussion-papers/dp18-2-transforming-culture-financial-services (archived at https://perma.cc/4JEE-Z3UL)

2 International Organization of Securities Commissions (IOSCO) Report (2017) IOSCO Task Force Report on Wholesale Market Conduct, IOSCO FR07/2017, iosco.org/library/pubdocs/pdf/IOSCOPD563.pdf (archived at https://perma.cc/N2GW-JCTR)

3 Miles, R (2017) *Conduct Risk Management: Using a behavioural approach to protect your board and financial services business*, Kogan Page

4 From authors' own (UK Finance) debriefing with Ms Chesterfield; also University College London (2020) Changing Minds webinar, 26 July, ucl-changing-minds.org/webinar/banking-on-behavioural-insights/ (archived at https://perma.cc/U5XX-S4PC); see also http://fairbanking.org.uk/ (archived at https://perma.cc/JT8D-VZD9)

5 IOSCO (2017)

6 Scott, S J and Cooke, M (2020) *Culture Audits: Removing the blindfold*, Starling Trust

7 Stiroh, Kevin (2019–20) New York Federal Reserve speeches on 'Cultural capital' and reform, at newyorkfed.org/governance-and-culture-reform (archived at https://perma.cc/N7GB-YFTN)

8 Reserve Bank of New Zealand governor Adrian Orr, cited in Scott and Cooke, *Culture Audits*, above

9 Financial Conduct Authority (FCA) (2020) Transforming Culture in Financial Services – Driving Purposeful Cultures: Discussion Paper 20/1, https://www.fca.org.uk/publications/discussion-papers/dp20-1-transforming-culture-financial-services-driving-purposeful-cultures (archived at https://perma.cc/7CTQ-YT4J)

10 FCA Discussion papers 18/2 and 20/1, both on Transforming Culture, fca.org.uk (archived at https://perma.cc/RB9N-6EBD)

11 Quoted in Scott and Cooke, ibid

12 European Commission (nd) EC consultation on reform of nonfinancial reporting, https://ec.europa.eu/info/law/better-regulation/have-your-say/initiatives/12129-Revision-of-Non-Financial-Reporting-Directive (archived at https://perma.cc/ZVQ2-BV2H)

13 De Nederlandsche Bank (Mirea Raaijmakers, editor) (2015) Supervision of Behaviour and Culture, https://www.dnb.nl/media/1gmkp1vk/supervision-of-behaviour-and-culture_tcm46-380398-1.pdf (archived at https://perma.cc/C87B-YHRN)

14 Dutch Justice Ministry [Justitie] (2006) De Tafel van Elf: een veelzijdig instrument, kcwj.nl/sites/default/files/Tafel_van_Elf__veelzijdig_instrument.pdf (archived at https://perma.cc/79RQ-NZCN)

15 Stiroh (2019–20)

16 Hayne, K M (2019) Royal Commission Report into Misconduct in the Banking, Superannuation and Financial Services Industry, royalcommission.gov.au/royal-commission-misconduct-banking-superannuation-and-financial-services-industry (archived at https://perma.cc/JG79-JQJT)

17 Hong Kong Monetary Authority (2020) Report on Review of Self-assessments on Bank Culture, May, www.hkma.gov.hk/media/chi/doc/key-information/guidelines-and-circular/2020/20200522c1a1.pdf (archived at https://perma.cc/36K6-MC3H)

03

The house is on fire

*How regulators' own research has
pointed to 'culture reset'*

COSETTE RECZEK

Introduction: evolving beyond deterrents

When first introduced, the earliest wave of conduct regulation tended to be seen by firms, by default, through a 'compliance lens'. As events of misconduct continued throughout the decade following the 2008 financial crisis, it was perceived that implementation of conduct regulation and guidance couldn't come soon enough to drive real behavioural change across the financial services industry. Even before the worldwide spread of Covid-19, the year 2020 boded badly for public trust in institutions of all kinds:

> None of the four societal institutions that the study measures – government, business, NGOs and media – is trusted. The cause of this paradox can be found in people's fears about the future and their role in it, which are a wake-up call for our institutions to embrace a new way of effectively building trust: balancing competence with ethical behaviour (Edelman Trust Barometer, January 2020[1]).

As will be seen in this chapter, regulators have mounted their own research projects over many years to enquire into why the new 'conduct regime' of behaviour-based controls seemed so slow to effect culture change within financial services firms. It emerged that the key to lasting change may lie in greater clarity in understanding the linkage of how culture drives behaviour, and how conduct and culture interrelate. Other regulated sectors (aviation, food) have had notably more success with reforming their regulatory dialogues and risk cultures.

This chapter takes a tour through how financial sector regulators have responded to this pressure to increase clarity with rising urgency following the 10th anniversary (in 2018) of the global financial crisis.

THEMES AND CONCEPTS IN THIS CHAPTER

acceptable and expected conduct – Annual Conduct Meetings – 'behaviour-at-risk' – 'behavioural clusters' taxonomy of misconduct – Banking Standards Board (BSB) assessment framework – behavioural science in the design of incentives – causal link between 'unhealthy culture' and events of misconduct – 'culture fatigue' – 'Culture Sprint' experimental space – Conduct Rules – deterrents theory/failure – economic and social function of the firm – effective financial regulatory reform (own vs other sectors) – fines as a 'friction cost of business' – Five Conduct Questions – formal Culture Audit guidelines in development (Institute of Internal Auditors) – 'the Gekko effect' – group influence effects – need for clarity in defining purpose – 'nudging' – post-2008 continuing financial sector scandals – principles-based regulation – psychological safety – 'regulatory void' between principles and practice – self-regulatory 'GSVR' – sub-culture (dissonance) – silos and tribes – systemic misbehaviour – 'vox populi risk' to regulator legitimacy

---

Regulatory fines seen as a 'friction cost of doing business'

As we'll explore in more detail in Chapter 6, there's a powerful 'vox populi risk' that doubts and questions the legitimacy of financial regulatory frameworks, and even of the governments that sponsor them. The wrath of consumers who lost so much in the 2008 financial crisis has only grown in the face of the relentless parade of subsequent scandals. As political realists, answerable to their sponsoring ministers in every case, financial regulators around the world increasingly recognized that even the historically severe fines levied against misbehaving firms seemed not enough to prevent continued wrongdoing.

'Vox populi' criticism (see box) is sounding louder than ever:

> I ceased believing Britain was capable of genuine reform years ago... We are overrun by our own pirates. [The FCA set] huge figures for fines... but it was all

'small beer' in financial terms in any case... I recall expert opinion termed such costs not as penalties, but as merely 'the cost of doing business'.[2]

It is hard to avoid concluding that conventional theory of deterrents – laws, detection and punishment including massive fines – for various reasons may not apply in the case of financial services.[3] If these instruments don't prevent systemic misbehaviour, what else might?

'**Vox populi risk**' is the set of impacts on a firm's business – or the 'business' of regulation itself – that result from public opinion turning against it. Public opinion is fast-changing and increasingly volatile, as has been seen with popular protests for policy change such as #notinmyname, #metoo, #blacklivesmatter, #taxpayersalliance, #didtheyhelp and #extinctionrebellion; and at a product level by the rise of citizen-supported comparison and critique forums such as Trustpilot, Glassdoor and Violation Tracker. Public changes of mood may rapidly redefine what now constitutes 'acceptable and expected' behaviour: the perceived legitimacy and social licence of firms, control agencies and governments.

An increasing weight of research, much of it commissioned by regulators, has suggested that where conventional deterrents fail, other forms of direct intervention to influence culture and behaviour might stand a better chance of gaining traction.

Early days: seeking progress beyond 'compliance' to culture mindset

At its inception in 2012, the UK's **Financial Conduct Authority** (FCA) expressed a conventional, principles-based view that:

Regulation has to strike the right balance between allowing the industry to thrive and ensuring it retains its integrity and delivers what consumers expect from it. We will set ourselves demanding targets for our own performance, as well as expecting high standards from others in this regard[4] (John Griffith-Jones, Chairman-Designate, FCA, 2012).

So from the boardroom to point of sale and beyond, firms' behaviour, attitudes and motivations must be about good conduct... Things need to change; industry and the regulator need to rise to the challenge of that change. The creation of the FCA is our opportunity to reset conduct standards for the financial services industry[5] (Martin Wheatley, Chief Executive-Designate, FCA, 2012).

The FCA soon (2015) introduced a simple yet effective tool to focus firms' discussion and evaluation of 'acceptable and expected conduct': The Five Conduct Questions (see Chapters 10 and 11). These questions initially formed part of the FCA's strategy for supervising wholesale banks. In 2016 the questions were incorporated into Annual Conduct Meetings (ACMs), introduced for the largest firms to help the FCA understand how these firms were engaging with the questions and what measures they were taking, prompted by the questions, to improve conduct in their firms.[6] Since 2017 the FCA has published a regular (not quite annual) review of firms' engagement with the Five Questions, encouraging firms to benchmark their own efforts and see how engagement with 'conduct risk' has evolved year on year.

Extending its intended agenda of robust supervision and enforcement activities, the FCA introduced conduct regulation creating individual accountability not only for board members and executives but also for all staff in financial firms. The Senior Managers and Certification Regime ('SMR'), first implemented in March 2016, introduced Conduct Rules applicable to all (excepting ancillary staff), together with ensuring that firms had processes to assess whether these rules had been breached, with breaches to be reported to the FCA and tracked on a central register.

CONDUCT RULES

Under FCA's Senior Managers and Certification Regime:

   Rule 1: You must act with integrity.

   Rule 2: You must act with due skill, care and diligence.

   Rule 3: You must be open and cooperative with the FCA, the PRA and other
      regulators.

   Rule 4: You must pay due regard to the interests of customers and treat them
      fairly.

   Rule 5: You must observe proper standards of market conduct.

The introduction of individual accountability rules sought to fill a perceived 'regulatory void', since enforcers have signally failed to catch up with business leaders allegedly responsible for serial misconduct before, during and since the 2008 market crash. From its inception, the FCA's view was that only personal accountability would concentrate minds and motives on good conduct.

Despite all this, misdeeds kept happening (see p 105), with 'behaviour-at-risk' recognized as a key contributory factor. To impress the importance of good conduct on each individual, leaders and colleagues needed to be asked to demonstrate how elements of good conduct are present within the daily working culture. The regulatory theory was that nudging social norms of good culture would create healthier 'rules of belonging' within teams, driving improved behaviour across whole firms.

Given the size and scale of the biggest financial services institutions, there could never be one universal culture. Diversity, geography, language, and the nature of the business activities themselves give rise to difference in perception of what good looks like. For example, 'you must pay due regard to the interests of customers and treat them fairly' could look different depending upon whether the customer is a typical retail customer or a professional, high-net-worth individual investor. These differences lead to multiple cultures within the same institution, which was borne out in research presented by Professors Elizabeth Sheedy and Barbara Griffin in their seminal **Macquarie University** research 'Empirical Analysis of Risk Culture in Financial Institutions: Interim Report.'[7] Most variations in risk culture occur at the business-unit level and are driven by the local team environment. This is consistent with the hypothesis that culture is a local construct and very much dependent on interactions with close colleagues and the immediate manager.

A related factor driving culture is rewards; it's no good preaching conduct values if those who bend the rules are remunerated regardless. Starting with blunt instruments such as failure to complete mandatory training, remuneration in financial services has evolved to introduce caps, clawbacks, and consideration not only of what has been done but also how it's been done (ie, performance and values ratings), including any conduct breaches.

Research recognizes linkage of culture to behaviour

The intersection of the legal and regulatory framework of conduct and the key roles of culture and behaviour within it were reflected in what is still today the most comprehensive regulatory approach encompassing both elements: the Dutch central bank **De Nederlandsche Bank**'s (DNB) risk-based supervisory cycle underpinned by behaviour and culture risk identification, assessment, and mitigation. Starting work on their approach in 2010, DNB recognized early that as guardians of financial stability, 'we must keep a close eye on anything that might put this financial stability in jeopardy. Naturally, this includes a financial institution's behaviour and culture.'[8]

DNB acknowledged that when they started down this path, 'this new strategy met with scepticism not just outside our organization, but internally.'[9] However, by 2015 DNB reported that their endeavours had been 'increasingly rewarding and that some countries are following suit. The initial scepticism has gradually made way for genuine appreciation, both from institutions whose behaviour and culture we examine and from our supervisory colleagues at home and further afield.'[10]

The **Federal Reserve Bank of New York** (NY Fed), citing the work of DNB, had begun to think along similar lines, in 2015 revealing that it had since 2013 been taking part in an international dialogue on the reform of culture in the financial services industry: 'new laws, regulations, and standards have done little to curb banker misconduct. Each post-Crisis episode demonstrates a narrow cultural focus on short-term gain and disregard of broader social consequences.'[11]

NY Fed then posed the question: Why culture?, suggesting that:

Environment drives conduct. What each of us learned from our parents governs some of our behavior, but not nearly as much as any of us who are parents would like to believe. Place ordinary people in a bad environment, and bad things tend to happen. That said, place someone in a good environment, and good things tend to happen. This is just part of being human. We observe and adapt.[12]

It also noted that culture is generally inconsistent within each firm, with subculture 'silos' and 'tribes', of whose presence we should be alert for 'warning signs' of behaviour incompatible with the firm's claimed values. Finally, NY Fed urged a 'relentless and sustained effort' for cultural reform through a process of continuous improvement:

... from the top of an institution to its most junior employees, and across all of the institution's business activities... [to cover] the full scope of an employee's career, beginning with recruiting and continuing with annual performance management, compensation and promotion decisions.

Also in 2015, in the UK the **Banking Standards Board** (BSB) was established to promote high standards of behaviour and competence across the UK banking industry. The original idea for the body emerged from the work of the **Parliamentary Commission** on Banking Standards which called for a new type of organization, different from traditional regulators, that would look at banking standards, culture and the root causes of poor behaviour.

The BSB has created an assessment approach intended to help firms achieve and maintain high standards of behaviour and competence, based on a framework of nine characteristics (honesty, respect, openness, accountability, competence, reliability, responsiveness, personal and organizational resilience, and shared purpose). Monitoring firms' engagement with and embedding of these factors, BSB expects to encourage good outcomes for member firms, their employees, customers/clients, investors and the economy and society as a whole; all those stakeholders who may and should be expected to benefit from a good culture in banking service provision.

The BSB published its first annual review based on this framework early in 2017. It included feedback from more than 28,000 employees in 22 institutions across the UK financial services industry, reached by surveys, focus groups, or deep-dive interviews. It identified key themes for further exploration, including:

- apparent mismatch between values espoused by the firm and the way some employees see business being done;
- developing a culture within the banking sector of responsibility and accountability rather than of blame;
- identifying practical steps to help promote employee resilience and well-being.

Strikingly, none of these relates directly to 'compliance', looking instead to banks' values, culture and the many possible variables of human behaviour that we may be able to track.

Global initiatives

BSB was by no means the only self-regulatory body (see sidebar: GSVR) established with the intention of changing financial sector culture and conduct. Among many other more or less formal groupings established in the decade of the 2010s in the UK and around the world, two are notable: the Global Foreign Exchange (FX) Committee and the Fixed-Income Credit and Commodities (FICC) Markets Standards Board.

DOES SELF-REGULATION ('GSVR') WORK IN THE LONG TERM?

GSVR, or 'government-sponsored voluntary regulation' is policy-makers' jargon name for codes of practice and similar industry-level efforts where regulatee groups take self-governing initiatives to pre-empt full regulation. Academic studies[13] dismiss many GSVRs as mere 'pledges', though they have enabled various industries to make progress answering society's concerns, for example on reducing fat content or salt levels in food and reducing the use of plastic bags. GSVRs are also found in the fields of environment and sustainability; public health; employment and skills; pricing; trading policy and social policy.

The **Global FX Committee** was formed in 2017 to promote, maintain and regularly update a code of practice, the FX Global Code (FX Code), and also to consider how best to support adherence to the Code. The first version of the FX Code was published in May 2018, emphasizing ethics, govern-ance, risk and compliance alongside execution, information handling, and other technical aspects of working in FX markets. It has membership from all the major financial institutions around the world.

The **FICC Markets Standards Board** (FMSB) began its work in 2015 to identify global market vulnerabilities, to develop best market practice and consistent approaches, and to drive global adherence. It too has membership from many of the major financial institutions around the world. Besides publishing standards and statements of good practice to drive consistency of market practices across FICC markets, it also undertook analysis of miscon-duct in various markets around the globe over a long sweep of time: a 200+-year global perspective.

The FMSB research concluded that market misconduct, when observed over time, could be grouped together into categories that FMSB calls 'behav-ioural clusters'. This analysis, published in July 2018,[14] found that a *limited number of recognizable patterns of misconduct recur* over many years, regardless of asset class or jurisdiction.

That being the case, how difficult should it then be to put controls in place to prevent or detect these recognizable, recurrent, patterned misbehav-iours? Harder than it at first appears, suggested the report, since behaviours adapt continually to new technologies and market structures – in other words, where there's a will there's a way (see Figure 3.1). That said, a natu-ral inference of the research is that by adopting and consistently using

FIGURE 3.1   Historically recurrent 'behavioural clusters' of misconduct events

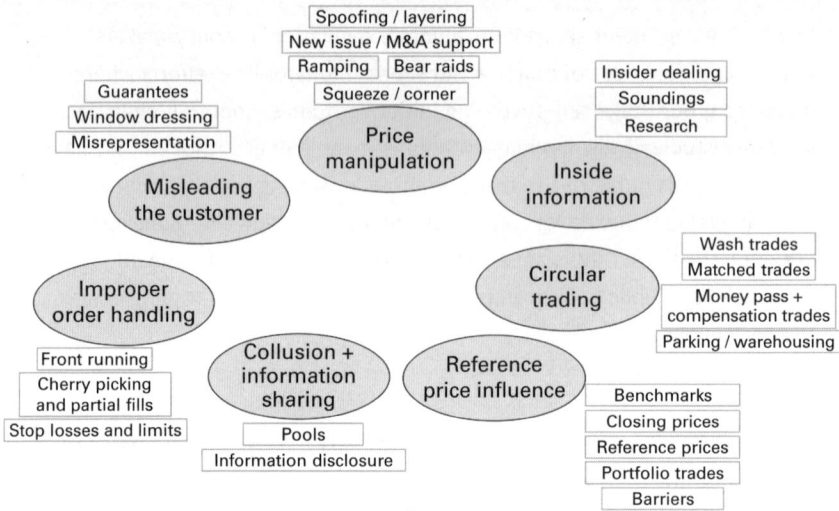

SOURCE   FICC research: Misconduct patterns in financial markets (July 2018)[15]

FMSB's good practice framework standards and statements, the industry could make more effective efforts to detect and prevent market misconduct.

Post-2018: now we're Woke?

The tipping point for the regulatory thinking about culture as a driver of conduct came in 2018 – the 10th anniversary of the onset of the global financial crisis. That year, a sustained campaign of speeches and statements culminated in a seminal research report published by the **Group of Thirty**.

Endorsing this, in February 2018 Central Bank of Ireland Director General Derville Rowland reflected on the legacy of Hollywood's fictitious corporate raider Gordon Gekko in the film *Wall Street* (1987); Rowland pointed to the significance of behaviour and culture in achieving good conduct. She noted that a NY Fed paper had referred to Gekko's character as being based on the real-life Ivan Boesky – the same Boesky who was convicted of insider trading and sent to prison. The author of the NY Fed paper, Professor Andrew W. Lo, had coined the term 'the Gekko effect' to argue that a corporate culture may transmit negative values to a firm's workforce in ways that make financial malfeasance significantly more likely.[16] He suggested a need to promote essential behaviours that can guard against the spread of a destructive culture, such as: willingness to admit mistakes, the refusal to respect unjust authority, the ability to consider the future rather than the immediate present, and the individual values of honesty, responsibility and independence of thought.[17]

A research digest published in February 2018 by the UK's FCA noted its findings on group effects in risk-taking:[18]

- People behave differently when they are in groups; rule-breaking depends on the culture and social norms within firms.

- Wrongdoing can be reduced by promoting a positive culture of compliance. Firms can do this through their tone of communication, training and the expectations they set for their staff, as well as by providing the right incentives, combatting negative ideologies and publicizing examples of good behaviour.

- Dealing with determined transgressors, with 'salient and vivid' punishment targeted against the individuals doing business, is likely to be more effective than punishments at the level of the firm.

It also set out the vital role of regulators in reinforcing the importance of individual morality and responsibility in decision-making; this view had in part informed the FCA's rollout of its senior managers accountability regime, SMR.[19] The regulator concluded specifically that financial sector *culture* 'is widely accepted as a key root cause of the major conduct failings that have occurred within the industry in recent history.'[20] It supported this with specialist research essays exploring topics such as:

- use of behavioural science to guide incentives and cultural change;

- looking beyond the role of leadership in effecting change;

- applying strategic focus to the continuous process for adapting culture;

- fostering environments of trust to encourage openness and learning; and

- applying a systems perspective in assessing both internal culture and external influencers.

Whilst the anthology presented firms with an invitation to consider, rather than mandating a set of rules, it made a clear connection between culture and individuals' behaviour within financial services firms.

By May 2018 the FCA launched a new core element of managing culture in financial services institutions: the need for employees to have psychological safety. In their Insight report 'Speaking Up Creates the Most Effective Teams', the FCA recognized Harvard academic, Professor Amy Edmondson's characterization that psychological safety is the willingness of people to express an opinion in the workplace.[21] In Edmondson's original definition, psychological safety is an employee's belief that they will 'not be punished or humiliated for speaking up with ideas, questions, concerns, or mistakes, and that the team is safe for interpersonal risk-taking.'[22] This describes an environment where senior leaders are committed to learning from mistakes; where no one feels afraid to raise concerns or fears negative consequences to their ego or career if they do.

Despite having acknowledged and noted these research outputs, financial institutions continued to struggle with plans for cultural reform. By June 2018, the head of NY Fed, John C Williams, in a speech urging 'Now is the time for banking culture reform', noted the approach of the 10th anniversary of the 2008 crisis (without apparent irony). The reader could be forgiven any cynicism about why 'now was the time', 10 years after the misconduct-driven crisis – and despite mighty attempts at change as that decade passed.

Part of the answer to this may be found in another NY Fed-published piece not long after, in October 2018, entitled 'The Complexity of Culture Reform in Finance'. This accepted that the industry had:

> ... moved beyond the questions about 'if' this is an important issue and statements about 'why' it is important. Rather, the focus is 'how' the financial industry – both financial firms and the official sector – can continue to make progress in improving culture and reducing misconduct risk.[23]

It tied together preceding years of research and acknowledged various culture intervention prototypes, including an initiative for culture assessment (citing BSB's research, which by now was inviting global participants), technology and big data analysis to detect behavioural patterns. It also highlighted the capacity of behavioural economics to draw together psychology and economics to:

> ... provide insight into why individuals may behave in a certain way and make decisions that may not be in their own economic best interest. For example, individuals often make choices that provide immediate recognition or satisfaction – higher status within a peer group, for example – often at the cost of a potentially better financial outcome in the long term. This type of human behavior is at the core of the complexity of culture reform.[24]

ENCOURAGING THE USE OF TOOLS TO MEASURE AND ASSESS CULTURE

Culture measurement was spotlit in a January 2018 keynote article in the *Harvard Business Review*.[25] This identified qualitative ways of measurement, such as language-based 'lexical register' analysis of email or Glassdoor, as well as other tools aimed at capturing a firm-wide and industry-wide cultural baseline, enabling measured progress against that baseline; this included, critically, a breakdown of teams to gain insight into pockets of local risk culture. Behavioural research think-tank and methods pioneer Starling Trust has also urged the audit function to 'remove the blindfold' and invest effort in getting to know and work with behaviour-at-risk diagnostics.[26]

One example of a 'culture benchmark' approach is CultureScope, an award-winning tool devised by iPsychTec with Wharton Business School (see Chapters 12, 14). This tool recognizes that whilst improving employee engagement can be a powerful force for driving organizational performance, engagement tends to rise and fall quickly in response to transient business choices, which affect employee feelings. In simple terms, CultureScope measures individual and organizational behaviours (and not feelings/sentiment) and links these behaviours to business outcomes to generate predictive analytics. It compares and contrasts individual behaviour ('the people') and organizational environment ('the place'), linking these to business outcomes and drawing insights for action to improve alignment.

The Institute of Internal Auditors (IIA) has recognized the difficulty of 'rating' idiosyncratic cultures at individual and firm level, not least due to 'individual belief systems and preferences of each employee – from line workers to the corner office'; it's a hard ask to define and assess 'intangible organization-wide qualities or aspects that comprise human belief systems, social norms, and other psychological factors.' These differences in individual motivation can lead to different interpretations of expected behaviours day to day. To help get under the hood on this, IIA has work in progress on an approach for Auditing Culture[27] – distinct and separate from its approach to Auditing Conduct Risk.

Other commercial tools for detecting and predicting culture challenges include EthicEyes, which enables firms to constantly monitor their own ethical well-being, fostering strong ethical awareness with real-time insight. Participants receive up to five binary (yes/no) text questions per week that probe dimensions of an ethical resilience model. The anonymous responses are collated by EthicEyes and displayed on a private dashboard, enabling managers to instantly see 'how things are' across the firm and identify where potential ethical risks are increasing or decreasing by department. This stimulates real-time feedback on culture and ethics, to reinforce positive behaviours and intervene to reverse unwanted trends, keeping culture a part of everyday conversation.

To seal 2018's change of direction, and as a resounding critique of the lack of progress over the preceding decade, **Group of Thirty** (G30) published its research, 'Banking Conduct and Culture: A Permanent Mindset Change'. This noted how banks' 'rapid… evolution in thinking' and a 'positive shift in their view of the importance of conduct and culture' had not been matched by practical commitment to change throughout whole firms:

> …much of the work has been done at the most senior levels of the organization – with 'tone from the top' receiving much more focus than 'tone from above'. For permanent and ongoing change to occur, banks now need to focus on embedding culture awareness and stewardship at all levels of the organization, with a particular focus on middle management and frontline businesses.[28]

It ultimately called for recognition that as 'society and the competitive landscape rapidly evolve', banks have been 'complacent about their trust and reputational problems'.[29]

The G30 report heralded the expansion, to a global scale, of the debate on culture assessment and related regulatory reform. Building on the continued (and laudably early) efforts in the Netherlands, and also the rising visibility of the debate in the UK and US, 2019 saw the establishment of a culture and conduct steering group by the **Monetary Authority of Singapore**. In Australia, a **Royal Commission** reported in February 2019 on sustained harms visited by banks on their customers.

The Central Bank of Ireland expanded its focus on culture and conduct through establishment of a GSVR-based **Irish Banking Culture Board**, with a majority of non-banking members and with some similarities to UK's Banking Standards Board. Irish consumers have been initially unconvinced, calling the Board 'an excuse for bankers and Government to pretend that they are doing something, when they are doing nothing', as reported by the *Irish Independent*.[30]

Playing a broken record?

Despite these various aligned efforts around the world, during 2019 it remained clear that there was a large gap between rhetoric and actual behaviour across swathes of the financial services industry. NY Fed, debriefing on its own 'culture initiative' research, noted continuing 'evidence of deep-seated cultural and ethical failures', with most progress made merely on 'creating greater awareness of the problem' and reforms only patchily implemented:

> Major misconduct continues in financial services across the globe ...[with] headline scandals [of] money laundering, bribery, international sanctions evasion, and consumer abuse. Not surprisingly, public trust in the industry remains extremely low.[31]

The striking point here is the phrase 'not surprisingly', as 11 years had then passed since the 2008 crash. Would the 2020s be different? And how long would it take to introduce real reform, to make culture assessment an effective tool of risk governance?

FLYING AND FOOD: DOING IT BETTER

How two other heavily regulated sectors improved safety and service by changing their cultures of risk reporting – in liaison with their regulators.[32]

Civil aviation (US/global)

The civil aviation sector's Safety Management System is based on a 'Just Culture' of non-punitive risk reporting, under which no individual employee is blamed for an 'honest mistake'. (If, on the other hand, there's proof of intent to 'wilful violation or gross negligence', that will still be punished.) The industry describes this as having moved from 'compliance-based to performance-based' risk reporting, encouraging open reports from the front-line staff who are best placed to 'detect weak signals' of hazard. The resulting good working relationships bring 'openness, support and mutual respect, behavioural consistency, sharing and delegation of control, and demonstration of concern', all of which helps to 'promote trust'.[33]

As detailed in Chris Hodges and Ruth Steinholtz's landmark study, 'Safety Regulation in Civil Aviation',[34] in the 15 years immediately following the 1968–71 regulatory amnesty necessary to effect this change of culture, aviation achieved (by one significant measure) a five-fold improvement in its safety, reducing the risk of 'near-miss' in flight from 42 events per million operations, to 8 events per million.

Food standards (UK)

Since the event of several food supply chain quality scandals in the 2000s (such as the 'horsemeat lasagna' events of 2013[35]) the UK's Food Standards Agency (FSA) has actively stepped up to improve dialogue between market participants and regulators. Launching a culture change programme (2016) with a strategic goal of 'Food we can trust', the regulator alerted firms that it would 'take account of all available sources of information' (looking to primary information sources to overcome the 'compliance games' of formal risk reporting).

    At the same time the regulator explicitly incentivized firms to take responsibility and cooperate, in two ways: 'Business doing the right thing for customers will be recognized', and '[We are] content to rely on businesses that earn a reputation for producing trusted [audit] data'.[36]

Will the '20s be different?

At the turn of the decade, 2020 – and as the world responded to the Covid-19 pandemic – more regulatory agencies than ever embraced the need for culture assessment, accepting the causal link between unhealthy culture and poor conduct. Following the introduction of its Managers-in-Charge requirements in 2017, the **Hong Kong Monetary Authority** (HKMA) instructed 30 banks (including all major retail banks and selected foreign bank branches with substantial operations in Hong Kong) to conduct self-assessments on their culture enhancement efforts and benchmark themselves against the findings of major conduct incidents outside Hong Kong. The HKMA reviewed the self-assessment reports from the selected banks to draw insights and published their report in May 2020. Whilst the HKMA acknowledged that banks had 'made significant progress in promoting sound bank culture', it found that 'more effort is required' to:

- tackle the key challenge of culture assessment to identify the gaps between current progress and desired culture;

- promote an environment which provides 'psychological safety' to encourage staff to speak up without fear of adverse consequences; and

- drive cultural changes – though being mindful of 'culture fatigue'.[37]

We might at this point question how, if firms are suffering from culture fatigue, they'd find the extra energy and focus needed to identify and close culture gaps and to promote psychological safety. The **Monetary Authority of Singapore** (MAS) didn't wait on an answer, but has conducted its own research on culture and acted directly on its findings. In May 2020, MAS, together with the Association of Banks in Singapore, established a **Culture and Conduct Steering Group** to promote sound culture and mandate conduct standards among its regulatee banks.[38]

In September 2020, MAS published guidelines on *Individual Accountability and Conduct*, emphasizing an overlay of responsibility and ethical behaviour rules on the legislation already in place. Of all the agencies issuing FCA-style SMR accountability rules, MAS's most directly mirror the UK regime, examining progress through a planned supervisory framework for culture assessment. As an island territory, Singapore is heavily dependent on its financial services economy. Any financial scandal there creates disproportionate pain, whether it's the Mercantile Exchange's inadvertent 'by-standing' during the rogue trader-driven Barings collapse of 1995, or more recent shocks such as an $8bn penny-share implosion in 2013, and commodity traders' $3bn market-wrecking antics in oil contracts, uncovered in 2020. There's clearly every incentive for this regulator to look to lead the way for the rest of the world.

The **Australian Prudential Regulatory Authority** (APRA) published its *Banking Executive Accountability Regime* (BEAR) in 2018 – during the middle of the Royal Commission's investigation into banking misconduct. Whilst not as all-encompassing as the UK's SMR, Australia's BEAR mandated greater accountability by senior leaders, with deferred remuneration.[39] When the final report of Australia's Royal Commission was published in 2019 (complete with 76 recommendations), firms found their formerly dry professional jargon – fees for no service, non-monetary default – translated into screaming headlines, including from the *Guardian*: 'charging the dead, kicking farmers off their land even though they'd made every payment'.[40] As at Q4/2020, over a year later and after billions of AU$ paid out in compensation, there's still uncertainty over whether Australia's government will enact all of the report's recommendations, putting any significant pressure on the country's discredited industry to mend its self-serving ways.[41]

In the UK, the FCA celebrated the arrival of 2020 by publishing another compendium of essays on transforming culture, this time linking culture to purpose as a unifying factor in driving behaviour and promoting psychological safety. Entitled 'Transforming culture in financial services – driving purposeful cultures', this second anthology stressed the primacy of articulating a 'clear, meaningful' corporate purpose as 'an important part of adopting a healthy culture' which plays 'a fundamental role in reducing potential harm to consumers and markets'[42] (see Chapter 10).

FIRMS GET TO BRAINSTORM CULTURE WITH THE REGULATOR: FCA 'CULTURE SPRINTS'

Launching a 'Culture Sprint' initiative in 2019 at the FCA, its head of supervision Jonathan Davidson pointed out that whilst 'you can design and manage your culture, it doesn't just happen to you'; the aim of CultureSprint would be to 'help firms identify healthy culture that they want to have and help them to understand how to get there.'[43]

The creation of the FCA's CultureSprint forum was to allow a safe space for practical input and creative thinking from the people who work in finance every day, alongside input from academics and researchers. The sessions brought together a range of experts from multi-disciplinary perspectives to work together in teams, exploring ideas and developing solutions to problems the industry is facing in relation to culture. Their focus has been on developing practicable solutions and firms who attend do so on the basis that they will take the solution developed within their 'sprint' workshop team back to their firm to test it within a team/business area.[44]

The first culture sprint was so successful that the FCA held others during 2019 and 2020 (including virtually, during Covid-19 lockdowns). The FCA publishes conclusions after each session.

After Covid-19 gripped the world, the FCA recognized both the challenges and opportunities for changes in conduct and culture whilst employees increasingly worked remotely. In an Insight article published in June 2020, the FCA noted that Covid-19 has:

> ... changed our world and the way that we work... it is far from certain that we will ever return to life exactly as it was before. Leaders [must be] able to move

from a crisis management mindset to thinking about how to run their businesses differently, with a strong focus on culture. Firms that... find ways to nudge behaviours in the right direction have the chance to build business models and resilient cultures that adapt to the new circumstances with positive outcomes for customers, employees and investors.[45]

In September 2020 the FCA published industry 'Feedback on 5 Conduct Questions' (by now an annual exercise).[46] It focuses on culture from the start, noting banks' 'substantial time, effort and financial resources' invested in 'global change programmes to improve conduct risk management and, ultimately, culture'. The 5 Conduct Questions, first raised in prototype form in 2015, had always been intended to support such efforts. Along with the rest of us, the regulator was curious as to how well the questions had succeeded in driving and embedding culture change among all staff in firms. The research highlighted 'progress still required' on such points as:

- identifying conduct risk (processes remain weak);
- too wide a range of practices in assessing remuneration and performance, which factors tend directly to drive culture and behaviour (and hence also conduct risk);
- that it's too often still unsafe to speak up;
- staff need more clarity as to purpose, principles and values.[47]

The September 2020 review iterated the vital relationship of purpose to culture and behaviour, attaching to four key drivers of culture: Leadership, People Policies (including speak-up culture and psychological safety), Governance (how decisions are made within a firm), and Purpose. Purpose (see also Chapter 10) is held to be a firm's description of its own:

> ... economic function, and how it makes money. On one level, this is just
> a description of a firm's business model. But... in order to understand how
> a firm's purpose drives its culture, you need to understand how a company
> describes, to itself and others, the essential purpose of the firm, its products and
> its services, and so its reason for existing, and why the world would be worse
> off without the value it provides. We are also critically concerned with how far
> we can see this purpose tangibly driving the decisions made at all levels of the
> firm.[48]

Noting that networks of trust are networks of value, financial industry think-tank Starling Trust uses research data-driven insights to help firms overcome culture- or conduct-related risks. Starling publishes an annual

'Compendium' on regulatory activities and priorities regarding culture and conduct supervision in the banking sector, noting in 2020 that conduct regulators are now focusing on 'how supervisory attention to culture and conduct risk is best operationalized, and how financial institutions are expected to better audit such risks and to evidence their success in related risk management and culture reform efforts.'[49]

Conclusion

Strikingly, soon after Covid-19 hit the UK in earnest and national lockdown was in place, the FCA's interim Chief Executive Chris Woolard cautioned that almost all commercial lending was still unregulated and his powers to ensure lenders treated businesses fairly relied solely on post-2008 safeguards governing senior managers' conduct.[50] Under the UK's SMR, introduced in response to the global banking crisis, individuals can be held accountable for their conduct towards customers. However, the FCA has so far taken little action under the regime and Mr Woolard admitted, 'This is the first real test of SMR... it gives us some kind of oversight, but we have to be realistic: our powers are limited.'

Conduct regulation was originally introduced at least partly to enable regulatory agents to prosecute alleged wrongdoers. Yet as seen throughout this book, after a flurry of large-looking early fines (although few levied against individuals), there is now a general recognition of limited achievement in enforcement under senior manager accountability regimes, or indeed other conduct regimes. As the research by regulators and GSVR bodies highlighted in this chapter shows, since 2018 thinking has rapidly moved on to recognize the criticality of culture, behaviour, and purpose in driving conduct and mitigating conduct risk. Yet despite initial efforts by some firms, most are achieving only mixed results in identifying 'behaviour-at-risk' and improving psychological safety. Meanwhile, alarmingly, reports of 'culture fatigue' – already – bode poorly for firms' efforts to introduce and sustain meaningful improvement.

As NY Fed ruefully noted in 2019, our collective success to date has been mainly in 'creating greater awareness of the problem' – in starting to raise better questions, as it were, but not yet answering them, let alone solving the underlying problems. After years of concerted effort, how content should we be that only 'awareness' has been achieved? Culture reform has been evident among a 'significant few', whilst 'major misconduct continues in financial services across the globe'. We might reasonably look in the mirror, collec-tively, and reflect on why. Is it fundamental misalignment in the tone from the top? Local risk cultures within teams? The variety in motivations and circumstances of each individual working in financial services (which may be less about culture and more about money and professional standing)? All of these, perhaps, and more?

Perhaps what's required is a dramatic approach as seen in other sectors (see Sidebar: Flying and food), or the collective response to probably human-ity's greatest existential threat, climate change. The climate change threat has faced similar challenges of struggling to gain traction appropriate to the scale of the problem. In financial services we would benefit from a Paris Accord-type agreement, where all countries the world over commit to a fundamental restructuring of the profession. Our house is on fire, too.

That said, by putting to work the recent research into psychological safety, culture measurement and culture audits for much-needed insight into local risk cultures and ways of working, it is hoped that by the end of the 2020s the financial services industry will have made progress beyond merely raising awareness of culture factors towards actually operating in a funda-mentally different way. The immediate task for the industry is to graduate past the 'awareness' stage into truly operating in a more customer-centric way. Knowing what we now know and have seen in this chapter, about tendencies for misconduct to persist, the difficulties with culture change from within and possible ways to combat both, it will be interesting to see how far the necessary change happens as we move forwards.

Notes

1 Edelman Trust Barometer portal, edelman.com/trustbarometer (archived at https://perma.cc/LHV4-YLFK)

2 Murphy, R (2020) Tax Research UK, respondent group comments to article, Money laundering is rampant and the government is refusing to put in place the measures to tackle it, 21 September, https://www.taxresearch.org.uk/ Blog/2020/09/21/money-laundering-is-rampant-and-the-government-is-refusing-to-put-in-place-the-measures-to-tackle-it/ (archived at https://perma.cc/7SBQ-E8R8)

3 For a more detailed analysis see Miles, R (2017) The roots of misconduct: Macro structural factors enabling bad behaviour, in *Conduct Risk Management: Using a behavioural approach to protect your board and financial services business*, Kogan Page, pp 100–105

4 FCA (2012) Journey to the FCA, October, p 5, fca.org.uk/publication/ corporate/fsa-journey-to-the-fca.pdf (archived at https://perma.cc/K2ZA-WGXR)

5 FCA (2012) Journey to the FCA, October, p 7, fca.org.uk/publication/ corporate/fsa-journey-to-the-fca.pdf (archived at https://perma.cc/K2ZA-WGXR)

6 FCA (2016) 5 Conduct Questions Feedback, p 3, fca.org.uk/publication/ market-studies/5-conduct-questions-industry-feedback-2016.pdf (archived at https://perma.cc/2RPD-ML5T)

7 Sheedy, E and Griffin, B (2014) Empirical analysis of risk culture in financial institutions: interim report, pp 2–3, researchgate.net/publication/314473817 (archived at https://perma.cc/5SNE-5APP)

8 De Nederlandsche Bank (DNB) (2015) Supervision of behaviour and culture: foundations, practice and future developments, pp 9–10, https://www.dnb.nl/ media/1gmkp1vk/supervision-of-behaviour-and-culture_tcm46-380398-1.pdf (archived at https://perma.cc/C87B-YHRN)

9 De Nederlandsche Bank (DNB) (2015) Supervision of behaviour and culture: foundations, practice and future developments, pp 9–10, https://www.dnb.nl/ media/1gmkp1vk/supervision-of-behaviour-and-culture_tcm46-380398-1.pdf (archived at https://perma.cc/C87B-YHRN)

10 De Nederlandsche Bank (DNB) (2015) Supervision of behaviour and culture: foundations, practice and future developments, pp 9–10, https://www.dnb.nl/ media/1gmkp1vk/supervision-of-behaviour-and-culture_tcm46-380398-1.pdf (archived at https://perma.cc/C87B-YHRN)

11 New York Federal Reserve (NY Fed) Speeches newyorkfed.org/newsevents/ speeches/2015/mus151123 (archived at https://perma.cc/99MV-3WLG)

12 New York Federal Reserve (NY Fed) Speeches newyorkfed.org/newsevents/ speeches/2015/mus151123 (archived at https://perma.cc/99MV-3WLG)

13 See Hodges and Decker, Oxford University Law Faculty, eg law.ox.ac.uk/sites/ files/oxlaw/a5-deckerhodges-voluntary-regulation.pdf (archived at https:// perma.cc/2Y35-FYBV)

14 FICC Markets Standards Board (2018) Behavioural cluster analysis: misconduct patterns in financial services, fmsb.com/wp-content/uploads/ 2018/07/BCA_v32_1.pdf (archived at https://perma.cc/D9UP-XSMQ)

15 FICC Markets Standards Board (2018) Behavioural cluster analysis: misconduct patterns in financial services, fmsb.com/wp-content/uploads/ 2018/07/BCA_v32_1.pdf (archived at https://perma.cc/D9UP-XSMQ)

16 NY Fed (2018) We continue to challenge the effectiveness of the underlying culture in banks – Director General Derville Rowland, centralbank.ie/news/ article/challenge-underlying-culture-in-banks-derville-rowland-7-February-2018 (archived at https://perma.cc/7XC8-HG57)

17 Lo, A W (2016) The Gordon Gekko effect: the role of culture in the financial industry, *NY Fed Economic Policy Review*, August

18 FCA (2018) Discussion Paper 18/2: Transforming Culture in Financial Services, fca.org.uk/publication/discussion/dp18-02.pdf (archived at https://perma.cc/4WXC-8Z52)

19 Iscenko, Z et al (2016) Behaviour and Compliance in Organisations, p 3, FCA, https://papers.ssrn.com/sol3/papers.cfm?abstract_id=2939687 (archived at https://perma.cc/D7FK-FGSD)

20 FCA (2018) ibid

21 Chesterfield, A and Smart, L (2018) Psychological safety: the secret to effective teams, fca.org.uk/insight/psychological-safety-secret-effective-teams (archived at https://perma.cc/5BPG-LP3P)

22 Edmondson, A (1999) Psychological safety and learning behavior in work teams, *Administrative Science Quarterly,* **44** (2), 350–83, https://doi.org/10.2307/2666999 (archived at https://perma.cc/X3MV-RDZH)

23 NY Fed (2018) Speeches, newyorkfed.org/newsevents/speeches/2018/sti181004 (archived at https://perma.cc/U2JE-CYUL)

24 NY Fed (2018) Speeches, newyorkfed.org/newsevents/speeches/2018/sti181004 (archived at https://perma.cc/U2JE-CYUL)

25 Groysberg, et al (2018) The leader's guide to corporate culture, *Harvard Business Review*, hbr.org/2018/01/the-leaders-guide-to-corporate-culture (archived at https://perma.cc/4CPW-BZRW)

26 Scott, S and Cooke, M (2020) *Culture Audits: Removing the blindfold*, Regulation Asia, 3 August, regulationasia.com/culture-audits-removing-the-blindfold/ (archived at https://perma.cc/GS5J-75XA)

27 See www.theiia.org/auditingculture (archived at https://perma.cc/6PUW-Y5HJ)

28 G30 (2018) Banking Culture Report, p 16, group30.org/images/uploads/publications/aaG30_Culture2018.pdf (archived at https://perma.cc/7HML-VBMX)

29 G30 (2018) Banking Culture Report, p 16, group30.org/images/uploads/publications/aaG30_Culture2018.pdf (archived at https://perma.cc/7HML-VBMX)

30 Weston, C (2020) Banking culture board is 'a waste of time', says campaigner, *Irish Independent*, 21 July, independent.ie/business/personal-finance/banking/banking-culture-board-is-waste-of-time-campaigner-39383895.html (archived at https://perma.cc/GS9C-YDG7)

31 James Hennessy (2019) We're Only Human: Culture and Change Management, Conference speech, 5 Sept, newyorkfed.org/newsevents/speeches/2019/hen190905 (archived at https://perma.cc/YYH7-DSPA)

32 For a more detailed comparison see Hodges, C and Steinholtz, R (2017) *Ethical Business Practice and Regulation*, Bloomsbury, bloomsbury.com/au/ethical-business-practice-and-regulation-9781509916375/ (archived at https://perma.cc/9SEG-TSEK)

33 See CAA training's Conditions for Just Culture, www.skybrary.aero/index.php/Just_Culture (archived at https://perma.cc/LLT3-LT9T)

34 Hodges, C and Steinholtz, R (2017) *Ethical Business Practice and Regulation*, pp 88–96, Bloomsbury, bloomsbury.com/au/ethical-business-practice-and-regulation-9781509916375/ (archived at https://perma.cc/9SEG-TSEK)

35 See for example www.bbc.co.uk/news/uk-21375594 (archived at https://perma.cc/KP79-RXGJ)

36 Food Standards Agency strategy document (2015) Food We Can Trust: FSA Strategic Plan 2015-20, www.food.gov.uk/sites/default/files/media/document/Food-Standards-Agency-Strategy%20FINAL.pdf (archived at https://perma.cc/5DUZ-PRA4)

37 Hong Kong Market Authority (2020) pp 4–5 www.hkma.gov.hk/media/chi/doc/key-information/guidelines-and-circular/2020/20200522c1a1.pdf (archived at https://perma.cc/BX6S-J398)

38 Monetary Authority of Singapore (2019) www.mas.gov.sg/news/media-releases/2019/new-industry-steering-group-to-elevate-culture-and-conduct-standards-for-banking-industry (archived at https://perma.cc/S2ZF-DQQF)

39 Reported in nortonrosefulbright.com/en-no/knowledge/publications/2e9a356e/australia's-banking-executive-accountability-regime (archived at https://perma.cc/5HZB-SPEV)

40 Butler, B (2020) Banking royal commission one year on: optimism over changes but banks fight back, theguardian.com/australia-news/2020/feb/01/banking-royal-commission-one-year-on-optimism-over-changes-but-banks-fight-back (archived at https://perma.cc/5K85-JZAF)

41 Butler, B (2020) Banking royal commission one year on: optimism over changes but banks fight back, theguardian.com/australia-news/2020/feb/01/banking-royal-commission-one-year-on-optimism-over-changes-but-banks-fight-back (archived at https://perma.cc/5K85-JZAF)

42 FCA (2020) Discussion Paper 20/1: Driving Purposeful Cultures, fca.org.uk/publications/discussion-papers/dp20-1-transforming-culture-financial-services-driving-purposeful-cultures (archived at https://perma.cc/5AAE-KRB8)

43 FCA (2019) CultureSprint transcript, September, fca.org.uk/publication/transcripts/video-transcript-culture-sprint-september-2019.pdf (archived at https://perma.cc/9M3B-BKZL)

44 FCA/CultureSprint (2020) CultureSprint: supporting and empowering managers to transform culture, fca.org.uk/events/culturesprint-supporting-and-empowering-managers-transform-culture (archived at https://perma.cc/KBV6-66Y7)

45 FCA/CultureSprint (2020) CultureSprint: supporting and empowering managers to transform culture, fca.org.uk/events/culturesprint-supporting-and-empowering-managers-transform-culture (archived at https://perma.cc/KBV6-66Y7)

46 FCA (2020) 5 Conduct Questions – Feedback on industry engagement, p 4, fca.org.uk/publication/market-studies/5-conduct-questions-industry-feedback-2019-20.pdf (archived at https://perma.cc/4NWS-FNAP)

47 FCA (2020) 5 Conduct Questions – Feedback on industry engagement, p 4, fca.org.uk/publication/market-studies/5-conduct-questions-industry-feedback-2019-20.pdf (archived at https://perma.cc/4NWS-FNAP)

48 FCA speeches (2020) fca.org.uk/news/speeches/regulatory-perspective-drivers-culture-and-role-purpose-and-governance (archived at https://perma.cc/9VPD-DACQ)

49 Starling Trust (2020) Compendium, April 2020, p 11, https://starlingtrust.com/the-starling-compendium/ (archived at https://perma.cc/GA46-QWUG)

50 As reported in *Financial Times*, ft.com/content/0ec16280-423f-405a-a081-b51fee20d6c7 (archived at https://perma.cc/HDA7-QPED)

04

What's the big idea? (1)

How conduct regulators use behavioural science

ROGER MILES

Introduction

This chapter will explore why we in the financial sector behave as we do – starting, parochially but importantly, with why regulators do what they do. It then delves into two key approaches to understanding human behaviour, using the science that conduct regulators themselves use when preparing their assessment frameworks.

Understanding the science not only alerts us to where the regulator is coming from, it helps us to see more clearly why we all do what we do, in the workplace and in life generally (especially when we wrongly assume we're doing 'the right thing'); how we make sense of the world at individual level; and the ways that we work together in groups. This not only keeps us ahead of the rules, it makes for a more robust and resilient business.

Next there is a summary tour of the essentials of brain science (neurology and psychology) – just those essentials that we need to understand narrowly, for now, what will be expected to feature on a firm's culture self-assessment of its progress in overcoming any harmful assumptions. Two relevant headline culture audit questions will be: How's your firm getting on at recognizing and overcoming the mental bias effects that drive people to make unsound decisions? How well are you building a purposeful culture, supported by psychological safety and cognitive diversity?

To get behind biases requires a basic knowledge of the cognitive science of risk perception. The version offered here is as summarized as I can make it for this narrow purpose; accordingly, apologies in advance: if you happen to be a trained medical doctor, psychologist or anthropologist, you'll find the first section of this chapter quaintly simplistic. On the plus side, as long as you're not from one of those professions this chapter will save you five years of doctoral study, or at least several days wading through the hugely important (but also quite hard going) work, *Thinking, Fast and Slow* by Daniel Kahneman.

The final part of this chapter takes three strands of science and shows how they have started to inform firms' (and regulators') efforts to intervene positively to improve culture. We'll take a first look at how they inform those key terms, purposeful culture, psychological safety and cognitive diversity as they'll be used by culture assessors. You may be assured that those three items are going to start featuring prominently in your firm's culture reporting from now on.

THEMES AND CONCEPTS IN THIS CHAPTER

biases: are they 'all bad'? – bias effects that distort decision-making – cognitive diversity – conduct conversation – 'floor-walk' culture assessment – financial vs non-financial misconduct – groupthink (collective blindness, motivated reasoning, assumed framing, fundamental attribution error) – 'healthy culture is good for business' – in-groups and out-groups – is 'de-biasing' possible? – psychological safety – purposeful culture – situational awareness ('tells') – Thinking, Fast and Slow (theory of dual-system brain) – three science 'keys' to culture assessment – unintended consequences of policies

Tying culture assessment to 'brain science'

As seen in Chapters 2 and 3, all around the world conduct regulators are busy developing new rules. Before diving into the deeper behavioural science that informs the shaping of the rules, there is a major piece of the 'mental landscape' of regulation that we really need to deal with first: what motivates all conduct regulators? In plain terms, why do they do what they do? Perhaps more saliently, once we know the answer to this, what can we do that will satisfy their expectations?

Over many years I've engaged with that question. To find fresh answers, one has to acquire – like Liam Neeson in *Taken*, but without the violence – a very particular set of skills. For me, these skills have included cognitive psychology, behavioural observation and language analysis.

As well as directly asking regulators what they do (then discourse-analysing their answers), I've interviewed many hundreds of attested senior managers about what Conduct means to them; watched, with an anthropological lens as regulatory case officers and financial practitioners interacted; and asked all kinds of financial practitioners to 'tell me a story about what just happened', soon after external shocks such as a market crash, pandemic, or a Section 166 notice (see box) – again then using thematic analysis to deconstruct their replies. And here's the result.

SECTION 166 NOTICE

The dreaded 'Section 166' warning from the UK Financial Conduct Authority, also known as a Skilled Person Review notice, is the regulator's way of compelling a firm to open its records and senior personnel to close scrutiny by an experienced independent inspector (the 'skilled person').

It may be issued simply on suspicion that an offence has been committed, when the situation is still unclear. The review is a form of extreme audit of the fitness-for-purpose of the firm's controls, processes and people. It's widely seen as a punishment, though not formally communicated as this; most firms regard it as a regulatory question mark against their reputation for good conduct, pending the skilled person's assessment.

What motivates all conduct regulators: seven key themes

As the conduct regulator talks to you, there are roughly seven themes, or motivations, whirring simultaneously in their head. And, by the way, with the 2021 arrival of culture assessments, regulators increasingly *will* want to talk to you and to others throughout your firm, one-to-one in person: see the 'floor-walk' section below.

Here are those themes:

- They want to **raise public trust** in financial providers, by encouraging the best possible customer/client outcomes and preventing harm; by keeping their political sponsors happy, and by maintaining orderly markets.

- They want the financial firms that they regulate to **give a better account to the public** of their own behaviour.

- As part of that, they want to see everyone in regulated firms **thinking for themselves** – not simply 'box-ticking', rote-learning or delegating conduct initiatives. This includes behaving (and showing you're behaving) in ways such as: involving senior managers, and then everyone, with a personal sense 'doing what's right'; welcoming challenge; and looking to improve, including learning from our (and others') mistakes.

- A big idea behind this is that **social purpose matters**; good behaviour – being 'pro-social' – is more important than just making money. People in a well-conducted firm will often reflect on the firm's wider purpose, how the firm is 'good for the world', not just paying its owners.

- Conduct regulators see it as an essential task of their own – since it's what they are striving to regulate – to understand the raw material of conduct through studying the **science of human behaviour**. To prevent future crises, these regulators believe, we must open-mindedly learn from behavioural science and look beyond the historic models assumptions of econometrics.

- The regulator expects each of us to put some effort into understanding and using that science to identify and mitigate the **mental biases** that disrupt sound decision-making.

- Finally, through programmes such as the Senior Managers Regime (UK's SMCR and its equivalents around the world – see 'Mandating personal responsibility', Chapter 5), they want to hold **each practitioner personally responsible** as a lever for improving behaviour industry-wide. How well are you working 'conduct-aware', they wonder?

Driving this agenda, conduct regulators get their ideas from many new sources of thinking but above all from the latest research findings in behavioural science. If you are serious about reporting on your firm's culture, as part of the wider task of conduct assessment, you need to acquire at least a basic working knowledge of the behavioural science that informs the framing of the new regulation – including the regulators' culture assessments.

In case you're wondering, 'Personally accountable for what?', let's cover one further headline point of understanding before we get into the science: What do regulators mean by 'misconduct'?

The bad behaviour that regulators want to prevent: two forms of misconduct

The central idea behind conduct regulation is to get everyone in finance to behave better and to better explain themselves: What are you all doing that's of any value to anyone other than yourselves? This means, at foundation level, making sure that no financial practitioners do anything that causes harm to customers or clients, or creates disorderly markets. Then, obviously, looking to practitioners to do a lot more than just 'doing no harm': that is, ideally to be showing 'exemplary conduct'.

Since regulation is now much more about how you behave generally – not just how you sell your products – the net of defining 'harm' is cast much wider to include how you behave among colleagues, in the markets, and even in your life in general. Regulators define misconduct – the behaviours they want to prevent – broadly in two forms.

Financial misconduct: As you may have guessed, this is any bad behaviour around selling your products. Common forms[1] include:

- **misleading customers** – such as taking unfair advantage of their ignorance to sell them something they don't need (an **inappropriate product**), or that's not going to give them the outcome they expected;

- **exploiting 'asymmetric information'**, that is, trading on private knowledge you have, that other participants don't (including customers), possibly with **collusion, inside information** or **undeclared conflict of interest;**

- **price manipulation,** which may also entail **manipulating benchmarks** (that is, market reference prices);

- **circular trading** – such as pumping up market prices artificially, by selling and re-selling the same contract for no good reason;

- **improper order handling** – not managing to give clients 'best execution' on an order, or wilfully or carelessly allowing poor client outcomes when executing their orders.

Then there's **non-financial misconduct.** This includes many forms of misbehaviour that don't relate directly to the business of selling products, although they may well affect how your team sets about making its sales. These include, but are not limited to, behaviours such as:

- **intimidation** – that is, threatening people; and similarly...

- **discrimination** in any of the ways you hire, promote, reward and recognize people's achievements – this might also include **favouritism, exclusion** or **ostracizing;**

- **sexual misconduct**, and sexual and other **harassment**;
- **bullying** – that is, making someone feel bad when they're simply trying to do their job.

You might well wonder, as most people in financial firms are doing, how any inspection or audit could find and report meaningful data on any of those 'soft object' human risks. If at this point you haven't yet come across the new form of conduct inspection practice, get set for a shock – but then push on through it to learn about the new reality.

The floor-walk: introducing a new style of regulatory assessment

Conduct regulators are now sending out specialist 'culture assessment' teams as part of their audit of firms; that may well be why you are reading this book. When the culture assessors visit your firm, they'll be looking to make direct observations of how you behave – by, shock horror, physically walking around in the business; or dropping in on teams' Zoom meetings; or inviting individuals from any level of your firm to a personal 'tea and a chat with the regulator' at their own offices. It's all about talking to people at the business end, one-to-one. This apparently new audit technique is actually a revival of a much older form of inspection, relying on direct observation rather than the proxy indicators reported in a paper audit. The 'floor-walk' will analyse your behaviour and view any supporting evidence of it through the lens of behavioural science[2] – and therefore so should you. Pre-empt it by starting now; this chapter, together with Chapter 5 and Chapter 10 will help to set you up.

That is the single most important point. Start your firm's 'conduct conversation' right now; don't wait for the regulator to ask you the first question when they visit you. (If the first time you consider the question is when the regulator is standing in front of you, asking it, it's clearly way too late.) In several jurisdictions,[3] regulators are already walking the floors of financial firms, or joining board meetings or team meetings. They are asking front-office staff, as well as senior managers, questions that probe their understanding of 'expected and acceptable' behaviour and conduct; the answers will be studied for signs of misbehaviour.

We'll look at the questions that culture assessors have asked, and that we know they'll be asking in future, in detail in Chapter 10.

It's not just inspectors in your back yard, by the way. There are other new alternative forms of remotely watching over what actually happens: direct surveillance and big-data pattern analysis by 'reg techs'. More on those in Chapter 12.

First, the science behind conduct and culture assessment: what do you need to know? Caveat: what follows is a very reductive summary, not the 'full science' version.

Why our brains sabotage good decision-making... and what conduct regulators want to do about it

Actually, this next bit is surprisingly fun and interesting to think about (or so say thousands of practitioners who've attended our workshops on this – and really, they weren't just being polite). You'll shortly find things out that change the way you see your life, as well as 'conduct risk' knowledge that helps your future work.

As we explore in more detail throughout the book, two major disruptions have triggered a crisis of public trust in institutions, including government and financial markets. The first trigger was the global financial crisis (GFC) of 2008; the second, the Covid-19 pandemic of 2020. Policy makers and regulators have fixed underlying problems of under-capitalization in financial markets following the GFC, but there remains a deep deficit of public trust in finance in general: its institutions, markets, governance and regulations. This is a long-term structural problem, and the popular resentment it generated is having even broader political effects in the real world, away from the sphere of finance.

Because after the GFC and again with the coming of Covid-19, citizens looked to government to put right perceived social injustices, financial regulators (who answer to government) were keen to find and use new tools to prevent a repeat of these financial crises. The old market controls based on econometric risk analysis clearly failed to curb misbehaviour; regulators therefore cast around for new methods of control which would address behaviour primarily, rather than simply 'value-at-risk' in market instruments.

If you need to understand how to control behaviour, it *really* helps to understand how behaviour itself works in the first place: meaning, the science of human cognition of risk, of how groups of people interact, and in particular how our brains make decisions.

Luckily for the new generation of 'behavioural regulators' launched in the 2010s, there have been rapid advances in behavioural science since the 1990s, just in time to enable their fresh approach to controlling conduct. Two pleasant surprises for the new regulators (and their political sponsors) were that (1) the 'nudge' approach to regulation is cheaper to administer than previous forms of complex legal framework and (2) that behavioural science's focus on observing how individuals take responsibility, or don't ('what actually happens') means that you can quickly levy large fines against corporates and individuals, meaning that the new regulation pays for itself – good if your national Treasury is running a huge deficit, as happened in 2008 and again, very much larger, in 2021.

Starting to look inside your head

Behavioural scientists have always been interested in what actually happens when people interact, not what a set of rules say *should* be happening. Rather, this type of scientist wants to see how people *actually* interact, and why humans don't always do what the rules say they should be doing. The science invites us to put some prep time into understanding things like:

- how **decision-making** can be compromised by bias effects (how the brain 'jumps to conclusions' rather than making rational choices), and helping to explain this dual-system theory of the brain (aka Fast and Slow Thinking, or animal brain vs rational brain);
- why **groups of people behave differently** from individuals, driven by group-acting bias effects to make herd emotional decisions, with collective overconfidence and group think.

This is a huge field of study, tracing its formal research roots back to the 1930s,[4] and the history of informal questioning of 'the madness of crowds' stretching back to the mid-19th century.[5] It has enjoyed a recent boost into the mainstream with several Nobel prizes and public recognition through pop-science books such as *Nudge*,[6] *Thinking, Fast and Slow*[7] and *Predictably Irrational*.[8]

Luckily for us, regulators don't require us to reach Nobel prize levels of insight. Remember, though, that conduct regulators and their culture assessor teams are avid readers of the latest behavioural science research. (Which is good for the authors of this book, by the way, because that's a big part of the work we do, and why we're happy to be sharing here our many years of expert practice in the field with you.)

Dangers of 'fast thinking': a quick explanation

Conduct regulation – and any regulation, come to that – has an inbuilt cultural problem of its own. The people who design rules and controls and risk analysis behave as if it's all about the numbers. If the statistics are the only thing you are looking at, then you will tend to miss the point that the stats are the *outcome* of what just happened; that is, they're the end result of what people do. If instead you can get closer to observing actual human behaviour in the moment – what people are doing, as they do it – then you'll get a better informed, more realistic picture of your firm's culture. And, you might hope, catch small bad habits before they turn into big bad group misbehaviours.

Most of the world's financial regulators realized in about 2012 (a few got there far earlier – notably the Netherlands) that trying to control behaviour by rational instruction doesn't work because that's not how the human brain actually works. Just appealing to logic and rationality is not an effective way to get people to reconsider their behaviour. We now need to get inside the human brain to see what to do instead.

A big part of conduct regulators' thinking about behaviour is to examine and try to resolve the tension between people's rational thinking and 'gut feel' decision-making – both on the selling side and the customer side.

Our intuitive 'animal brain' tends to take shortcuts when making decisions. We call these shortcuts by various names such as rules of thumb, or jumping to conclusions; or, if you're a behavioural science nerd, heuristics and bias effects. Modern understanding of how our brains jump to conclusions was developed by various behavioural scientists from the 1960s onwards, notably Daniel Kahneman who won a Nobel Prize (with Amos Tversky) for research on how biases work. This research led to Dual-System Brain Theory, which is better known as Thinking, Fast And Slow. Kahneman's book on this, though it's a popular science summary, still runs to nearly 400 pages, so why not let's summarize it here in a couple of pages.

First of all, here's a slice through your brain (Figure 4.1). Even if you don't have any previous knowledge of how the human brain works, you can instantly see there are different textures in it. One eye-catching little bit of it is right in the middle, looking like a nut, which you'll see is attached to a long 'pipe'.

The pipe is important because it carries both the power supply to the brain and the data supply to and from it. The power supply is the flow of blood (the brain is a big organ that needs lots of blood, especially when it has a lot of work to do). The data of course takes the form of electric impulses, nerve impulses posting into the brain information received by the

FIGURE 4.1   Brain cross-section: amygdala and spinal cord

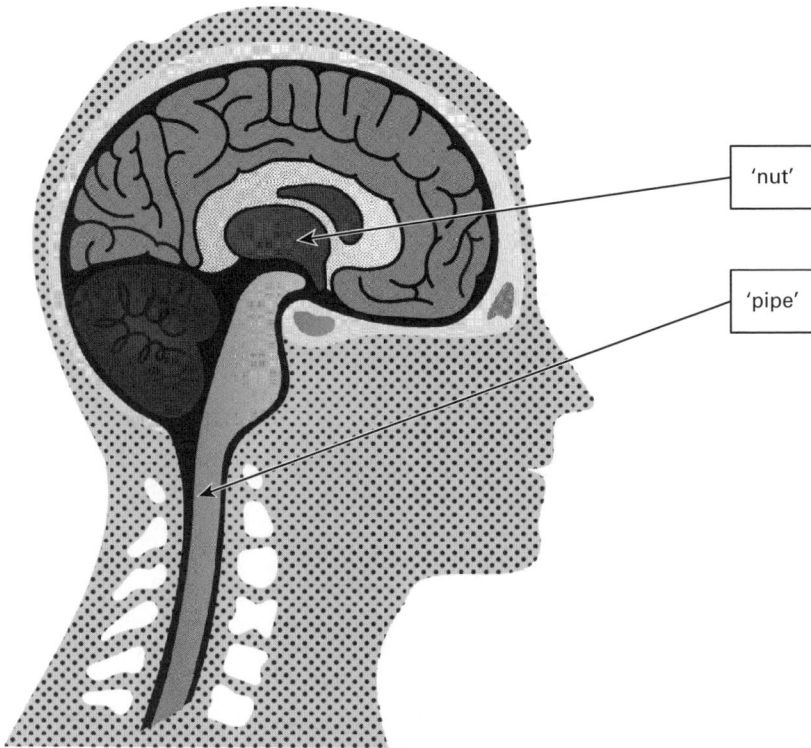

body (touch, taste, etc) and sending out from the brain signals to control the body (moving your muscles etc).

Then there's one other part of the brain we need to be aware of for now: the squishy bit at the front (Figure 4.2).

Now we know that the pipe is the power supply and the main data conduit, one thing is clear: placed where it is, that little nut is getting the most direct access to the power and data supplies from the pipe. The squishy bit, meanwhile, is further away from the pipe, so it doesn't get first dibs on either the power supply or the data.

So now let's give these parts their proper names (Figure 4.3). (By the way, this is a very short summary that really doesn't do justice to proper brain science. On the other hand, if you don't plan to spend several years at medical school to acquire the proper brain science, stick around.)

Now, let's give those parts the names we'd use as non-scientists (Figure 4.4):

The **intuition** part of the brain was the earliest piece of our brains to evolve. It controls our responses to life's most urgent needs: staying safe,

FIGURE 4.2   Prefrontal cortex

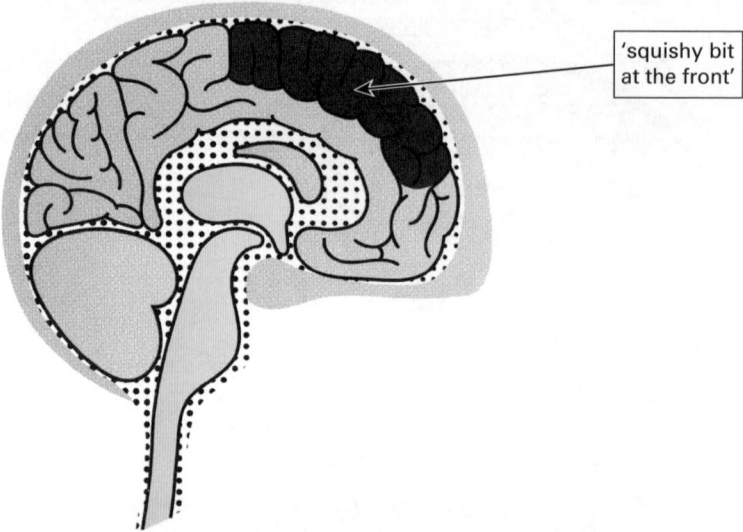

'squishy bit at the front'

FIGURE 4.3   Brain with science labels

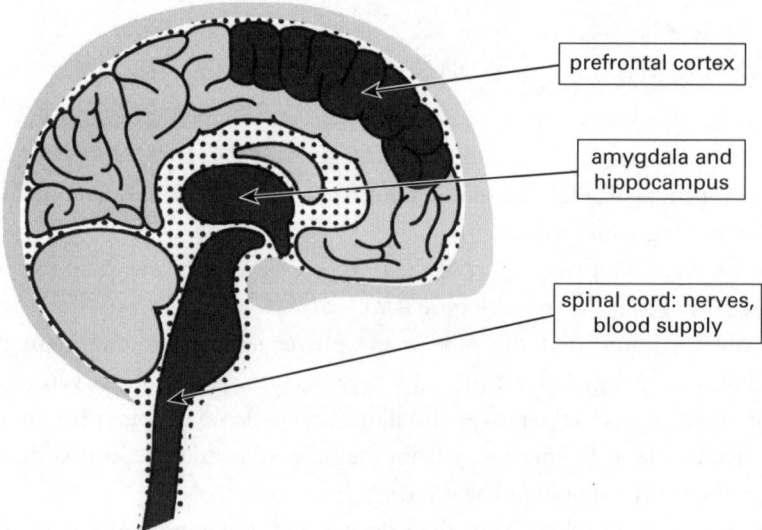

prefrontal cortex

amygdala and hippocampus

spinal cord: nerves, blood supply

eating, reacting to threats, pleasure or pain. Meanwhile on the outer edge, the rational part of the brain does the heavy lifting of solving complex **logic** problems, working out maths challenges, and so on.

And here's the big point we were heading for: because the animal brain is right next to the power supply, it runs at roughly 10 times the 'clock speed'

FIGURE 4.4   Intuition and reason

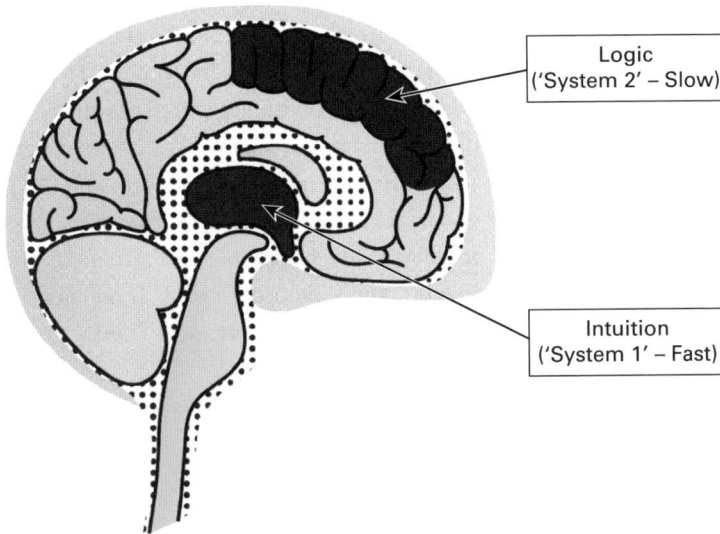

of the rational brain. Hence 'Fast' (animal intuition) and 'Slow' (rational) brains. Important outcomes follow from that difference in speed. When you think you're making a rational decision, actually your animal brain has already taken over, yet you don't even know it. The animal brain runs ahead of your rational brain, making decisions usually based on biases (more on these shortly – for now, think of them as mental shortcuts or assumptions).

The consequences of this are serious. Whenever we imagine that we're solving problems in a fully rational way, it is highly likely that our animal brain has already made our mind up for us; it has already decided, subconsciously, what we are going to do. Significantly also, the animal brain is 'always on', whilst the rational brain needs a conscious effort to engage. Kahneman published a list of characteristics of the two parts of the brain:

TABLE 4.1   Fast-brain/slow-brain characteristics

INTUITION – Fast	LOGIC – Slow
Associative	Rules-based
Automatic	Controlled
Effortless	Wilful, strenuous
Emotional ('affect')	Neutral
Multi-task (parallel)	Single-task (serial)

SOURCE   Miles, after Kahneman and Kawachi

The final point on each list is important. The animal brain juggles all sorts of intuitive conclusions, super-fast – it multi-tasks. You might think that your rational brain can also multi-task, but what it's actually doing is processing little chunks of problems in sequence, serially.

How does all this brain science help us with regulated conduct? Easy. In a nutshell, the kind of person who designs rules, laws and controls tends to assume that everyone's rational brain is dominant; that is, that most people will rationally assess rules and risks around every decision they make. As we've just seen, that isn't what actually happens at all. To take a simple example I like to quote,[9] here is your lunchtime snack from the point of view of a regulator, in this case the food regulator, who thinks this is how you also view it (Figure 4.5):

FIGURE 4.5   Regulator's view of your snack

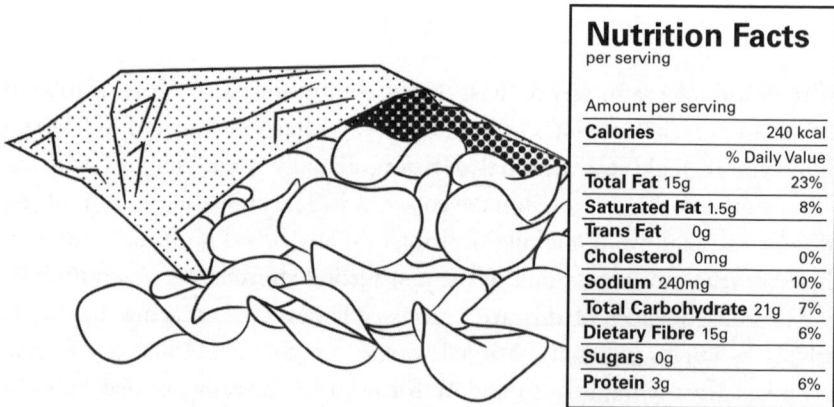

Nutrition Facts
per serving

Amount per serving	
Calories	240 kcal
	% Daily Value
Total Fat 15g	23%
Saturated Fat 1.5g	8%
Trans Fat 0g	
Cholesterol 0mg	0%
Sodium 240mg	10%
Total Carbohydrate 21g	7%
Dietary Fibre 15g	6%
Sugars 0g	
Protein 3g	6%

I am fairly sure that the way you actually engage with this packet of crisps is just to open it and eat the crisps.

It's a classic regulator instance of 'expert bias' (we could also call it 'spotlight thinking' or solecism) to assume that ordinary people will think in the same way as the person who designed the rule, or the control measure. Thinking, Fast and Slow warns us that this isn't at all like how people normally think. If we want to make sound decisions, and to bring colleagues with us when we're trying to achieve anything at work, we need to be much more aware of how our biases – and theirs – may be compromising those decisions.

Biases, a primer: which ones do conduct regulators most care about?

(There's lots more about biases in another book of mine, *Conduct Risk Management: A behavioural approach*, so I won't repeat it all here, just recap some highlights.)

The animal brain, as it works super-fast, doesn't want to hang around while the slower rational brain gets into gear (even though it's a matter of microseconds): animal intuition fills in the time-lag by jumping straight to a decision. Bias is the result of the tension (dissonance, often) between the fast and slow brain, a conflict that the fast brain tends to win; intuitive decisions are often right, but they're also often wrong, sometimes with catastrophic consequences. As you might expect, conduct regulators are very interested in any form of bias that leads people to underestimate a risk, or to mis-buy a contract, or to be (perhaps unwittingly) colluding in activity that distorts fair market-making.

BIASES GOOD, BIASES BAD?

There's a big academic row between two research camps, roughly summed up as (1) 'Biases are bad' (Kahneman, Ariely and others[10]) and (2) 'Biases are brilliant' (Gigerenzer and others[11]). Of course, they're both right, and both wrong, in various ways. Many academics make a career out of arguing with other academics.

If biases are so destructive, you might reasonably ask, what's the point of them; what are they *for*? Actually, a lot of biases are helpful to us.[12] For example, when you need to cross a busy road, you don't pause to make a complex rational calculation of traffic speeds and trajectories; you 'sense' the safest time to cross, and go. Most of the time, your animal brain is rather kindly saving the rational brain from the headache of having to calculate every step you take. The fast brain saves the slow brain a lot of energy by using biases to lessen the cognitive load (think brain-ache). You don't consciously realize that this is happening, but it happens all the time, and particularly in five situations (see Figure 4.6).

1   When we face too much incoming information (so we skim through it).

2   When the information that's available to us doesn't explain what we need to know (so we fill in the gaps).

FIGURE 4.6   Five triggers for bias

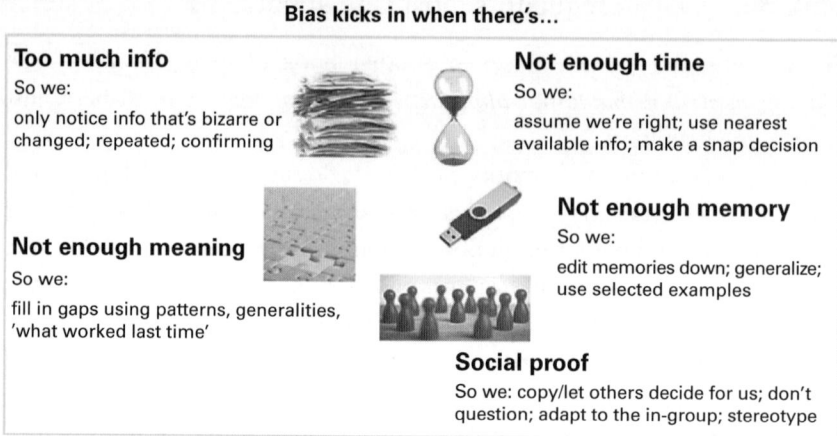

Bias kicks in when there's...

Too much info
So we:
only notice info that's bizarre or changed; repeated; confirming

Not enough time
So we:
assume we're right; use nearest available info; make a snap decision

Not enough meaning
So we:
fill in gaps using patterns, generalities, 'what worked last time'

Not enough memory
So we:
edit memories down; generalize; use selected examples

Social proof
So we: copy/let others decide for us; don't question; adapt to the in-group; stereotype

3   When we're short of time (so we 'cut to the chase').

4   When personally or as a group, we can't remember all the details (so we recall just a few examples, or generalize from the bits we do remember).

5   When everyone else has already decided what they're going to do, and it's easier if we 'go with the flow'.

Triggered by one or more of those five pressures, we know that there are various forms of bias that kick in. Let's start by highlighting a few of the commonest, most dominant bias effects – which by the way are the ones that conduct regulators are also most often interested in. (We could even say that they have a bias towards looking for these, except maybe that's a cheap shot.) In Table 4.1 there's a list of those big-hitting biases. First, a little more context.

Where biases get really interesting – and they're a pretty fascinating topic anyway – is when they cause problems with financial firms selling the wrong products to customers and clients. Some of the problem is on the buyer side, some on the seller side, but on both sides the regulator would like us to get aware of how biases disrupt good business decisions – and preferably to 'de-bias' ourselves. But that's hard (see box). The best we might do is get to know the main biases that might affect our work (see Table 4.1) and consciously try to avoid them catching us out.

'DE-BIASING'? BEWARE THE MUNCHAUSEN PROBLEM

You can't 'de-bias' yourself; it would be like trying to save yourself single-handedly from drowning. In the fairytale *The Tall Tales of Baron Munchausen*,[13] our hero (who's a pathological liar) describes a time he saved himself from drowning in quicksand by 'pulling himself out by his own bootstraps'.

Remembering why biases occur – it's your fast intuitive brain overriding your slow rational brain – Table 4.2 shows a quick list of 15 biases that conduct regulators seem to be most exercised about. For each bias, I offer a handy diagnostic, a brief definition, and a couple of examples, like this:

- *The verbal 'tell'*: how you might recognize, from what somebody just said to you, that there's a bias effect going on.

- *What it does*: summary definition of how the bias works. Yes, there are hundreds of learned articles and millions of words written about cognitive bias research; you're welcome to find them, just not here, for the sake of brevity and keeping moving.

- *Examples*: H: where you might see the bias playing out in a domestic setting; M: where you may see the bias playing out in the form of misconduct (customer/client detriment) in a financial service setting.

Incidentally, groupthink is such a huge topic that it needs whole books to itself. One important point to note about groupthink is that it doesn't simply mean – as it's commonly misused to mean – 'people agreeing with each other as expedient'. The groupthink bias effect is much subtler and is all about status, 'in-groups' reaffirming their in-ness in a deliberately exclusive way, and a thing called 'expert bias', where people with any form of expertise use it as a way to exclude others from the debate – sometimes with (as you'll have guessed) disastrous consequences.

There are 180-ish other biases[15] (many in the Glossary at the end of the book).

We all need to be wary of biases affecting decision-making. Conduct regulators expect us to be aware of these biases and the risks they represent, when we're selling, or designing products, or simply working together and making day-to-day business decisions. There has only been space here to highlight a few of the key bias effects, but it's a hugely enjoyable topic to read up on, so do hunt for more among the reading resources listed at the back of the book.

TABLE 4.2 Bias types and their unintended outcomes[14]

Bias name	How it sounds (verbal 'tells')/what it does	Examples (home life/misconduct)
Present bias	'Live for the moment – tomorrow's another day.' Focusing only on payoffs that are closer to now.	H: Maxing out your credit card, because why not? M: Hit-and-run sales practices.
Confirmation bias	'I have (just one) bit of evidence that proves I'm right.' Seeking out or evaluating information in a way that fits with what you already believe.	H: 'Google says I'm right (or at least, the second page I found there did)'; social media echo-chambers. M: Letting the customer stay 'loyal' to the brand they bought before, rather than making an informed choice of change.
Loss aversion	'I'd just rather not, thanks all the same.' We shy away from a likely loss, more than we'd seize the chance of (the same) likely gain.	H: Remembering someone for when they criticized you, rather than when they praised you. M: Keeping customers in a low-return account, when better paying products are available at the same level of risk.
Affect	'I'm going with my gut feel on this.' Basing a decision on the momentary pain/pleasure you get at the moment you decide.	H: Snack time: doughnut, not celery. M: Encouraging the customer to buy (possibly the wrong) product because they 'feel good about it'.
Overconfidence	'Don't stop me, I know what I'm doing.' Being far more certain than you should be, given what (little) you know.	H: Assuming your last-minute booked holiday will all be fine, because it's your holiday, right? M: Managers' undue faith in their own abilities; believing your controls all work just fine, or that you'll never get caught.
Projection	'It'll be fine – just look at our last set of performance figures.' The idea that the future will bring 'more of the same' and that our own tastes and preferences will be constant.	H: Splurging on buying that lovely new home/outfit/car/gadget because you're sure that your expected pay rise will cover it – it did last year, right? M: Taking out a payday loan without considering possible future upsets.

(continued)

TABLE 4.2 (Continued)

Bias name	How it sounds (verbal 'tells')/what it does	Examples (home life/misconduct)
Anchoring (reference dependence)	'Of course this is a good buy – just look at the headline interest rate.' Clinging to the first item of information you saw about something.	H: Buying stuff (that you don't really need) in the sales, because the price tag says they're cheaper than the recommended retail price. M: Buying a complex product based on a summary headline rate of return.
Selective attention	'Red cars are generally faster than blue cars – not that I know anything about cars.' Believing what you want to believe; tuning out any details that conflict with your view, or that don't seem to you to matter.	H: Cherry-picking from the fruit bowl: eating only the ripe fruit, leaving the over-ripe. M: Showing the client, first, a reason to buy this product – skipping over any reasons not to. Using carefully edited statistics to make your case.
Endowment effects	'This is how we like to do it, no questions.' Feeling oddly attached to something you've owned for ages, or a project you've spent a lot of time working on.	H: He may be a psychopathic leader, but he's *our* psychopathic leader. M: Keep on using old compliance practices, even though they don't really work.
Regret, and cognitive dissonance	'Don't make me have to think about it.' Ignoring the nagging sense (from your rational brain) that you just made a bad decision, such as something you bought.	H: Buying a massive, polar explorer-specified 4x4, that you only ever use for school runs and shopping trips. M: Customer knows they're locked into a contract that doesn't seem right for their needs, but can't quite explain what's wrong.
Framing (limited attention)	'Would you prefer to die in poverty, or buy this pension?' The answer you get depends heavily on how you present the question.	H: Your family is deeply dysfunctional; but in the photos you share, everyone is smiling. (That's framing in both senses, by the way.) M: Cancelling an inconveniently loss-making trade by invoking a rule-based manual override such as 'Last Look'.

(continued)

TABLE 4.2 (Continued)

Bias name	How it sounds (verbal 'tells')/what it does	Examples (home life/misconduct)
Mental accounting	'In my head, we can't spend that as I already have a plan for it – not that the budget mentions it, of course.' Imagining how any lump sum of money you have is divided up into things you're going to spend it on.	H: Thinking of a sum of cash in your account as 'already spoken for' as you'll be spending it soon on a holiday/utility bill/whatever. M: Customer looks at investments one at a time, rather than considering their portfolio as a whole
Groupthink (motivated reasoning)	'Experts like us need to back each other up.' Supporting others' decisions because it feels like a way to reassure your (and their) status as all senior people/having some shared special insight.	H: The whole household goes on a trip to somewhere that no one actually wanted to go, because everyone thought everyone else wanted to go there. (Yes, it happens.) M: Everything corporate! In boardrooms: voting for a decision (that you don't personally agree with) because you'd like the board to look united on this one. In political parties: being sure that you're right (and the voters are wrong).
Social proof	'Everybody does it.' Feeling comfortable in your decision because it's not really a decision, you're just going with the flow. (Yes, this one's both a trigger [input] and a bias outcome.)	H: Buying the same type of wheels/pet/holiday as your next-door neighbour. M: When the auditors come round, you hide your trading losses on your team's (special, private) 'back book' – because that's just what we do here.
Stereotyping (aka performance attribution bias and [wrongly] 'unconscious bias')	'They'll be good at this, because they're like me – and I'm good at this.' Giving a person credit (and maybe a job) for being good at things, when actually it's just that they resemble you in some ways, which gives you a warm feeling of recognition.	H: Having friends who are all 'people like me' – same school/university, same skin colour, who only like the same stuff you like. M: Only hiring and promoting people who went to the same school/university as you; or (far worse) of the same gender/ethnic/social background/sexual preference as you. Ignoring the achievements of anyone who doesn't fit your preconceived idea of 'an OK person'.

Once you have mastered a knowledge of the basic biases, it's useful then to expand your understanding by learning a bit about the behavioural science of 'situational awareness', which you might have heard informally called 'tells'. 'Tells' are subtle signs that people give – by the words they say or (more often) don't, but show by what they do – that reveal when various forms of potentially harmful bias or other socially hazardous behaviour are present. (See box below for two sets of clues that will start you off on that journey by looking at 'tells' for non-financial misconduct; see also the research debrief at Interlude 3 for a vivid set of misconduct 'tells' from financial firms surveyed during 2020.)

THINKING SMARTER: SPOTTING OTHER INFORMATIVE 'TELLS'

In searching for evidence of good behaviour and/or misconduct, we need to learn to look in new places for phenomena that we hadn't considered before and which may not at first seem measurable. Here are some favourite anecdotal examples, from my observational research in many firms:

- Is there **laughter** (not maliciously) in your workplace? That's a good (positive) proxy for *psychological safety.*

- Nobody ever volunteers for anything? Do people around you tend to be **bystanding**? It's a proxy for lack of *moral courage or challenge.*

- **Google autocomplete**: Try typing in the search phrase 'Why did [your firm's name]…?' and see what comes out. Free research into what the public's top concern is about you, today.

- **Internal mobility** – the more that staff can move around the firm and are encouraged to pursue careers across different business functions, the better the impact on staff retention (lower attrition and associated replacement/ training costs). This could be a positive proxy for cognitive diversity (challenge, problem-solving), helping to overcome tired business assumptions.

- People are prepared to share their private concerns with you (good) – but only if you talk to them one-to-one and '**off-campus**', where nobody else can see or hear your meeting. At that meeting, in the coffee shop, their conversation often starts with, 'I've never said this to anyone else, but…', or 'Everyone knows this is a problem but no one talks about it…'. Good that you find out, not so good that there's so much fear.

- Nobody gets any credit for '**self-reporting**' of process problems (not just 'technical breaches'). How often has anyone in your firm been praised, in any form, for saying they need to resolve a problem? A great indicator for lack of a healthy environment for controls and socializing of risk.

- '**Loud voices** and long shadows' – that in the meeting room or on the Zoom call, the conversation is dominated by those who simply talk the loudest and/or or use status to dominate: talking over others, ignoring alternative points of view, violating expected norms of taking turns to speak around the (virtual) table.

- Another version of the above power-play is the '**blink game**' – who blinks first? An aggressive speaker simply expects others to concede to them. In financial firms, this is often apparent where powerful, sales-side people 'bulldoze' other functions; and in 'entitled behaviour' among in-groups generally.

- High levels of staff '**sickies**' (questionable medical leave) as a proxy for unmanaged *workplace stress*.

- Is there anecdotally a perceived history of '**shooting the messenger**' – that is, people talk about 'giving a hard time' to anyone who raises a problem or reports a control breach? A useful negative indicator for psychological safety.

- There are a lot of **workarounds** – people doing temporary fixes to patch up systems and processes that aren't working properly, rather than properly addressing an underlying problem. This is not just an IT issue; you can see behaviour patterns of 'cutting corners' in almost any field of work.

- **Whispering** and **language-switching** on the phone, or abrupt **channel-switching** (eg from voice line to online chat room) as 'tells' for *fraud*.

- **Late registration**, **late arrival** and/or **non-attendance** at compliance training as a proxy for *disengagement*.

- **Personal credit score falling** as a tell for mis-selling.

- Call centre staff **waiting an extra ring** before answering incoming calls, as a proxy for *demotivation*.

- **Sitting down at the desk** at exactly 9:00 am every day, no sooner or later, as a 'tell' for *presenteeism* (demotivation, possible future 'wrecking' behaviours).

- **Never takes a holiday**, as a 'tell' for fraud.

- **Voluntary demotion**, as a proxy for concealed reporting of misconduct or fraud; also known as *'juniorizing'*, as a way of avoiding regulatory responsibility.
- Clusters of staff **dismissals with aggressive gagging orders** (injunctions/ superinjunctions) as a proxy for *abusive conduct* by the manager concerned.

Finally in this chapter, let's take a first look at three factors that various scientific research says – and regulators now say – vitally shape the way that 'culture assessment' tests will determine whether your firm's culture is suitably healthy. Rest assured that these themes (and more detail about them) will appear in the course of the following chapters.

Three science keys to a positive culture assessment for your firm

Three strands of scientific research – in economics, neuroscience and social anthropology – have recently emerged as informing conduct regulators' thinking on what are the most important tests within a 'culture assessment'. Though we'll explore the data-gathering side of all this in Chapters 8 and 9, it's useful here first to get an idea of why these three topics are so influential, and to note the research behind them.

Management science: the business value of 'purposeful culture'

The regulator has spelled out that a 'healthy culture' is purposeful, psychologically safe, diverse and inclusive; future culture assessments will examine:

> … how effective four culture drivers are at reducing the potential harm
> arising from a firm's business model: purpose, leadership, approach to people,
> and governance. The 'people driver' concerns whether firms are building
> a psychologically safe environment [and] how effective their diversity and
> inclusion is at promoting 'speaking up' and driving behaviour that reduces
> potential harm to customers.[16]

We will explore in more detail what this means in practice throughout this book. For a practical approach to the specific tasks of articulating your firm's purpose and then using this formulation in your conduct reports and culture assessments, see Chapters 5 and 10.

Brain science: psychological safety

Conduct regulators are keen to promote psychological safety as an essential quality of the 'exemplary' firm. In a February 2021 briefing, Jonathan Davidson, a leading FCA advocate of culture assessment, described the difference between merely 'speaking up' and having psychological safety in a firm thus:

> While effective whistleblowing is incredibly important, it isn't a substitute for psychological safety. Leaders need to educate themselves on what it is and how to… lead by example [of] how they cultivate psychological safety.[17]

On first introducing this important indicator, it's useful to define it, so we can keep it in mind during the rest of the book. There are three overlapping definitions, each of which speaks to a slightly different assessment function. First from Harvard's Professor Amy Edmondson, who has led research in this field since the late 1990s:

> A belief that one will not be punished or humiliated for speaking up with ideas, questions, concerns, or mistakes, and that the team is safe for interpersonal risk-taking.[18]

Two useful others:

> A climate in which team members are not afraid to express themselves, feel accepted and respected; a fertile environment for thinking, creativity, innovation and growth, that leads to more collaborative relationships and an overall improvement in team productivity.[19]

> Not being exposed to 'social rejection' which 'triggers a stress response that compromises our cognitive abilities', suppressing 'higher, logical brain activity [such as] thinking, creativity, decision-making and self-control', inducing 'a stress state in which we can find it difficult to concentrate, make decisions or control our emotions.[20]

Evolutionary anthropology: the power of cognitive diversity

Cognitive diversity is potentially the most interesting of all the new indicators being considered by conduct regulators. It reaches significantly beyond the conventional indicators for diversity (such as gender, ethnicity, social origin) and even some of the newer framing concepts such as neurotype. The UK's regulator (FCA) has described this factor as 'leading to better decision-making and enabling firms to meet the needs of consumers from diverse segments of society.'[21]

Cognitive diversity is variety in styles of thinking, especially as these challenge more entrenched modes of thought. As the social psychology analyst Matthew Syed cogently addresses the problem in his book, *Rebel Ideas*: a core problem of the workplace is a result of human evolution through early tribal societies. The workplace fosters 'tribal' behaviour – that is, the risk of informal groups splitting into 'subcultures':

> 'It is comforting to be surrounded by people who think the same way, who mirror our perspectives, who confirm our prejudices. It validates our world view. It stimulates the pleasure centres of our brains... like a hidden gravitational force.'[22]

As now widely agreed – not least by Syed, many of the world's conduct regulators, and the author panel of this book – diversity of thinking styles is a vital quality in a firm, to prevent 'collective blindness' (groupthink, motivated reasoning). By encouraging any kind of team to look beyond its own assumed framing of any given problem, cognitive diversity strongly improves the chance of finding alternative solutions, whilst also restraining excessive confidence of an 'in-group' (see Stephen Scott's analysis of the 'cool crowd problem' in Chapter 6). Perhaps best of all, it's an anti-bias mechanism for challenging the 'fundamental attribution error' effect: the bias problem of too readily assigning blame to individuals rather than acknowledging complex causes. It's related to a stereotyping problem: that people – particularly in status-conscious groups, as during a board meeting – tend to credit 'a person like me' with greater insight than 'a person not like me'. It's not hard to see how in a room full of, shall we say, board members of a certain (un-diverse) age and gender profile, and who perhaps all went to the same university (maybe even at the same time), may not be a particularly diverse-thinking group of people.

Conclusion

In Chapter 5, we'll start to unravel the mysteries of the regulatory call for 'purposeful culture'. Now that you're familiar with some of the core material that regulators use to frame their own thinking, and their motives as they develop culture assessment tools and 'better questions', you should feel more comfortable understanding where the questions come from – and will come from, as they continue to evolve.

On arrival at Chapters 9 and 10, you'll find these further support your confidence in the tasks of drawing together and categorizing sets of suitable indicators for expressing purpose and assessing culture. Along the way, let's keep in mind the regulator's motives and the three touchstones of purposeful culture, psychological safety and cognitive diversity. All of this will contribute to your own efforts in developing your firm's culture reporting framework. Let's leave the last word to the regulator, one more time:

> [Some] leaders are taking ownership of their firm's culture... because they understand the benefits of a healthy culture. [It] delivers long-term sustainable benefits for employees, consumers and shareholders, and helps firms avoid large-scale risks from crystallizing... and to be more innovative. In short, they understand that healthy cultures are good for business.[23]

Notes

1 For a longer list see FICC-FMSB Behavioural cluster analysis which identifies the 25 most common patterns of misconduct over the past 210 (yes, 210) years
2 Miles, R (2017) *Conduct Risk Management: Using a behavioural approach to protect your board and financial services business,* Kogan Page
3 At time of writing (Q4/2020), UK, the Netherlands, Ireland, Australia, South Africa, Japan, Hong Kong and Singapore. I confidently predict that others will follow suit.
4 Merton, R K (1936) The unanticipated consequences of purposive social action, *American Sociological Review* (Harvard) 1 (6), pp 894–904
5 McKay, C (1841) *Extraordinary Popular Delusions and the Madness of Crowds*
6 Thaler, R H and Sunstein, C R (2009) *Nudge: Improving decisions about health, wealth and happiness,* Penguin
7 Kahneman, D (2008) *Thinking, Fast and Slow,* Penguin
8 Ariely, D (2008) *Predictably Irrational,* HarperCollins
9 With the author's thanks to Prof Ishiro Kawachi at Harvard School of Public Health, who first shared a version of this with him; with all due acknowledgement to Prof Daniel Kahneman as the originator of the theory.
10 See for example Dan Ariely, as above
11 See for example Gerd Gigerenzer (2002) *Bounded Rationality: The adaptive toolbox,* MIT Press
12 The 'bounded rationality' theory – see Gigerenzer, G (2002) *Bounded Rationality: The adaptive toolbox,* MIT Press
13 See Library of Congress, https://blogs.loc.gov/international-collections/2017/08/the-tall-tales-of-baron-munchausen/ (archived at https://perma.cc/4G8R-2YTS)

14 See also IOSCO paper FR05/2019, April 2019

15 Many online resources, eg teachthought.com/critical-thinking/the-cognitive-bias-codex-a-visual-of-180-cognitive-biases/ (archived at https://perma.cc/4AXG-AKLV)

16 Jonathan Davidson, FCA Executive Director of Supervision (2020) speech: The business of social purpose, 26 November, fca.org.uk/news/speeches/business-social-purpose (archived at https://perma.cc/JG58-VJK4)

17 Jonathan Davidson (2021) quoted in CISI Briefing: Ask the Experts, February 2021, www.cisi.org/cisiweb2/cisi-news/ (archived at https://perma.cc/M48R-6L9E)

18 Edmondson, A (2018) *The Fearless Organization: Creating Psychological safety in the workplace for learning, innovation, and growth,* Wiley

19 Radecki, D, Hull, L and McCusker, J (2018) Psychological Safety, BBL Academy, www.academy-bbl.com (archived at https://perma.cc/Q4Z2-8BV7)

20 Lupien S J et al (2009) Effects of stress throughout the lifespan on the brain, behaviour and cognition, *Neuroscience*, 29 April, 10 (6), pp 434–45, europepmc.org/article/MED/19401723 (archived at https://perma.cc/E5NH-5F6B)

21 Davidson, J (2021) Interviewed in *CISI Review*, February, cisi.org/cisiweb2/cisi-news/the-review (archived at https://perma.cc/AQ9L-SHWT)

22 Syed, M (2019) *Rebel Ideas: The power of diverse thinking*, John Murray

23 Davidson, J (2021) Interviewed in *CISI Review*, February, cisi.org/cisiweb2/cisi-news/the-review (archived at https://perma.cc/AQ9L-SHWT)

Interlude One
From poacher to gamekeeper to poacher... to scientist: a supervisor's tale

CHRISTIAN HUNT

Editor's note

It has been an immense pleasure working with Christian Hunt over several years – he's a breath of fresh air in the usually stuffy environment of Compliance. Christian's story here explores being one of the first regulators (and businesspeople) to 'get' the behavioural science link with culture. His personal account here doesn't represent the official policy, guidance or views of any of the institutions mentioned. It's livelier than that!

KEY CONCEPTS IN THIS CHAPTER

action bias – bad apple defence – behavioural regulator – behavioural science – bystanding – compliance processes – conduct regulation – counter-cyclical – design of controls, instructions and training – enforcement vs supervision – expressive enforcement – global financial crisis – human risk – investment bank – 'light-touch' vs interventionist regulation – nudging vs enforcement – proxy indicators of behaviour – prudential vs conduct regulation – regulatory capture – regulatory reform – regulator's watchlist – rogue trader – rule-maker's rationale – supervisor/ supervision – surveillance technology – 'the naughty step' – unauthorized trading event – unintended consequences – 'walkabout' culture audit – wilful vs inadvertent non-compliance

A new broom?

In 2011 – although it was three years since the world's markets had crashed – the UK still had its old, pre-'behavioural' regulator, the Financial Services Authority (FSA). I joined them as a supervisor September that year.

It had never been in my career plan to become a banking regulator, but having seen the 2008 global financial crisis (GFC), it was clearly somewhere that would provide me with exciting work. It was arguably also *because* it hadn't been in my career plan, that the regulator was interested in hiring me. Although conduct regulation was still on the drawing board at that point, I'd heard interesting rumblings about a possible new behaviour-based regulatory approach which would stand to benefit from some fresh minds; a view I firmly shared.

In my early career, I'd worked in investment banking and seen firsthand how the industry operated. During that time, I'd been on secondment to The Takeover Panel, a regulator that oversees takeovers and mergers and protects the interests of shareholders. Established in the 1960s, it operated on a rather unusual, but effective basis: a rulebook underpinned by key principles, where the rules could be disapplied, if applying them led to a breach of the principles. It was a form of regulation I liked; a recognition that the world isn't always codifiable and that focusing on outcomes could be more effective than dogmatic adherence to rules.

After Her Majesty's (Labour) Government fell in 2010, partly as victim in the aftermath of the 2008 financial crisis, traumatized British voters elected what turned out to be a Conservative-Liberal coalition government. This new administration's new idea was to break up the FSA, which had been a sole regulator for the entire financial services industry, into two separate bodies. One of the new agencies would now focus on prudential regulation: in simple terms, protecting the stability of the financial system by stopping firms from failing in a disorderly manner and causing chaos. The other agency would focus on conduct: preventing bad behaviour and socially undesirable outcomes.

The change from traditional to 'behavioural'

In fact, the idea wasn't so new. Japan had regulated financial practitioners' conduct since 1998 – having experienced its own financial crisis in the 1997.[1] Also, in 1998, Australia had separately decided that it made sense to relieve its old single regulator of the hard task of trying to police both prudential and conduct objectives. Australia's rationale was plain: in 'bad times' a single regulator might over-focus on prudential risk, in 'good times' on conduct (losing sight of counter-cyclical prudence). Or these two objectives might conflict; trying too hard to keep a struggling firm afloat might well incentivize poor conduct.

By the time I was hired by the UK regulator in 2011, plans to split the FSA had been finalized and the countdown to what was called 'Legal Cutover' in 2013 had begun. On joining, I knew I'd be moving to the new Prudential Regulation Authority, a soon-to-be established subsidiary of the Bank of England.

The work of a supervisor

I headed a supervision department, the part of the regulator that directly faces off against firms, where my remit was to cover international banks. 'International' here meant foreign banks operating in the UK, rather than UK firms with an international footprint. This distinction matters a lot to the regulator, and here's why: when you have a firm that is based in your country, with its head office and registration there, legally and practically you have way more influence over it than you would if it's simply a foreign bank branch or subsidiary.

I was, then, dealing with the UK businesses of foreign companies. We of course looked at these firms in the context of their wider group activities geographically, since if we'd only kept an eye on what was happening in the UK, that would give us only part of the picture. As we had all seen with Lehman Brothers, firms operated globally, but when they failed, it happened locally. To keep ahead of this risk, we coordinated our supervision with other regulators. You can't supervise a global firm only from one location; rather like a balloon, if you put pressure in one place, the activity you're squeezing moves elsewhere – here meaning, to another jurisdiction.

I'd been given a portfolio of Swiss, Japanese and American banks to look after. These were far from being a homogenous collection of firms; there was a massive difference between the global wealth management and investment banking businesses of Swiss banks such as Credit Suisse and UBS and the less speculative businesses of the US custody banks like Northern Trust and State Street.

Accordingly, when I started as a regulator, the first question I asked myself was where I should focus my efforts. I was acutely aware that the risks posed by the banks I was responsible for supervising certainly wouldn't present themselves neatly in a nicely wrapped package. Things could happen very quickly, and I'd need to be across my entire portfolio. With some apprehension, I reviewed supervisory responses to events from just a few months earlier, April 2011, when Japan had experienced 'the Great Earthquake' (the Fukushima earthquake and tsunami) which had profoundly affected many of their firms.

An abrupt audit of the regulator's readiness

Barely a week after I started, I had my answer. UBS, the Swiss bank, had discovered that a London-based trader called Kweku Adoboli had incurred unauthorized losses of over $2bn.[2,3] He was arrested, the firm had to respond quickly to an emergency, and I was pitched into a crisis that was to become a defining point in my regulatory career – all just as I was getting used to a new commute, new office and new colleagues.

When I first heard about the incident, I'd simply presumed that there would be a regulatory playbook labelled 'Rogue Traders'. Wrong. But as it turned out, not having a playbook was actually a very smart strategy, as well as a major life lesson for us all. Every incident is different. Open-mindedness is vital. Much as we'd wish there to be, there aren't necessarily salient patterns of facts from previous incidents that help us to understand the current one you're dealing with. While we like to think of rogue traders as being in some form of homogenous risk 'group', actually they're individuals, with individual motivations. At the same time, every firm is different; the scale of the challenge, and the impact of the damage, is different in each case.

For the next two years my regulatory experience was heavily driven by this one case of unauthorized trading, as I spent far more time looking at UBS than I would otherwise have done. It's an interesting position to be in; on the one hand, you're not having actually to deal with the issue, you're merely supervising how a firm responds to it. On the other hand, there are questions to be answered around whether you, as a regulator, could have done something to prevent it, and there's a considerable amount of public scrutiny around the exercise.

Clamping down on bad barrels

An understandable temptation in this type of situation is to focus on the individual, rather than the organization. From the perspective of any firm that's been hit by a rogue trader, it is appealing to view it as 'one bad apple' (in the jargon, an 'unauthorized trading' event), rather than really reflecting on the role of the barrel in the incident. Unsurprisingly, as charged with a solemn responsibility for ensuring good governance, a prudential regulator may be expected to inspect the barrel with greater care than ever.

There is also a great temptation, as a regulator, to fixate on visible remediation: implementing new controls, enhancing monitoring and oversight programmes and increasing the level of mandatory training. It plays well to our natural human urge to 'do something' – what behavioural scientists call 'action bias' and political scientists call 'expressive enforcement'. It also feels like a sensible solution to a problem of bad behaviour. As in: if people are out of control, we need to rein them in with a combination of a more watchful eye and louder warning shots, in the form of stronger mandatory training and credible deterrents ('salient and vivid punishment'[4] – ie the messages that [a] they're likely to get caught and [b] it will hurt a lot when they are).

This is also most regulators' natural tendency. Regulators have biases of their own, in particular an action bias, though they're loath to admit it. The old regulators (notably the FSA) were criticized for being too 'captured' – letting firms set the agenda – and 'light touch', intervening only after things turned bad. The new regulators want to avoid being accused of that, hence they like to be seen always to be doing something. From a regulator's point of view,[5] being visibly active helps keep their sponsor happy (that's the government, remember) – besides public opinion, which still regards regulators as complicit in 'stealing' taxpayers' money to bail out the banks post-GFC. Accordingly, it made all kinds of strategic sense to come down harshly on firms who had demonstrated that they couldn't be trusted to get things right on their own.

Watch out for the watchlist

As a supervisor, I wasn't responsible for enforcement; that was handled by a separate team who meted out any due punishments. These usually took the form of fines that were eye-watering for the average person in the street, yet sometimes felt more like a rounding error when you looked at the amount of money that some serially offending firms were making.

In this incident UBS was fined the, in layman's terms, enormous sum of £29.7m for their 'unauthorized trading' event, which was deemed to be a failure of systems and controls.[6] This was a fine against the firm. Since 2018 the policy thrust of conduct regulation through the Senior Managers Regime (UK) and its international equivalents, has been to fine individuals for misconduct, rather than firms: making each penalty 'salient and vivid' for the individual concerned.

But my responsibility was to strike a balance in how we as supervisors engaged with firms, weighing up the merits of carrot versus stick. On the one hand, a good supervisor should work with firms to solve legacy problems, which sometimes aren't of their own making. Beating up those firms and project leaders who are simply trying to clean things up, isn't the most productive path towards the outcomes you're looking for. On the flip side, you won't want to be seen to be a pushover. You know you're publicly accountable to your chief regulator, and ultimately to the government, and perhaps worst of all, to the court of public opinion for how the firms you deal with respond to your urging them to put things straight.

Even less apparent to outsiders, perhaps, is the regulator's own internal scrutiny of its supervisors who have miscreant firms on their watch. Not the supervisors as individuals, but their supervisory approach. As a supervisor you might find one of your firms placed on the watchlist (the regulator's rolling list of any banks that are currently deemed to pose a significant risk to regulatory objectives[7]). If that happens, you'll find you're going to have to do a lot more internal reporting about them. It actually is what it sounds like: a list of firms who are on the 'naughty step'. The regulator tells them as much, partly to incentivize them to get themselves off the step.

The watchlist isn't just a tool the regulator uses to denote firms who've just had a big misconduct incident occur. It was then, and likely still is now, used by the regulator as a psychological tool to nudge firms into line; a tool that's also usually bolstered by a more blunt and painful instrument: additional capital charges. Together with added capital charges, the whole package is a form of 'bad behaviour tax' on the errant business.

A clear view of 'what the regulator wants'

When we think of regulation, we tend to think of rulebooks, and box-ticking compliance requirements. Working in supervision, I was surprised instead to find that regulation is very much a person-to-person business.

While the interlocutors on both sides are only granted personal authority to interact because they are nominated as proxies by their respective organizations, ultimately much of what works in everyday practice is achieved on this human one-to-one level. It's a little like trade agreements or political horse-trading – albeit that the odds are now increasingly stacked in favour of the regulator, in a way they might not have been in the past.

I spent two years as a supervisor, both at the FSA and at the PRA. At which point, I was appointed COO, responsible for the operations of an independent subsidiary of the Bank of England. It was an interesting challenge. One look at the architecture of the Bank of England will give you a clue: it was, at least in 2013 when I took the role, generally reliant on being a black box that would only release information such as interest rate decisions at pre-ordained times. Coincidentally, in 2013 the Bank of England's new governor Mark Carney arrived, intent on greater transparency of bank decision-making.[8]

At that time, banks hadn't yet seen much of the new regulatory 'walkabout' style – much discussed throughout this book – of the central bank's subsidiary sending its junior staff out into regulatees' offices, where rapid decisions regularly needed to be made; this wasn't what firms were used to. (It's rather different now, as 'walkabout' direct observation tests become a core supervisory tool under the new culture assessments.)

Taking the insight outside: regulatory staff move to practitioner firms

On the Bank of England side, meanwhile, came a different kind of culture shift: higher staff turnover, of around 12 per cent (somewhat higher in the supervision teams) as people crisscrossed between the regulator and regulatees. This was viewed with some disapproval by the more Civil Service types in the rest of the Bank of England, where staff turnover was materially lower, mainly to/from academia and other governmental bodies and into retirement. Now, although many countries don't allow people to move from regulator to regulatee, in some – notably including the UK and France[9] – it's seen as being helpful.

Perhaps inevitably, I became part of the exodus.

I ended up, also somewhat inevitably, at UBS. Having spent so much time interacting with the firm, I'd come to know them well, and they knew me well, so that both sides knew to a fair extent what they were getting. I also respected that, having seen them from the outside in, this was a firm that wanted to do the right thing.

Post-regulatory indigestion

It can be all too easy, when you leave the regulator, to find yourself working for a firm that wants you to act as a spin doctor for bad behaviour. That wasn't for me; I wanted to go somewhere that was making a tangible effort to do right.

Regulators joining firms typically find themselves in either Compliance or Audit, and I was no exception, joining UBS's Compliance and Operational Risk Control team. One of the positive outcomes following the Adoboli affair was that there was understood to be merit in bringing together the function responsible for ensuring the firm followed the rules, Compliance, with the function that was responsible for managing many of the risks that those rules sought to mitigate, Operational Risk.

Much as we like to think of Compliance as a binary exercise – that you either are, or are not compliant – the reality is subtler, more scalar. Some rules are speed limit-like in nature; for example, whether or not you have breached sanctions or reported your trades on time. Many others are not, though: it can be very challenging to try, for example, to codify conduct regulations without creating unintended consequences.

On becoming Global Head of Compliance and Operational Risk Control in a firm's asset management business, the change of perspective was fascinating and a little unnerving. Having been the responsible UK regulator, I now realized that I'd effectively been part of the team of architects of many requirements imposed on the firm. I was, not to put too fine a point on it, having to eat my own regulatory cooking – frankly, it didn't always taste good. In some cases rules clearly designed and applicable for banking activities could unintentionally block legitimate asset management business activities.

The practical consequences can be challenging. If you're in a compliance role, then you're understandably required to lead by example; so I'd lead online training for regulations that weren't strictly relevant to me and comply with the tightest of requirements that we imposed on our business colleagues. Another culture shock that many Heads of Compliance will recognize is to find how many things are done in your name (including to you yourself), such as receiving emails from yourself, sending yourself on training and reminding you about new policies you owned.

A light dawns

It was then that something struck me: if, as a Compliance person, I found the 'Compliance process' a tough subject to sell, then how must my colleagues in the front office feel? After all, they didn't have the word Compliance in their job title, and they weren't former regulators. What on earth must they think?

There was also increasing evidence to support the need for a fresh approach, following this question. The fact that policies were being issued and (oxymoronic) 'invitations to mandatory training' being sent in my name, meant I had to take responsibility – which could take the edge off my best intentions. At worst, I might feel like the proverbial protestor outside the White House with a 'not in my name' banner.

In case I needed further evidence to confirm my hunch that the target audience might not like this situation, there's nothing like sending out a clunky, compliance-y email to test the impact you're making. If you're approachable, which I like to think I am, and if said clunky emails are sent out in your name, you can bet that people will come and find you to discuss them if they don't like what they're seeing. Yes: they did come and find me. And yes, they didn't always like what they were seeing.

The second realization was that we were putting a lot of effort into getting people to behave in a particular way; my function's primary purpose was to drive people's behaviour. Aha! We were in the business of influencing human decision-making. After all, you couldn't just tell an organization to be compliant. Inanimate objects don't respond much to instructions; people respond rather better, as long as the instructions are well presented. If you want to have a firm be compliant, then it's down to whether the people within that firm do the right thing. Equally, Operational Risk Control was also the business of influencing human decision-making. When things went wrong, there was always human involvement, either causing problems in the first place or making them worse by the way they reacted to them.

Compliance is good business – not just 'rules'

What my unique set of experiences had set me up to realize was that actually – trigger warning here – the main business of Compliance isn't rules. It's the business of influencing people. All too often, the methods that are used are designed using a theoretical basis of 'how we would like people to behave', and 'what a rational person (ie a person like me, the rule-maker) would do', rather than the way that other real people are likely to actually behave.

If a Compliance function treats employees like forced – or enforced – consumers of lists of prohibitions, we risk ending up with our precious human assets merely doing trivially measurable things, the stuff we can monitor, rather than engaging thoughtfully in problem-solving for the benefit of the business and its customers. As we see repeatedly in well-run business, and advocate throughout this book, giving staff the opportunity to engage intelligently in a conversation about 'why we do things the way we do' – and whether those things can be done better – is a far better route than blind enforcement of rules and rote-learning. It took me 10 years, and twice jumping the fence between business and regulation, to realize how much this matters.

Bringing behavioural science to compliance

As ever in life, once you see something, it is very hard to 'unsee' it. In my case, the moment I saw my role through a behavioural lens was the point of no return. I began to analyse every aspect of Compliance as an 'intervention', an attempt to influence human decision-making. It occurred to me that if we were in the business of influencing other people, then we should shamelessly borrow the techniques that are successfully deployed by others who are in that same business; most obviously advertising, but also transport authorities and (whisper it) governments. What works for selling washing powder, managing passenger behaviour on the London Underground and getting people to live healthier lives, could inform how we did Compliance.

It helped that, for some time, I'd had a frankly nerdy interest in the emerging field of behavioural science, which studies why people do what they do – the actual drivers of human behaviour. And I stress the *actual* drivers, rather than the ones we tell ourselves and others are behind our decision-making. To be honest, I probably spent more time exploring behavioural science than some of the other subjects I was officially supposed to be studying earlier in life; in my mind it was, in many respects, a solution looking for a problem. And Compliance was an enormous problem. One behavioural science was ideally suited to help solve.

In a large global organization, I wasn't going to be able to do this myself. The title Global Head of Compliance and Operational Risk Control suggests a degree of power that the reality sometimes belies. There were absolutely things I controlled, and could and did change. But equally there were lots of things that were imposed on a firm-wide basis that I didn't control. Things for which I would need the support of those who owned firm-wide programmes and policies.

Benefits of dropping the 'Compliance' brand

Advertising was also to provide me with an idea for how to solve that challenge, as we'll see. My mission, and by then it had become a mission, would need a slogan and a brand. Riffing off a highly memorable advertising slogan from the early 1980s for Italian brand Zanussi ('the Appliance of Science'), I came up with the slogan 'Bringing Behavioural Science to Compliance'.

Whilst many compliance people extol the virtues of artificial intelligence, robotics and machine learning as their tools of the future, I'd say they are only right up to a point: many aspects of compliance officers' work could and should be done by machine. But it's not a humanly engaging solution; people will still be essential to risk management, doing things that machines can't. Most glaringly, you need people to help manage the risks posed by... other people. From that came the idea of Human Risk; an intentionally broad term, covering everything from wilful wrongdoing to honest mistakes. Farewell, in my mind, to the awfully uninspiring 'Compliance' brand and a warm welcome to 'Human Risk'.

This re-positioning of the function worked better than I had expected. As I pushed for the firm to embrace the idea of Human Risk, I was offered and accepted a firm-wide role as Head of Behavioural Science within Compliance. That allowed me to take a detailed look at processes that we don't often pay much attention to, but are highly significant from a behavioural perspective.

Driving the internal change

Such as: induction training. We all intuitively know that first impressions count, yet how much attention do firms pay to genuinely making a good first impression on their new employees?

I attended as an observer and was fascinated to see that the slides the person giving the training was required to deliver didn't contain much information it would be useful for the attendees to have on day one of their new careers. No one starts a new job wondering, 'What does the firm's operational risk framework look like?' or 'I wonder what precise number of offices it has around the world?' Yet that's typically what these presentations contain.

Induction training isn't a marketing pitch. Or rather it is, but it's to an audience that's already bought the product, so needs reassurance they've made the right decision and help adapting to their new environment, not a second viewing of the corporate advertisements they probably watched while applying for the role. To their credit, the trainer intuitively realized this; they swiftly closed the gap between the slides' boilerplate content and the practical information the recruits really wanted (like 'where can I get coffee?', 'when will I get my passport back?'). Wouldn't it have been better, I mused afterwards, if the presenter had been able to do that *with* the prepared slides, rather than in spite of them?

Looking in new places

I began to find interesting behavioural insights in unexpected quarters.

One day, someone in the building management team called me, having heard about my line of work. They explained that they wanted to improve levels of staff participation in waste recycling in a building that was otherwise extremely environmentally friendly. Could I help? We don't often think of recycling as a compliance exercise, but it is. Employees might not be environmentally engaged, but the firm was, so while they were at work, there was an expectation that they would behave in an environmentally friendly manner. Might recycling serve as a visible signal of people's adherence to corporate values, and so a potential proxy indicator for adherence to conduct requirements that were less visible?

On the face of it, yes. There were variations in take-up of recycling, between different floors. Was this a predictable outcome, not from 'bad people' but 'poor control design' (unclear signage, bins not visible), with different floorplans driving different outcomes? A well-intended sign told people that 'none of our waste goes to landfill'. What if people read that sign as saying 'we're really good at managing waste' – implying that the firm had things covered, behind the scenes, so no need for you personally to do anything? Did the sign accidentally induce 'bystanding'?

There's a lesson there for all compliance officers about the risks of shouting too loudly about how effective your frameworks are; it might just make people who already assume that compliance is 'not my job, anyway', disengage even further. For each message, think outside-in and user-test it.

Just as important, there were no practical 'nudges': the physical environment didn't make recycling easy. The office canteen provided packaging for people to take their lunch back to their desks. Yet it was unclear which bin to put the packaging in. A common packaging item, a foam box, didn't seem to fit into any of the recycling slots. Were people not recycling simply because we'd made it really hard for them to do? A simple compliance lesson about nudges: people's propensity to follow a rule often correlates to how easy (or hard) it is for them to follow it.

Reframing the problem

It's very tempting, when you have people breaking a rule, to conclude that you have a 'people problem'. But if lots of people aren't complying with a rule, then it's more likely that there's a problem with the rule itself. Perhaps it's inadvertently stopping a legitimate activity, or there's been insufficient or poorly timed training on the rule. If one or two people fail to comply, then you've got a people problem. If lots of people fail to comply, there's something in the rule that needs looking at. As you do that closer look, you can identify the people who are wilfully non-compliant and those who are just inadvertently non-compliant.

It was easy – but an assumption – to conclude from the low level of recycling on some floors that those employees didn't care about the environment. Yet in truth, there were lots of practical reasons why they might not be compliant. Remove those hurdles, and you get some very valuable intelligence on which areas of the business might, just might, have less propensity to ignore other rules.

From Compliance... into Science

Fast-forward to the present day and my mission continues: I've taken Human Risk 'on the road'. Unsurprisingly, what works within Financial Services is also working well to solve Compliance challenges in other sectors.

Notes

1 Nasako, H (2001) The financial crisis in Japan during the 1990s: how the Bank of Japan responded, www.bis.org/publ/bppdf/bispap06.pdf (archived at https://perma.cc/5FPU-XVX9)

2 Adoboli's confession email to an auditor, as evidence in Court, https://assets. documentcloud.org/documents/520177/kweku-adoboli-email.txt (archived at https://perma.cc/Q5WG-ESNZ)

3 BBC News (2012) From 'rising star' to rogue trader, 20 November, bbc.co.uk/news/uk-19660659 (archived at https://perma.cc/UMT4-6SH2)

4 Financial Conduct Authority (2016) Behaviour and Compliance in Organisations, Occasional Paper 24

5 See Miles, R (2017) on dimensions of 'the regulatory problem', Chapter 4 of *Conduct Risk Management: Using a behavioural approach to protect your board and financial services business*, Kogan Page

6 BBC (2012) UBS fined £29.7m by FSA over Kweku Adoboli case, https://www.bbc.co.uk/news/business-20492017 (archived at https://perma.cc/EDR3-GMYL)

7 FCA and PRA (2018) Tackling Serious Failings in Firms: Explanation of FCA and PRA 'Watchlists' and other Special Powers to be invoked following 2014 UK Parliamentary Review on Banking Standards, fca.org.uk/publication/corporate/tackling-serious-failings-in-firms.pdf (archived at https://perma.cc/FYQ7-536H)

8 https://www.bankofengland.co.uk/news/2013/february/mark-carney-questionnaire-for-the-tsc (archived at https://perma.cc/F5DB-LQ7N)

9 The French use the delightful term *pantouflage* to denote the practice of ageing civil servants obtaining pre-retirement sinecures in the private sector

05

What's the big idea? (2)

Regulators' challenge to firms: framing 'purposeful culture'

COSETTE RECZEK AND ROGER MILES

Introduction: what's your purpose?

After wide-ranging debate around the 'social usefulness' of financial services and the primary purpose of financial regulation, there is increasing agreement on the need for the industry's public reporting to answer a core challenge: explain what you do and why, in a way that recognizes the value to society of what you do.

The new watchword is to 'define purposeful culture'. In this chapter we will see how that has come about, what forms of progress (and stumbles) there have been along the way, and how your firm might best approach this challenge from now on, starting by using some simple lenses to focus on what it means in practice.

THEMES AND CONCEPTS IN THIS CHAPTER

Australian inquiry into misconduct in banking (Royal Commission) – 'bad apple' hypothesis – Banker's Oath – Banking Standards Board annual assessment – cognitive diversity – capital cover – conduct and culture Annual Report dashboards, absence of – corporate purpose – Covid-19 as opportunity to reappraise cultural failings – culture assessment framework – culture benchmarking – culture conversation – culture models – 'Dear CEO' letter interventions – exemplary conduct – financial indicators vs behavioural indicators – 'grey areas' and 'acceptable behaviour' assumption – industry-level culture change – key drivers of behaviour and culture – leadership and management competencies – legitimacy of rules – MacQuarie Risk Culture Scale – pillars of conduct assessment – post-2008 financial sector scandals – priming – principles-based guidance – psychological safety – public harms – purposeful culture – reputational risk – response effects – rewards, recognition and incentives – self-diagnosed sentiment v observed behaviour – self-regulation ('government-sponsored voluntary regulation'/ GSVR) – Senior Managers' accountability regimes, UK and other – Supervision of Culture approach – 'tone from the top' insufficient – value-at-risk vs behaviour-at-risk

Regulators' 'culture challenge' to firms

In 2018 the UK's Financial Conduct Authority (FCA) discussion paper 'Transforming Culture in Financial Services'[1] opened with:

> *Culture in* financial services is widely accepted as a key root cause of the major conduct failings that have occurred within the industry in recent history, causing harm to both consumers and markets.

The paper ranged loosely across themes including: is there a right culture?; the role of regulators; and the role of reward. It included varied and sometimes conflicting contributions from financial business leaders, consulting firms, external auditors, and academia. In a follow-up paper in 2020 which added 'Driving purposeful cultures' to the original title,[2] the FCA highlighted links between culture and purpose. Introducing the 2020 paper, the FCA's head of retail supervision Jonathan Davidson reflects on a regulator's own purpose and motivation:

> My purpose at the FCA is to bring about a transformation in the business models and culture of financial services... We wanted to surface... outstanding issues that are preventing the adoption of healthy cultures in financial services, and encourage leaders to reflect on their firms' cultures and to continue, or in some cases, start, taking action.

At that point, more than 12 years had passed since the 2008 global financial crisis (GFC), described as a 'generation-defining event' (this was, of course, before Covid-19 struck). Regulators used the 2020 culture anthology to express a sense of 'shock' that many financial services firms had not yet addressed the deeply rooted culture issues that the paper discussed. Davidson called on firms to make and show real progress:

> Purpose is the gravitational force that draws in and aligns teamwork, engagement, inspiration and creativity. To do this, the stars of employee purpose, social purpose, firm purpose and shareholder purpose all need to align. But… for many years, the stars haven't aligned. And the fault in the stars has created unhealthy cultures.[3]

There's a difficulty from the outset, of course. Each firm's culture is unique and there is no one-size-fits-all model. So the regulator – reasonably enough – doesn't set out to prescribe what any regulated firm's culture should be. However, regulators see that it is a firm's culture that shapes its conduct outcomes for both consumers and markets.

Rather than offering practical pointers or a developed reporting framework, the 2018 and 2020 FCA discussions conclude with no prescription for reporting on culture. Instead, quietly during the course of 2020 the regulator began to weave into its existing conduct assessment framework a suggestion of further overseeing four key drivers of culture within firms, aligned with the pre-existing conduct 'pillars': Purpose; Leadership; Approach to rewarding and managing people; and Governance.[4]

To 'deliver culture change', the regulator would continue to support both academic and industry research into the transformation of culture, as well as engaging with independent culture assessment initiatives such as the annual assessments carried out by the Banking Standards Board.[5] In webinars and less formal industry roundtables, the 'four key drivers' of culture were sometimes also described as Purpose; People management; Governance; Systems and controls. Under these headings we began to hear about framing concepts for culture measurement, notably psychological safety, leadership and management competencies, recognition and incentives, and cognitive diversity.

As we see throughout this book, the 'culture conversation' in financial services is not unique to the UK. It is a global response primarily to the 2008 financial crisis and continuing industry scandals since, and to the economic and social shocks of the Covid-19 pandemic in 2020. These events are seen as having had in all too many cases a catastrophic impact on individuals, families and businesses – exacerbated on the supply side by too many financial service providers' failure to acknowledge their role in causing public harms.

Challenging poor cultural outcomes of self-regulation

Way back in 2014, a team at Oxford University undertook significant research into the culture of regulatory dialogues around the commonest method of self-regulation, so-called 'government-sponsored voluntary regulations' (GSVRs).[6] GSVR has been described as 'pledges' made between businesses and the government. Example outcomes from GSVR in other regulated sectors include food producers reducing fat content and salt levels in food, and retailers reducing the use of plastic bags. GSVR has also been used in policy domains such as the environment and sustainability, public health, employment and skills, pricing, trading policy, and social policy. In financial services we have seen it in, for example, the old (1990s UK) Banking Codes and more recently in the work of the Fixed Income, Currencies and Commodities Markets Standards Board (FICC-FMSB)[7] and the Lending Standards Board.[8]

The Oxford study's authors, Dr Chris Decker and Professor Christopher Hodges, noted that a major motive for a business to engage with GSVR is 'reputational', since it may be adversely affected by news and social media comments about its (non)compliance, even though the 'pledges' are not legally binding rules. Yet if the business is within a market where other providers routinely ignore the 'pledge', reputational risk is lower, since in the public view 'they're all as bad as each other'; and government may or may not have the political will (or bandwidth) to convert a voluntary code into binding statute law. Dr Decker and Prof Hodges recommended that upcoming GSVRs should at least be evaluated in the same way as full legislation; HM Government duly announced that GSVR should be subject to regulatory impact assessment, as formal laws are.[9]

Other jurisdictions have started to take more forceful action to improve financial services culture. Since 2015, all Dutch bankers have been required to swear an Oath of Good Conduct (see box below) with eight integrity vows,[10] backed by legal sanctions to enforce it. This oath draws on both the behavioural science principle that *priming* can have a strong benign influence on conduct, and the conventional principle of deterrents – backed by strong threats of detection (with alert surveillance) and enforcement (with tough penalties).

Ironically, the Dutch oath was developed from a voluntary Banking and Finance Oath introduced in Australia in 2013, which although at the time was the first of its type in the world, unfortunately suffered from minimal take-up. It has been suggested that Australian finance's reluctance to sign up 'could have been a result of bankers feeling conflicted about their actions'.[11] Cultural drivers of this reluctance became clearer with the later (2019) scathing findings published by Australia's Royal Commission inquiry into misconduct in financial services.[12]

DUTCH BANKERS' OATH – FULL TEXT

I swear/promise that within the limits of the position I hold at any time in the banking industry:

- I will execute my function ethically and with care.
- I will draw a careful balance between the interests of all parties associated with the business, being the customers, shareholders, employees and the society in which the business operates.
- When drawing that balance, I will make the customers' interests central.
- I will comply with the laws, regulations and codes of conduct that apply to me.
- I will keep confidential that which has been entrusted to me.
- I will not abuse my knowledge.
- I will act openly and accountably and I know my responsibility to society.
- I will make every effort to retain and improve trust in the financial sector.

So help me God/This I declare and promise.

The oath/affirmation was taken/made in the above form on [date], at [place], before [name of person who administered the oath] in the presence of [name of other representative of the business or industry or professional organization].

Furthermore, [name of the person] confirmed his/her acceptance of the enforcement of the codes of conduct by the Disciplinary Committee and the exercise of authority by the Director General pursuant to the disciplinary scheme in the banking industry codes of conduct.

Name [signature]

Culture change remains a 'slow, uphill battle'

In 2018 the Group of Thirty (G30), an international group of leading finan-
ciers and academics, observed that 'Ten years after the global financial crisis,
trust in banks remains low', publishing the second of two global-view
reports on conduct and culture in financial services.[13] G30's reviews addressed:
(1) How much progress has the banking industry made in culture and conduct
since the financial crisis, particularly since our last report? and (2) Where do we
go from here?

G30 noted that 10 years after the 2008 financial crisis, despite many new
regulations, the banking industry still suffered from a negative reputation,
that trust still needed repairing because serious conduct and culture failures
continued, and that public mistrust of the industry persisted (see Table 5.1
below). Worse, pushing against well-meant initiatives for culture change, the
industry's desire to 'get back to business', with an onset of 'culture initiative
fatigue', meant that change programmes wouldn't gain traction. The main
conclusion was that bank conduct and culture are, at best, facing a 'slow,
uphill battle' for external trust.

Progress since the 2018 industry-wide assessments

That slow, uphill battle for trust seems to have become more like a trek up
the K2 mountain with no view yet of the summit. The FCA recognized this,
in the diplomatic phrasing of its 2019 review of firms' progress in responding to five conduct questions (for detail see Chapter 10):

> As firm CEOs will attest, the effort to shape and improve conduct and culture
> does not have an end date. The more complex, long-term challenge of achieving
> sustainable firm-wide mindset change still lies ahead.[14]

The Chair of the European Central Bank's supervisory board observed that
banks' culture and governance needed a rethink as they continued to devolve
blame for the GFC and subsequent scandals onto a few 'bad apples', distanc-
ing themselves from the problem.[15]

Purposeful culture: regulators make new sense of 'mission'

The answer, as G30 sees it, lies in improving firms' focus on (socially useful)
purpose in decision-making:

TABLE 5.1 Timeline: financial sector scandals continue through the decade *after* the 2008 crisis

2011	**Rogue trader:** UBS trader undertook US$2bn of unauthorized trades
2012	**Sanctions violations:** Standard Chartered violated U.S. sanctions against Iran, Libya, Cuba and Sudan
	Reference rate manipulation: Barclays, UBS, Rabobank, Deutsche Bank, RBS colluded to manipulate LIBOR submissions to benefit trading positions
	Mis-selling: Lloyds, RBS, HSBC, Barclays mis-sold payment protection insurance and other complex financial products to customers
	Money laundering: HSBC allowed drug cartels to launder US$900mn through its U.S. banks
	Rogue trader: J.P. Morgan 'London Whale' accumulated US$2bn worth of derivatives positions
	Insider trading: Nomura leaked non-public info on firms undergoing IPOs to favoured fund manager clients
2013	**Bribery:** J.P. Morgan awarded more than 100 jobs and interships to 'princelings' referred by government officials in Asia
2014	**Market manipulation:** UBS, RBS, HSBC, Citibank, J.P. Morgan. Bank of America colluded over six years to manipulate foreign exchange spot markets using exclusive chatrooms and coded language
	False tax returns: Credit Suisse assisted US taxpayers in hiding offshore accounts
	Reference rate manipulation: National Australia Bank, ANZ, Westpac and Commonwealth Bank manipulated Australian Bank Bill Swap Rate (BBSW) benchmark
2015	**Mortgage fraud:** ABN-Amro mortgage advisors forged client signatures in revised documentation on mortgages
	Fraudulently opened accounts: Wells Fargo opened millions of fraudulent savings and checking accounts without customer consent
	Unsuitable financial advice: Commonwealth Bank encouraged more than 3,500 clients to undertake risky, inappropriate investments
2016	**Loan fraud:** ICBC, Postal Savings Bank of China granted loans to criminals who illegally pledged gold of low purity as collateral
2017	**Aggressive sales targets:** TD Bank increased overdraft protection amounts and credit card borrowing limits without customer authorisation
2018	**Fees for no service:** Commonwealth Bank (Aus) and AMP charged thousands of customers for financial advice that was never given
2019	**Money laundering:** Standard Chartered Bank fined over £100mn for anti-money laundering breaches

SOURCE Research from G30[16]

Repair measures thus need to focus on the fundamental drivers of decision-making... first and foremost, culture. Decisions are always embedded in and guided by culture... Tone from the top has an important role to play, but it is not enough: a sound culture has to be embedded at all levels of the organization, with particular attention to middle management and frontline business. A working environment has to be created in which staff are not afraid to speak up and challenge decisions.[17]

The European Central Bank in 2020 noted 'with particular concern... deteriorating scores driven by limited effectiveness of management bodies' in improving governance and culture.[18] Past episodes of bad behaviour had pointed to patterns of subcultures within large, complex financial institutions, acting in their own distinctive ways; acknowledging this, it looks even harder for senior managers to translate well-meant 'tone at top' into a coherent culture that resonates across the organization.[19] (Design of a programme to overcome this challenge is addressed directly by a behavioural analytics expert in Chapter 7.)

Locally in the UK, the Senior Managers Regime (SMCR), as successor to the Treating Customers Fairly initiative, impresses on firms that a culture change must be embedded throughout the organization. Customers recognize that a firm's culture is driven from the top down but is expressed to customers primarily through front-line service staff. Leaders of financial firms need to ensure that their culture change programmes and aspirations reach from the top to the bottom of their organization, reviewing every aspect of it to ensure that it promotes a customer-centric culture.[20]

Yet, how far do firms' staff actually modify their behaviour in response to 'tone from the top' messages? Not much, if at all, as it turns out. Local managers and team leaders have far more direct influence, whilst many board pronouncements are dismissed by front-line staff as 'just rhetoric' (see box, page 108: Tone from the top isn't enough).

The difficult task of how initially to approach a framing of the firm's collective purpose is addressed in a section on culture models (see Chapter 10).

THE RISK COALITION

In December 2019, the Risk Coalition, a network of not-for-profit professional bodies and membership organizations committed to raising the standards of risk management in the UK, published *'Raising the Bar: Principles-based guidance for board risk committees and risk functions'*,[21] to support banks in raising the general standard of risk governance and oversight practice within UK financial services.

The principles and guidance were published to establish a common understanding of the purpose, role and activities of the board risk committee and risk function; they offer a benchmark against which board risk committees and risk functions can objectively self-assess. This promises to drive evolution of the general standard of risk governance and oversight practice within UK financial services.

The Risk Coalition also provides GABI – a new online Gap Analysis and Benchmarking Insights service to enable self-assessment and benchmarks for industry-wide good practice.

Outside the UK, other regulators have published findings and expectations for culture in banks. In their 2018 paper 'Behaviour and Culture of the Irish Retail Banks'[22] the Central Bank of Ireland (CBI) (co-authored with DNB) tied improvement in decision-making and risk management to expanded diversity in the boardroom and throughout the professional population. The CBI set out to work with each bank individually to establish a plan to achieve this diversity. Each plan would have clear expectations, stretch measures and implementation targets with effectiveness measured against suitably ambitious outcomes and targets. To aid this, the five banks focused upon in the 2018 CBI report helped found an independent body dedicated to making banking in Ireland trustworthy again: The Irish Banking Culture Board. Yet in November 2019 it was recognized that banks must play 'a long game if the aim is to rebuild trust and change culture in any banking sector', posing the question, 'Why is it so damn difficult to change culture?'[23]

From Q1/2021 the CBI has brought in a new framework for individual accountability, the Senior Executive Accountability Regime (SEAR), analogous to the UK's regime (SMCR). Placing this on a legislative footing, as in the UK and elsewhere (see box: Mandating personal responsibility) will help drive forward CBI's mandate to ensure positive culture change across the financial services sector.[24]

MANDATING PERSONAL RESPONSIBILITY: EXAMPLE CONDUCT REGIMES HOLDING MANAGERS PERSONALLY ACCOUNTABLE, AS AT Q1/2021

- **Australia**: Banking Executive Accountability Regime (Australian Prudential Regulation Authority).
- **Hong Kong**: Supervision of Bank Culture (Hong Kong Monetary Authority).
- **Ireland**: Senior Executive Accountability Regime (Central Bank of Ireland).
- **Japan**: Strengthened Misconduct Governance (Japan Financial Services Authority).
- **Netherlands**: Banker's Oath, and Financial Markets Amendment Act (Netherlands Authority for the Financial Markets).
- **Singapore**: Individual Accountability (Monetary Authority of Singapore).
- **UK**: Senior Managers & Certification Regime (Financial Conduct Authority)

TONE FROM THE TOP ISN'T ENOUGH: THE DEMANDING REALITY OF RISK CULTURE

If a bank's board affirms a universal expectation of staff for risk culture and conduct behaviours, can it reasonably expect consistent uptake of these throughout the firm? What are the drivers of potential internal differences in risk culture and conduct? Elizabeth Sheedy and Barbara Griffin researched this using the Macquarie University Risk Culture Scale™ examining risk culture in 113 business units across three major banks.

Strong risk culture (higher scores for Valued, Proactive, Manager and low scores for Avoidance) was generally associated with more desirable risk-related behaviour (eg speaking up) and less undesirable behaviour (eg manipulating controls).

Personal characteristics were also important. Staff with longer tenure, those who were less risk tolerant and those with positive attitudes to risk management were more likely to display desirable risk-related behaviour. Those with high personal risk tolerance were more likely to behave 'undesirably'. Senior staff tend see their firm's culture far more positively than junior staff. This highlights the importance of anonymous and independent risk culture assessments where staff feel safe to reveal their true beliefs.

Good risk structures (policies, controls, IT systems, training, remuneration systems) appeared to support strong culture and reduce undesirable risk behaviour. However, good risk structures alone do not guarantee good behaviour; remuneration and other factors are all interpreted through the lens of culture.

Culture scores varied most widely at business unit level, driven by the local team environment. Culture would seem to be a local construct, highly dependent on interactions with close colleagues and the immediate manager.[25]

Covid-19 and 'Dear CEO...'

Against this background of mostly slow progress, the onset of Covid-19 in early 2020 saw regulators reappraising firms' social engagement and accountability. The FCA wrote a series of letters to the CEOs of financial firms during April–June 2020,[26] restating the case that the key root causes of harms are unhealthy culture and the (often) non-financial misconduct that results from this. How a firm handles non-financial misconduct is 'indicative of its culture' generally; the remedy is for firms to embed healthy cultures within which the 'identifying and modifying of key drivers' of misconduct is a priority. Where SMCR was the first opportunity and a catalyst to transform culture, Covid-19 presented more of a 'last call' to the industry.

The letters explained that non-financial misconduct generates 'tells' – indicators of poor culture that are evident in day-to-day observable behaviour such as discrimination, harassment, victimization and bullying. Obstacles to improvement include fear of speaking up, and a lack of diversity and inclusion.

The 'Dear CEO' Covid-era letters also show early signs of the FCA's pivot towards championing firms that show 'exemplary conduct' (rather than only being seen as a prosecutor of misconduct): firms are exhorted to sustain socially useful services such as trade finance and insurance cover for small businesses, and to be more conscious than ever of the needs of and challenges facing vulnerable customers during a time of social stress.

Suggested 'positive signs' in these 'Dear CEO' letters somewhat obviously include: senior managers visibly taking responsibility for what happens; that it is safe for anyone in a firm to speak up (with evidence of events of this happening); that the firm has an external reputation for keeping good staff;

and that the firm's decisions on risk and other business matters are long-termist and well informed.

The event of the externally imposed crisis of pandemic – as opposed to the largely self-inflicted crises of misconduct throughout the 2010s – was seen by the regulator as a form of fresh test of culture, allowing well-governed firms a new, if unplanned, opportunity to shine.

Early examples of firms' self-assessed culture reporting (pre-2021 culture assessments)

At the end of the 2019 business year (reporting Q1/2020), banks had self-reported their progress on culture development, in line with their 'best guess' understanding of regulatory and customer expectations (see examples in Chapter 10 and case study, Interlude 2). Here's a flavour of what we know about major banks' pre-emptive work on culture reporting, from their announcements about it.

Santander measured its achievement of its 'Simple, Personal and Fair' manifesto through surveys and interviews with employees, shareholders, and customers across all segments. Its 2019 Annual Report laid out a three-phase culture transformation journey (started in 2015) which shares a number of qualitative objectives and achievements to demonstrate progress.[27]

Deutsche Bank refers to culture change as 'a multi-year journey... By aligning our people and business processes we support the long-term, sustainable anchoring of our values across the organization. We recognize that our senior managers in particular play a key role in living the values and acting as role models. However, each and every employee is encouraged to help shape our new culture in order to earn the trust of clients, shareholders and society at large.'[28] Culture remains a critical lever in its future strategy, mapping onto compensation, diversity and inclusion, and risk management in the bank's Annual Report.[29] Culture is discussed more robustly in its own right, noting specific achievements in a Non-Financial Report. This discusses assessment against objectives such as Speak Up, Listen Up, and Grey Areas in Ethical Decision-Making, and narrates achievements against across these objectives, referring to (but not showing any specifics of) dashboards for culture and conduct metrics.

HSBC annual reporting refers to past transgressions, fines paid, and activities past and present to enable a responsible business culture to restore trust. Beyond this, there is limited reference to broader culture and conduct measurement.[30]

J.P. Morgan Chase's 2019 annual report does discuss its global Code of Conduct but does not reference culture directly.[31]

National Australia Bank, one of the principal objects of the Australian Royal Commission's investigative report on banking misconduct (published in final form in February 2019), undertook its own culture self-assessment as a mechanism to determine a culture and conduct improvement programme. The self-assessment, the action plan and its progress were published and referenced in the bank's 2019 annual reporting cycle.

These are anecdotal rather than a fully representative sample research of all reported efforts across the industry. It's notable that banks – who have been first into the 'culture space' as a result of being the first subsector to face SMCR enforcement action – appear to be the earliest providers to get to grips with (or at least discuss) the prospect of assessed culture reporting.

As at Q1/2021, we're not yet optimistic of material progress in the 'uphill battle'. There again, much of the industry still has some serious prep to do on understanding how culture *can* be measured, and even before that, to get its collective head around the linkage between corporate purpose, culture and enacted conduct. With that in mind, we'll now move to introduce a few essentials of culture measurement, concepts of purpose, and a first look at regulator-friendly reporting indicators. (Plenty more detail later in the book, but first, some little steps.)

CONDUCT GREY AREAS

A persistent concern among financial compliance people and lawyers is that what's 'acceptable behaviour' is a moving target. Whether what your firm does is the 'right thing' may possibly depend on the whims of enforcers, on political pressure, on any conspicuous misbehaviour among your subsector peer group, and (invidiously) on social media-fuelled public 'moral panics'.[32] Business practices which were assumed to be acceptable may abruptly fall victim to new case precedent.

Test *causes célèbres* have included the Last Look case (2015);[33] a Mexican case for alleged bond trade 'pumping' (2018);[34] and a case brought by Australia's Competition regulator against six banks for alleged collusion to manipulate prices by 'holding back' issued shares during a share offering (2020).[35] In the UK, banks' concerns about the possibility of conduct infractions arising out of routine business activities led to a research study (Cambridge

University and Cass Business School, London) of 'conduct grey areas'.[36] Sensitivities explored in an initial scoping study[37] included:

- Could 'customer detriment' include:
  - Foreclosing on SMEs in arrears/default?
  - Precautionary de-risking of high-net-worth client lists?
  - Denying travel insurance to chronically ill people?
  - Failing to spot a customer's changed circumstances?
  - Brexit-forced change of business entity?
- Cyber risk arising from simple human error.
- Tax advisory: avoidance or evasion?
- Price transparency.
- Clients' preferential access to research.
- Sector variances in 'acceptable behaviours' (eg between retail and commercial banking).
- Robo-advice: no longer waived as 'execution only'.
- Mission creep among enforcers:
  - criminalizing of previously civil offences;
  - will rules be applied retroactively?

How culture could be measured: BSB shows one way

Since 2015 the UK's Banking Standards Board (BSB) has been addressing this question through an annually published survey of (in the 2020 report) more than 81,000 employees in 29 banks.[38] Reflecting on this 'outcome-based approach to assessing organizational culture',[39] the BSB recognizes that 'understanding a firm's culture matters because it is fundamental to the way in which a strategy agreed in the boardroom actually takes effect'.

Each firm has its own unique, individual culture. This makes any attempt to superimpose industry-standard metrics, benchmarks and reporting dauntingly complex. The real question, then, may be not how to *measure* culture but how to *assess* it as rigorously, consistently and usefully as possible.

In other words, a practicable approach is not so much to measure (an abstract construct of) the culture per se of a firm, but the outcomes generated by that culture within the firm. To measure, report, and benchmark culture in banks, the BSB proposes a nine-element framework with Shared Purpose at its core, and eight associated elements:

- Honesty
- Competence
- Reliability
- Responsiveness
- Respect
- Openness
- Accountability
- Personal/Organizational Resilience

Through an annual questionnaire and benchmarking process, the BSB objectively surmises progress for culture within the banking sector. The FCA notes that the BSB framework does not (yet) assess Leadership Character explicitly. However, across the four years that the survey has run, BSB identified notable waypoints in the rolling culture assessment, including:

2016:

- Many firms have an apparent mismatch between their stated values and the way that some employees see business being done.
- The challenge is to develop a culture of responsibility and accountability rather than of blame. How to create an environment in which mistakes are learned from, ideas encouraged, professionalism prized and a diversity of views valued and fostered, as well as personal resilience and well-being.
- All of which goes to ensure that employees of UK banks and building societies are able to serve their customers, members and clients well.

2017:

- Year-on-year improvement overall.
- Responsibility and accountability is key and, within this, speaking up and challenge. A healthy organizational culture needs employees to feel able and willing to speak out if they see something that is at odds with the firm's aims or values, or that can be improved.

- Actually speaking up is very difficult, however. Human beings are primed to conform – this is, after all, what supports a group culture – and speaking up, by definition, entails going against the tide.

- Many banks and building societies are, and should be, expanding the speak-up programmes, some bringing in behavioural expertise and reframing questions.

2019 (published 2020):

- Little change on previous results. This followed a similar tendency in 2018, meaning that – over the four years in which the assessment has been run to date – the overall picture is one of initially improving scores in 2017 but then no further improvement.

- Following many firms' efforts to understand and manage their organizational cultures, this lack of change is 'disappointing'. Firms may feel they have been 'running hard to stand still' or that 'actions taken… take time to show results; culture change rarely happens quickly or in a straight line.'

Starting to look for the 'new MI': alternative indicators of corporate health

As the BSB's nuanced, qualitative indicator sets suggest, to assess culture we need to look beyond traditional financial performance indicators. As financial people we're of course used to assessing performance by measures such as dividend yield, efficiency, capital cover and profitability. None of these is of much, if any, value for the task of assessing culture. (We could attempt to make an argument connecting the two tasks, but it would be self-serving and convoluted.)

It's easiest to focus again by starting with what the conduct regulator's interest is: not value-at-risk (fair market contract pricing), but behaviour-at-risk (how far people treat each other fairly). Indicators for behaviour are all about the extent to which our firms support people (staff and customers) becoming the best version of themselves. These human factor indicators emerging from our discussions with regulators are likely to include, at the very least:

- psychological safety
- cognitive diversity

- leadership character and competence
- anti-bystanding (aka moral courage)
- social value

On a related point, although almost all firms now use staff surveys as the core of their effort to assess their people's engagement with values and/or purpose and/or culture, and there's a huge industry of staff survey advisers and administrators... there are several serious limitations to this approach. We need to acknowledge these limitations at the outset of the culture assessment task if we are to overcome them and move on.

Less sentiment, more observation

The classic form of staff survey is an assessment of **sentiment**. It asks – albeit in lots of different ways – the essential questions, 'How do you feel?' and 'What do you want?' These questions go to people's own opinion of their own state of mind; an individual, expressed attempt to make sense of one's own motivation and preferences.

But as we've seen with reference to biases in Chapter 4, human beings are notoriously unreliable at making sense of their own preferences and choices – let alone analysing them objectively. Each of us is generally the worst person to judge ourself dispassionately, to attempt to self-assess *why* we think and do as we do. Remember all those animal-brain effects (biases) we looked at (Table 4.2, pages 74–76)? So, a ticked box next to 'engagement?' in a staff survey may indicate genuine engagement – or, equally possibly, that the respondent is trying to second-guess the right answer, to please some imagined (or real) career assessor in the background.

Trying to prevent these so-called *response effects*, of people 'gaming the test' or simply reacting to the knowledge that they're being measured, is one of the big design challenges of behavioural science. That's one reason why creating such testing is not for novices; but it's not a reason to give up on trying. Read on to learn more of how to overcome the problem yourself, but also be prepared occasionally to draft in expert help – as more and more firms are now doing.

The way that behavioural science overcomes the challenge of respondent subjectivity is to be more 'empirical': that is, not so much to ask a person to express an opinion about why they feel or behave as they do, but to make an **observation** of *what they actually do*. The ideal observation is discreet, meaning the subject of the assessment doesn't know they're being assessed. But that, of course, raises a bunch of related ethical concerns about consent and privacy. For example, what if a behaviour assessment takes the form of watching someone remotely, such as through their laptop camera when they're working from home, without their knowledge? In 2020, one bank tried doing exactly that and quickly found itself on the wrong side of UK Data Privacy law (GDPR)[40] – not to mention angry staff.

What behaviour observation does achieve, however, is a much more robust and objective focus on 'How do people really behave here?' It sees and assesses what is visible and demonstrated – how organizational culture is made manifest in *action*; what real people actually do. There's further analytical discussion of the value of observing actual behaviour, rather than assessing sentiment, from one of the world's most highly awarded developers of behavioural analytics, in Chapter 7.

As a working premise throughout the rest of the book, let's now concentrate on finding more robust, empirical evidence of how people behave and what actually happens – and not fool ourselves into expecting alignment with formal rules and controls. As explored in detail in Chapters 6 and 7, a more productive way to approach assessing culture is to see how closely the behavioural norms of the firm ('the place') fit with, or clash against, each person's changing expectations ('the people'). Actual behaviour – as opposed to the version that senior managers fondly imagine is happening – is usually driven more by informal social pressures of 'belonging' than by formal corporate instructions. Towards the end of the book we'll introduce some really impressive analytics – hold that thought.

SECTOR CULTURES AS EXPRESSED IN DIALOGUES WITH THEIR REGULATORS

Following on from his research into failures of self-regulatory arrangements ('GSVRs') in various industries, Professor Christopher Hodges, together with Ruth Steinholtz, in 2017 published the seminal work *Ethical Business Practice and Regulation: A behavioural and values-based approach to compliance and enforcement*.[41] It observes 'what actually happens' in organizations in a range of regulated sectors, including pharma, aviation, public healthcare, and financial services, through the lens of their dialogues with government. Despite being a magisterial tour of the topic over a 30-year view, it offers brisk, punchy but deeply wise conclusions for all regulated activities. As a taster:

- 'A healthy culture both protects and generates value. It is therefore important to have a continuous focus on culture, rather than wait for a crisis.'
- 'Shareholder value is an *outcome*, not an *objective*.' (See Chapter 10, page 227 onwards.)
- 'We must leave the blaming approach behind as it does not enable us to learn and improve. Instead, focus on fixing the problems and decreasing the likelihood that they will recur.'
- 'People are prepared to cheat. They can cheat and still feel good about themselves by rationalizing that bad behaviour.'
- To be 'good' (to have 'legitimacy'), a rule 'must be made fairly, applied fairly, and correspond to individual [practitioners'] internal moral values.'

Moving beyond self-reporting: culture change mandated by top-down rules

From March 2016, the UK FCA's individual accountability rules, known as the Senior Managers & Certification Regime (SMCR, or SMR) started to regulate conduct at board level and for executive leadership. This requires senior leaders with customer-facing roles to face regulatory questioning and to have to certify their own competence, fitness for the role, and propriety of character; ultimately all regulated financial service sector staff under their management must also adhere to its conduct rules. Any senior managers' breaches of conduct rules are reported to the FCA and tracked in the form of regulatory references with six years of history – the intent being to track 'bad apples' as they move from one firm to another.

As Chapter 11 explores, SMR has yet to achieve significant traction, if judged by its track record of enforcement (as at Q2/2021). However, the regime is seen by many directors to have ushered in more positive attitudes in boardroom conversations, strengthening challenges and perhaps calling time on the era of over-mighty, over-confident (and sometimes just plain arrogant) leadership.[42] Although the 2008 financial crisis produced no criminal prosecutions in the UK, SMR provides for fines, prison, and bans on working in the financial services industry. Managers must document 'reasonable steps' taken to remedy any wrongdoing and to institute robust controls.

The FCA had also announced an intended Thematic Review of Culture in banking, but dropped this proposal in favour of, from 2021, culture assessment based on firms' self-reporting. Some British parliamentarians suggested that the abandoning of a potentially Australia-style grand enquiry into culture may have been politically motivated – a 'surrender to big banks'.[43]

Adding reputational risk to the culture supervision view

Although it's not yet enshrined in conduct rules, central banks have started to identify **reputational risk** as a significant element in banks' capital cover (that is, their resilience to GFC-type market shocks). A bank's reputation is a part of its 'idiosyncratic' capital value, say the Basel III Pillar 2 capital adequacy arrangements, in recognition of the growing importance of this and other strategic and legal risks. Under this regime of capital assessment, banks should consider:

> Risk arising from negative perception on the part of customers, counterparties, shareholders and other stakeholders that can adversely affect a bank's ability to maintain normal business practice.[44]

These negative perceptions could result from, for example, failures of routine service and systems (such as IT system outage); perceived failure to properly serve vulnerable customers, as during a pandemic; or the reputational impact of regulatory enforcements (such as fines and suspensions for misconduct).

Capital, reputation and trustworthiness are now explicitly linked within the supervisory framework. Given a historic regulatory tendency to 'mission creep', we may expect this linkage to be extended into supervisory assessments of culture and conduct; after all, as we see throughout this book and especially in Chapter 6, politically a big driver for the conduct agenda is to get financial firms to accept past cultural failings and make efforts to improve their reputation with a disillusioned public.

Two healthy culture essentials (1): psychological safety

How far 'people feel secure at work, in teams they belong to, with colleagues and leaders they trust'[45] is now seen by conduct regulators as fundamental to firms' good engagement with employees, and in turn for sustainably good business performance. As the FCA reminds us,[46] healthy cultures are both purposeful and safe; for a culture to be healthy, leaders at all levels need to foster an environment in which employees feel comfortable to express their opinions and are listened to when they do so. Without the backing of psychological safety and an actively inclusive culture, the value of diversity would be lost. The practical challenge for banks and others has been how to measure these factors in a reliable, let alone meaningful, way.

Some firms have responded by addressing psychological safety explicitly, asking staff (through anonymized surveys) to identify where shortfalls lay. In plain terms: where are there problems with abusive individuals, or teams working in a culture of fear? Typical in many firms has been a well-intended historic culture of polite conservatism. In such firms, hierarchies made challenge difficult, frustrating the possibility of any transformation through 'cognitive diversity' – such as the encouragement of intelligent questions from, say, junior staff and new arrivals. This left cosy senior management assumptions untouched.

Even before Covid-19, the more progressive firms had already started to consider defining 'what good looks like' in terms of everyday good behaviour, making psychological safety a lived reality by encouraging everyone to share opinions, speak freely, and constructively challenge without being blamed. The financial sector is now actively and continuously hunting for reliable indicators[47] that will enable firms to report consistently on their success with these efforts.

Following Covid-19 we may expect desire for psychological safety to attach to many areas of business (and other human) activity. In a time of turmoil we remember the importance of healthy cultures being purposeful as well as safe: how many organizations will be able to say that they have truly supported their employees and customers?

Two healthy culture essentials (2): cognitive diversity

A related, and again already much debated, indicator of a firm's ethical qualities is its approach to talent, and specifically diversity and inclusion. Social protest shockwaves, such as about gender pay disparities and #blacklivesmatter, add urgency to this topic. Yet these questions still feel untried and their answers elusive to many organizations grappling with them as part of a structured 'culture assessment'. For example, how far do your colleagues feel that they can bring their 'whole selves' to work, without fear of being judged or sidelined?

Cognitive diversity has been defined as 'differences in perspective or information processing styles. It is not predicted by factors such as gender, ethnicity, or age'[48]. An aspect of it that's hugely important to firms is how individuals think about and engage with new, uncertain, and complex situations. Lack of it shows most obviously in the tendency of firms to hire 'people (socially) like us' rather than cast the recruiting net wide for all available talents on a meritocratic basis.

As rated by a related measure, 'reflexivity' – that is, how quickly an institution responds to changing circumstances – inevitably, governance institutions throughout history have often fallen short. Their slowness of response always becomes more evident with hindsight, of course[49] – as with many national governments' seeming collective deafness to the lessons of SARS, MERS and Ebola which left them unprepared for the predations of Covid-19.

In the financial sector, lack of diversity of cognitive skills became clear during the 2008 GFC as the assumptions underlying econometric risk models failed: the wholesale collapse of hopeful model predictions about 'self-correcting' pricing[50] contributed significantly to the depth and the severity of the financial crisis that ensued.[51] Come the event of Covid-19, many financial firms encountered a nest of still prevailing problems: groupthink, intellectual arrogance, expert bias, over-confidence, motivated reasoning and cultural cognition; 'bystanding' and insufficient challenge amid a culture of fear or complacency; continued over-reliance on legacy reporting systems and weak controls; and risk assessments that use narrow models, self-reporting audits, or other forms of fragile assumption.

Regulator-friendly MI: what might future good reporting practice look like?

Recognizing that each financial firm has its own culture, the UK regulator is now holding firms' culture to account by a mix of visit-based culture assessments (within the existing conduct assessment framework) and review of firms' own self-assessments. As of the turn of 2021, although firms await guidance as to what specific data a good culture self-assessment report might be populated with, we may expect the focus of future regulator-approved conduct assessments to include measures of speak-up and other challenges to prove good decision-making; diversity and inclusion; and the evidenced rooting out of bullying, discrimination and other patterns of abusive behaviour. These may be expected to co-locate with existing (reiterated in the FCA's 2020/21 Business Plan[52]) conduct assessments of 'four key culture drivers': Purpose, Leadership, Approach to rewarding and managing people, and Governance – and how well these are acting to identify and reduce harms.

All conduct regulators may be expected to develop further tools using behavioural science techniques to question how far customer outcomes are 'acceptable and expected' across a wide range of products, markets and jurisdictions (see the author's *Conduct Risk Management: A behavioural approach*[53]). Philosophically similar to the approach used by the UK's Banking Standards Board, the regulators' new approach includes top-down culture audits, interviews with staff about their experiences, and product fairness analysis.

There are multiple ways in which managers can gather information about their employee attitudes and behaviours. Traditionally, surveys have been a key part of the toolkit. But surveys can mask what employees really think, and employees can say what they anticipate the bank wants to hear. In addition, employees may be reluctant to be candid with their concerns for fear of reprisal.[54]

Designing out 'response effects'

A significant challenge in compiling any form of behavioural indicator is what behavioural scientists call Goodhart's Law, or more simply, *response effects*: that anyone who knows they're being observed is very likely to change their behaviour in response to the fact of being observed. This may take the form of, say, people second-guessing 'the right answer' to a staff survey question. In ordinary life, it's like the way that when you're driving along and a police car appears behind you, you start driving super-cautiously.

Regulators are actively looking for ways to overcome response effects, experimenting with 'unobvious indicators' and various forms of remote observation, including tech-based monitoring of speech and internet activity (see box: Regulators' experiments with new indicators for culture). This is further examined in Chapters 10 (on 'better questions') and 12 (on reg techs).

REGULATORS' EXPERIMENTS WITH NEW INDICATORS FOR CULTURE

In a September 2019 *Insight* paper, 'Measuring Culture – Can It Be Done?', FCA behavioural scientist Alex Chesterfield observed that if culture 'needs to be managed, then it needs to be measured.'[55] Her paper reflected on alternatives for culture measurement including an Unobtrusive Corporate Culture Analysis Tool (UCCAT) – an experimental tool for benchmarking corporate culture. Rather than making assessments via employee interviews and questionnaires, UCCAT analyses publicly available data, such as annual reports, financial records, press releases and databases, that are indicative of a company's cultural 'footprint'. These data points are termed 'unobtrusive indicators of organizational culture' (UICs).[56]

Reflecting on the representativeness of new data-gathering techniques, the paper asked rhetorically whether in future we might expect to see if 'firms themselves, auditors or investment analysts should take on this task of their own volition, or whether legislators and regulators need to take the lead?'

Other new culture indicators that we're aware have been tested in the regulatory 'labs' – not without controversy – include:

- To assess **cognitive diversity** and **reflexivity**: a scalar indicator for active open-minded thinking about evidence (AOT-E)[57]

- To assess **performance attribution bias** (stereotyping of eg job candidates, often [wrongly] labelled as 'unconscious bias'): Implicit Association Test (Harvard IAT test).[58]

Dutch thought leadership

The Dutch central bank (DNB) has continued to follow a uniquely strong and distinctive path, although its underlying aim is the same as any other conduct regulator: restoration of trust in financial services. DNB's focus is ethical culture, sound remuneration policies and sustainable business models of banking institutions. DNB concluded from the 2008 financial crisis that an organization's behaviour and culture had a significant bearing on the level of risk in the banking system and initially careless risk-taking in individual banks. From 2011, DNB started explicitly supervising behaviour and culture, forming an expert team focusing on two key areas:

- What influence do individual actions on the one hand and group dynamics on the other have on financial performance, risk and integrity of the institution, and how does the prevailing culture facilitate desirable behaviour and restrain undesirable behaviour?

- What measures are needed to mitigate the risks related to human behaviour?[59]

As noted in the above discussion of risk governance, DNB observed that boards did not generally have sufficient expertise in behaviour and culture, and the stated intentions of the management were not convincing. Proposed measures did not always go far enough and were not consistently implemented. Executive directors did not sufficiently abide by the values they themselves set for their organization.

FIGURE 5.1   Summary of four DNB approaches to culture assessments

Board effectiveness	Risk culture
• **Asks: How far do Board group dynamics impact prudential and risk performance?** • **Observes directly (on site)**: Board's decision-making, leadership, communication, group dynamics • **Indicators**: Any factors that 'impair effective Board performance, or sound and principled business operations'	• **Asks: Are there behaviour patterns that could compromise risk-taking decisions, risk-aware working, and management of risk?** • **Observes directly (on site)**: Behaviour patterns of all staff • **Indicators**: Any behavioural factors having a 'potentially detrimental impact' on risk management and sound decision-making

Change effectiveness	Root cause analysis
• **Asks: Is firm able to implement organizational and cultural change programmes?** • **Observes directly (on site)**: Firm's capacity to change • **Indicators**: Strengths/weaknesses in translating vision into action; willingness to change; implementation in practice; examples of ability to learn	• **Asks: Are there underlying behavioural and cultural explanations for a firm's persistent problems?** • **Researches remotely (off site)**: Causes for risks at behavioural, group dynamic and mindset level • **Indicators**: Behaviour and culture 'explanations' for issues underlying persistent problems; pressure-points where supervisor may 'intervene' against drivers of unsound and ineffective behaviour patterns

SOURCE Miles-UK Finance; after DN

In 2015 the behavioural expert team at DNB, led by Mirea Raaijmakers (co-author of Chapter 6 of this book), published the landmark *Supervision of Behaviour and Culture: Foundations, practice and future developments*.[60] It's a regulator's guide to identifying behaviour and risk culture, assessing and mitigating risk across areas such as decision-making, leadership, communication, group dynamics and change. This is in effect a manifesto, urging a constructive response from the world's regulators and firms to develop their own culture reporting frameworks. By focusing on these key areas and the behaviours driving them, DNB seeks to drive tangible positive change. Figure 5.1 shows, for example, how the first three of these four DNB tools for culture assessment are based on direct observation rather than 'paper audit'. It is becoming normal for conduct case officers/'culture assessors' to 'walk the floor', holding direct conversations with firms' staff, and to attend board meetings. No firm should assume any more that assessment is to be achieved by remote or paper-based reporting.

Conclusion

Later chapters will explore in detail how firms can pursue the better design and population of conduct and culture reports, with practical case examples from a range of firms and analytics compilers.

Firms' immediate task, as regulators remind us, is to define, then align, purpose, measurement and incentives. During Chapters 6–10 we'll look more closely at how to put that good intention into practice, for the benefit of the business (and as more than simply 'conduct compliance').

Notes

1 FCA DP 18/2 (2018) Transforming culture in financial services, fca.org.uk/publications/discussion-papers/dp18-2-transforming-culture-financial-services (archived at https://perma.cc/SH29-R4JU)

2 FCA DP 20/1 (2020) Transforming culture in financial services: driving purposeful cultures: https://www.fca.org.uk/publications/discussion-papers/dp20-1-transforming-culture-financial-services-driving-purposeful-cultures (archived at https://perma.cc/N4FA-9YBB)

3 FCA DP 20/1 (2020) Transforming culture in financial services: driving purposeful cultures: https://www.fca.org.uk/publications/discussion-papers/dp20-1-transforming-culture-financial-services-driving-purposeful-cultures (archived at https://perma.cc/N4FA-9YBB).

4   FCA (2015) Culture and governance, fca.org.uk/firms/culture-and-governance (archived at https://perma.cc/QE8B-QGM5)

5   Banking Standards Board (2019) Assessment Results 2019, banking standardsboard.org.uk/assessment-results-2019/ (archived at https://perma. cc/32QE-ZWD4)

6   One of the study's authors, Prof. Christopher Hodges, is a contributor to this book.

7   fmsb.com (archived at https://perma.cc/34NA-F83U)

8   LSB (nd) The Standards of Lending Practice, lendingstandardsboard.org.uk/ the-slp/ (archived at https://perma.cc/CSE7-GGNX)

9   University of Oxford (nd) Government-sponsored voluntary regulation, law.ox.ac.uk/research-subject-groups/research-index/impact-index/government-sponsored-voluntary-regulation (archived at https://perma.cc/7BWE-U2TE)

10 Aitken, R (2014) Dutch bankers swearing an oath to God...whatever next?, *Forbes*, forbes.com/sites/rogeraitken/2014/12/23/dutch-bankers-swearing-an-oath-to-god-whatever-next/ (archived at https://perma.cc/NW9L-UWVC)

11 Myer, R (2019) The bankers' oath that can't be enforced and has never rubbed out a member, *The New Daily*, thenewdaily.com.au/finance/finance-news/2019/ 02/14/the-bankers-oath-that-cant-be-enforced/ (archived at https://perma.cc/ 95HZ-MJGU)

12 Australian Royal Commission (2019) Royal commission into misconduct in the banking, superannuation and financial services industry, royalcommission. gov.au/sites/default/files/2019-02/fsrc-volume-1-final-report.pdf (archived at https://perma.cc/U8VZ-JH9J)

13 Group of 30 (2015) Banking conduct and culture: a call for sustained and comprehensive reform; (2018) Banking conduct and culture: a permanent mindset change, group30.org/images/uploads/publications/aaG30_Culture2018. pdf (archived at https://perma.cc/H4F3-YVAN)

14 FCA (2019) 'Progress and challenges': Five conduct questions, fca.org.uk/ publication/market-studies/5-conduct-questions-industry-feedback-2018-19.pdf (archived at https://perma.cc/B7P6-WWHG), page 3

15 European Central Bank (2019) Just a few bad apples? Speech by Andria Enria, https://www.bankingsupervision.europa.eu/press/speeches/date/2019/html/ssm. sp190620~f9149fe258.en.html (archived at https://perma.cc/YQ8B-X42G)

16 Group of 30 (2015) Banking conduct and culture: a call for sustained and comprehensive reform; (2018) Banking conduct and culture: a permanent mindset change, group30.org/images/uploads/publications/aaG30_Culture2018. pdf (archived at https://perma.cc/H4F3-YVAN)

17 Group of 30 (2015) Banking conduct and culture: a call for sustained and comprehensive reform; (2018) Banking conduct and culture: a permanent mindset change, group30.org/images/uploads/publications/aaG30_Culture2018. pdf (archived at https://perma.cc/H4F3-YVAN)

18 European Central Bank (2019) The supervisory review and evaluation process in 2019, www.bankingsupervision.europa.eu/banking/srep/2019/html/aggregate_results_2019.en.html (archived at https://perma.cc/H7PB-GQU6)

19 Engler, H (2018) Bank culture forum: Behavioral science gains role as banks address culture, conduct, *Reuters*, reuters.com/article/bc-finreg-bank-culture-forum-behavioral/bank-culture-forum-behavioral-science-gains-role-as-banks-address-culture-conduct-idUSKBN1HU1PW (archived at https://perma.cc/J9JB-3JNF)

20 FSCP (2016) Consumer panel position paper – banking culture, fs-cp.org.uk/sites/default/files/bank_culture_position_paper_final.pdf (archived at https://perma.cc/7FEL-UTMV)

21 The Risk Coalition (nd) Raising the bar, https://riskcoalition.org.uk/the-guidance (archived at https://perma.cc/P4A7-UDWK)

22 Central Bank of Ireland (2018) Behaviour and culture of the Irish retail banks, centralbank.ie/docs/default-source/publications/corporate-reports/behaviour-and-culture-of-the-irish-retail-banks.pdf?sfvrsn=2 (archived at https://perma.cc/AL2R-MCC8)

23 RTE (2019) The long and winding road to changing Irish banking culture, rte.ie/brainstorm/2019/1108/1089488-the-long-and-winding-road-to-changing-irish-banking-culture/ (archived at https://perma.cc/WGQ3-WT72)

24 CBI Annual Report 2019, lexology.com/library/detail.aspx?g=28f42da2-2976-47b2-8da7-e4a372aebc21 (archived at https://perma.cc/8PHX-QY9P)

25 Sheedy, E and Griffin, B (2014) Empirical analysis of risk culture in financial institutions: interim report, pp 2–3, researchgate.net/publication/314473817 (archived at https://perma.cc/C24U-3HGV)

26 FCA: 'Dear CEO' letters regarding pandemic response, eg fca.org.uk/publication/correspondence/dear-ceo-ensuring-fair-treatment-corporate-customers-preparing-raise-equity-finance.pdf (archived at https://perma.cc/8MXJ-WS4Q); fca.org.uk/publication/correspondence/dear-ceo-insuring-sme-business-interruption-coronavirus.pdf (archived at https://perma.cc/2DDT-VKXY)

27 Santander 2019 Annual Report, santander.com/content/dam/santander-com/en/documentos/informe-anual/2019/ia-2019-annual-report-en.pdf (archived at https://perma.cc/WQ2L-MYKF)

28 Deutsche Bank (2020) Cultural change at Deutsche Bank: questions & answers, db.com/cr/en/concrete-Cultural-change-Questions-and-Answers.htm (archived at https://perma.cc/729V-FHES)

29 Deutsche Bank Annual Report 2019, db.com/ir/en/download/Deutsche_Bank_Annual_Report_2019.pdf (archived at https://perma.cc/KZG7-VBTG)

30 HSBC Annual Report 2019, hsbc.com/investors/results-and-announcements/annual-report (archived at https://perma.cc/TV72-3EJ8)

31 J.P. Morgan Chase Annual Report 2019, jpmorganchase.com/corporate/investor-relations/investor-relations.htm (archived at https://perma.cc/A2EE-5NCH)

32 'A public overreaction to forms of deviance or wrongdoing believed to be threats to the moral order' (Oxford): see the work of Marshall McLuhan and the research career of Stanley Cohen, eg *Folk Devils and Moral Panics* (1972)

33 Schmerken, I (2016) A hard look at last look in foreign exchange, *Flextrade*, flextrade.com/a-hard-look-at-last-look-in-foreign-exchange/ (archived at https://perma.cc/M6D8-CKUK)

34 Lasky, A (2020) Case Spotlight: Mexican government bonds antitrust case reaches preliminary $20.7m settlement, *FRT Bulletin*, https://frtservices.com/case-spotlight-mexican-government-bonds-antitrust-case-reaches-preliminary-20-7m-settlement/ (archived at https://perma.cc/SPF2-8UL9)

35 Australian Financial Review (2020) ACCC slams banks' cartel defence, afr.com/companies/financial-services/accc-slams-investment-bank-cartel-defence-a-furphy-20200722-p55eey (archived at https://perma.cc/5PG2-PGAB)

36 McCormick, R, Stears, C and Miles, R (2018) Conduct risk: scoping the grey areas (privately sponsored research through Cambridge Judge Business School/Cass Business School)

37 McCormick, R, Stears, C and Miles, R (2018) Conduct risk: scoping the grey areas (privately sponsored research through Cambridge Judge Business School/Cass Business School.)

38 BSB Assessment Results 2019, bankingstandardsboard.org.uk/bsb-assessment-results-2019/ (archived at https://perma.cc/EJU7-HJLL)

39 The UK Banking Standards Board (nd) An outcome-based approach to assessing organisational culture, https://bankingstandardsboard.org.uk/the-uk-banking-standards-board-an-outcome-based-approach-to-assessing-organisational-culture/ (archived at https://perma.cc/G7GW-GKDC)

40 Barclays faces employee spying probe, InfoSecurity briefing, bankinfosecurity.com/barclays-faces-employee-spying-probe-a-14796 (archived at https://perma.cc/VK4H-NFJG)

41 Hodges, C and Steinholtz, R (2017) *Ethical Business Practice and Regulation*, Bloomsbury, bloomsburyprofessional.com/uk/ethical-business-practice-and-regulation-9781509916382 (archived at https://perma.cc/FA48-TEVM)

42 Miles, R (2020) Research among financial sector Boards, 2018–20, for Board Performance & Effectiveness (BP&E Global Ltd): Debrief, bpandeglobal.com/Uploaded/1/Documents/Articles/BPE-Key-differences-in-Board-Effectiveness-across-financial-services-sectors.pdf (archived at https://perma.cc/AMC8-6VRT)

43 Edwards, A (2016) It's no House of Cards: the FCA's decision to drop its banking culture thematic review, aoinvestigationsinsight.com/xxxx/ (archived at https://perma.cc/29PF-ZESD)

44 Basel Committee on Banking Supervision (2019) bis.org/bcbs/publ/d465.pdf (archived at https://perma.cc/W97X-KGKJ)

45 Amy Edmondson (2019) *The Fearless Organization*, Wiley

46 FCA DP 20/1 (2020) Transforming culture in financial services: driving purposeful cultures: https://www.fca.org.uk/publications/discussion-papers/dp20-1-transforming-culture-financial-services-driving-purposeful-cultures (archived at https://perma.cc/N4FA-9YBB)

47 UK Finance Conduct and Culture Focus roundtables: Measuring Your Conduct, https://www.ukfinance.org.uk/events-training/measuring-conduct-and-culture-new-regulatory-reporting (archived at https://perma.cc/7CRN-Q8QY)

48 Reynolds, A and Lewis, D (2013) Teams solve problems faster when they're more cognitively diverse, *Harvard Business Review,* March, hbr.org/2017/03/teams-solve-problems-faster-when-theyre-more-cognitively-diverse (archived at https://perma.cc/GQ4X-83K5)

49 Syed, M (2019) *Rebel Ideas, Chapter 1: Collective Blindness*, John Murray

50 Kay, J and King, M (2020) *Radical Uncertainty: Decision-making beyond the numbers*, W W Norton

51 Andrew Haldane, Bank of England speech to BIS (October 2017) Rethinking Financial Stability

52 Stevenson, C et al (2020) FCA Business Plan 2020/2021, womblebonddickinson.com/uk/insights/articles-and-briefings/fca-business-plan-20202021 (archived at https://perma.cc/TNN5-APPE)

53 Miles, R (2017) *Conduct Risk Management: Using a behavioural approach to protect your board and financial services business*, Kogan Page, London

54 Engler, H (2018) Bank culture forum: Behavioral science gains role as banks address culture, conduct, *Reuters*, reuters.com/article/bc-finreg-bank-culture-forum-behavioral/bank-culture-forum-behavioral-science-gains-role-as-banks-address-culture-conduct-idUSKBN1HU1PW (archived at https://perma.cc/J9JB-3JNF)

55 Chesterfield, A et al (2019) Measuring culture – can it be done? *Insight*, fca.org.uk/insight/measuring-culture-can-it-be-done (archived at https://perma.cc/8RS3-LHK8)

56 Chesterfield, A et al (2019) Measuring culture – can it be done? *Insight*, fca.org.uk/insight/measuring-culture-can-it-be-done (archived at https://perma.cc/8RS3-LHK8), and www.akofoundation.org/wp-content/uploads/2017/11/2_0_ako-capital-corporate-culture-project-background-and-methodology.pdf (archived at https://perma.cc/MW6S-JS6U)

57 Example research by Pennycook et al (2020), published in *Judgment and Decision Making*, 15 (4), July pp. 476–98, http://journal.sjdm.org/20/200414/jdm200414.pdf (archived at https://perma.cc/82RB-LQVX)

58 Methodology explained at Harvard Project Implicit, implicit.harvard.edu/implicit/takeatest.html (archived at https://perma.cc/QFD5-P6SS)

59 FRC (nd) De Nederlandsche Bank – supervising culture directly, frc.org.uk/
directors/the-culture-project/case-study-de-nederlandsche-bank-%E2%80%93-
supervising-cu (archived at https://perma.cc/D3NR-WDPM)

60 DNB (2015) *Supervision of Behaviour and Culture: Foundations, practice and
future developments*, https://www.dnb.nl/media/1gmkp1vk/supervision-of-
behaviour-and-culture_tcm46-380398-1.pdf (archived at https://perma.cc/
CS6R-89VV)

06

A 'behaviour-at-risk' agenda emerges

Questioning purpose, lost trust and cultural coercion

STEPHEN J SCOTT, ROGER MILES AND MIREA RAAIJMAKERS

Introduction

We humans at first *survived* as a species largely thanks to our ability to cooperate with trusted others. We later *thrived* as a species once we learned to collaborate with strangers, at scale, as a presumed behavioural norm. Humanity amplified and maintained such successes by creating institutions that serve as a sort of 'trust infrastructure'. In the 21st century, arguably, our single greatest challenge is the sharp drop in public trust in many of those very institutions. An erosion of their reliability undoes the very basis for shared peace and prosperity (Figures 6.1 and 6.2).

The collapse in trust follows a popular perception that risk governance has failed in several sectors, notably finance and public health. In this chapter, we will suggest how everyone – citizens, institutions and regulators – might get along better, whilst promoting public goods. Along the way, we will challenge some convenient but mistaken assumptions of modern management science and propose better approaches, including new ways to manage nonfinancial risks around firm culture and the conduct that it encourages.

We'll also look to understand causes and consequences of human behaviour, reaching into a range of research disciplines and viewing the challenge through three 'lenses': the Present (as found); an Alternative Present (with

FIGURE 6.1   Perception factors driving trust in an institution

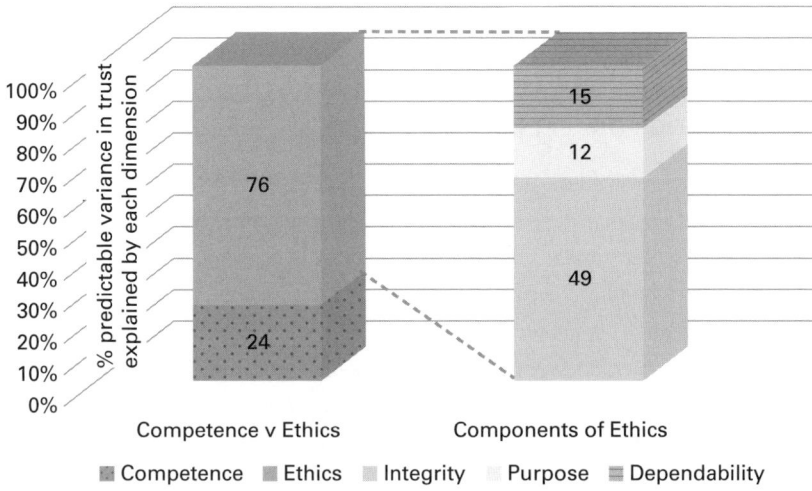

DATA   Edelman Trust Barometer 2020[1]

FIGURE 6.2   No institution seen as both competent and ethical

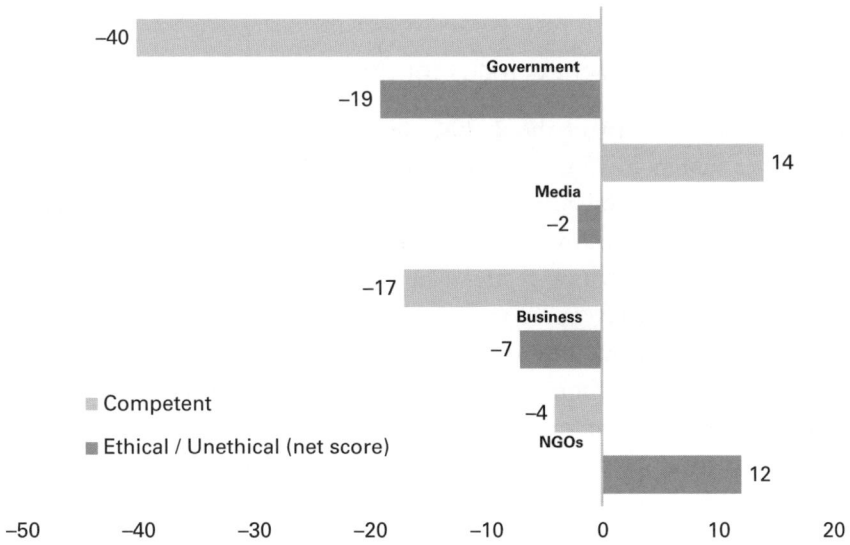

Data   Edelman Trust Barometer, 2020

greater emphasis on 'social licence'); and a better Future (where awareness of risk and of cultural values are transformed, in ways we'll shortly see).

THEMES AND CONCEPTS IN THIS CHAPTER

behaviour at risk – 'Conduct costs' – central bank supervision of behaviour and culture – coercive competition – cognitive biases and heuristics – corporate purpose – the Dunbar Number – expert bias – failure of collective imagination – formal organization vs informal groups – group identity – group norms – human co-operation as an evolved trait – human-factor risks – identity priming – in-group and out-group – institutional trustworthiness – metacognition – 'normal people' vs classical economists – public goods – 'reg tech' and computational social science – 'relentlessly empirical' observation – rational maximizing vs social influences – reputational capital – social 'licence to operate' – social proof (of 'normal' behaviour) – social signalling – societal expectations – sub-cultures – 'tone from the top' – trust as a 'currency' – 'trust infrastructure' – trust dynamics – trust modelling – vox populi risk – 'What Actually Happens'

A new focus for governance

Until almost the turn of the 2020s, corporate governance practices gave priority to shareholder interests over those of stakeholders. Businesses could dimly see, yet often failed really to grasp, that they have social as well as financial functions and related expectations. In our proposed Alternative Present we'll look at how recent challenges are overturning old assumptions: people routinely question corporate purpose (what each firm is *for*) and identity (what the firm actually *is* – for example a collection of 'trust relations' among collaborative peers). We'll see how important an element Trust is, both at market (macro) level and the personal (micro) level. We will trace Trust from its origins among our tribal beginnings as a cooperative species, to the point where we have come to thrive globally by building networks to share intelligence among remote but trusted peers. Anyone tasked with managing behavioural risk in an organization should give some thought to how easily social cooperation can mutate into a 'coercive competition' that challenges what they seek to achieve; this chapter concludes by suggesting how best to manage this.

All of this needs us to take a more multi-disciplinary view and to bring the same rigour to non-financial risk management as has been regularly applied to assessing and mitigating financial risks. This is especially important in efforts to diagnose and mediate the 'human-factor' risks of culture and conduct that are of such contemporary interest to our new cadre of regulators assessing human behaviour. Until financial firms properly appreciate this human risk dimension, they will continue to be sucked into the crisis of public trust which is itself rooted in a wider failure (on the part of business and government leaders) to recognize that behaviour is shaped by a human-animal need for identity, rooted in social groups.

We rely on interaction with other people for 'social proof' that our behaviour is 'normal' – that is, in keeping with group norms. These norms shape our individual and collective identities, setting and re-setting what we see as boundaries of acceptable and expected behaviour. Employees in a firm experience the same standard-setting of norms for the workplace. Conduct (and misconduct) follow partly from *formal* systems, such as incentive schemes and 'tone from the top', but far more strongly from *informal* influences gathered by observing 'what actually happens' among close colleagues. These formal and informal normative forces may work together to shape certain behaviours. More often, however, we may see them pulling employees in opposed directions. We define this circumstance as a 'coercive competition'.

New tools in the domain of 'computational social science' have made it possible to examine this tension, and to reveal patterns of formal and informal coercion that create behavioural predilections. Our Future view suggests that, over time, firms will devise new interventions to better manage culture and conduct related risks, in part through the adoption of these tools, and to work collectively to restore popular trustworthiness in financial (and other) institutions.

Present era (as found): questioning trust and purpose

We humans like to believe that there's something about our species that's different, special, better, other. True, but only up to a point. We have some distinctive capacities, for sure. One of the greatest is our love of narrative – especially of an inner kind: the stories we tell ourselves about ourselves, about one another, about our world, and about our place within it, all to make sense of what it means to be alive – *and* live amongst a group of confederates. We are our own protagonist as these inner stories question why we do what we do.

Humankind's wonderful capacity for self-questioning ('metacognition') sets us apart from other animals but also inflicts on us a form of existential curse. In the 21st century, we seem to know everything and yet nothing: the answer to every conceivable question is just a Google search away, yet we face an epidemic of alienation, loneliness and distrust that's shredding our social fabric. It can feel as if we're living in a society where 'the network of relationships and connection and trust that everything else relies upon – is failing'.[2]

Business, like all collaborative undertakings, is an inherently social endeavour: at the simplest, someone has to sell and someone else to buy. It makes no sense, then, to think about business governance except in a social context: businesses fashioning productive human connections (or failing to). In the 2020s, business leaders seemingly awoke to this idea, that, as social creatures, our enterprises thrive or fail within 'shared communities'.[3] In its 2018 manifesto on governance and *the purpose of a corporation*,[4] the US Business Roundtable (CEOs at 200 prominent firms) reversed its historic stance that 'There is one and only one social responsibility of business – to use its resources and engage in activities designed to increase its profits'.[5] Overturning decades of shareholder primacy, this new purpose supports a multi-stakeholder model in which firms commit to 'creating value for customers, investing in employees, fostering diversity and inclusion, dealing fairly with suppliers, supporting communities and protecting the environment'[6] – all listed ahead of shareholders.

Also in 2018, investment management giant BlackRock's founder Larry Fink told global brands' boards that 'to prosper over time, every company must not only deliver financial performance, but also show how it makes a positive contribution to society'.[7] Those who don't, he warned, 'will ultimately lose the license to operate from key stakeholders'.[8] He later noted that we're alive during a historically huge wealth transfer: in US terms, $24 trillion is moving from baby boomers to millennials. The new generation has wholly different views on what makes an acceptable investee business. Environmental, social, and governance issues (ESG) will only become more 'material to corporate valuations'.[9] In this context, corporate purpose is to unify management, employees and communities, to drive ethical behaviour and to create:

> ...an essential check on actions that go against the best interests of stakeholders. Purpose guides culture, provides a framework for consistent decision-making, and, ultimately, helps sustain long-term financial returns for the shareholders of your company.[10]

Purpose here serves to root all effective corporate governance. Only behaviour consistent with a firm's purpose will reliably advance the interests of its shareholders and wider stakeholders.

Since the Great Depression of the 1930s, critics of free-market capitalism had argued that the old economics of quarterly dividends sidelined any need to support human well-being. This was a tale of binary opposites: stakeholder versus shareholder primacy. Come the 1990s, the social purpose debate began to be more nuanced,[11] with think-tanks such as Tomorrow's Company and New Economics[12] highlighting 'social licence to operate'. Although the early 2000s' Labour (UK) and Democratic (US) surges made people more aware of the new economics, it was mainly the coming of the global financial crisis (GFC) in 2007–8 that brought forward urgent public questions about the balance of social goods. Ironically it has taken the public health crisis of the 2020 pandemic, rather than financial market abuse, to spur the next stage in governance reform.

Alternative present: reframing the debate

The new corporate governance, then, asks not only 'For whom is the firm?' (eg the legal primacy of shareholders versus stakeholders) but also 'For what is the firm?' (balance of economic and social purpose).[13] Together, these hark back to an even more basic question: 'What is the firm?'

In the 1930s, Coase had suggested that businesses had settled into a mechanistic and bureaucratic view of the firm as a set of contractual obligations that work to minimize 'transaction costs'.[14] This view prevailed for 80 years, until a new cadre of self-styled 'behavioural economists' brought insights from psychology to question the assumptions made by classical economists. One of these new economists, Colin Camerer, in 2003 bluntly suggested that the old guard should spend more time talking to 'normal people' and less time playing with econometric models.[15] These same classical economists perhaps weren't listening, as during the 2008 GFC they proceeded to lose the confidence of those 'normal people' (in this case, the voting public), having stuck with reductive theories and model assumptions that 'prized elegance over real-world applicability'. As so often in the history of science, expert bias had struck: established practitioner-members of an in-group had rejected potentially useful learnings from other disciplines such as behavioural science[16] until it was too late – leaving classical economists distrusted.[17]

Trust was at first too abstract a factor to model, at least using classical econometrics. This changed as behavioural science began to grow during the late 20th century. In 1972, Kenneth Arrow alerted economists to the significance of trust for business-as-usual, as almost all transactions entail 'an element of trust', especially 'over a period of time... much of the economic backwardness in the world can be explained by the lack of mutual confidence'.[18]

In the 21st century, trust is seen increasingly as a proxy form of 'currency' that smooths exchange, supports cooperation, even acts as a social glue that maintains public order and expedites all sorts of group enterprises. Think of the firm less as a 'nexus of contracts' between different parties, more 'the opposite: a nexus of relations... built on trust'.[19] Trust is the single greatest determinant of business value, argues Oxford University-based reputation analyst Rachel Botsman, who notes how, in the age of TrustPilot, reputation is 'a currency more powerful than our credit history'.[20] Trust is a core component of 'reputation risk' that's reflected in share price, capital adequacy and competitive advantage. Eighty-five per cent of the US S&P 500 stock worth lies in intangible value ('reputation premium'); that's US$21 trillion in value added simply from consumers' trust in each S&P 500 company's brand.[21]

If trust adds such huge value to them, it's all the more worrying how far businesses worldwide are in a crisis of declining public trust. Criticism grew sharply louder during the 2008 GFC and again in the 2020s as citizens question the credibility of firms' responses to the pandemic, to civil rights protests and to populist leaders' jibes about the 'swamp' of hidden political influence. We have seen related bouts of 'vox populi risk'[22] as voters rally to support isolationist and separatist policies. This is alarming because trust is 'the lifeblood of any economy';[23] we may be suffering collective 'trust deficit disorder', says the United Nations, backing an OECD initiative to recover Trust in Business.[24]

This all might look like a modern, post-industrial problem, but its roots lie deeper. We should take a wider view of social history, as Yuval Noah Harari does:[25]

> We assume that a large brain, the use of tools, superior learning abilities and complex social structures are huge advantages. But humans enjoyed all of these advantages for a full two million years during which they remained weak and marginal creatures.[26]

What changed was our tribal and social culture after the invention of agriculture, when we organized into 'mass cooperation networks';[27] farming, and later manufacturing, needed us to develop ways of institutionalizing relations of trust by proxy, first with family and tribe, later with strangers.

Evolutionary anthropologist Robin Dunbar identified the brain physics behind our tribal, social behaviour. Our human 'social brain' is wired to let us maintain active relationships with up to 150 people (the 'Dunbar Number').[28] These social relationships are arranged in a kind of hierarchy, with the most emotionally intense being the strongest, moving towards weaker links as we go from the 'centre' to the 'edge' of our social group. The five people closest to us 'between them... account for around 40% of all our social effort and our emotional capital. The outermost [150] layer accounts for less than 20% of our social effort'.[29]

This human trait of investing emotional energy in a small, core set of trusted peers helped us to evolve: 'It takes a tribe to raise a human... evolution favoured those capable of forming strong social ties'.[30] By seeking reliable information about who could be trusted, small tribal human groups were able to grow into larger interdependent social groups: we 'could develop tighter and more sophisticated types of cooperation'.[31] And so we survived and thrived as a species (Figure 6.3).

FIGURE 6.3   Dunbar dynamics

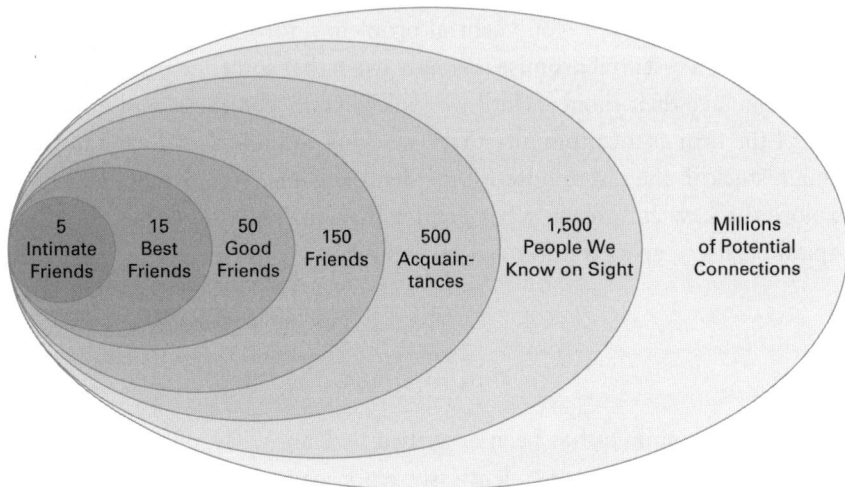

SOURCE Starling

What we're all looking for, now

Mainly, we thrived because we had worked out ways to use proxies for trust: how to trust someone at one remove from our direct acquaintance. In this way we could massively widen our human circles of trust. I trust a guy who trusts a guy who trusts a guy; my enemy's enemy is my friend. Trust is not only bilateral: two people's trust for one another also usually engages with a web of trust between each of them and others they know.[32]

Strangers can quickly develop trust with a virtual or physical check on cultural signals and behavioural norms around 'belonging' to an institution. In a potential life partner, say, we can quickly check out a family's belief system, a home town, a place of education, and any choices of cultural expression (what music, movies, food, social life, social media, and so on, they like).

The same goes for choice of workplace. It's almost as if we had set up employer firms to serve a function of 'social signalling': they are one form of conduit for trust, enabling humans to cooperate productively and flexibly with vast numbers of strangers.

All of which is why humankind rules the world, suggests Harari. We are at our cleverest when we exploit collective (not personal) intelligence, in social groups. Dunbar agrees: 'Shared knowledge itself is a good marker of community membership.' Of course, we pay a price for this as it exerts a bias influence on how we perceive the world around us. Since our individual knowledge is tied to that of others, the community shapes our attitudes and understanding of risk – with sometimes unwanted or even tragic consequences.

This is a core quality – and central problem – for financial businesses. A financial firm's essential promise is simply trust: that someone trusts someone else to manage their money. Until we look beyond 'contracts' and grasp the idea of the firm as a community that's working to build social capital, we'll remain stuck in the old mindset of dividend streams. To move on, let's now explore the new culture of 'we is greater than me', as traditional, financial capital begins to give ground to social capital.

Future view

Behavioural economics has been described by Dan Ariely, one of its brightest stars, as the science of 'relentlessly empirical' observation – or What Actually Happens, as we prefer to call it – though it's not only modern (behavioural) science that looks for such proof. Mid-20th-century economist Milton Friedman urged colleagues to judge economic models by their ability to predict behaviour correctly: the most important test of a model is 'comparison of its predictions with experience'.[33] By this measure, classical economics crashed and burned spectacularly in 2008. After the GFC, Queen Elizabeth II famously asked at the London School of Economics, 'Why did nobody notice it?' The economists later responded somewhat sheepishly that they'd suffered 'a failure of the collective imagination of many bright people... to understand the risks to the system as a whole'.[34] Classical economic models cut us off from nuances of human behaviour. We hadn't joined the dots between balance-sheet maths (econometrics) and what real people do (social psychology). We needed to explore this junction.

For a start: any human organization is a complex system, bringing us together in a network of interactions with others. These interactions – and our expectations of how future interactions will go – influence how we behave. Our behaviour in turn influences how others respond to us, and so on, in a ripple effect. Each person has their own response to external disruptions and pressures, but also responds to other people's responses. There's a ceaseless series of interactions, layering up either to reinforce old patterns of outcome or prompt new ones, perhaps altering how a whole system works. Though we may be (just about) able to perceive directly this network of interactions, it's hard to convert all this complexity into any kind of workable action plan to try to bring about purposeful change. Instead, we tend to 'tolerate complexity by failing to recognize it'.[35] Until the coming of culture assessments in the 2010s and 2020s, most management plans preferred to skate over the complexities of human behaviour. Unsurprisingly, as a result, many businesses couldn't make any meaningful change in culture.

To make better sense of this, we can pull together insights from social and natural sciences.

In- and out-groups

Social science teaches us that we have a powerful human drive to belong[36]. We've evolved such a strong protective need for this that it can be seen from infants onwards. Any prospect of being socially excluded triggers a deeply fearful response; being ostracized can bring physical pain, depression and lasting feelings of helplessness and hopelessness.[37] Even a hint of possible social exclusion can demolish self-esteem.[38]

Natural science, meanwhile, teaches us that fear and anxiety live in the amygdala part of the brain, which is also the seat of aggression; it's super-sensitive to any socially unsettling situation. The same brain circuit that gives a disgust response (as when, say, seeing a cockroach) also engages when we experience *someone* as disgusting. In pre-civilization tribes, this disgust protected us against potentially hostile neighbouring groups, our brains unconsciously sorting other humans into 'us' and 'them'. Of course, it's only a short – but problematic – step from this to a bigger modern social consequence: 'in-groups' and 'out-groups'. In behavioural research, time and again it is found that 'us versus them' responses are triggered, even in young children who've been given a choice of two different coloured shirts, as an arbitrary marker: even with arbitrarily assigned groups, 'in-group affection and out-group hatred seem entangled'.[39] To avoid the disgust associated with being ostracized, we cooperate with our peers to 'fit in'. We observe and adopt their established norms of behaviour ('normative compliance'), such conformity allowing for us to remain welcome in our trusted peer group. More than anything, it seems, 'we crave reward (engagement) and fear punishment (exclusion) from other members of our group'.[40]

So it is that natural science and social science agree: we are social beings to our core.

As such, much of our personal identity stems from our social interactions, and any threat to cut off our social connections may feel like a threat to our sense of self. It's clear from their start that group norms established a behavioural ideal to support group formation and maintenance. Loss of group membership or access creates 'a loss of utility', in the language of classical economics. This can be problematic as, far from being stable, our personal sense of identity can be awfully prone to change according to the situation we're in.

There is a stack of experimental proof of this. As one example, we tend to order more food in a restaurant if our waiter is obese; the waiter's physical appearance signals to us a norm for extra consumption.[41] And another, also food-related: when we order the same dish as one another in a restaurant, we're later more inclined to trust one another.[42] At any given moment, our individual behaviour tends to depend strongly on how we see ourselves and what others do, in the social context of who we're with at the time. To have any hope of understanding aggregate culture in a corporate setting, we need to get to grips with this core behavioural factor.

You may have already realized that there's a dark side to this. A stack of bias drivers (repetition, recency, proximity, self-interest, misperceived causation, constrained representation of self) push us towards the expedient conclusion that 'What's common is what's right'; the so-called 'common is moral' heuristic. Our actions and self-judged 'right or wrong' are much less about our conscious moral views than we may have hoped. Rather, the behaviour we accept as 'right' is what we see happening among peers – and the more often it is seen, the more right it must be (there's that repetition effect again). As we string along to get along, experiences repeated over time ('instrumental conditioning') breed *conditional dishonesty*. People will start to act unethically – even contrarily to their own sincerely held moral views – as long as the action serves to maintain the status quo, meaning in-group status and related sense of identity. Multiply this up and it creates systemic effects at sector level (see box below).

ARE BANKERS PRIMED TO CHEAT?

In a major, if depressing, study of 'identity priming',[43] researchers recruited a range of bank employees then asked them to toss a coin 10 times and report the outcomes, winning either $20 or nothing for each task depending on whether they reported 'heads' or 'tails'. The researchers deliberately designed in self-reporting, so that participants knew they were unobserved, as well as giving participants an open opportunity both to cheat and to claim the 'alibi' that they'd simply had a lucky winning streak. (Earlier studies had shown that people usually have an 'honesty norm' – needing to maintain a positive self-image of being a good person – so that they won't take advantage of such a loophole.) Here, however, researchers added an extra twist: before tossing the coin, participants had to fill out one of two short surveys, either about their work at the bank, or their home life. This activity 'primed' them either to be conscious of their professional identity as bankers, or their family life.

The 'identity priming' survey triggered an amazing skew in the reported outcomes of the coin-toss test. The 'banker' group cheated, reporting a 58.2 per cent success rate; the 'home life' group reported only 51.6 per cent (allowing for error, statistically in line with the true rate of 50%). Those self-identifying as bankers on some level seemed to feel that this identity 'allowed' them to cheat. As the researchers concluded, this suggests that the sector's 'prevailing culture... favours dishonest behaviour'.

Group behaviour, then, has a dark side. Misbehaviour can be contagious and misconduct that's socially reinforced tends to be sticky. As with rites of passage, from frat-house 'hazing' to criminal gang 'induction tests', there is a play on the *endowment bias* of passing a moral 'point of no return': the very factors that helped you resist misconduct before starting to do it – high among them, fear of social rejection – perversely become reasons for sticking with the misconduct after you've started it. We reshape our behaviour to gain admittance to the group. The group senses this and may impose, through peer pressure, a trigger to our animal brain, which is desperate to belong to a tribe. Soon enough, we internalize our changed behaviour and will even start to defend norms that, as an individual, we'd never have supported. Most workers identify far more with their immediate workgroup than with the firm as a whole. They interact not so much with people they consciously choose to relate to, but rather with those who most strongly represent a local 'in-group' identity – for better or worse.

If we're to make any decent attempt to change behaviour, we must 'first deal with [employees'] existing web of relationships, rather than treat people as isolated individuals'.[44] The persistence of misconduct scandals suggests that management science hasn't quite recognized this yet; it seems that most of the people responsible for risk management still have a serious gap in their own perception of human risk.

Whatever next? Preparing to govern human-factor risk

Though many factors account for collapsing public trust in institutions, we'd suggest – challengingly – that two of the biggest are our industry's own failure to improve dynamic observation and governance of 'behaviour-at-risk' (aka 'What Actually Happens' evolving rapidly in real time), and failure to explain itself more plainly to the public.

Although risk governance leaders may not think of their work as politically and societally important, it is. Where risk controls fail to act fairly, the implications are huge: 'When the fairness of… rules grows questionable and the benefits of the system are distributed too unequally, the consensus for free market meritocracy can collapse'.[45] Sceptical citizens see public corruption and corporate misconduct as one and the same disease, of 'elites' who, when charged with running institutions, repeatedly seem to place their own interests before those of the people they are meant to serve. Social trust in infrastructure fades; faith in the system is lost.

If we only debate legal governance mechanisms, this leaves the public sceptical that the sector is not addressing any real concern over social purpose and actual behaviour, merely solving problems in a mechanistic way. A firm is far more than just a collection of managers, shareholders and some indistinct mass of connected stakeholders. More than ever in a knowledge economy, it is made up of people. Risk governance leaders will be seen to be failing in their duty unless they seek to understand the human side of the firm, moving beyond a past focus on contracts towards managing the 'nexus of relations' that enlivens a firm's purpose, as employees collaborate in support of that purpose.

As we've seen, employees come together in clusters of highly trusted peers. These peer trust networks ('informal groups') often have little to do with the formal intended ordering of the firm as set out in reporting-line charts or public reports (the 'formal organization'). The purpose of various informal subgroups, with their own subcultures, within the firm may well be inconsistent with the stated mission, purpose and values of the business.

Orthodox economics – the pursuit of 'rational maximizing of utility' – failed to notice that in-group identity can exert far more influence on behaviour than financial reward alone. Past industry templates for risk governance failed to curb cultures of misconduct; trust in the sector continued to erode. Risk governance will only improve once we get better at factoring in the social nature of the human animal and when we add – separately but in parallel with risk governance – an explicit, scientifically informed focus on risk behaviour and the social mechanisms that drive that behaviour. With this in mind, let's home in on a core problem: how coercive behaviour corrodes conduct in work groups.

Taking on coercive competition

We might all agree that a big part of what drives economic success in a business is its 'human material'.[46] We'd also then agree that helping this human asset to be the best it can be, would be one of the best ways to improve business performance. What often frustrates attempts at this across a whole firm is the way that sub-cultures in one group conflict with those of other groups. Whichever way you define 'group', there may be tensions: among senior managers, the C-suite, middle managers and business heads, between salespeople and audit people, functional departments, wider stakeholders investing in, employed by or supplying the business. Each of these sectional

FIGURE 6.4   Coercive competition 1: framework

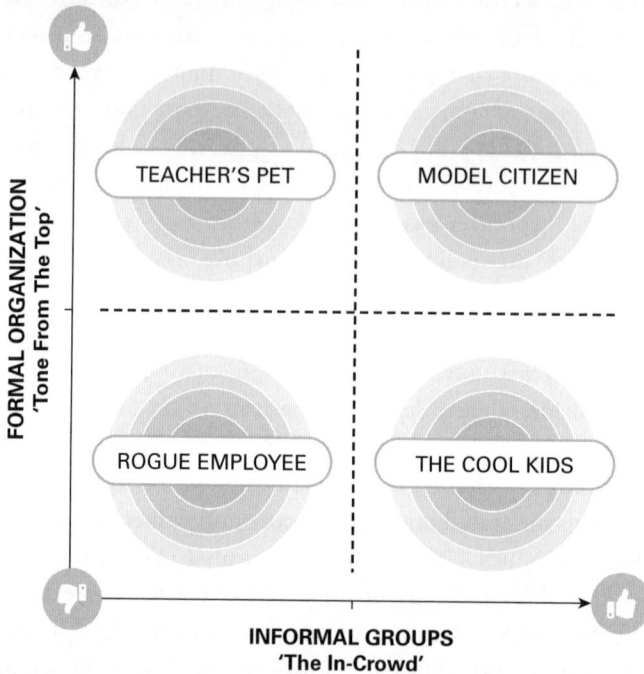

interests will have its own norms of behaviour but the force that these norms exert dissipates the further we move away from the centre of a given individual's most trusted (informal) peer network. Each individual will be subjected to 'coercive competition' between various informal groups' different norms. This may be best understood through a simple graphic (Figure 6.4) predicting how an employee will tend to behave when torn between the social or group norms of two or more communities close to them.

The Y axis shows normative pressures from the formal organization (official workplace rules and structures). The X axis shows pressures to conform to informal (and possibly 'misbehaving') norms in a closely trusted peer group. An employee will be rewarded for compliance, and punished for lack of compliance, in line with normative pressures along either axis. Depending on how the employee acts to balance these competing pressures, there may be one of four possible contrasting outcomes – in this admittedly very simplistic model:

- **Teacher's pet** (aka 'climber', 'goody-goody'): The employee conforms to the formal organization's dictates and rejects any alternatives coming from closely trusted peers.

- **Rogue employee:** The employee disregards the behavioural norms urged by both the formal organization and by their immediate peer group. This is the 'malicious insider' most sought after by compliance, surveillance and monitoring teams.

- **Model citizen:** When (if) it's possible for a person to behave in a way that aligns with both the formal organization and closely trusted peers' norms, there may – just – be an ideal outcome.

- **The cool kids:** Where the trusted peer group's norms clash with those of the formal firm, it's all too easy to succumb to the pull of 'our gang' – our innermost Dunbar social circle – adapting behaviour to conform to our peers' expectations, at the expense of the firm's rules.

Of course, this overly simplistic model lacks nuance; the following chapter on culture assessment tools (Chapter 7) explores in more detail the tensions and behavioural drivers of 'person versus place'. The above model ignores, for instance, that each of us belongs to several different communities, within and outside the workplace – just as we'd identify ourselves with a different label depending on where and how we're being asked about it, such as adult, parent, by gender, by professional qualification, by job title or discipline, or as a voter, book-lover, gym member, by preferred provider of news media, and so on. Simple as it is, this framework will guide us towards some useful headline conclusions about engaging with culture and behaviour change.

Resolving conflicted cultures

The main task facing firms may well be to create broad cultural coherence and, specifically, to prevent coercive competition from distorting employees' natural sense of good behaviour. For a start, this means learning how these behavioural dynamics work. Let's start by creating a scatter plot that places each employee separately within our 'coercion' box. This itself might immediately suggest where to act to intervene against abuses.

Here first (Figure 6.5) is the scatter in a healthy firm with broad cultural cohesion.

By contrast, here's (Figure 6.6) a company at war with itself (as when in a firm there's tension between front office and compliance, or in a school between 'nerds' and 'jocks').

When we tested a version of this culture model with bank leadership, one telling reaction was that 'we'd expect to see it looking more like this [Figure 6.7] – and the cool kids are the ones that keep me up at night'.[47]

FIGURE 6.5   Coercive competition 2

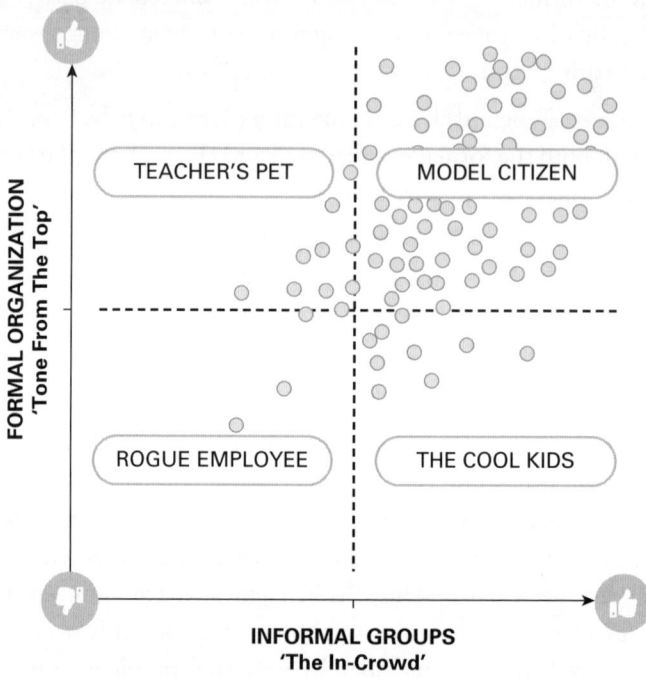

FIGURE 6.6   Coercive competition 3

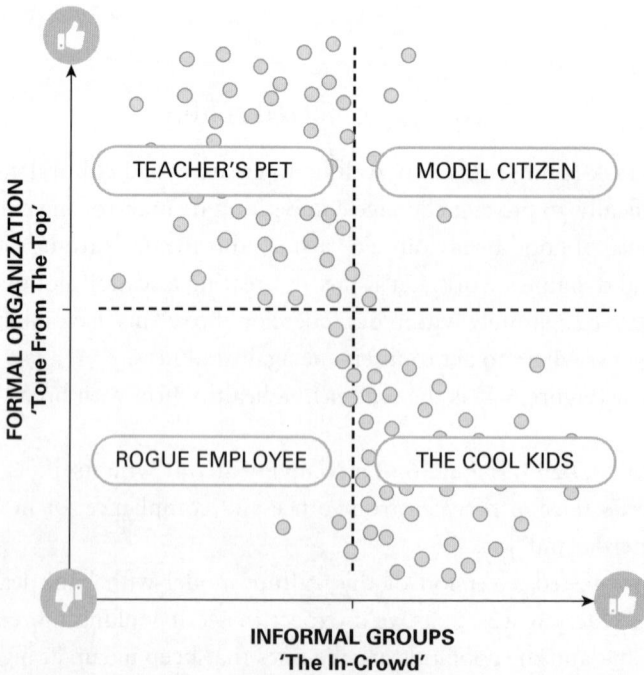

FIGURE 6.7   Coercive competition 4

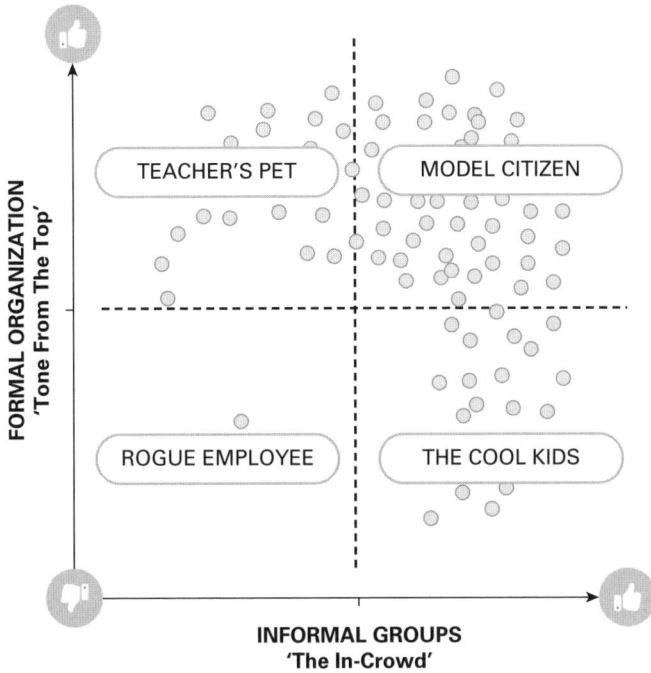

FIGURE 6.8   Coercive competition 5

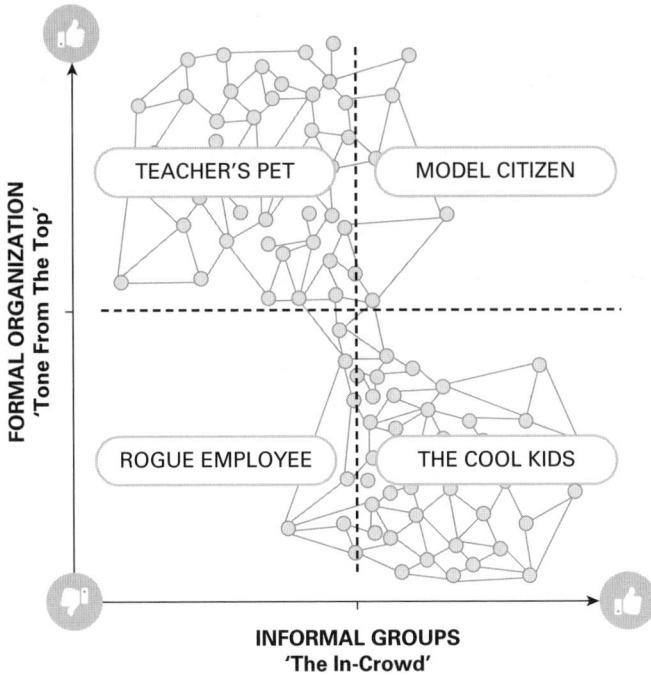

We can add extra dimensions to the model, such as to show how each employee exists within several networks (Figure 6.8). Again simplistically, here's that idea in graph form.

It can help to consider employees as atoms interacting to create molecules with differing properties – the same atoms might combine to form coal, graphite, or diamond. Similarly, as a social group self-assembles, its structure may have many different properties – selfish, altruistic, community-minded, disengaged. Different informal groups (social networks) within organizations will exhibit different behaviours according to their norms and current members. All of which, we'd hope, should be of serious interest to forward-thinking business leaders.

What this approach tells us

We see four drivers of coercive compliance that push employees along each axis of our chart (Figure 6.4):

1 **Institutional pressure:** The firm's rules and marketplace laws aim to induce compliant behaviour, pre-empting and preventing misconduct by threatening sanctions, offering incentives, and pointing to a high probability of detection for misconduct (top two quadrants on Y axis, Figure 6.4).

2 **Security systems:** These work 'after the fact' to catch events of misconduct – as with surveillance, forensic and audit systems, using monitoring to spot the 'rogue employee' in the model. Although a malicious insider can cause great harm, only a tiny number of people in any firm may be sociopaths, let alone full-on psychopaths (empathy deficients who override behavioural norms in both the firm and the peer group).

3 **Moral pressure:** Coming from 'inside our own heads', this is deeply tied to self-identity. If it works at all,[48] this is where 'tone from the top' in firms' codes of practice, Town Hall meetings and training programmes may have their moment. That is when these formal practices are combined with group behaviours based on the desired moral norms. Insofar, it pushes towards the top right quadrant.

4 **Reputational pressure:** A subtler but stronger internal ethical pressure, this comes from how each of us reacts to other people's response to our actions. This driver pulls hardest between top left 'teacher's pet' and

bottom right 'cool kids'. You might by now have guessed that for many people, the 'cools' exert by far the strongest coercive force – which risk managers ignore.

Conclusion: better managing coercive culture

If we've failed historically and collectively to manage culture- and conduct-related risks within financial firms (and elsewhere), this is in no small part due to our failure to grasp how coercive competition re-shapes individual behaviour. Because it's a strong force, produced by millennia of human evolution, if we're serious about managing it we must understand how it works within the 'nexus of relations' in any firm.

There is of course a wider economic message here too. The Dutch central bank (DNB) introduced its pioneering approach of supervising behaviour and culture in 2011.[49] At the core of this approach are targeted deep dives that systematically identify behavioural patterns of key groups in financial institutions. It is highly regarded amongst regulators and firms as a very effective approach that has surgical precision locally – yet is much harder to apply on a bigger, more global scale. As related technologies improve (see Chapters 7 and 12), we'll get better at identifying, tracking and measuring organizational networks on a large scale, and so better anticipating and preventing any wayward behaviour. Just as no serious company would be run without a financial accounting system to draw together results from all its business units, in future we'd expect to see any self-respecting firm similarly assembling behavioural observations.

Regulators are very interested in 'how innovation and enhanced technology will support the measurement of risk culture', with firms routinely combining 'broader data to make stronger predictions about potential misconduct and behavioural risk.'[50] With data-based and other tools, we may now map interpersonal trust networks and measure how they are shaping behaviour, pulling forward predictive signals from readily available datasets, revealing previously invisible drivers of conduct, and permitting for *proactive* risk mitigation efforts.

Researchers deployed one such tool to analyse bankers' peer email communications, finding that these reveal three distinct paths of 'enculturation' that strongly predict individuals' future career progress in the firm. Whilst all new employees use email language that is initially misaligned with organizational norms, they soon learn and exhibit one of three different 'word signature' norms – essentially (1) accept and adopt, (2) reject and eject, or (3) reject and defect. (As it happens, these paths correspond with trajectories identified in one author's study of UK senior risk managers' careers.[51]) The 1s have higher job satisfaction and motivation, make more discretionary efforts, enjoy greater and longer attachment to the firm and perform better both as individuals and in teams. The 2s and 3s either didn't 'rapidly conform to cultural norms' and were 'rejected by... colleagues and ultimately forced to exit' or at first fitted in well but later lost 'cultural fit... appeared to be detaching from the organization' and ultimately resigned.[52]

New social science tools have the power to transform how firms might investigate cultural dynamics and behavioural tendencies, starting now by using commonly available, firm-owned data sets. In the near future we may expect them to produce sharply predictive insights into the drivers of employee behaviour and organizational outcomes. 'Reg tech' (regulatory technology) providers are already developing 'computational social science' techniques to identify and mitigate behaviour-at-risk that is not yet well captured by standard metrics and governance processes.[53] Over time, these will transform the corporate, risk governance and analytical reporting landscape.

With better understanding of how coercive competition occurs, leaders will have behavioural early warning systems and will be able to intervene earlier to encourage desirable group and individual behavioural norms. They will also be enabled to drive out behaviours that don't align with their firm's purpose and values. Done right, this will work to prevent unnecessary 'conduct costs' to shareholders, customers, employees and society, and may eventually (whisper it!) help to restore trustworthiness to our vital institutions.

Notes

1   Edelman (2020) Global Trust Barometer, https://www.edelman.co.uk/research/edelman-trust-barometer-2020 (archived at https://perma.cc/7RGE-72CX)

2   Brooks, D (2018) The New Cold War: the forces of division and the forces of connection, *New York Times*, 29 October

3   Elbot, N (2013) An Expanded Community of Fate: Senior Fellow Margaret Levi on Unions on Political Action, Watson Institute of Public Affairs, Brown University.

4   Business Roundtable (nd) Statement on the Purpose of a Corporation, Business Roundtable, https://opportunity.businessroundtable.org/ourcommitment/ (archived at https://perma.cc/SP9J-4EZY)

5   Friedman, M (1970) A Friedman Doctrine: the social responsibility of business is to increase its profits, *New York Times Magazine*, 30 September

6   Business Roundtable (nd) Statement on the Purpose of a Corporation, Business Roundtable, https://opportunity.businessroundtable.org/ourcommitment/ (archived at https://perma.cc/SP9J-4EZY)

7   Ross-Sorkin, A (2018) Black Rock's message: contribute to society or risk losing our support, *New York Times*, 15 January

8   Ross-Sorkin, A (2018) Black Rock's message: contribute to society or risk losing our support, *New York Times*, 15 January

9   Ross-Sorkin, A (2018) Black Rock's message: contribute to society or risk losing our support, *New York Times*, 15 January

10 Ross-Sorkin, A (2018) Black Rock's message: contribute to society or risk losing our support, *New York Times*, 15 January

11 RSA (Goyder, Ed.) (1995) Tomorrow's Company inquiry, www.tomorrowscompany.com/wp-content/uploads/2016/05/RSA-Inquiry-Tomorrows-Company-1995.compressed.pdf (archived at https://perma.cc/3HAQ-6UY3

12 See for example the think-tanks neweconomics.org (archived at https://perma.cc/MH7C-XS4Q) and economicpluralism.org (archived at https://perma.cc/T8BV-W226)

13 *The Economist* (2019) Big business is beginning to accept broader social responsibilities: pursuing shareholder value is no longer enough, it seems, 22 August

14 Coase (1937) *The Nature of The Firm*

15 Camerer, C (2003) The behavioral challenge to economics: understanding normal people, Caltech, www.researchgate.net/publication/5027243 (archived at https://perma.cc/6CR5-8CYE)

16 El-Erian, M L (2019) Why economics must get broader before it gets better, *Project Syndicate*, https://www.project-syndicate.org/commentary/mainstream-economics-must-learn-from-others-by-mohamed-a-el-erian-2019-03?barrier=accesspaylog (archived at https://perma.cc/VYF8-5UVG)

17 See for example Robson, D (2019) *The Intelligence Trap: Why smart people do stupid things*, Hodder & Stoughton

18 Arrow, K J (1972) Gifts and Exchanges, *Philosophy & Public Affairs*, 1: pp 343–362

19 Meyer, C (2018) *Prosperity: Better business makes the greater good*, Oxford University Press

20 Rachel Botsman, Said Business School, Oxford University, quoted in *The Reputation Game* (Waller and Younger, 2017).

21 Berman, B (2019) $21 trillion in US intangible assets is 84% of S&P 500 Value – IP rights and reputation included, *IP Close Up*, 4 June

22 See for example Tina Fordham (2016) Vox populi risk: a future where aggregate economic growth no longer guarantees political stability, *Citigroup*, https://reports.weforum.org/global-strategic-foresight/tina-fordham-citigroup-vox-populi-risk/ (archived at https://perma.cc/2GQL-B7ER); see also Cambridge Judge Business School's Global Risk Index series at https://www.jbs.cam.ac.uk/faculty-research/centres/risk/publications/managing-multi-threat/cambridge-global-risk-index/ (archived at https://perma.cc/SNY7-NJ8Z)

23 IMF (2018), Annual Report 2018: Building A Shared Future (Part 2)

24 OECD Trust in Business Initiative, http://www.oecd.org/daf/ca/trust-business.htm (archived at https://perma.cc/QGF7-CEK8)

25 Harari, Y N (2015) *Sapiens: A brief history of humankind*, Signal

26 Harari, Y N (2015) *Sapiens: A brief history of humankind*, Signal

27 Harari, Y N (2015) *Sapiens: A brief history of humankind*, Signal

28 Dunbar, R (1992) Neocortex size as a constraint on group size in primates, *Journal of Human Evolution*, **22**, p 469

29 Dunbar, R (2016) *Human Evolution: Our brains and behaviour*, OUP

30 Harari, Y N (2015) *Sapiens: A brief history of humankind*, Signal

31 Harari, Y N (2015) *Sapiens: A brief history of humankind*, Signal

32 In the wise words of the Spice Girls (1996): 'If you wanna be my lover, gotta get with my friends', Wannabe (Virgin Records)

33 Mark Thoma (2006) Milton Friedman: the methodology of positive economics, *Economist's View*, 26 November

34 Letter from University of London professors Tim Besley and Peter Hennessy to Her Majesty the Queen, United Kingdom 22 July

35 Sloman and Fernbach, ibid

36 Baumeister, R F and Leary, M R (1995) The need to belong: Desire for interpersonal attachments as a fundamental human motivation, *Psychological Bulletin*, **117**, pp 497–529

37 Williams, K D (2006) Ostracism, *Annual Review of Psychology*, **58**, pp 425–52

38 Zadro, L, Williams, K D and Richardson, R (2004) How low can you go? Ostracism by a computer is sufficient to lower self-reported levels of belonging, control, self-esteem, and meaningful existence, *Journal of Experimental Social Psychology*, **40**, pp 560–567

39 Gallagher, B (2019) Humans are wired for good, *Nautilus,* 22 Aug

40 Schneier, B (2012) *Liars and Outliers: enabling the trust that society needs to thrive*, Wiley

41 Doring, T and Wansink, B (2017) The Waiter's weight: Does a server's BMI relate to how much food diners order? *Environment and Behavior*, **49**, pp 192–214

42 Woolley, K and Fischbach, A (2017) A recipe for friendship: similar food consumption promotes trust and cooperation, *Journal of Consumer Psychology*, **27**, pp 1–10

43   Cohn, A et al (2014) Business culture and dishonesty in the banking industry, *Nature*, **516**, pp 86–89

44   Chu, J (2011) Searching for balloons in a social network, *MIT News*, 28 October

45   Zingales, L (2012) *A Capitalism for the People: Recovering the lost genius of American prosperity*, Basic Books

46   Veblen, T (1898) Why is economics not an evolutionary science? *Quarterly Journal of Economics*, **12**, pp 373–97

47   Starling Trust; unpublished in-house research.

48   Sheedy, E and Griffin, B (2014) The Risk Culture Project, lse.ac.uk/accounting/assets/CARR/documents/Previous-Seminars/2014/Sheedy-Risk-Culture-Paper-Nov-14.pdf (archived at https://perma.cc/6AAN-ACHM)

49   Raaijmakers, M et al (2015) Supervision of Behaviour and Culture, *De Nederlandsche Bank* (DNB) https://www.dnb.nl/media/1gmkp1vk/supervision-of-behaviour-and-culture_tcm46-380398-1.pdf (archived at https://perma.cc/5DYR-8KRR)

50   Kevin Stiroh, Executive Vice President, Federal Reserve Bank of New York (2019) Reform of culture and finance from multiple perspectives; remarks at GARP conference, 26 February

51   Miles, R (2012) From Compliance to Coping: The role of the Chief Risk Officer in UK banks, 2007–9, Senate House, University of London; and Miles, R (2012) Banks, Regulation and Rule-Bending in *Operational Risk: New Frontiers Explored*, Davis E, Ed, Risk Books, London

52   Goldberg, A et al (2016) Enculturation Trajectories and Individual Attainment, Institute for Research on Labor and Employment, Working Paper 107 (archived at https://perma.cc/K7AT-NCYG52)

53   UK-FCA used the term *behaviour-at-risk (BaR)* in 2019 to describe dynamic tracking of fast-changing conduct risk in firms. See page 8 of FCA (2019) 'Progress and Challenges': 5 Conduct Questions Feedback https://www.fca.org.uk/publication/market-studies/5-conduct-questions-industry-feedback-2018-19.pdf (archived at https://perma.cc/39KV-M3B5)

07

The new mindset and language of culture

Assessing financial and non-financial conduct

HANI NABEEL AND ROGER MILES

Taking a wider view of misconduct

'Financial misconduct' typically relates to defined conventional offences – crimes or acts or omissions which at least heavily imply criminality: fraud or dishonesty; financial market abuse; handling the proceeds of crime; or the financing of terrorism. The language of financial misconduct is, largely speaking, the language of the law. Your actions were legal or illegal; you knew, or you should reasonably have known.

In an increasingly complex and information-rich world, 'legalese' is no longer up to performing this task. It tends to be unduly rationalistic ('System 2 thinking', if you're a student of Thinking, Fast and Slow – see page 69), trying to reduce behavioural nuance to black-letter codex, focusing on the punitive and lacking aspiration for a regulatory generation that looks increasingly to partner rather than officiate.

A finer focus on culture and non-financial misconduct reflects the latest evolution of regulators towards a more sophisticated approach.

THEMES AND CONCEPTS IN THIS CHAPTER

better questions, better answers – bystanding – 'Culture lens' perspective on measurement – conduct 'coaching' by regulators – conduct regulation as 'positive mindset' – direct observation of behaviour – drivers of behaviour – excessive conformity – exemplary conduct vs misconduct – financial and non-financial misconduct – healthy vs unhealthy culture – inclusiveness – legal-rational thinking vs behavioural thinking – new indicators for positive mindsets (diversity, social purpose, active learning, expressive) – perceived justice – predictive validity – sentiment surveys vs direct observation – strong correlation – 'virtuous alignment' indicator

CONDUCT REGULATORS' PIVOT TOWARDS CULTURE ASSESSMENT

As the UK's Financial Conduct Authority (FCA) has said:[1]

> Poor culture... can lead directly to harm to consumers, market participants, employees and markets... How a firm handles non-financial misconduct throughout the organization, including discrimination, harassment, victimization and bullying, is indicative of a firm's culture. Lack of diversity and inclusion, and non-financial misconduct [are] obstacles to creating an environment in which it is safe to speak up, the best talent is retained, the best business choices are made, and the best risk decisions are taken.

Conduct regulation moves towards a positive mindset

The shift is clear: conduct regulation is no longer simply about enforcers catching you doing a certain thing wrong; it is about regulators as 'coaches',[2] working with firms to discover the root causes of why you do what you do – and to make sure these are healthy, and working to support a healthily customer-centric culture. In fact, we'll now call all of the above: Culture.

For firms now taking on board the regulator's own culture shift, the challenge seems an abstract notion that's even harder to define in legalese than financial misconduct. The industry has tended to look at culture in one of two ways: Either, to say it is 'not a thing' and focus on more tangible metrics – letting culture happen without a plan in practice. Or, to try to define it simplistically as 'sort of, doing everything right', without any rigor-ous evaluation of how people actually operate and how group norms influence individuals' behaviour.

If the abstract concept of culture is to be useful to our thinking, it needs to be made observable. To improve our understanding, we need a mindset and language around culture in firms which is specific, quantifiable, accurate and useful, but which captures the richness of all that we collectively know about organizational culture.

Healthy and unhealthy culture

The new dynamic in the regulatory partnership is more aspirational. It brings organizations towards the ideals of a healthy culture and shifts focus to encourage the right behaviours, not just to punish the event of the wrong ones. It also provokes a much richer adult conversation about what a healthy culture is that goes far beyond, 'one that commits little financial miscon-duct'. It allows organizations to define and make sense of pivotal questions such as:

- How inclusive are we?
- What is our purpose and our value to society in general?
- Are we fostering an environment of psychological safety?
- Do we show moral courage, or are we 'bystanders'?
- Does cognitive diversity inform and improve our decision-making?

You are what you do: observing actual behaviour

Human behaviour lies at the root of the healthy/unhealthy culture focus; specifically, presence or absence of encouraging ('exemplary') or concerning ('misconduct') behaviours. Focusing on observed behaviour as the core metric for culture could allow organizations to grapple with the nuances of how they operate in a less simplistic legal/illegal way. Now that behaviour patterns can be reliably identified – as we'll see in this chapter – this allows us to stay focused on specific, tangible elements that we can measure, track and influence for the better. We have reached a stage where we can pass culture guru Edgar Schein's test of whether behavioural data is 'observable and useful', giving us the prospect of roping in the big questions such as, 'Are we inclusive?', grounding our answers robustly in what actually happens in real life.

Put simply, the behaviour that is present and absent in an organization is the best and truest measure of its culture. Our individual and collective behaviour represents all the deeper organizational myths, habits and beliefs about what is acceptable and unacceptable, consciously and unconsciously. It reflects what we find familiar and reassuring, are uncomfortable with and wary of, what we admire, resent and above all assume.

Behaviour also reflects the inherent forced-choice nature of real life. We may tell ourselves the mythos that we are straightforwardly 'a good person' but the truth is far more nuanced. We tell 'white lies'; we gently (sometimes not-so-gently) bend inconvenient rules. In our actual behaviour we constantly make choices to prioritize ourselves over others – or not. Does a person choose to be less considerate to another's needs than they could be, and/or less forthright about what they believe needs to be said? A person cannot sit in the comfortable (and normal) self-delusion that they are always all of both at the same time, to suit their preferred self-image; it's not practically possible. Manifest behaviour is the acid test, the indicator that shows what we are really inclined to do, especially when under pressure, individually and collectively. Observed behaviour is therefore the ideal lens through which to consider the near-constant everyday ethical micro-dilemmas that the focus on non-financial misconduct has brought forward.

Critically, the new focus on behaviour lets us consider the richness of context. Past simplistic approaches tried to chase the chimaera of a single 'ideal' way of operating. That's clearly not realistic. An organization whose business model is focused on rapid expansion may need to be encouraging very different behaviours to one consolidated in a very mature and stable market. A business seeking to disrupt with a small, new customer base can experiment, whereas a big firm with formal responsibilities to many customers must focus on meeting all of its pre-existing obligations.

The focus on behaviour can thread the needle – looking for common themes that typify a healthy culture whilst at the same time appreciating that different behaviours are needed in different settings, and different things work in different places. It can also allow for an open, adult dialogue between organization and regulator. As conduct regulators recognize, what's healthy in some settings (such as, say, singing raucously, because you're at a bachelor party) might be a red flag in another context (singing raucously in response to a tricky question at a job interview).

Where and how to draw the line? Let's look closer.

Indicators for mindsets that reduce non-financial misconduct

Regulators' view of how to create a mindset for reducing non-financial misconduct is, at the turn of the year 2021, focused on a few thematic clusters, notably:

Purpose and social value

As a theme throughout this book, firms are increasingly expected by employees, customers, stakeholders, regulators and society at large, to find purpose and meaning. With clear purpose, a person is more likely to persevere under pressure when they believe in what they're doing. In defining purpose, it's more important to 'teach a leader to fish rather than give them a fish'; for them to have innate purpose to guide acting appropriately without external stare. As organizations have not traditionally promoted such 'meaning makers' as the archetype of a strong leader, many businesses remain cynical or insecure about values, culture and what good looks like.

Diversity and inclusion

Although it seems redundant (and somewhat ironic), we suggest that this topic provokes differing views and interpretations. In two areas, mindset shifts are needed to meet the test of promoting a healthy culture to displace non-financial misconduct: socio-economic inclusion (creating opportunity for people of all demographics and backgrounds) and experiential and cognitive diversity (incorporating voices with different ways of thinking). There is clearly overlap between these two, but there are differences as well. Key healthy cultural behaviours indicating the required mindset include:

- A non-hierarchical operating model: authority is granted to junior and middle management; people are trusted and encouraged to make decisions.
- Group-over-individual team ethos: the firm actively promotes the need to work and succeed together, and encourages engagement in 'conduct conversations' and setting goals collectively.
- Meritocratic decision-making: ideas are considered and valued on their merits rather than who they came from; over-emphasis on status and prestige is actively discouraged.
- Challenging and forthright: speaking up and (constructively) challenging authority is actively encouraged and seen as valuable. The firm makes

space for dissenting voices; loyalty is framed as based on honesty rather than blind obedience.

- Possibility-seeking: the firm makes space for possibilities and untested ideas. People habitually explore new perspectives and avoid using the excuse of 'compliance' to justify sticking with existing practices.

These indicators signify openness to change. By embracing them, we both break down tired norms created by overrepresented groups and dispel leadership groupthink, improving the firm's decision-making in fast-changing contexts.

Well-being and psychological safety

There's a shift in regulatory emphasis towards encouraging the conditions for healthy operations, with psychological safety a key to this. It's not just about calling out obvious abuses such as bullying and harassment; people are often formally authorized to act but in practice nervous to do so, uncertain whether their authority is real, and/or intimidated by certain individuals or groups. The cognitive science labels for this problem (impostor syndrome, bystander effect, diffusion of responsibility) provide a clear hint: many people simply don't speak up spontaneously, for fear of being conspicuous, or embarrassed, or facing some form of retribution.

Here a focus on actual behaviour can be a big help in improving outcomes. Do people actually speak up? When do they and don't they? When they do speak up, are they admired and held up as role models, or undermined, ostracized, even punished for 'troublemaking'? Is bullying tolerated, or (insidiously) discouraged in name but not in deed – or is it confronted with visible consequences?

New methods for a new mindset: beyond sentiment surveys

The more sophisticated mindset around healthy culture demands more nuanced methods. To be effective, and ultimately predictive, behaviour analysis needs to be quantifiable and to identify accurately what actually happens – not filtered through perceptions or opinions coloured by hidden cultural influences.

Traditionally firms have relied on internal sentiment surveys based on job satisfaction, well-being and general attitudes, as well as organizational engagement often reflected in town halls, initiative participation rates, and HR data such as absenteeism. Externally the metrics of choice have tended towards net promoter scores, other customer satisfaction data and shifts in market penetration. Each of these have their limitations, however, when the 'quantifiable, predictive, reflective' test is applied.

Sentiment surveys are often held up as the most rigorous and data-driven approach. However, they elicit subjective opinions; they don't report objective observations of actual behaviours. They measure what people 'think they think'. Few use standardized definitions, and even fewer ask respondents to make hard choices between competing virtues or priorities (eg 'Who gets listened to the most around here: the most knowledgeable or the most creative?', 'What do you see more of around here: punishment or celebration of success?'). As such, they give a limited picture of what happens in an organization culturally in reality.

Town hall discussions can also try to cover a wide range of organizational factors, but are filtered by the dominant culture, raising lists of issues rather than building the full coherent picture of a firm's culture.

Measuring behaviour through a 'culture lens'

To improve on previous efforts, then, culture assessments need to catalogue, characterize and quantify the key behaviours that make up the firm's culture. They need to retain, from sentiment surveys, a spirit of enquiry and openness to the employee perspective. But they also need to draw out distinct, measurable differences that can be used to classify and compare a culture either to other cultures or to an aspiration developed with staff and with an encouraging regulator.

This moves the firm beyond sentiment tracking (what I think) to behaviour tracking (what I/we actually do); from the barely meaningful 'Is this a good or bad culture?' towards richer, more realistic questions like 'Do we have a culture that encourages speaking out?' or 'Is this more of an inclusive, receptive culture or more of a wait-to-be-told, status-driven one?'

Behaviour assessment systems are developing this more nuanced approach. The model used here (CultureScope) has distilled extensive behavioural factor research down into a critical set of variables: 30 behavioural factors, in 15 paired dimensions in tension with each other. It assesses how people see their own behaviour versus the dominant behavioural norms in the organization around them. Rather than rating what they like or do not like, as with most sentiment surveys, employees are asked to make choices about which competing behaviours are more or less present. This creates a robust profile of the behavioural tendencies which represent an organization's culture, rather than simply a set of ratings and likeability scores. It also ties the data back to clear, consistent definitions which can be compared and contrasted across and between firms.

This approach shifts the mindset from 'Did you get a perfect score on culture?' to 'To what extent were healthy or unhealthy cultural factors present or absent in our firm?', pinpointing human intent. It also notes many different behaviours that cluster together to produce higher-level cultural influences. For instance, we can identify behavioural factors that are sub-elements of inclusion. By measuring and then clustering those five or six factors, we can see precisely how far a firm's culture is exhibiting underlying behaviours that create an inclusive culture.

This represents a huge improvement on previous efforts to assess culture. Rather than just asking people, 'How inclusive do you think your firm is…?', we can find behaviour factors that reflect and predict inclusivity, then we can statistically evaluate how far these are present and absent. We can then analyse other outcomes across the whole firm, to identify which behaviours best predict, for example, whether people are willing to speak up when they see misconduct around them. This system easily and reliably identifies causal links, without resorting to 'hypotheticals'.

As we've seen, a vital element of non-financial healthy culture is the confidence and comfort to speak up in an environment that gives people a voice: psychological safety. This includes actively discouraging bullying, harassment and autocratic cultural practices which disempower colleagues, diffuse responsibility and induce bystanding. The case example at the end of this chapter offers a worked culture assessment of this problem, complete with behavioural drivers and remedial actions.

BYSTANDING

Especially when there's a culture of fear in a firm, people tend to wait for others to act, seeing it as not their job to confront the situation and hiding in the more literal and defensible safe ground of financial misconduct ('I didn't do anything wrong, it's not my place to address what my bosses' boss might have done…'). Behavioural science research on the 'bystander effect'[3] notes that it gets worse the more people are present. Where we might intuitively expect that having more people to witness the misbehaviour would *increase* the likelihood that someone will call it out, in practice more witnesses all too often leads to greater diffusion of responsibility ('One of these [many] other people will sort this out, so I don't have to put myself to the trouble of stepping in/I can turn a blind eye to it'). This is one example of where behavioural research shows us a *counterintuitive* conclusion, rather than going with the 'common sense' we might expect.

The behavioural roots of key cultural factors

As a case example at the end of this chapter shows, there is a powerful positive effect on employee engagement when good leaders demonstrate the behaviours needed to build trust. But that is not the whole story. Good leadership also needs good followership – trust in leadership is almost four times higher when 'virtuous alignments' (between the place and the people) are stronger.

The case example also shows that there is a core set of behaviours that underpin trust, well-being and employee voice. We can summarize these six behaviours that, between the people and the place, are found to drive higher employee trust in leaders, higher employee well-being and substantially higher levels of comfort in speaking up and sharing opinions and ideas at work (Figure 7.1).

Expressiveness will seem intuitively obvious (that is, a 'no-brainer'). A characteristic willingness among employees to share opinions, and the firm's encouragement to do so, is a behaviour pattern that obviously supports the sharing of employee voice.

The other behaviour pattern, **active learning**, may seem less intuitive; behavioural science has shown that getting the best benefit from speak-up (employee voice) very much depends on whether speaking up is seen by staff to lead to a general engagement in solving problems. Speaking up is no good if it's a solitary, unlistened-to voice. The firm needs not only to encourage speaking up but to recruit and promote actively open-minded people, and to encourage active learning through experimentation and managed risk.

Four of these six behaviours operate as complementary pairs. Again, one pair is highly intuitive in that voice is more likely to be received positively when it is shared in a way that is seen to be focused on building and strengthening partnerships within the workplace rather than just for the benefit of the individual sharing their voice. This is how we see **collective** operating in

FIGURE 7.1   How 'the people' and 'the place' behaved to build trust, well-being and employee voice

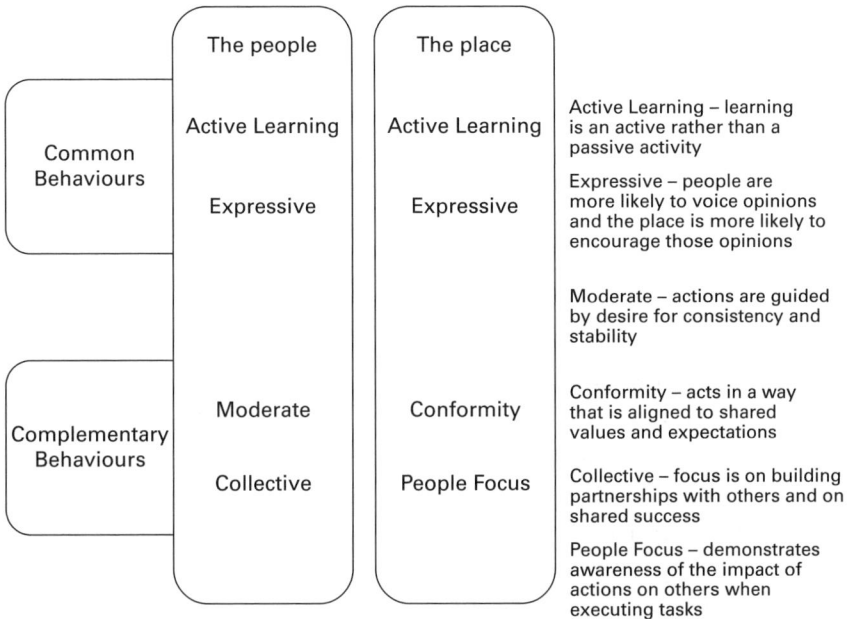

the predictive model and how it plays through the actions of leaders to build trust among employees. That behaviour from the perspective of the people is complemented and strengthened in workplaces by demonstrating an awareness of the impact of actions on others when executing tasks and achieving objectives, which the analysis calls **people focus**.

Another complementary pair examines trust, which needs to be synergistic between 'people' and 'place'. In short, trust depends on expectations of others, such as their reciprocity, and whether others can be expected to act in ways that are predictable. That view of trust is where the behaviour factor **moderate** fits in: from the 'people' side, how employees behave through their expression of voice; from the 'place' side, **conformity**. Conformity here does not just mean abiding by the rules, though that is important in employees having faith that there is justice in the workplace. It also indicates that leaders are consistent in paying attention to the employee voice. This explains the levels of higher trust in leaders seen in the case example, where conformity in the place was higher.

PERCEPTIONS OF JUSTICE IN THE WORKPLACE

Models of organizational justice show that perceptions of justice in the workplace depend on whether employees see that the processes by which decisions are reached are fair (procedural justice), whether the distribution of rewards is fair (distributive justice), whether the involvement of people is fair (relationship justice) and whether the sharing of information is fair and reasonable (informational justice).

Better questions get better answers

The case example at the end of this chapter shows how new forms of analysis can go far further in asking the more sophisticated questions that underlie issues of non-financial misconduct. The old 'sentiment approach' gave us only subjective opinions, and even then only opinions about things we thought to ask or could anticipate in advance. By using behavioural analytics we can answer richer, more layered questions. Vitally, we can find the answers we never even knew we needed, and help ourselves to see that we were not even asking the right question in the first place. We can also reassess the assumptions about what might constitute a healthy or unhealthy culture in different settings and then reinterpret the data we already have based on this new set of ideals and behavioural priorities. The whole topic of asking better questions to generate new MI is expanded in detail in Chapter 10, pages 235–246.

The new approach can be seen as a shift in intent, specifically to focus on healthy culture, which is inherent in analysis of non-financial forms of conduct: better questions get better answers. Understanding culture with a clear quantitative foundation allows better diagnosis and more relevant and useful action. It also provides a clearer basis for firms to present evidence that they're meeting the spirit of the conduct regulator's intent.

Conclusion: using the new mindset and language as we develop culture assessment practice

This richer analytic approach can be the cornerstone of the shift from financial (mis)conduct to financial AND non-financial (mis)conduct – from policing legal compliance to encouraging a healthy culture that promotes desirable behaviour. With it, organizations can show themselves to be meaningfully embracing the spirit and intention behind the shift from the regulator. They can also go much further to ensure they are asking searching, robust questions about their true cultural health. They can also potentially make huge gains in reducing events of financial misconduct and promoting the 'exemplary conduct' that regulators (and the public) so keenly desire to see.

Punishing the crime can be far more resource-intensive than diagnosing and addressing the symptoms early on. Robust behavioural analysis can be the organizational health screen that picks up potential problems early and brings them front and centre.

They can also introduce a new, more qualitative, nuanced and less simplistic language into the firm's conduct conversation. Once the behaviours are identified and understood, then they can exist as an internal language where people actively discuss 'striking a balance between Innovate and Consolidate', 'creating Active Learning Opportunities' or 'reviewing our processes from an Empower point of view'. In this way the language and mindset combine to provide a lens to view behaviour in the firm, even when not using the survey technology itself.

In terms of conduct regulators' major thematic concerns such as Psychological Safety, Moral Courage, Leadership Character, Diversity and Inclusion, these can also be used to create consistent definitions and understandings of what these things are, where the organization is, and where it wants to be. The firm can then track these understandings and aspirations consistently over time through regular surveys and a robust internal discourse.

The increased rigour and predictive validity of this system could also generate greater interest and buy-in from senior leaders historically inclined to be somewhat sceptical and contemptuous of sentiment data. This is particularly true in financial services. Finance leaders have grown up with empirical data as an important part of how they navigate ambiguity and make decisions. The huge step up from subjective sentiment data and feedback can have a powerful impact on getting leaders to change attitudes and mindsets in this traditionally neglected element of good governance. In time, we can expect it to come to play a big role in driving home the regulator's central point: the health of your culture is as tangible and important as any specific instance of misconduct.

METHODOLOGY NOTE ON ASCERTAINING STRENGTH
OF CORRELATION

Many researchers use Jacob Cohen's correlation effect size benchmarks to
gauge the strength of relationships. These benchmarks are 0.2 for a small
effect, 0.3 for a moderate effect and 0.5 for a large effect. The results of our
model for predicting employee voice would benchmark as a large effect size
(R=0.496). More recent research suggests that the size of an effect varies
depending on what is being studied and that different benchmarks reflecting
different fields of study are required. We obtained our 80th percentile
benchmark for research on employee attitudes from the following source:

Bosco, F A et al (2015), Correlational effect size benchmarks, *Journal of Applied Psychology*,
100, pp 431–49

CASE EXAMPLE
*Assessing psychological safety and speaking up in a global retail
and investment bank*

A global bank had concerns about their own culture in relation to new regulatory
definitions of financial and non-financial misconduct. They were not confident their
people would speak up and do the right thing beyond the narrower limits of specified
direct responsibilities. They felt they might not be able to pass the new culture-based tests
of conduct. They had invested in various initiatives to promote employee voice over
several years, but felt they had achieved at most mixed success and were frustrated about
the difficulty of establishing a metric to address this critical but hard-to-define area.

They engaged an external culture analysis team, using the CultureScope tool to
examine employee voice and speak-up culture more directly, for self-diagnosis and
to guide their culture change efforts. The team then sought to understand the bank's
culture more deeply, and to identify root causes of dominant patterns of behaviour
that their leadership had struggled to understand and shift.

There is often observable conflict between how the firm behaves overall ('the place')
and how individuals typically behave ('the people') – the natural behavioural posture of
each employee. That conflict tends to induce and create opportunities for misbehaviour
in the workplace, derailing efforts to achieve work goals and the firm's strategic aims.

Like many organizations, the bank had regularly surveyed employees to gauge
attitudes and sentiment. Quarterly and annual surveys included questions on
whether the employee felt able to share opinions and to speak up without negative
consequences ('Speak Up' measure), believed that there is mutual trust between
employees and leaders ('Mutual Trust' measure), and whether line managers take
into account the well-being of employees ('Well-being' measure).

IS MANAGER INTEREST IN EMPLOYEE WELL-BEING A SUFFICIENTLY 'STRONG PROXY'?

One limitation of this project was the framing of the survey question asked of employees about their well-being at work. The specific question used asks whether the manager is invested in the employee's well-being rather than the well-being the employee generally experiences at work. However, we feel that it is a reasonable inference that employee well-being is correlated with the extent to which an organization, through its managers, is concerned about and invested in employee well-being.

The analysis tracked the pattern of results from employee surveys over three consecutive quarters to develop a predictive model through two waves of analysis. The first explored the relationship between the three sets of survey questions to understand the functional relationships between them. Through testing the fit of various models to the survey data, the culture analysts arrived at a model in which **mutual trust** and **well-being** were confirmed as acting most powerfully as drivers of whether employees reported comfort in speaking up.

The team then developed and evaluated a model that linked the behaviour of the people and the place to trust and well-being at work, and used that model to understand the direct and indirect impacts of the behaviour of the people and the place on employee voice.

In the end, finding a relationship between culture, trust, well-being and speaking up was not where the surprise lay. The surprise was in the strength of the predictive relationships found and how this helped to identify and expand the set of behavioural drivers behind employee attitudes in the workplace. Various waves of the bank's own in-house surveys had shown that employee attitudes were fairly stable and, on the surface, potentially reassuring for the bank. We already know that research studies from the 1990s onwards have shown that the normal odds of an employee speaking up at work have sat stubbornly at around 50:50 (that is, 'evens'). This bank's surveys showed that, overall, 60 per cent of employees reported high or very high comfort in speaking up: 10 percentage points above the baseline set by those three decades of wider research.

Yet there was also a persistent 16 per cent or around 1 in 6 of employees who reported low or very low comfort in speaking up and sharing their opinions at work, and a further 24 per cent, or around 1 in 4 employees, who reported uncertainty about the value of stating their opinions at work. This is where using behavioural analytics helped the bank to get under the skin of these survey statistics. The culture factor analysis found:

- Below the surface of the employee survey results lay a very strong 'driver' relationship between the behavioural profiles of the people and the place; a relationship only apparent once behavioural diagnostics were overlaid on the employee attitude surveys.

- That relationship remained strong up to nine months after the behavioural analytics had been deployed and explained why employee sentiment remained so consistent. If behaviours do not change, then (unsurprisingly) employee attitudes, including the likelihood of speaking, up are unlikely to change. In this case, there was a specific set of common or complementary behavioural drivers which enabled the bank to narrow down its focus for intervention action.

- 'The place' had an overriding impact specifically on levels of mutual trust; impact of behaviour was around four parts place to one part people. The place (workplace culture overall) acted as a direct driver of employee voice and, through employee well-being and mutual trust, as an indirect driver.

When it comes to mutual trust in the workplace, it's not simply about whether people, employees, naturally trust others but about whether they trust and feel trusted by their leaders where they work. For employee voice (see Figure 7.2), the surveys had captured both promotive voice (sharing ideas and opinions aimed at improving team and organizational performance) and prohibitive voice (speaking up to stop harm to others and the organization). The data

FIGURE 7.2 Key drivers of employee voice in a client organization

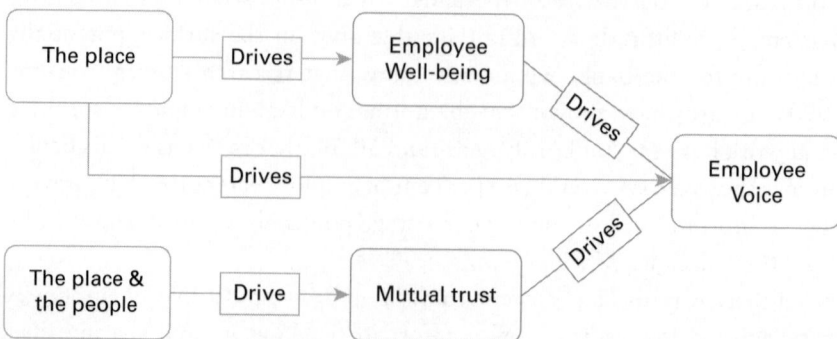

showed lower endorsement rates among employees for promotive voice, which was of concern to the bank at a time when competition in their industry had increased with the arrival of challenger banks using new customer service models and technologies.

Alignment proven to encourage healthy culture

Employees' comfort about **sharing voice** in the workplace is many times greater when personal and workplace values are stronger and aligned. While there is some comfort in sharing voice even when the place is weaker in its support for employee voice, the strength of that endorsement is exponentially higher when the place is stronger in those critical behaviours that drive employee voice (Figure 7.3).

For the quadrant we may call **virtuous alignment**, employees were 13.6 times more likely to report comfort in sharing opinions. In contrast, the odds for that comfort were 1.8 times less likely in the opposite quadrant (that we'll call **double negative**), and the ratio of those two numbers produces a factor of 7.5 times higher comfort for when the workplace has observed behaviours strongly aligned with values.

Assessing **well-being** (Figure 7.4), there was a similar pattern in the impact of the place. Employees in the virtuous alignment quadrant were 6.7

FIGURE 7.3   Employee comfort about sharing voice

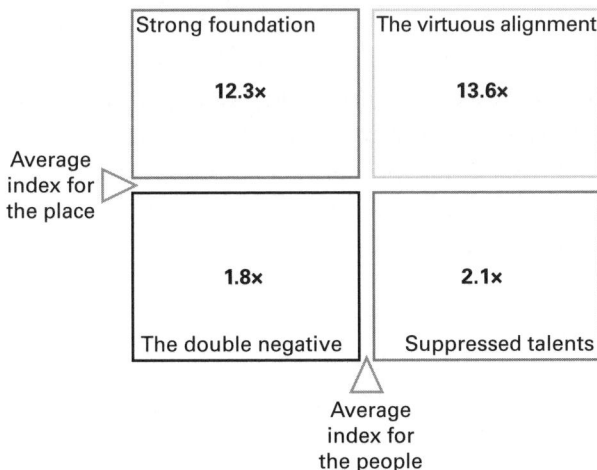

FIGURE 7.4   Employee comfort about well-being

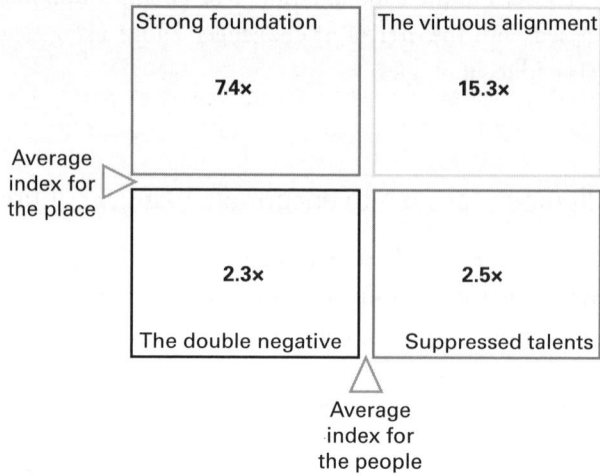

times more likely to report higher well-being than those in the double negative quadrant. The difference between employees in the quadrant we have called **strong foundation** and the virtuous alignment quadrant suggests an opportunity to intervene to develop employees' awareness and practice of behaviours that support their own well-being at work. Rather than look to the line manager as the sole driver of employee well-being, the analysis suggests an opportunity for the bank to explore how employees in the strong foundation quadrant can become more active agents in supporting their own well-being at work. By combining behavioural analytics and employee survey data, the bank was able to understand where most effectively to intervene to promote employee well-being and, once having well-being, employees becoming more willing to share opinions.

Another discovered culture driver of speak-up was **trust in leadership** (Figure 7.5). Here we see a direct impact of both the people and the place such that employees in the virtuous alignment quadrant were 17.2 times more likely to report high comfort in speaking up than employees in the double negative quadrant.

The synergistic impact on trust of both the people and place can be seen by another comparison among the four quadrants. In contrast to a quadrant identifying **suppressed talents** where the odds for reporting trust in leaders is 4.3 to 1, the odds for employees reporting high trust in leadership in the strong foundation quadrant are 14.7 to 1 – more than three times higher.

FIGURE 7.5   Employee comfort about trust in leadership

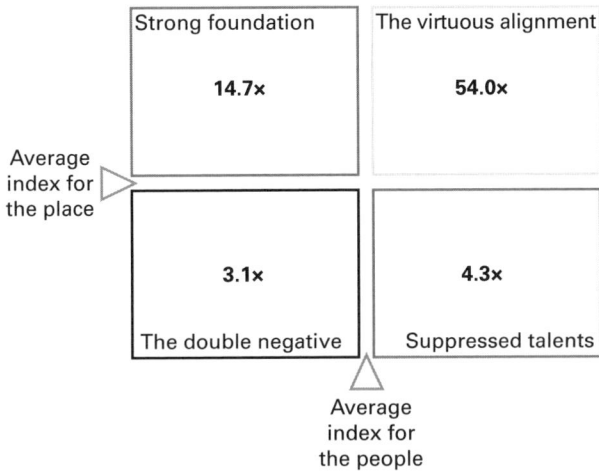

	Strong foundation	The virtuous alignment
Average index for the place ▷	14.7×	54.0×
	3.1×	4.3×
	The double negative	Suppressed talents

Average
index for
the people

Conversely, this indicates how firm-wide culture (the place) may act to suppress employees' propensity to build trust between themselves and leaders in the organization.

Notes

1 FCA 'Dear CEO' letters to insurance firm principals (2020): https://www.fca.org.uk/publication/correspondence/dear-ceo-letter-non-financial-misconduct-wholesale-general-insurance-firms.pdf (archived at https://perma.cc/RY9U-KETK)

2 Ted MacDonald, FCA, briefing to Securities Houses Compliance Officers Group (SHCOG), 2016, author's own collection

3 Darley, J M and Latane, B (1968) Bystander intervention in emergencies: Diffusion of responsibility, *Journal of Personality and Social Psychology*, 8 (4, Pt.1), pp 377–83, https://doi.org/10.1037/h0025589 (archived at https://perma.cc/7KYT-KR3C)

08

Audit basics

*How the practice of culture audit differs
from conventional auditing*

ELIZABETH ARZADON AND ROGER MILES

Introduction

As recently as 2010, the idea of inserting behavioural and social scientists into traditional audit functions to assess culture directly was hugely innovative. Indeed, organizations that have taken this path remain at the forefront of behaviour and culture risk management insight and practice. Through ongoing evidence-based audit work, regular reporting and improvement efforts, organizations applying this approach are at various stages of embedding a norm where all staff feel accountable for creating an environment that manages risk well.

Why did this relatively small number of firms (and some supervisory bodies) decide that culture was worth assessing as an audit activity? They did so because they realized that while auditors deliver enormous value, conventional auditing – focused on hard controls and numbers – was not enough. Even after completing a conventional audit, risks remained that they 'could not put their finger on'. In simple terms, the audit gave the impression of 'all clear', while losses and misconduct were still occurring.

In this chapter, we will look at what culture audit is, how it interacts with conventional audit, and how it can be used to reduce risk. It should be noted that the term 'audit' as used in this chapter refers to internal audit, not external audit.

THEMES AND CONCEPTS IN THIS CHAPTER

behavioural observation, 'floor-walk'/'virtual visit' – behavioural science in culture audit – behavioural science principles – bias in risk appetite – biased decision-making – business benefits of culture audit – cognitive bias – 'conduct risk appetite zero' fallacy – content analysis techniques – control design gaps – conventional audit vs culture audit – culture auditors – culture dashboards – culture risks ('vox populi' and others) – evidence, evidence-based – 'games of compliance' – 'holding up the mirror' – internal audit – interviewing technique – judgement-based reporting – poorly framed controls – rating systems: arguments for and against – response effects and 'Goodhart's Law' – root cause analysis – sampling – staff surveys, value of – triangulating to independent sources – unconscious non-compliance – understanding how to drive culture change – unreliable self-reporting – 'what actually happened' – 'what good looks like' standard – wishful control designs (incl self-reporting, attestation)

Why does internal audit exist?

According to the Global Institute of Internal Audit, internal audit aims 'to enhance and protect organizational value by providing risk-based and objective assurance, advice and insight'.[1] This nicely articulated mission statement seems a bit more exciting than the visual many people have of auditors as calculator-wielding police officers, but basically the function has a fairly simple mandate: to make sure management isn't taking more risk than the board is comfortable with.

Whilst this sounds straightforward, there are some deeper assumptions built into the goal of internal audit, such as that:

- boards benefit from having an independent view of risk, separate from management's view;
- risk is an issue that can be highly prone to bias, compared with other management topics, so it's vital for the board to have an independent view of it;
- with a wider perspective, internal audit may be better placed to understand and evaluate risk than those in the business itself;
- internal audit can influence outcomes, despite having no authority over them.

Built into all these assumptions is the idea that line managers' perceptions of risk may be skewed, compromising good management of risk. The role of internal audit therefore requires two steps. Firstly, internal audit needs to use its unique objectivity to develop a more valid assessment of:

a the inherent risks facing a business;

b how well the controls designed to mitigate these risks are working; and

c whether or not the resulting level of residual risk is in line with the board's appetite.

Secondly, if residual risk is beyond the board's appetite, it needs to fix the situation appropriately.

Let's turn to the question of how internal auditors actually achieve these goals – both traditionally and in the more modern world of culture auditing.

How do conventional audit and culture audit differ?

In general, *conventional* audit is primarily focused on the hard controls and financial operations of the organization. It evaluates the effectiveness of processes and systems designed to manage risk. This includes assessing the design of these processes and systems and the way they are functioning in practice. If gaps are identified, conventional audit aims to ensure they are addressed within a reasonable timeframe and informs management and the board as appropriate. Conventional audit tends to be conducted by auditors with an accounting and/or finance background.

In general, *culture* audit evaluates the extent to which behavioural norms within a group reinforce effective management of risk and are supported by the organizational environment. It includes consideration of the board's stated risk appetite for all key risks and examines behavioural norms that help or hinder maintenance of that risk appetite. Importantly, culture audit places particular emphasis on the systemic nature of behaviour and its root causes. Action plans designed to drive improvement tend to be multifaceted, addressing both the formal and informal factors underpinning problematic norms. Culture audit tends to be conducted by those with a behavioural sciences and/or social sciences background, and an understanding of how to apply these disciplines to the management of risk.

How are conventional audit and culture audit similar?

At first glance, conventional and culture auditing may appear quite different. But scratch the surface and some similarities emerge. Ultimately, as they're both forms of internal auditing that try to identify, evaluate and mitigate risk within a business, they both need a clear mandate, accurate diagnosis of reality, and the ability to influence. No surprise then, perhaps, that we find the techniques that each use conform to some very similar principles:

Evidence-based

Both conventional and culture audit rely on evidence as the basis for analysis and assessment. This is because both strive to provide an objective perspective that is valid and reliable. Conventional audit evidence can take a variety of forms, usually related to process compliance and outcomes – for example, alignment between process documentation and walk-through results. Culture audit often includes such process and outcome evidence but also requires insight on mindsets and behaviour. Hence, it typically includes qualitative data on these dimensions, systematically gathered and sometimes quantified in order to aid analysis and reliable comparison, such as interview quotes, observed behaviour, survey responses and incident descriptions.

Sampling

Although technology is beginning to offer new tools for continuous monitoring, most audits still collect and routinely analyse data by hand. Many risk controls are not in constant use, and although 100 per cent compliance might seem a worthy aim, many also accept a certain rate of failures or exceptions. When human auditors collect data themselves, they will generally need to extrapolate results to assess how material their findings really are. Of course, this concept of sample testing is common in conventional auditing. In culture auditing, careful sampling can be even more significant; it's vital to verify whether the behaviours observed or discussed during the course of a review are the 'norm' under regular business conditions. To address this, many culture auditors look to cross-reference (triangulate) results from sampling (such as interviews and observations) with wider data (such as surveys or email language analysis tools).

Insightful

In most cost-conscious organizations (and which ones aren't?), there's constant pressure for audit to demonstrate value. Whilst some internal audit activities are mandated by regulation, there are business benefits too:

auditors can add value by seeing an issue or a solution others don't. Conventional auditing does this by systematically using rigorous, fact-based tools to analyse activities in ways that line managers perhaps don't, applying professional judgement often gained through experience and observing many organizations, and bringing an outsider's fresh point of view to interpret facts neutrally.

Culture auditors bring an extra natural advantage of fresh insight because behavioural science practitioners are still, at least for now, few and far between in financial firms. This makes it relatively easy for culture auditors to offer insight that's novel and valuable: reassessing the organization to highlight systemic obstacles and weaknesses in controls; applying a behavioural lens to reveal richer and more accurate data to highlight previously unseen issues; designing behaviour-change interventions that really deliver improvement.

Measurement against standards

Auditing should hold itself to a high ethical standard: a yardstick that describes 'what good looks like'. Standards ensure expectations are clear for both auditors and auditees and they also support reliable, consistent judgement across time, auditor and business area. Conventional audit relies on various reference points: laws, regulations, policies, standard operating procedures and risk appetite statements. Its goal is generally, through testing, to assess compliance with the standards.

Culture auditing also has criteria: sometimes developed specifically (such as behavioural indicator forms), sometimes already existing (such as with similar standards used in conventional audit, but also including new evidence on expected behaviour such as leadership capability frameworks). Culture audit's assessment aims to compare against a pre-agreed behavioural standard and highlight any resulting outcomes.

Ethical

It may seem obvious to note that ethical conduct underpins professional disciplines. All the same, it is worth dwelling on reasons why ethics are particularly important for culture audit methods in practice. As a control function, auditors are in a position of power. Their views will carry some weight simply by virtue of their role as part of the governance framework. Auditors are duty bound not to misuse this power, even inadvertently.

Conventional audit includes maximum terms in leadership positions, regular rotation of staff, internal QA processes and external audits.

Culture auditors occupy a similar ethical context, but with an added dimension of concern: that behavioural science is seen by many general managers as a 'black box' art, offering any unscrupulous culture auditor an opportunity to exploit deference to expertise and information asymmetry. Best practice culture auditing responds with various tools to uphold ethical conduct: standard operating procedures for managing ethical scenarios, standards related to analysis methods, transparency of data, record-keeping, and peer review.

As we've seen, then, conventional and culture auditing principles are similar in their shared mandate and organizational constraints. We'd suggest that this is an excellent foundation for bringing together certain elements of the two internal audit approaches. Despite the common ground, however, there are also fundamental differences. It has taken some time, but there is rising awareness that most conventional auditing techniques are at best an awkward fit, and at worst create additional issues when applied to cultural risk. Let's consider these.

What's missing from conventional auditing when it comes to cultural issues?

A key starting point in conventional auditing is that risks can be controlled through well-designed mechanisms. Tests examine whether controls are adequate, both as to design (*should* the control work) and execution (*did* the control work). Controls that are well designed but fail in practice might be examined further to determine why: did human limitations play a part? Mostly, though, conventional audit focuses on two behavioural dimensions that seem best to explain shortcomings in execution ('what actually happened'):

- Skill – requiring more training or better systems to make compliance easier and better.

- Will – requiring reminders, to make accountability clearer, or to introduce penalties.

Though these approaches cover many aspects of non-compliance, they ignore a wide range of other cultural drivers that therefore remain unexplored and unaddressed. Here are some of these:

Biased risk appetite decisions

Most conventional auditing assumes the risk appetite agreed with the board is the appropriate starting point for evaluating the effectiveness of controls: that is, 'good' controls should ensure risk stays within the pre-determined level. But what if the decision-making that led to that risk appetite is somehow flawed? The Dutch central bank (DNB) has been examining decision-making processes in financial institution leadership teams since the early 2000s, and has identified a range of behavioural patterns that may undermine effectiveness.[2] These include issues related to:

- leadership style (eg automatic deference to a dominant CEO);
- cognitive bias (eg normalization of 'rule-gaming' and other deviant activities); and
- group dynamics (eg conflict avoidance).

Any of these issues could compromise decisions on risk appetite, but they are left unexamined by traditional audit techniques and therefore unaddressed.

Poorly designed controls (from a behavioural perspective)

Those of us who work in behavioural research are constantly surprised by the level of blind optimism that's evident in the design of many controls. Whilst a risk manager and their auditor might think that mandating a 'standard operating procedure' is sufficient to guide everyone's good behaviour, it doesn't take too much imagination to recognize how flimsy such a control really is – especially when context is taken into account.

NOT AFFECTING BEHAVIOUR? SUPERVISORY ATTESTATIONS

A classic example of wishful control design is supervisory attestations in trading businesses. Imagine yourself as a trading desk head and consider the various incentives, both subtle and overt, that you face to sign the daily attestation that your team has complied with all the necessary rules and regulations. And now consider how well you really think that attestation has controlled the actual risk of trader compliance. Did the fact that as a supervisor you signed an attestation really mean you know the trader did nothing inappropriate all day?

At best, such a control provides a named person to hold accountable if things go wrong. At worst, it lulls management and the board into a false sense of security regarding the apparent 'control' of rogue trade risk. Controls such as this are often widely accepted but rarely questioned as traditional measures utilized across the industry over time. Auditors of both kinds need to look harder at 'what actually happens', rather than simply assessing broad risk management outcomes.

A second example of poorly designed 'control' is the rising popularity of 'zero tolerance' conduct risk appetite statements. While some parties argue that the concept is useful as it helps to focus attention on zero tolerance of misbehaviour, we are firmly against this. Risk appetite statements should be tools for controlling actual risk decisions, not theatre for the purpose of managing perceptions with regulators. Yet more often than not, boards and management teams feel compelled to set conduct risk appetite to zero because they believe regulators expect it. In reality, the cost of *genuine* 'zero tolerance' for misconduct risk would make many commercial decisions non-starters, if only because judgement of 'good conduct' rests so heavily on unpredictable and ever-shifting community expectations. As with the attestation example above, conduct risk appetite statements that skirt genuinely difficult tensions between conflicting priorities (revenue maximization vs conduct risk) and simply state (but don't robustly uphold in practice) a zero-tolerance stance are at best pointless, and could give a worrying sense of false security to a range of stakeholders.

Unexpected gaps in well-designed controls

We're often impressed (and appalled) to see how imaginative humans can be if faced with an opportunity to skirt the rules for self-interest. Conventional audit methods approach the assessment of control design logically and systematically, often with the aid of data analytics and statistics. These are of course valuable ways to identify technical gaps based on theoretical control models. But staff who are motivated by performance-based rewards have a powerful incentive to 'game the system'; they can often find ways to circumvent or manipulate controls to their advantage – whether or not they use them.

Sometimes the intent of such behaviour is benign, or rationalized as acceptable when 'the letter of the law' has been followed; staff may even be unaware of the unconscious benefit they are gaining through their non-compliance. What about, for example, the 'victimless' crime of not probing for the right information about a credit application, to ease through the approval of a loan? The financial benefit to the banker may not be significant but the emotional boost from making a customer happy feels rewarding.

Often it's hard for conventional audit to identify gaps in controls when the official process is well known – walkthroughs may show no issues and staff may easily explain away as honest oversights any shortcomings in written controls. To really understand broader cultural factors that create systematic non-compliance we need an approach of thoughtful questioning, to bring to the surface both conscious and unconscious beliefs and mindsets. These techniques are rarely part of the conventional auditor's toolkit.

Judgement-based reporting

Many conventional auditors have been reporting on culture for decades, using their professional judgement as a basis for conclusions. Seasoned internal auditors develop experience and intuition, observing and analysing business activities across different time periods, leaders, and operational contexts. Reasonably enough, they use this intuition to supplement and interpret data, especially on qualitative issues such as culture. Since they are structurally independent, internal auditors' opinions are often perceived as more valid on issues that may be seen as inherently subjective. Indeed, many internal audit departments have report formats dedicated to sharing their opinion. These reports are usually intended to convey early impressions of emerging issues that may not have been formally audited.

However logical and well intentioned, though, such judgement-based (rather than evidence-based) opinions on culture can backfire. First, without robust triangulations to check data against multiple sources, nuanced issues may not be fully understood and it's all too easy for stakeholder discussions to descend into 'he-said-she-said' debates. Second, although professional judgement is a legitimate basis for insight, evidence remains the keystone of audit objectivity – ignoring this principle tends to undermine the function's credibility. Finally, personal judgement can be difficult to frame in a constructive way – let alone action points based on it. Usually judgement is based on surface-level observation rather than deep understanding of underlying mindsets and the organizational environment driving behaviours.

As we'll shortly see in detail, cultural audit findings that are evidence-based and robust carry far more weight than those that rely on one conventional auditor's subjective judgement.

Not the best way to drive improvement

Above all, conventional audit structures simply aren't well suited to driving culture change. For example, one of the most powerful levers internal audit has to enact change is to escalate issues of concern. What needs to change is usually pretty clear – but getting the required focus and investment may not happen until those above apply pressure on management to act.

On matters of culture, the big barrier to improvement often isn't a lack of focus or investment, but a basic lack of understanding about how to drive cultural change. Although escalation may alert senior leaders that there is an issue, that alone won't help the shift much. Second, conventional audit moves slowly, with a time frame geared to meeting legal deadlines rather than to expediting cultural change. Third, the norm of rating risk issues – useful as a way of ranking the materiality of audit issues – can be positively unhelpful when reporting on culture-related problems. This is because culture change always requires some form of personal support and usually behavioural change on the part of the leader – yet a leader who is fearful and defensive of a poor rating won't be in the right frame of mind to accept and prepare to make personal changes. In short, conventional auditing is good at identifying, evaluating and addressing shortcomings in formal mechanisms, but notably poor at achieving the same for cultural issues.

Using behavioural science to audit culture

Now that we've described how conventional auditing struggles with the issue of culture, what is the solution? Behavioural and social scientists have been applying their skills and knowledge to the field of culture auditing since around 2011. While early progress tended to occur in pockets, now, thanks to the international outreach work of bodies such as the Dutch central bank, De Nederlandsche Bank (DNB) and the International Organization of Securities Commissions (IOSCO), there is an increasingly centralized consensus of research and experience identifying the best audit techniques for collecting, analysing and reporting on cultural issues and also which issues might need to be approached with particular care to achieve good outcomes. Let's now look at some of the strengths and pitfalls of various principles and methods commonly applied in culture audit programmes using behavioural science.

Behavioural science principles

Non-judgement

In any science, whether physics or psychology, avoiding bias is a core aim. This concept has vital practical implications for culture auditing. Being deliberately neutral helps interviewers remain curious, open and empathetic towards the views and experiences an interviewee might disclose; it makes the interview more reflective and more honest. It's important to note that the term non-judgement here refers to an attitude towards the interviewee at a personal/human level and does not mean we shouldn't develop an informed opinion of particular behaviours as acceptable or unacceptable within the context of a business's operations.

A good cultural auditor takes care to avoid over-empathizing with the experience of auditees – after data has been collected and the audit moves into its evaluation phase, it is the role of auditors to assess the impact of behavioural norms on effective management of risk, which does require judgement.

Confidentiality

The protocols of conventional auditing don't pay much attention to confidentiality of sources – indeed, staff involved in the process are usually very aware they are 'on the record' with regard to information they provide. However, on sensitive issues, one of the most important conditions for disclosure is psychological safety. If staff feel confident their individual feedback will be kept confidential, it improves the probability they will be open and honest.

Providing an assurance of confidentiality should not be taken lightly, however. In our experience, it can be necessary to make great efforts to protect the committed sources, including setting expectations with stakeholders prior to the audit, explicitly setting out the limitations that might apply to the interviewee (for example, on disclosing any illegal activities), anonymizing quotes used to illustrate theme findings, and removing any personal or business-line identifiers from all forms of interview notes.

Inductive process

Inductive research methods start by observing the phenomenon in question, then examining the environment thoroughly to understand what factors might be reinforcing it, without any predetermined theory of cause (hypothesis). This approach contrasts with deductive approaches that start with a hypothesis and look for evidence to prove or disprove it. Both research methods are used in behavioural science and indeed in culture auditing. However, inductive processes are particularly well suited to the multifaceted, systemic nature of culture and also reflect our relatively early stage in understanding about how culture influences risk management effectiveness – hypothesis-based methods might run the risk of overlooking new but important dimensions.

Data collection methods: what works and what doesn't

Staff perception surveys

Surveys are still one of the most common techniques used in culture audits. They are an efficient way to obtain anonymous feedback from staff, and offer a population measure to supplement sample-based data. Well-constructed surveys can also be used to monitor progress across time and identify areas of relative strength and weakness across an organization.

However, surveys also have significant drawbacks. Most notably, questions need to be carefully designed to avoid skewed response patterns (for example, 'Socially Desirable Responding' where participants answer questions in a way that portray themselves favourably) and staff need to feel confident their responses will really be anonymous. The closed structure of most survey questions (requiring a pre-determined 'yes/no' or percentage agreement response) can also raise more questions than they answer. People are often poor judges of their own emotional states and preferences: as the marketing guru David Ogilvy put it, 'The trouble with [asking people what they prefer] is that people don't think what they feel, they don't say what they think, and they don't do what they say'.[3]

Finally, self-reporting also tends to preclude any probing for less conscious mindsets and beliefs. On the whole, however, surveys can provide a valuable component of a culture audit, as long as they are not the main foundation for it.

Interviewing

The style of interviews we use as behavioural and social scientists differs markedly from conventional auditing. Besides the non-judgemental stance, effective culture audit interviews tend to use a semi-structured design based around a small number of topics rather than a fully prescriptive list of pre-determined questions. The interviewer's aim is usually to facilitate a discussion that explores the interviewee's experience and observations, typically focusing on a particular cultural 'level': behaviours, mindsets or root causes. Various props may be employed to support consistency across interviews, for example behaviour statement cards shown to every interviewee to prompt the discussion. Interviewing is a core skill of most social science practitioners but it can still present challenges.

A proficient interviewer takes care not to ask leading questions (which might simply confirm the interviewer's preconceptions) or show judgement (which can quickly undermine candour). A special skills challenge for the interviewer is the need to establish rapport very quickly and create an environment that aids candid self-reflection and insight. Verbatim notes are critical to ensure that systematic content analysis of the discussion is possible so a dedicated note-taker or audio recording (later transcribed) is usually necessary – again with clear assurances and safeguards on confidentiality. As a key technique for gathering information on culture and its effects on management of risk, interviewing usually requires an experienced, qualified practitioner to achieve the best results.

Behavioural observation

In a general sense, observation is a technique used by all auditors. As the behavioural scientist Dan Ariely reminds us, we should all be 'relentlessly empirical',[4] meaning to deliberately observe the evidence of all our senses and not to rely overly on proxy indicators or second-hand accounts. A classic form of observation used by conventional auditors – and now also used by conduct regulatory inspectors in many jurisdictions – is the 'walk-through' (or 'floor-walk' or 'virtual visit' by Zoom): staff are asked to perform a process or control as they would normally, so that the auditor can assess whether it conforms to expectation or not.

Alternatively, the inspector may simply get up from the formal audit meeting and request to walk the (real or virtual) front-office floor, interviewing members of the customer-facing business units more or less at random and requiring them to express an opinion about engaging with purpose, values, conduct and/or culture issues. Of course, staff are usually hyper-sensitive to an inspector's (physical or virtual) presence and likely to take special care in following appropriate procedures or attempting to give 'model answers'. In the case of culture audit, a pre-rehearsed 'model answer' is highly unlikely to be what the regulator wishes to hear; rather, they are looking for the employee's own opinion and insight as evidence of engagement with a programme for promotion of exemplary conduct.

Observing culture needs a different approach, such as multiple or prolonged observations of business as usual over several hours or days, to decrease observer effects. This helps the observer become less obtrusive. There's an obvious bias-check to be done here: an observer must guard against the tendency to over-weight behaviour they have personally witnessed when developing conclusions. Using a structured checklist to collect data in a standardized format for later analysis helps combat this. There is always the possibility that behaviour will be influenced by the effect of being observed (so-called 'response effects'; in extremes, an effect called 'Goodhart's Law' may occur – that any effort at measurement becomes worthless because so many people are aware of it and 'gaming' it).

Due to these constraints, observation as a culture audit method is mostly limited to collection of data on behaviour – 'what actually happens' – rather than internal mental factors such as mindsets and beliefs. Overall, observational data is an excellent complement to balance against methods that generally rely on self-report and perception.

Data analysis methods

Triangulating to independent data sources

Culture is often regarded as a subjective topic and indeed to some extent it is. Individuals within a particular culture will have their own valid perception of reality and we could simply say that a cultural auditor's task is just to provide a fair representation of these various perspectives. Besides embracing different perspectives, though, culture also reflects and is influenced by 'facts': events that objectively occurred, complaints made, words spoken, processes and systems implemented. So that we can draw robust conclusions on culture, it's useful to cross-validate multiple types and sources of data. It may be possible to misinterpret or dismiss a single person's comment, but a far more compelling basis for a conclusion can be made based on, say, 20 similar interview comments, 80 per cent of survey respondents saying the same thing, lengthy data on 'average days to report error', multiple critical incidents arising from unreported errors, and substantial evidence of an incident reporting tool being underutilized.

On a practical level, social scientists sometimes lean more towards perception-based data as the starting point for conclusions, yet triangulation of data can provide an excellent opportunity for collaboration with conventional auditors, who are often more experienced with quantitative, fact-based data and analysis.

Root cause analysis

Root cause analysis (RCA) is often part of conventional auditors' toolkits. But proceed with care: typically, the goal of traditional RCA is to identify the *single* root cause of a control failure. Thinking about the multi-dimensional nature of culture, RCA within a culture audit *should* aim at identifying as many as possible, if not all, of the interconnected contributing factors. Usually RCA in this context starts with a particular behavioural norm and explores the formal and informal factors that mutually reinforce the norm.

The RCA needs to be based on evidence collected throughout the audit, not just theoretical drivers. A thorough understanding of what's reinforcing a behavioural norm is a critical first step when you're looking to develop effective improvement actions.

Of course, not all drivers will be controllable – history, for example – but you're unlikely to make any real changes without also doing something to mitigate the effect of environmental reinforcers. Cultural RCAs can help give insight into the likely time and effort required to achieve a shift – usually in a more nuanced way than using a simple training or compliance reminder.

Content analysis

Content analysis is a process for transforming qualitative data such as interview transcripts or free text survey comments into qualitative data that can be systematically analysed.

The process usually starts with several analysts independently generating and coding the same sample of text and data according to themes or other insights they might be interested in – for example key mindsets, perceived leadership characteristics or team dynamics. The output from each analyst's independent coding is then compared and discussed, with additional samples also independently coded, building up until there is a high level of alignment in how each analyst is coding similar blocks of text. This step is important to improve the accuracy and consistency of how we interpret source data and identify themes. Once a solid level of inter-rater agreement is achieved, the full set of text data is distributed amongst analysts for complete coding.

Coded data then offers a range of possibilities for assessing how far isolated observations may constitute norms, differences between groups, and teams that might be particular outliers.

Social science offers several commonly used techniques (thematic analysis, discourse analysis, content analysis, morphemic analysis), some of which are relatively easy for generalist auditors to train in, offering a good opportunity for conventional audit teams looking to incorporate some aspects of behavioural science into their programmes.

Reporting methods

'Holding up the mirror' (HUTM) workshops

Whilst varying in length and style from company to company, most conventional audits are reported in a written format, usually after discussion with the auditee. They typically include key information such as the background to the audit, summary of work conducted, any issues identified by the audit, and overall conclusion and audit report rating. By contrast, a HUTM session is becoming a common way of communicating the findings from a culture review, the materials from which are then attached to a short executive summary for escalation to the board.

The goal of such sessions is to 'show, not tell' the auditor's conclusions by illustrating the breadth of evidence on which findings are based. This approach reduces senior management's (sadly common) tendency to dismiss even the most rigorous cultural observations as subjective and potentially biased. It also provides rich information to management about the nature, impact and drivers of culture within their business. Sessions usually follow a similar agenda, including background to the review, methodology used (including sampling), key issues, evidence for the impact, norms and drivers of each issue, and areas to prioritize for improvement.

It takes sensitivity to balance all elements when facilitating these sessions: On the one hand, it may well be necessary to confront reluctant leaders with enough data to ensure they recognize that their view of 'reality' may not be complete (if issues being raised are not already well recognized, that is). On the other hand, it's equally important not to overwhelm leaders to the point where they become defensive and/or feel helpless to achieve improvement.

This kind of reporting reflects a distinctive characteristic of culture audits: improvement is almost impossible without fundamental buy-in from leaders and from other stakeholders, notably front-line staff and middle managers.

Senior managers' mere acceptance of the audit point is not enough; cultural change almost always requires some degree of effortful behavioural change on the part of leaders. That's unlikely to occur unless the leader or leaders truly believe in the need to personally change. HUTM sessions are designed to ensure that culture audit findings have the best chance of improvement once identified.

Unrated reports

The rating of audit issues and overall reports has a long history in conventional auditing. Ratings provide a standardized method for communicating how concerned senior leaders should be about an issue and/or business relative to others across the organization. However, ratings can also cause significant conflict with auditees and often induce elaborate, distracting 'games of compliance'. Higher ratings generally attract significant direct or indirect consequences – hence the 'gaming' – and the ultimate decision is at the auditor's discretion.

Although the argument for persisting with ratings is generally compelling in conventional auditing, several factors create a strong case for avoiding them when it comes to culture audits. First, recall the critical nature of leadership buy-in to achieving genuine cultural change if required. Petty arguments and departmental turf wars about ratings can stall any attempt to improve, with a real risk of disengaging stakeholders before the report is even issued. Second, it is often difficult to judge an appropriate rating for cultural issues and reports until culture auditors have built up enough of a body of evidence to enable true assessment and comparison. Third, there are ways to mitigate the risk of not rating issues and reports. Some institutions with a limited number of culture audits on their plan each year choose to escalate every report to the board. This avoids one key reason for including a rating (to determine how far the report is escalated).

Culture metric dashboards

Especially in the financial sector, regulatory jurisdictions around the world continue to raise the bar on board and executive accountability for culture. With a range of high-profile cultural standards issues rocking corporations in all sectors, many boards are also concerned with the question of how to gain comfort that they won't be the next in line. With boards seeking consistent assurance, a common solution is a dashboard: a key set of metrics that are monitored against risk appetite levels and reported on a regular basis.

Responsibility for culture dashboard reporting can sit in any line of defence, and other chapters in this book examine the issue of culture metrics more generally. In the context of internal audit, perhaps the most important tension to resolve is the framing of a culture dashboard within the broader audit toolkit.

In general, dashboards that attempt to explain culture via a top-down selection of standardized metrics do not align with the inductive, evidence-rich, qualitative methods described above. Individual pre-determined 'proxy' measures can pinpoint where culture may be problematic, but generally struggle to explain why the issues exist, and therefore the difficult and unnecessary steps required to change.

However, as a 'helicopter view' of systemic issues, the culture dashboard can play a very important role in culture audit programme reporting. First, dashboards can be designed to reflect the more objective factors related to inherent cultural risk – pressures on a business that are likely to increase the likelihood of problematic behavioural norms developing, such as multiple changes in leadership, poorly integrated mergers, restructuring of reporting lines, geographical expansion, or high levels of staff turnover. Such reporting is forward-looking and can help management and auditors focus their attention on high-risk areas before issues arise. Second, dashboards can also be used to collate indicators of emerging residual cultural risk – evidence that problematic behavioural norms are emerging. Data on frequency and severity of risk incidents, policy breaches, client complaints, regulatory action and so on, are usually reported in other places but not always with a cultural risk interpretation. As with inherent risk reporting, this kind of dashboard often provides an evidence-based rationale for conducting a dedicated culture audit.

Opportunities for culture audit

Before 2010, anywhere other than in the Netherlands the idea of embedding teams of behavioural scientists into audit functions to assess the culture on risk outcomes would have been seen as strange or at least 'bravely' innovative. Even in the 2020s, institutions that have taken this path remain at the forefront of insight on the issue of culture rather than in the mainstream, sadly. Through ongoing evidence-based audit work, regular reporting and improvement efforts, some pioneering financial businesses have gradually embedded a norm where people feel accountable for creating an environment that manages risk well both consciously and unconsciously.

And yet... we also note that many other organizations continue to struggle not only with how to assess and change culture, but even with defining it and articulating what good looks like. One outcome from this ongoing confusion is continued examples of cultural failure as seen in scandals at leading corporations such as Wells Fargo, Boeing, Volkswagen, and Wirecard. Even as some institutions have made immense progress in auditing and improving cultural risk, at a broader level much more progress remains to be made.

Firms at earlier stages of maturity and seeking to strengthen their culture audit programmes can gain insight and inspiration from the experience of more advanced peers. But what about those firms who are already leading the field and might be wondering how to evolve further? Finally, then, let's look at three opportunities culture auditors might consider in their quest to keep innovating.

Use of continuous monitoring data to highlight cultural risk

The rapid growth in technology, AI and big data techniques offer immense opportunities for culture auditors to expand their toolkits, as explored in Chapter 12. At the same time, the pace of change and frequency of disruptive events – notably the global pandemic, radical climate change and human capital 'vox populi' protests such as #metoo, #blacklivesmatter and #okboomer – have created constantly shifting pressures on behavioural norms and cultural development. The old concept that culture is ingrained, slow moving, an essentially stable phenomenon that only needs measurement every few years, looks increasingly wrong-headed. Instead, boards and management teams need to find new ways to stay up to date, daily, with shifting cultural issues, norms and expectations.

Knitting these two trends together, one idea gaining traction is the use of real-time data gathered in various electronic systems within an organization (for example, email, messaging services, customer chat platforms, incident logging systems). Factors such as frequency, tone and cadence of interactions can be analysed to continually monitor levels of pressure driving cultural change. Over time, this data can then be used to predict where behavioural issues are most likely to emerge and become embedded as cultural problems, allowing early assessment and intervention by culture auditors. The industry handbook *Conduct Risk Management: A behavioural approach*[5] provides a 'behavioural lens' to enable firms to predict when they may be about to face stakeholder accusations of 'unacceptable behaviour', or simply face the need for culture change to meet society's changing expectations.

It is probably safe to suggest that most culture audits currently examine areas where a cultural challenge is known or suspected to exist. One future avenue for culture auditors is to collaborate with data scientists to capture the *leading* nature of culture by predicting outcomes early so that action can be taken to protect organizational value. As the UK FCA noted at the end of 2020:[6] 'Firms are beginning to do the "rear-view mirror" of conduct and culture assessment quite well, but now need to refocus on the way ahead: the (dynamic and predictive) "view through the windscreen forward".'

More active role in challenging leadership culture

One of the most consistent insights from culture auditing is the disconnect that so often exists between senior leadership and frontline perception and reality. For example, senior leaders are often immersed in managing risk in the abstract, at one remove: attending risk committees, reading risk registers and reports, and collaborating with risk colleagues on controls, issues and requirements. This can make them feel risk is significantly embedded into their corporate culture. Yet at the same time, the experience of frontline staff of business risk-taking can be dramatically different – although a salesperson might rarely utter the actual word 'risk' unless it's to complain about having to complete the annual compliance training. Culture audits give senior leaders rich insights into the frontline reality which can be difficult to obtain any other way.

What about, though, the cultural challenges that might exist at the leadership level itself? Since the advent of conduct regulation in the early 2010s a few progressive regulators such as the DNB have focused on identifying cultural norms in board and executive teams that may lead to suboptimal risk and conduct outcomes due to poor decision-making, leadership and team dynamics. Having regulators drive towards universal culture audit introduces a number of challenges, especially at times when trust between business and regulation may be strained, as in the aftermath of the pandemic. Throughout this book, and especially in its conclusion (Chapter 15) we reflect on how Covid-19 has changed regulatory expectations and firms' engagement with the conduct agenda.

Despite the challenges, an internally driven, self-directed process has many benefits in terms of possible openness to findings. Looking ahead, this seems to be a key opportunity for culture auditors to apply their techniques and experience to the assessment of leadership team culture, to facilitate self-awareness, improve business reflexivity and resilience, and address natural blindspots and group bias effects.

Increased focus on demonstrating improvement

As behavioural scientists, culture auditors tend to have a strong interest in measurement and assessment. In 2021, the idea that culture can be systematically and robustly evaluated is – almost – a given truth. Not so long ago, it was generally accepted that culture was essentially a subjective issue on which auditors might comment more credibly due to their independence, but certainly not with any scientific rigour. This shift may have only been possible due to the surprisingly aligned methodologies developed and implemented to assess risk culture by a determined group of regulators and enlightened financial institutions. The consistency in principles, techniques and messaging (much of it independently developed) has in our view helped to clarify industry expectations and best practice. We are delighted to be involved in such cross-industry promotion and knowledge sharing.

We should be careful that, amid all the focus on measurement and assessment, we don't neglect to think about how best to facilitate change. In conventional auditing, there's generally a range of formal mechanisms to ensure that audit points are acted upon: standard deadlines for action points, assessments of how effectively an implemented action has worked, approval processes for closing the issue.

Helpfully, many culture auditors are already well placed to take on this future challenge, with strong skills in supporting cultural change as well as assessment. As culture analysts we should be cheering on the best initiatives in action plan design but also pointing to where best to intervene to make lasting improvements. Although as culture auditors we've collectively made great progress with test designs, the fact that we continue to see cultural failure suggests it might be time to shift our focus from identifying and escalating culture issues, to making sure that they really are fixed. In the following chapters you'll find plenty of suggestions for how to go about this!

Notes

1 Global Institute of Internal Audit (GIIA)

2 Dutch central bank (DNB) (2015) Supervision of Behaviour and Culture, https://www.dnb.nl/media/1gmkp1vk/supervision-of-behaviour-and-culture_tcm46-380398-1.pdf (archived at https://perma.cc/5DYR-8KRR)

3 As reported by Rory Sutherland (2019) in *Alchemy*, WH Allen, p 43

4 Ariely, D (2009) *Predictably Irrational*, Harper

5 Miles R (2017) *Conduct Risk Management: Using a behavioural approach to protect your board and financial services business*, Kogan Page, koganpage.com/product/conduct-risk-management-9780749478612 (archived at https://perma.cc/AU3A-854H)

6 FCA (2020) 'Messages from the Engine Room': 5 Conduct Questions. Industry Feedback for 2019/20 Wholesale Banking Supervision, fca.org.uk/publication/market-studies/5-conduct-questions-industry-feedback-2019–20.pdf (archived at https://perma.cc/AV25-U43F)

09

The new management reporting information (MI) for culture Part 1

Getting past the old MI

ELIZABETH ARZADON AND ROGER MILES

Introduction

The concept of corporate culture emerged during the 1950s as analysts sought to describe the differences in group norms displayed by factory workers. As management theory evolved, consulting firms developed models to explain how certain cultural characteristics seemed to help some firms perform better than others. Not only was culture a factor in performance, some said it was the secret sauce; famously that 'Culture eats strategy for breakfast'.[1]

By the 1990s, businesses began to seize on the notion that culture could be reframed as a source of competitive advantage. Instead of simply observing culture, the idea grew that business leaders should manipulate and control this intangible asset. Leaders no longer had to accept a 'given' culture; they could deliberately create a culture that delivered better results. However, before you could manage it, you had to measure it. Welcome to the era of organizational culture surveys.

THEMES AND CONCEPTS IN THIS CHAPTER

benchmarking – big data potential – 'culture of misconduct' – cross-functional collaboration – culture as threat vs. culture as opportunity – culture MI (management information), old and new – culture surveys – data vs. narrative research – employee surveys, limitations of – 'gig economy' effects – 'Glassdoor effect' – HR-led culture initiatives – identifying what's 'acceptable and expected' behaviour – intrusive regulation – over-reacting vs. under-reacting – psychological contract – public critiques ('normal people', 'demand to know') – real-time dynamic observation vs. historic data collection – reputation as a currency – reputational impacts – sentiment surveys vs. observing behaviour – situational awareness – six systemic drivers of culture failure – 'tail vs. average' viewpoint

Culture as a threat to business value: 'systemic' drivers of culture failure?

It is mainly since the 2008 global financial crisis (GFC) that leaders and stakeholders have started to focus on culture as a possible *threat* to corporate value. In the early 2000s, scandals such as Lehman Brothers, Arthur Anderson and Enron were broadly viewed as case studies in cultural disaster, but their criminal status positioned them as outliers – the 'bad apples' of the corporate world. Since the GFC, bank (and other financial sector) culture has become more and more synonymous with poor conduct, a perception fed by a continuing series of scandals. Far from viewing culture as a key tool for unlocking value, 'a culture of misconduct' is more often discussed in relation to risk and regulatory requirements. Almost every major bank has been implicated in some form of systemic misconduct in the decade following the GFC, ranging from entrenched mis-selling to market manipulation to soft-pedalling on strategies to address anti-money laundering.

On one hand, the sheer continuing number and scale of such incidents has desensitized citizens' view of the banks: 'they're all as bad as each other', say many people. On the other, as the challenges appear to be systemic, regulators have increased the intensity of focus, oversight and supervision. Nobody (except possibly their legal teams) now believes the provider firms' usual defensive argument, that each one of the many incidents was only the fault of an individual bad apple who subverted an otherwise pure environment. Rather, the litany of misconduct events has added weight to the view that, culturally, institutions have broken down because they are operating in a corrosive system. Could it be that institutions (and the executives in charge of them) are *disincentivized* from investing in a culture that would drive good conduct? It's a challenging theory, unsatisfying to many because it implies that we may deflect blame onto a system, rather than identified individuals. However, it is also worth considering that by acknowledging the power of systemic drivers in past failures, we gain some insight into their continuing influence in the present and – if unchecked – the future. Here are the six main systemic drivers of culture failure in financial services:

Corporate longevity: The financial sector retains many 'veteran' brands. Employees in a long-lived megabrand acquire a distorted perception of what is significant in the wider world outside; they may come to believe that 'regulation doesn't matter' since their brand survives regardless.

Depth of resources: As with longevity, megabrands have deep pockets; a firm whose global capital and cash outgun any local sovereign government that's trying to regulate it, may get arrogant.

These two are pungent ingredients in a recipe for *regulatory capture*, where firms outmanoeuvre control agencies.[2] The others are:

Abstraction: Financial products mostly take the transactional form of electronic pulses. They're abstract; we can't see or touch them. People become more uneasy around products that are complex, physically remote, virtual, subcontracted, or secondary-traded (derivative) – like many financial contracts. On the plus side, the virtuality of a contactless card transaction feels painless (even as it may increase your overdraft). On a darker note, regulators may be less likely to act against a wholesale derivative trader, as it's 'too obscure' to gather all-important public support. The governance of obscure banking activities may not have felt as if it mattered to the senior managers responsible, but as regulatory and stakeholder challenges have shown – notably Australia's Royal Commission – this was not a sound assumption.

Absence of concerted challenge: Despite continuing scandals, compared with other sectors financial services for a long time escaped concerted challenge from external critics. It still faces weaker commercial competition than, say, tech manufacturing or car making. Except in Australia, it has deflected protest from consumers, and political-regulatory interventions (see Chapter 11). To effect change, protestors need to pick on a social harm that's plainly defined and easy to see. There's little political capital in attacking products that ordinary citizens can't understand – or could it be a strategy of consciously making products incomprehensible? The post-2008 landscape of complex credit derivative failures presented few easy-to-find targets for citizen protest.

Not territory-dependent: Unlike traditional retail, its virtual nature often means that a financial service business doesn't need to be located anywhere in particular. This may breed a culture in the firm that 'because we don't need to be here in this country, we don't need to worry about its laws'. Not being dependent on any one country for infrastructure, financial firms' senior management shop around – typically for the cheapest labour and the lightest supervision: so-called 'regulatory arbitrage' or 'jurisdiction-hopping'. Hence also the 'offshore' financial service economy happily markets itself as a place to bring 'complex financial deals which might not otherwise happen onshore'.[3] It's a short step from rationalizing jurisdiction hopping as 'good for cost control', to a wider culture of being ethically flexible. Why worry about rules in any one jurisdiction, if other easily moved-to jurisdictions offer greater flexibility? A determinedly 'flexible' firm sets up shop only in territories that offer the most favourable version of the law. In one of the authors' research, there is a startling eyewitness account of a global financial firm's board meeting at which a senior leader directly threatened a Cabinet minister in the host country government, threatening to 'offshore' thousands of (tax-paying) workers.[4] It may be that post-Covid-19 we'll see radical rethinking on the acceptability of such behaviour.

Granular regulation: The more the detail, the more the loopholes; so-called 'granular regulation' offers the aggressive rule-gamer more opportunities for gaming the 'spaces in between the rules'. There's a deeper structural factor here too. These authors' research notes a universal weakness of regulation; regulators generally can't acquire the same resources of information or intellect that financial firms do. Regulators must usually co-opt regulatees' resources to acquire the information that creates opportunities to prosecute misconduct. There is plentiful evidence that this is ineffective[5] – succeeding only in creating a mountain of reporting information that the regulators' staff will never have time to read or analyse. In other chapters we explore the oxymoron that is 'self-regulation'; unsurprisingly, regulatees are rarely in a hurry to incriminate themselves by self-reporting any problems.

These six structural factors have continued to influence many financial institutions, delaying cultural progress. Studies of recurrent abuses note that behaviour-based regulation hasn't yet attacked the root problems identified above.[6] Against this background, it's all the more important to make cultural change an achievable goal, as public perceptions and greater access to information lead to questioning of these historic structural factors as never before. Cultural change is not only possible, but an imperative.

During this transition period and beyond, data will be the transformative factor. Where past systemic factors *prevented* scrutiny, new systemic factors now do the opposite. They will compel 'cultural MI' in new forms, more thorough and robust, encompassing the 'who', 'what', 'how' and 'why' of behaviour and culture.

Ignorance is not an option

Before examining why a higher standard of data on culture is so necessary, let's look for a moment at why a *lack* of data on culture has become so problematic. The answer lies in a simple culture change that has already happened in many contexts: the single biggest issue driving change in the financial sector is that ignorance of cultural issues has become unacceptable. Although, legally, there may still be some recourse for senior leaders to plead ignorance, the court of public opinion is not so forgiving. Not to mention the world of group action civil suits close on their heels. Various factors within the system are reinforcing the expectation, however unrealistic it may be, that senior leaders should know about cultural issues and should resolve them *before* they become dirty laundry. Let's explore some of the factors that have created this situation.

Demand for immediate public knowledge

It seems reasonable to expect that organizational insiders should know about issues – such as errors, 'near misses', customer complaints, litigation and industrial issues – before outsiders do. Indeed, such information is traditionally considered sensitive and confidential and is carefully managed internally, let alone externally – unless/until it becomes (perhaps inadvertently) public. The argument for maintaining discretion around such events is reasonable enough: without the context of an issue being publicly known, facts may be interpreted in ways that are inaccurate and unnecessarily damaging. Hence, events and data that may be considered 'early warning signs' of cultural risk are often communicated among insiders carefully, couched among information designed to help make judgements about materiality, representativeness, and root causes. Such framing takes time.

In parallel with this traditional *formal* approach to managing sensitive information, the pace of *informal* information sharing is now hectic and insatiable. Social phenomena such as 'FOMO' (fear of missing out), increasing distrust (especially of public institutions) and ready accessibility of information are just a few of the reasons for society's incredible appetite for information.[7] Despite being awash with information, much of it remains hidden in plain sight – humans still have a finite capacity for absorbing new data. However, in among the cat memes, political cartoons, TikTok dance routines and holiday Instagram shots, it is still the information people would prefer to 'keep quiet' – scandalous conduct, gross human error, major oversights – that is most likely to rise to the top. There is power, and social kudos, in sharing stories of shocking customer service, leakage of personal data, or underpayment of staff. And these stories are valued even more if the information can be shared *before* those responsible have had a chance to frame the story in a palatable way. Perhaps this is because there is an unconscious recognition that the faster such information is shared the less opportunity there will be to do so. When such events do enter the public domain, leaders find themselves caught between an ethical rock and a capability hard place. That is, if they *did* know about them, why didn't they say anything to a public who has the right to know? And if they *didn't* know, why didn't they? In short, the speed of information sharing has upped the ante when it comes to data on cultural risk.

Increasingly intrusive regulators

Once upon a time (before the 2008 GFC), financial system regulation attracted little public attention. Regulator strategies often erred on the side of gentle influence – a long-term approach, based on trust and respect, aimed at encouraging good behaviour and outcomes. Seasoned leaders of all persuasions generally recognized the limitations of authoritarian micromanagement.

Post-GFC and post-Covid-19, however, the 'gentle influence' approach has been pushed aside in favour of strategies prescribing intense oversight and enforcement. Incident after incident within the financial sector had called into question the effectiveness of gentle influence. A series of inquiries and reviews have suggested that supervisory bodies need to bring to bear far greater scrutiny, pressure and sense of consequence to the entities they oversee. Around the world, agencies have been given the tools to apply enormous penalties, in the hope that if 'name and shame' doesn't achieve change then fear of financial consequences will. Where once the person on the street would not have known the difference between the main financial regulators (say, conduct [FCA] versus prudential [PRA] authorities), in the 2020s public opinions of both agencies are debated confidently in letters to the editor of the *London Evening Standard*. It is perhaps understandable, given how the behaviour of so many institutions has let down so many people – often including the most vulnerable – that frustration and anger have brought about a punitive mindset.

Regulatory bodies have responded to this shift in expectations with varying levels of vigour, but it's fair to say that, overall, there has been a significant upwards shift in regulatory scrutiny – and not only in traditional areas of regulatory interest such as compliance and capital adequacy. Issues once considered management tools for achieving required outcomes – accountability, governance and culture – have moved into the regulatory spotlight.

While many regulators do not directly examine culture, there are some around the world that have been doing so for more than a generation already; notably the Dutch, who have a strong tradition of combining behavioural research with political science when developing statute laws. Other jurisdictions have announced an intention, or have already started, to conduct culture-related examinations of individual entities and/or entire industries, notably in Ireland, Australia, Hong Kong, Singapore and Canada. In these jurisdictions, regulators are not simply asking boards or CEOs what they're doing to better manage culture; they are stepping in to form their own evaluations. This involves using behavioural and organizational experts to directly interview, survey and observe staff right down to the frontline, triangulating data with internal reporting, seeking feedback from other stakeholders (such as customers, partners and investors), and utilizing a range of other qualitative and quantitative techniques.

Especially for financial firms active in places where such examinations are already occurring, there is a real possibility that local conduct regulators may unearth insights that even the firms' own leaders were unaware of. This is a situation no board or executive team wants to find itself in – particularly considering that, in some jurisdictions, prudential and/or corporate governance guidelines *require* directors to have a clear view of the culture of their entity and to take action to address any shortcomings. The desire to avoid unpleasant surprises, especially those delivered by a regulator, has created a far greater impetus for internal culture reporting: forewarned is forearmed.

Implications of the gig economy

Once upon a time, employees sought a job for life; now, people may typically have 12 employers over their lifetime.[8] Changing employers every three to five years isn't exactly 'gig economy' territory, but the trend away from permanent employment is definitely growing – especially among the young (millennials and 'Generation Z'). In a 2017 study in the UK, 4.4 per cent of the population reported being engaged in the gig economy (56 per cent of them aged between 18 and 35).[9] Within two years, the number of gig economy workers had more than doubled, to 9.6 per cent.[10]

Whether it is the 12 employers for the average employee or innumerable employers for the gig worker, the 'job for life' concept is long dead. One big implication of this shift for culture reporting is the eroding of the traditional psychological contract between employers and staff. Denise Rousseau first coined the term 'psychological contract' in 1989 to describe the tacit agreement that exists between employers and employees: mutual obligations, beliefs and perceptions about the work relationship, generally representing some degree of loyalty.[11] When a psychological contract is positive and strong, employees tend to display more alignment to, investment in and commitment to their employer and its goals. It is not simply transactional. Based on characteristics such as trust, empathy, fairness and respect, a psychological contract requires time to develop and/or an expectation of an ongoing relationship.

So, what happens when employees have no intention of an ongoing relationship with an employer, or indeed when the relationship as a short-term contractor is explicitly transactional? For one thing, employers should perhaps not assume that their staff will stay silent about the less pleasant aspects of their working life! Enter, at this point, Glassdoor (see box).

THE GLASSDOOR EFFECT

Since 2008, the Glassdoor website has allowed employees to rate and review their current or previous workplace. It now hosts reviews of over a million employer organizations. Reviews are anonymous, offering the opportunity to be brutally honest. As with any social media platform, one should make some allowances for 'fat tails' in the distribution of reviews; the very disgruntled and the very happy will tend to express themselves most forcibly. But although fewer than 5 per cent of current employees rate themselves 'Very Dissatisfied' or 'Extremely Dissatisfied' with their employers, thanks to the way that our risk perception works it's not the proportions of the responses that hold one's attention so much as the qualitative comments of the dissatisfied. Numbers are huge: a large employer can have thousands of reviews. The existence and sheer volume of the published data attracts an audience: 50 million unique visitors every month. A firm described there as a 'bloodsucking company, long work hours, minimum pay' or with 'highly unethical behaviour... HR is a spectator' isn't exactly getting great references as a prospective employer. While unhappy staff have always existed, it is only now that they have this global platform for airing grievances. In a world of increasing transparency and decreasing employee loyalty, firms may find themselves the last to know about brewing cultural issues. Moral: don't rely too heavily on internal reporting.

Reputation is the new black

Why might these websites be a problem? And how valid are the views expressed on them?

Although it's tempting to dismiss social media criticisms as just a small, unrepresentative number of people venting grievances, that's too easy an assumption. Yet it's also fair for boards and executives to feel concerned, or possibly perplexed, about how much weight should be given to social media channels as a source of information about behavioural norms and risks within their business, particularly where the opinions expressed clash with the carefully explained, informative version provided by the management team. The overall impression of unhappy stakeholders seems skewed, since disgruntled staff and customers are more likely to air their story than happy ones, aren't they...?

Yet that inherent skew, and validity, don't really matter to the viewer. Ratings platforms such as Glassdoor – along with DidTheyHelp.com, Violation Tracker and other new arrivals – do offer 'unvarnished' insights. Business leaders shouldn't disregard such data, as reputation is all; with profound implications, as Oxford University reputation analyst Professor Rachel Botsman says: 'Reputation is becoming a currency that will be more powerful than our credit histories in the 21st century'.[12]

Public trust in institutions is critically low. Edelman's 2020 Trust Barometer report showed that only 38 per cent of respondents believe business institutions are 'honest and fair', while the same percentage believe they are 'corrupt and biased'.[13] Only 47 per cent rate CEOs as very/extremely credible, as against 61 per cent of people rating 'a person like yourself' as very/extremely credible (see box).

'NORMAL PEOPLE'

By 'a person like yourself', culture surveyors mean what behavioural scientists somewhat condescendingly refer to as 'a normal person'[14] – as in, someone without any professional vested interest.

Reputational impacts on recruitment and other stakeholder interest

More and more, 'normal people' see institutions as having a moral obligation to treat all of their stakeholders, including employees, fairly. Employees' negative Glassdoor reviews imply an untrustworthy employer. Prospective employees also take this view into account, which, together with the more generalized public suspicion of financial providers, is now creating a bigger problem for the industry: a potential crisis of quality in recruitment. Younger job applicants now rank job satisfaction priorities differently. Where previously 'money motivation' (salary package) ranked highest, now there's a more balanced set of concerns including ethical conduct, diversity, and reputation.[15] The financial sector can no longer count on getting first pick of the brightest and best candidates. Will it respond by giving a better ethical account of itself?

Customers and investors also look beyond transactional metrics to shape their decisions about which institutions they want to buy and invest in. In an environment where many people already view corporate reporting with scepticism, it is not hard to see how apparently objective and unmediated alternative social sources of opinion such as Glassdoor may be given greater weight. The elephant in the room is that a disgruntled current or ex-employee is far from unbiased and may self-interestedly seek to misrepresent the organization. However, most of the time this factor tends to be weighed more lightly than a more salient and prevalent distrust in corporate messaging.

If most outsiders are suspicious of management's reporting on ethics and culture, perhaps it's because internal culture reporting is undervalued. Senior leaders might save themselves a lot of effort on complex culture data collection by first looking to the same ratings as the general public does. Of course, managers are accountable for change, in a way that external stakeholders are not. Customer and employee ratings do tell part of the story, but they don't tell the whole story. External stakeholders such as regulators and potential investors don't necessarily need to understand the drivers of culture – though they'll quickly and intuitively decide whether a firm's actions meet their personal definition of 'acceptable and expected behaviour'.

To effectively shape and influence culture, meanwhile, managers need deeper insight into its real drivers and behavioural norms. Valid, evidence-based analysis and reporting is key. Externally observable outcome indicators are important, to keep senior leaders attuned to outside stakeholders' expectations. But it's hard information on root causes that will enable them to respond swiftly to issues and to navigate any potential regulatory and public backlash. With this in mind, let's look at a range of current attempts to gather such information.

Current MI on culture

We've just seen that *ignorance* about cultural issues is no longer an option. If senior leaders fail to proactively inform themselves of behavioural risks within their business, as seen through the eyes of external stakeholders, they will find out soon enough – whether by customer, employee or regulatory feedback. Moreover, failing to stay ahead of emerging cultural challenges exposes leaders not only to accusations of inauthenticity and denial but also robs them of the insight needed to respond effectively.

Of course, many leaders would argue they are far from ignorant of the state of culture within their organizations. They point to a range of internal reporting mechanisms they rely on to track their performance in this domain. In theory, organizations with formal culture reporting mechanisms are ahead of the curve – though, as noted above, not all organizations have these.

Internal MI on culture is imperative for the deep insight needed to predict and inform change. But just because information exists does not mean it's effective. Such 'found MI' may either be answering the wrong questions or asking the right questions but not managing to get meaningful responses.

What, then, are the most common forms of reporting on culture (when they exist) and how well do they meet the challenges highlighted above? The following metrics and techniques are common in the current world of culture MI.

Updates on HR-led culture initiatives

In many organizations, the human resources function 'owns' culture. Hence reporting often takes the form of updates to the board on investment in culture-related activities led by this function, such as employee engagement, diversity and well-being. More mature organizations might also set targets for, monitor and report progress against outcomes from these initiatives (Employee Promoter Scores, adapted from the Net Promoter Score concept commonly used to measure customer satisfaction), percentage of minority groups in leadership roles, absenteeism and the like.

Definitions, not actions

Some organizations fall into a rut of trying to define the terminology and models of culture and its relationship to other management dimensions. In a quest to gain clarity around the apparently 'fuzzy' topic of culture, reporting can centre for years on seeking executive and board approval for the perfect way of describing culture within their organization, without taking any real action. More mature organizations may progress to aligning views on a target culture.

Averages, not outliers

Reporting the 'average' is a common method for describing quantitative data. In the realm of culture, reporting sometimes gathers together various quantitative metrics with some relationship to behavioural norms, such as employee survey results, customer feedback ratings or complaint resolution timeframes. Reporting averages on these culture-related issues may have some logical foundation. For example, behavioural 'norms' are often considered a manifestation of culture, and hence the 'average' behaviour may also be considered a good representation of culture. However, averages can be deceptively reassuring, smoothing over outliers and hotspots that should potentially get more attention, or at least examination.

Benchmarks

Many metrics – such as change over time, differences between groups, or evaluations against a target – are difficult to interpret without a source of objective comparison. When it comes to culture, benchmarking against other organizations is common, especially for surveys of staff engagement and, in some jurisdictions, risk culture. Results are generally reported in relation to quartiles or percentiles. Benchmarks can offer a helpful yardstick when determining how challenging certain issues may be (such as embedding psychological safety). However, when it comes to culture and conduct in many parts of the financial services sector, being ahead of a benchmark is not necessarily evidence of outstanding performance.

Opinions

Less common, but still lingering in some organizations, is the idea that culture is purely subjective. Some boards and executive teams therefore seek reporting on culture in the form of qualitative opinions from a part of the organization considered to be more independent than others such as internal audit. This style of management information tends to draw upon observations and information gathered as part of the function's usual role, as well as the professional judgement of the auditors, to highlight areas that are concerning, improving or notably strong.

Employee surveys

With a long history of perceived 'subjectivity', culture MI often relies heavily on perception-based data, particularly employee surveys. Strictly speaking, the term 'climate' refers to perceptions of norms within an organization, while 'culture' is a broader concept encompassing both fact-based and perception-based data. Significantly, although perception often shapes behaviour, it is not always grounded in reality; how staff say they feel (sentiment survey) isn't the same as 'what actually happens' (observed behaviour). Understanding whether, for example, 'consequence-free non-compliance' is fact or just perception can help determine appropriate action. Unvalidated, perception-based reporting on culture can miss key context related to factual outcomes, formal mechanisms and historical events.

Frequency of reporting

Culture takes time to change. This may be why reporting tends to occur annually or semi-annually – that is, more frequent reporting is unlikely to demonstrate significant change (uncomfortably for leaders in organizations undergoing transformation programmes, where reporting needs to demonstrate progress). Moreover, the time taken to collect and analyse data often limits the frequency of reporting. There are several side effects of this cadence in reporting. First, survey and other data may have been gathered some months prior to reporting, offering a ready explanation for unfavourable results (e.g. 'They don't take into account progress we made since implementing X initiative'). Second, while culture may not change overnight, behaviours and their stressors can. Delayed reporting can miss significant signs of emerging issues and risks.

A new approach to culture MI

You may have noticed an 'action gap' between our opening discussion ('ignorance is not an option', in the eyes of society) and the later observation that firms' typical approaches to culture MI aren't (yet, generally) very effective. We'd suggest that, in a world where leaders are expected to demonstrate deep, real-time insight and curiosity about the views and behaviours of staff at all levels of their organization, culture reporting is arguably still in the adolescent stage. There are various inherent challenges to resolve before it can be considered mature.

Key among these challenges is for culture reporting to 'grow up'. During its quest for maturity, much culture reporting has borrowed its formats and goals from more traditional forms of reporting. Static point-in-time data, simplified for dashboard optics and designed to reinforce perceptions of management competence, is one common example. The result is an approach that does not meet the genuine demands of the current reality. As the FCA remarked to us, firms are still using the metrics of 'the rear-view mirror, rather than looking through the windscreen at the road ahead'.[16] Management and boards need reporting a mindset that looks beyond tracking of past events, towards present, dynamic situational awareness (see box).

Situational awareness is a human perceptive skill of intuitively 'seeing' the range of likely threats in a given setting (business or public). It can be trained to a higher level, exercising one's dynamic sensing – practice at locating a significant source of risk from among a mass of assorted incoming information or signals. The skill is common in some professions (test pilots, renal surgeons, the most successful entrepreneurs, submarine commanders) but, we observe, less so in financial boardrooms, whatever directors may claim.

Table 9.1 summarizes what this new mindset might be.

This shift in reporting mindset has big implications and represents not only a new attitude towards reporting but also towards management culture itself. To survive in the new world, this transition seems less like a choice than a necessary adaptation required to align internal and external realities. Below, we suggest a number of alternative reporting mechanisms.

Focus on actual behaviour

The new approach to culture MI puts examples of actual behaviour front and centre. While frameworks and models are useful tools for developing structure and common language around the topic of culture, they aren't the main game in a world where currency and reflexivity (responsiveness) are key. Instead, reporting should make for transparent discussion of actual behaviour in every part of the organization. A focus on actual behaviour is usually assisted by a bottom-up (inductive) method for collecting evidence, rather than a top-down (hypothesis-driven) approach. This is because top-down methods inherently seek to confirm how well 'reality' is meeting expectations and will often err towards confirmation bias, as well as overlooking issues outside the scope of the framework. Although hypothesis-driven methods can seem more efficient, inductive methods simply require a process to sample, collect and organize behavioural examples. There's a range of technological tools emerging that can dramatically reduce the time and effort required for this process (see Chapter 12 for examples).

TABLE 9.1   Culture reporting mindset

From	To
Control	Insight
Management driven	Board driven
Static	Dynamic
Manage the message	Radical transparency
Reactive	Proactive
Single narrative	Multiple realities
Report confidence in current state	Report risks to current state
Judgement	Observations
Seeking approval	Seeking input
Deterministic	Probabilistic

Deep-dive information on behavioural drivers

The new approach to culture MI simultaneously explains symptoms *and* their drivers. Information about actual, observed behaviour is the first step in culture reporting – you can't fix something if you don't know about it. Once you know about it, it's also critical to understand *why* it's occurring in order to respond effectively. Organizations no longer have the luxury of lengthy programmes to sequentially identify, evaluate, analyse, implement and monitor cultural remediation improvement plans, with reporting in between each step. Stakeholders expect root cause insight and action on a far faster turnaround than traditional transformation processes allow. Essentially, as soon as behaviours emerge, leaders are expected to understand why they are occurring and how they will adjust to drive different outcomes. Hard to achieve from the starting point of traditional cultural change programmes, this is far more achievable if systems are set up for continuous monitoring, rather than ad hoc data collection and reporting on the formal and informal drivers of behaviour. To succeed in it, organizations need to spend time and money establishing internal resources that will take responsibility for these tasks, not outsourcing them periodically to consultants, or adding them at the periphery of risk managers' existing responsibilities.

Information on the tail and the average

The new approach to culture MI doesn't just focus on average behaviour but also highlights outliers. Although culture itself is generally reflected in behavioural norms (or averages), norms don't appear overnight. They usually start in isolated pockets, then gather momentum and grow into typical behaviour of larger groups due to reinforcement and/or lack of intervention. If a major purpose of MI is to empower executives to *proactively* manage culture, then the horse has bolted by the time initial behaviours have developed into norms.

This is why boards are surprised when widespread issues emerge that they previously had no idea about. In reality, widespread issues take time to become that way – they can be better anticipated and acted upon, if we can get earlier and clearer sight of them. Too often incidents are reframed after the event as 'bad apples', when in reality they offer useful evidence of emerging cultural issues, reinforced by systemic factors.

A key challenge for those reporting culture MI is determining how representative these outlier behaviours may be and how 'mainstream' they are becoming, as well as the factors that may be underlying them. Businesses need to adopt robust techniques to evaluate the representativeness of behavioural patterns and the surrounding organizational environment. Executives and boards can then form an evidence-based view of whether such behaviours already constitute a norm that is outside the bounds of 'acceptable behaviour' and/or formal risk appetite, and how to respond if the behaviour is outside these but not yet a norm.

Real-time information

The new approach to culture MI allows for at least some element of real-time data. Certain data on culture, such as staff surveys, interview data and incident analysis, requires time to gather. This data is valuable as it has the robustness of a tried-and-tested method and provides direct insight into the way culture is experienced by staff and other stakeholders. As we've seen, though, the lag time between data collection and reporting can present challenges and limit management's response options. By contrast, new forms of data analysis – including text analysis of electronic communication, relational/social network analysis, and language analysis of audio data (e.g. of customer-staff interactions) – offer the ability to continuously monitor and report trends, emerging issues and impacts of external and internal events in real time. Then again, it would be wise to validate any newer techniques continuously against traditional data sources for some time. Culture dashboards that triangulate real-time and historical data deliver the best of both data types.

Data vs narratives

The new approach to culture MI provides data that provokes questions rather than providing comfort. When leaders are expected to see and respond to emerging issues faster than external stakeholders, not only is transparency crucial but so is constructive challenge: active engagement and curiosity. Those responsible for traditional culture MI typically explain the inclusion of commentary as helping leaders to navigate and interpret data by providing context. In reality, these narratives all too often (if unconsciously) lead the reader towards a pre-determined conclusion. This inhibits leaders from contributing their own perspective and wisdom on the data put before them.

Having said this, offering data alone can be risky. At the very least, to ensure data is used effectively, a few core elements are needed: validity and reliability; careful and balanced selection of metrics that reflect key outcomes; accompanying data on representativeness, and a dynamic of trust and respect between layers of management. Where these factors are present, culture MI offers a window into the reality of an organization at all levels and acts as an excellent tool for comparing and contrasting with other forms of MI.

Potential pitfalls of the new approach

Change is never without risk. Executives raised in a world where skill in 'managing upward perceptions' was the key to career success are likely to feel anxious about 'warts and all' reporting on behaviour within their areas of responsibility. Similarly, boards conditioned to being fed good news stories are likely to respond with alarm when suddenly a larger percentage of what they are told focuses on concerns and risks. New skills will be required on both sides – those generating the culture reports and the leaders receiving them – to realize a more transparent, dynamic, raw approach to culture reporting that is constructive rather than harmful.

We identify here the main pitfalls that organizational leaders should foresee and overcome as they move to embrace this style of reporting.

Not acting

If there is anything more reprehensible to the public and regulators than a leader who couldn't see there were cultural issues within their own organization, it is one who was given information about cultural issues but failed to take action. In several jurisdictions, conduct regulators explicitly expect boards to not only form a view of cultural strengths and weaknesses but also show they've addressed any points of weakness found. Implementing a culture MI programme that gives direct, extensive, real-time data on a range of robust behavioural dimensions increases the opportunity for leaders to gain early insight into nascent behavioural problems. With that insight comes responsibility – a responsibility to examine the data carefully and to ensure that areas of potential concern are fully explored and addressed as necessary.

Over-reacting

Critical feedback from the frontline can feel confrontational, especially if it wasn't shared in the past. How leaders respond is key: focusing on blame, shame and punitive consequences won't help future transparency and may even prompt a 'crackdown' reaction disproportionate to the risk. MI therefore needs to incorporate mechanisms that add context and perspective on factors such as representativeness, reliability and trajectory of change. Even in instances where problems are evident, a constructive response is crucial to maintaining a dynamic of candid openness within the organization. To keep a balance between accountability and psychological safety requires clear alignment of purpose, trust and respect on all sides.

Mischievous reporting

Related, but somewhat different to, the issue of over-reacting is how to manage deliberate misreporting of behavioural issues by staff or other stakeholders. Mischievous/malicious reporting is not necessarily new, and identifying and resolving instances where it has occurred should be relatively straightforward if data is triangulated, validated and followed up appropriately. However, social media, intense regulatory pressure and heightened public and political interest in the conduct of financial sector leaders increase the risk in relation to managing reports that may (or may not) be deliberately misleading. Whereas in the past leaders may have been 'protected' from such reports, new approaches to culture MI should include them – if only as indicators of probable stress and risk. Sensitive, respectful treatment is a minimum requirement, along with steps to manage a complete picture of the reputational risks, not just the legal ones.

Managing anonymity

A fundamental dilemma of research ethics – and internal trust – when seeking feedback on culture is that sometimes illegal and/or unethical behaviour is disclosed by individuals under promise of anonymity. Assurances of anonymity are often necessary to encourage candour but if MI includes examples of criminal misconduct or immoral behaviour, is there an onus on leaders to identify and pursue those responsible? Leaders need to understand the ramifications of whichever strategy they decide to apply, keeping in mind that certain options may have problematic side effects.

Unrealized potential of artificial intelligence and big data

Data scientists already offer a wealth of robust options for identifying, measuring, evaluating and monitoring behaviour and culture within organizations. Some firms have been delivering solutions for many years and continue to develop new methodologies and techniques that offer significant insight. However, the full sector-wide potential of data science solutions has been more difficult to realize than anticipated. Challenges in cleansing data, navigating privacy requirements, managing data security and bridging the communication divide between data users and scientists has scuppered the big data dreams of many culture MI initiatives. This is without even considering that, after decades of anticipation, genuine predictive validity and human-level content analysis is still a work in progress for many data analytics initiatives. Continued investment in this technology is necessary for progress. Organizations need to be aware that, for these technologies to add value, most require considerable investment of time and money, and at present are best positioned as supplements to traditional data sources rather than replacements for them.

Conclusion: the three factors leaders need

We have highlighted how it's essential for financial sector leaders to maintain a crystal-clear line of sight across all facets of behaviour within their institutions. This imperative requires culture MI that is far more transparent, real-time, holistic and unfiltered than traditional reporting mechanisms have been able to offer. It is clear that to make this transition, leaders must shift both mindset and processes, and that these shifts come with some risks. For those willing to head down this path, there are three factors that will see the new approach succeed: curiosity, ownership and collaboration.

Curiosity, not fear

The new approach to culture reporting requires an attitude towards behaviour that delays judgement as long as possible, in order to observe and understand the connection between norms and the system. By creating a psychologically safe environment, with an attitude of constructive curiosity, leaders are more likely to recognize genuine root causes underlying behavioural patterns; not by attributing blame to individuals, who are often simply responding to their environment. Unfortunately, external environments can all too easily push leaders into hasty attribution of fault; these include accountability regimes, public and political pressure, and the natural desire for quick and defensible solutions to reputational risks and incidents. Firms that can navigate these pressures, aspiring to maintain firm-wide curiosity around the topic of behaviour and culture, are far more likely to increase transparency and responsiveness than those that default to fear, control and punishment.

Ownership

It is common wisdom that leaders have a significant impact on culture. When cultural issues emerge, leaders are often expected to 'fall on their sword' in recognition of their accountability for the problem, if not their role in its occurrence. Yet if they are to achieve a transition to a new form of reporting that is courageously transparent, dynamic and responsive, leaders must display ownership of their role in culture, not just accountability for it. They must respond constructively to the arrival of challenging new information, accept feedback on their role in problematic patterns of behaviour, and take responsibility for action to effect changes if necessary. This might seem obvious, but in reality many leaders secretly believe that cultural issues are not really their *personal* fault (while sometimes accepting they might be the fault of their peers). Staff and other stakeholders easily spot such inauthenticity and respond with cynicism and lack of trust; they become disillusioned with the idea of giving transparent feedback. Leaders who can open their minds to the reality that they really *do* play a personal, individual role in the norms that are created, and who visibly display recognition of that role, will be in a much better position to reinforce transparency and change.

Collaboration between functions

Functional turf wars are common in the field of risk culture. For some reason, it is rare to see effective and constructive collaboration among the various functions involved in culture reporting – typically human resources, risk, internal audit, communications, conduct, integrity and governance. The default is often for a single function to own the framework, which inevitably skews the scope of culture reporting towards the primary priorities of that function's remit. Organizations that successfully transition towards a new approach to culture reporting will need to bridge silos and engage in true collective problem-solving to identify data sources, mechanisms and insights that intersect multiple functions. This requires leaders to let go of ego and adopt an orientation that focuses more on external priorities than internal ones. Once achieved, this new approach benefits far more than just the organization's culture MI programme!

Ultimately, leaders of financial firms can no longer ignore the issue of culture or treat it as a 'soft' issue. Customers, regulators, investors and politicians demand rapid insight and responsiveness when issues emerge. Traditional reporting methods are ill-equipped to support leaders effectively, largely because they are designed to control and attenuate harmful narratives around culture rather than open issues up for genuine exploration. Shifting to a new approach of course entails risks but, managed effectively, improves 'clear sight' that both supports better management of risk and builds sustainable business performance.

Notes

1 A phrase originated by Peter Drucker and subsequently made famous by Mark Fields, President at Ford Motor Company, Inc

2 Bloor, D et al (2006) Unicorn among the cedars: on the possibility of effective 'smart regulation' of the globalized shipping industry, *Social and Legal Studies*, December, https://journals.sagepub.com/doi/10.1177/0964663906069546 (archived at https://perma.cc/LK43-WTX4)

3 Platt, S (2015) *Criminal Capital*, Palgrave MacMillan

4 Miles, R (2012) From compliance to coping: experiences of chief risk officers in UK banks 2007–9, Senate House/King's College London

5 Summarized in R Miles (2012), From compliance to coping: experiences of chief risk officers in UK banks 2007–9, Senate House/King's College London

6 Such as G30's Banking conduct and culture: a call for sustained comprehensive reform (2015); G30 Update on Conduct and Culture (2018); Financial Stability Board Misconduct risk progress report (2018).

7 For commentary see for example Edelman Trust Barometer annual series: 2020 edition here: cdn2.hubspot.net/hubfs/440941/Trust%20Barometer%20 2020/2020%20Edelman%20Trust%20Barometer%20Global%20Report. pdf?utm_campaign=Global:%20Trust%20Barometer%202020&utm_source= Website (archived at https://perma.cc/8WBE-F284)

8 US Bureau of Labor (2019): *Number of Jobs, Labor Market Experience, and Earnings Growth: Results from a National Longitudinal Survey* (August 2019), www.bls.gov/news.release/pdf/nlsoy.pdf (archived at https://perma.cc/7XGW-YQZC)

9 UK Department for Business, Energy & Industrial Strategy (2018) *Characteristics of those in the Gig Economy* (February 2018), p 5, https://assets.publishing.service.gov.uk/government/uploads/system/uploads/attachment_data/file/687553/The_characteristics_of_those_in_the_gig_economy.pdf (archived at https://perma.cc/6TDF-Q7RW)

10 University of Hertfordshire (2019) *Platform Work in the UK 2016–19*, www.feps-europe.eu/attachments/publications/platform%20work%20in%20the%20uk%202016-2019%20v3-converted.pdf (archived at https://perma.cc/VFZ9-TKZF)

11 Rousseau, D (1989) Psychological and implied contracts in organizations, *Employee Responsibilities and Rights Journal,* 2 (2). Prof Rousseau identifies a psychological contract based on 'individual beliefs in a reciprocal obligation between the individual and the organization' and probes the 'development and… violation of psychological and implied contracts'

12 Quoted in Waller, D and Younger, R (2017) *The Reputation Game*, Bloomsbury

13 Edelman Trust Barometer (2020), cdn2.hubspot.net/hubfs/440941/Trust%20Barometer%202020/2020%20Edelman%20Trust%20Barometer%20Global%20Report.pdf?utm_campaign=Global:%20Trust%20Barometer%202020&utm_source=Website (archived at https://perma.cc/57A6-CHR5)

14 For example the classic behavioural science paper by Prof Colin Camerer (2003) The behavioral challenge to economics: understanding normal people, Caltech/Federal Reserve Bank of Boston

15 Deloittes (2018) Survey of Millennial Prospective Employees

16 FCA (2020) Private briefing to these authors before release of its engagement review: Five Conduct Questions: Industry Feedback for 2019/20

10

The new reporting Part 2

Developing the framework: from culture
models to better questions and indicators

ROGER MILES

Introduction

In this chapter, starting with the conduct regulator's challenge to firms to frame 'purposeful culture', we will explore some of the most useful models that can help us to conceive purpose and culture, and an elegant 'culture dashboard' concept which usefully gathers these.

There's then a tour of indicators that are useful for culture assessment. This starts by looking at a selection of existing indicators that firms are using, then compares those with the future indicators that regulators have experimented with and which we expect firms to need to use from H2/2021, as regulated culture assessments become routine.

Finally, taking its cue from the Five Conduct Questions that the UK conduct regulator uses to examine firms' response to the culture challenge, this chapter offers sets of plainly phrased practical questions. Unlike the sometimes clunky language of regulators' formulations, these questions are suitable to use right across your firm – especially with business-facing teams who don't always present the most willing face to anything that hints of a compliance request. These 'better questions' will help to engage everyone in a positive 'conduct conversation' that promotes healthy culture and exemplary conduct.

An unanswerable challenge?

In case you'd been concerned that culture is a hard topic to pin down, it may be consoling to know that much of the academic research literature agrees with you. One academic study of 600 evidence-based studies of 'purposeful culture' and ethical behaviour[1] went so far as to describe the cumulative impression of them in colourful terms: 'When it comes to stopping unethical behaviour, the continued investment in elaborate "risk culture frameworks and measures" is like hitting a nail with a cucumber.'[2] Many consulting firms' efforts at culture assessment, expensively paid for by banks and other financial firms, were found to be 'faddish and there is no science behind it… it is decoupled from the real risk factors'.

You might be surprised to hear that this author agrees. The challenge facing firms is how to find meaningful management reporting information (MI) that is reliable and consistent. By the end of this chapter, you'll have plenty of material to make a proper start, free from the 'faddish' and self-serving offers prepared by (for the most part) unqualified would-be advisors.

Far from being unanswerable, this is a challenge we can address simply and rationally. It just requires looking at old sources of information in new ways, asking some intelligent questions about data-gathering assumptions, and not listening to the sometimes deafening noise from vested interests keen to repackage their own conventional audit-based offerings. Bearing that in mind, let's focus on two important starting points.

First, conduct regulators want to see *firms thinking for themselves*, not 'outsourcing' culture initiatives to external firms. By all means buy in measurement tools; several of the best are described in this book. But don't delegate out the task of *embedding* culture engagement and change; that's a piece of prep that can only properly be achieved within your own firm. If a change programme only works for as long as an external advisor is maintaining it by 'holding your hand', it hasn't really worked at all.

Second, *you already have* a lot of the raw material you need. The financial sector has a powerful action bias towards buying in 'shiny boxes' to address its problems, because said boxes look like solutions. Providers of reg tech and other solutions are only too ready to play up to that bias – remember we talked about this in Chapter 4? The biases don't only act inside-to-out, they can work outside-in as firms buy in little more than a lovely-looking promise of a solution to an abstract-looking problem. Working at industry level, this book's authors don't buy into the shiny box assumption; we genuinely want firms to do for themselves what they should be doing.

Accordingly, what follows is our gift to you, at least for the price of the book – a selection of problem-solving frames and practical tools that have proved most consistently helpful in getting firms started on their conduct conversations and culture assessments. Though there are some big ideas, this isn't an advanced course. The point is to get everyone properly and productively started, to make this work your own. That's not only what conduct regulators want; it's what will add the most business value. Let's explore.

Picturing purposeful culture

In this section we will consider how reporting frameworks may be informed both by regulatory 'nudges' and by getting to know (and use) the most influential culture models.

Conduct regulators have issued the 'culture assessment challenge' in a variety of forms since 2016. One of the punchiest – from the FCA's Occasional Paper 24 commentary on 'beliefs, biases and morality'[3] challenges firms to overcome entrenched bad habits of misconduct, which are the product of a combination of biases and simple self-serving greed.

Here's a quick list of those bad habits. For each one, I've first listed what the FCA (and its science advisors) called it, often quoting the science jargon;

then a plain language translation of what they mean in practice – that is, what the regulator wants us to measure and manage.

Biases and bad habits to measure and overcome

'**Misaligned incentives**': this means, in its plainest form, rewarding mis-selling. Do your structures for incentives (pay, bonuses, promotion) give the greatest rewards to the people who simply sell the most stuff? What about customer or client satisfaction, or 'product fit' (how appropriate the product they've bought is, for the situation they're in)?

'**Negative ideologies**': are people's loyalties mostly set by their need to 'belong' in their team, no matter what? Does this lead to misplaced loyalties where, say, a sales team will do whatever the head of sales says, no questions asked? Or in the boardroom, the groupthink that says that the chief executive must be right, just because, well, they're the top dog so they must be right, right?

'**Moral evasion**': when people 'reason away' something dodgy that they've just done. For what it's worth, huge chunks of research on criminology and psychopathy[4] make the point that badly behaved people are quick to find 'reasons' that 'explain' what they do – whether to the courts, the psychiatrist, or indeed a public enquiry into industry misconduct.

'**Selective attention**': only looking at the things that it suits you to look at; clinging to processes and controls that you know don't really work.

'**Lack of challenge**': this isn't an invitation to you to have 'challenging behaviour', as in coming on like an obstreperous child; rather, it's that there's no sign of anyone ever putting a hand up to question anything. How will you address that?

'**Contagious rule-breaking**': where little habits of 'cutting corners' or 'workarounds' over time morph into full-on breaking of the rules. This happens because of the 'social proof' bias – that if 'everybody's doing it, it must be OK'. The regulator's analogy of rule-breaking being like a disease is appropriate, if chilling, given the events of 2020.

'**Overconfidence**': this comes in three kinds: (1) That you know what you're doing (even if actually, you don't). The posh science jargon has various far more colourful names for this, including 'failure of metacognition', 'insufficient intellectual humility', or 'Dunning-Kruger effect' (which you might know better as 'delusion of adequacy'). (2) That you won't get caught for doing the naughty thing that you know you're doing (aka 'detection denial'). (3) That even if you do get caught in mid-naughtiness, any penalty (such as a fine) won't really hurt (see 'Regulatory fines seen as a "friction cost of doing business"', Chapter 3, page 35.)

The shape of culture

How did such bad habits and beliefs become entrenched? Time to pull back the focus and look at some basic principles of how an organization's culture gets set, often unconsciously. What follows – rather like my shamelessly simplistic crash course in elementary neuroscience (Chapter 4, from page 65) – is of necessity a really short pop-science version of a huge stack of proper science. In this case, we're talking about social anthropology and the psychology of group interactions. Again, just to flag that this is presented very plainly, with my apologies to any social anthropologists or behavioural scientists who happen to be reading. The essential point here is just to help you to start getting your head around the concepts, in case this is the first time you've encountered them; or, if you've seen these before, it's to help remind you what matters most in the task of culture assessment.

The unchallenged thought leader on organizational culture is Professor Edgar Schein at MIT Sloan School of Management. (In a straw poll of all the co-authors of this book, this was agreed unanimously.) His influence is so great that you have probably already seen some of what follows, even if you didn't realize where it comes from. We're not going to get beyond 'Organizational Culture 1.01' here, but I can think of several conduct regulators who'd be impressed if you can show that you've read some of Schein's work (see Recommended Reading, page 386).

Like a lot of the best science, Schein pointed out something that we recognize intuitively as soon as we hear it: that if you want to understand the culture of any organization, you need to see both what's there at a surface level, and what's below the surface. Famously (the bit you might already have seen), he proposed an 'iceberg model' for this (Figure 10.1). As with an iceberg, the bit you can see is only a fraction of what's happening. (A real iceberg is 90 per cent underwater. Graphics of this model often represent it as more like a 30/70 divide. You choose, based on what you know about your own firm.)

Above the waterline are what Schein calls **artifacts**: things you can experience directly with your senses – you can see, hear, or touch them, and so on.

FIGURE 10.1   Schein's 'culture iceberg'

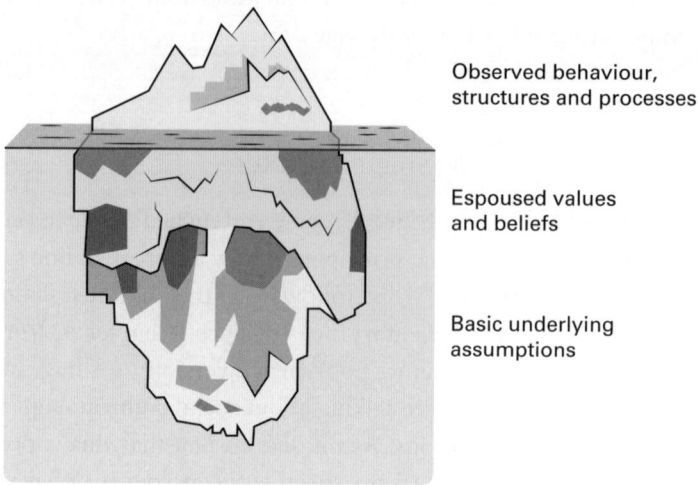

Observed behaviour, structures and processes

Espoused values and beliefs

Basic underlying assumptions

These elements include stuff like your office building, its furniture, and how people dress and speak to each other (including informal conversations and 'banter'). All these and more are recognizable to anyone in the firm; most of them are also readily apparent to anyone who looks in from outside the firm.

At the next level down, just below the waterline, are **espoused values**. These are your firm's stated values and any formal or informal 'rules of behaviour'; the way that people who work here represent the firm to themselves and to others. This includes official 'mission and values' bullets, formal corporate identity visuals and statements, corporate philosophies (on approach to paying out insurance claims, or buying and selling funds under management, for example). As with mission statements, it may be aspirational (such as 'to become our customers' most trusted partner') more than as-found, intending to draw people in a certain direction. Where aspirations run into trouble is of course…

At the second level down, the **shared basic assumptions**. These may differ from the closer-to-the-surface espoused values. Just as every organization has both a 'formal' form (the official line) and an 'informal' form (what actually happens), these deeper tacit assumptions can blow large holes in any attempt at official narrative. The lowest-level, deeper underwater assumptions are mostly tacit (nobody talks about them), and so much part of 'just what we do here' that even people inside the business may not notice or think about them.

How, you might ask, does knowing that affect my relationship with a conduct regulator? Very directly, as it happens.

Using the iceberg and other exercises
to generate 'questions of purpose'

Before moving on to consider how a firm's purpose shapes its culture, we need to pause to look at the purpose itself. There is a *lot* of regulatory speech-making about purpose, such as that 'To understand how a firm's purpose drives its culture, you need to understand how a company describes, to itself and others, the essential purpose of the firm, its products and its services, and so its reason for existing'.[5]

Luckily, the rhetoric all boils down to a few essentials, which we'll see shortly.

First, a few exercises in how to bring a clear head to the task of considering your purpose. Imagine yourself standing on top of a mountain (Figure 10.2), contemplating the world stretched out in front of you, as you ask the eternal question: what are we put on earth to achieve? Now hold that thought during the next two pages.

FIGURE 10.2   Contemplating your wider purpose in the world

Articulating purpose: prototypes and a 'Scrooge Test'

Culture assessors at the FCA cite a 'growing consensus' premise[6] that a firm's purpose – its collective 'why are we here?' – is more than just its conventional scheduling of 'economic function, and how it makes money'. Indeed, we're specifically asked to look beyond the business model.

To get this conversation started, at the UK Finance's Conduct Academy we developed a thought experiment that we called the 'Scrooge Test'. As you might recall, Scrooge is the anti-hero of Charles Dickens' novelette *A Christmas Carol*, who dreamed that he had died and could see people celebrating the event of his death. Here's the experiment. Consider: if your firm collapsed tomorrow, who (besides you and possibly your staff) would mourn its passing? If the answer is 'nobody much', then whose good is the firm serving? So, where is your wider purpose to be found? The regulator recently (Q1/2021) echoed this test, in their version suggesting you ask, 'Why would the world be worse off without the value your firm provides?'[7]

Conduct regulators – and indeed all kinds of stakeholders – are also deeply interested to see how far we can show that any such purpose is 'tangibly driving the decisions made at all levels of the firm'.

Financial regulators' suggested framings for defined purpose

To help financial firms along the way with the task of articulating purpose, several regulators and think-tanks have already helpfully offered various definitions of the purpose of financial services firms. Some highlights of these:

- 'A purpose beyond just making money.'[8]

Yes, that's a rather negative definition to start with. Here are some more positive ones:

- Channelling and guiding the investment and funding with which our economy is built.[9]
- Diversifying risks and providing affordable financial support to those in need by advancing credit.[10]
- Vital infrastructure: facilitating every single economic transaction through the payments system.[11]
- Delivering long-term sustainable benefits for employees, consumers and shareholders.[12]

- Sustainable custodianship and stewardship of assets.[13]
- Supporting markets, and mediating between savers and borrowers.[14]
- Delivering fair value to customers and long-term value for shareholders.[15]

These purposes are almost all high-level expressions of a firm's wider social function: its benefit to the economy as a mediator, employer, transmission system and social enabler. To probe this further, let's delve into two highly influential approaches to exploring people's 'intrinsic motivation' in the workplace and life generally, then look at a prototype culture reporting framework that puts the model views into a context of everyday practice.

'Why are we here?' An intrinsic motivation approach

Focusing now on 'purposeful culture', here are two of the most powerful approaches that reframe the 'Why are we here?' question in a fresh way. With differing approaches, they both go to the heart of *intrinsic vs extrinsic motivation* – that is, how far anyone in the firm is doing anything because they want to do it, or because they're forced to do it.

First, Abraham Maslow's **Hierarchy of Needs**[16] (Figure 10.3).

FIGURE 10.3   A hierarchy of human needs [after Maslow]

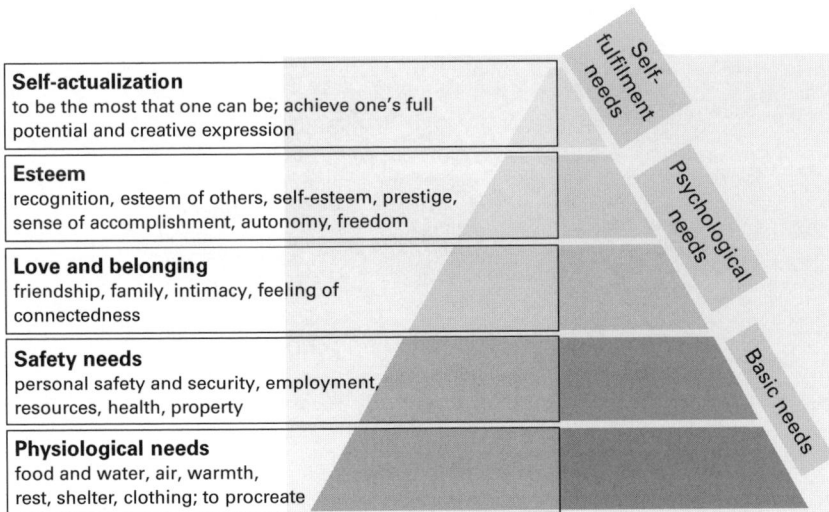

SOURCE Miles, after Maslow's *Theory of Human Motivation*; 'hierarchy of needs'

The psychologist Abraham Maslow argued (in 1943) that people's motives for doing anything they do (their 'enacted behaviour') may be best understood in terms of a 'ladder' or hierarchy of what they need in life. Starting at the bottom, as each need is satisfied, we can aspire to the next step up. The most basic need is immediate survival ('physiological'), followed by staying safe. Once these needs are taken care of, we seek satisfaction of ever-higher social and psychological needs: the need not to feel isolated but part of some kind of tribe or group ('belonging and love'); then to be seen to have accomplished something within the group ('esteem'); finally to become the 'best version of yourself' ('self-actualization').

More recently in Japan (2018), psychologist Michiko Kumano has promoted a mapped approach to a traditional philosophy of life purpose, **ikigai**[17]: 'reason for being'. It seeks to capture an essence of purpose in life, a meaningful direction that informs a sense of one's life being made worthwhile. To realize ikigai, we must consider both the spontaneous and purposeful actions we take towards achieving a sense of satisfaction and, cumulatively, a meaning to life (Figure 10.4). Ikigai is achieved when four intrinsic and extrinsic motivations align.

FIGURE 10.4   Reasons for being (personal or organization)

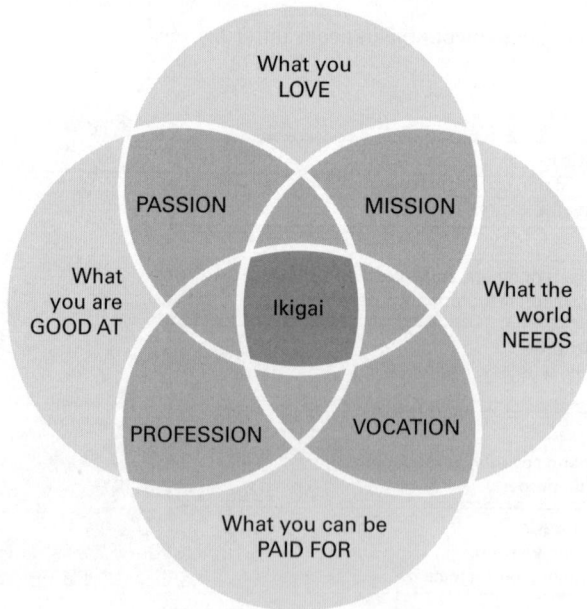

SOURCE Miles, after Kumano[18] and Marlow[19]

FIGURE 10.5   Preliminary sketch for a culture dashboard (1): headline level

Clients	Be client-centric	Individual owner
Our people	Value everyone's skills and diversity; invest in careers to drive performance	Individual owner
Culture (conduct, risk)	Balance risk-taking; be aware of consequences of our actions	Individual owner
Society, Economy	Play a meaningful part in the economy and society as a whole	Individual owner
Firm, Investors	Create sustainable profitability	Individual owner

SOURCE Miles/UK Finance

Finally in this subsection, here's an outline for a **culture assessment approach** that very elegantly combines themes from Maslow, Ikigai and 'stakeholder capitalism'. This is my own, reductive version of an approach to purpose and culture used by a global investment bank, that's been out there, impressively, since before the advent of the Senior Managers Regime (SMR) in 2016. When I first encountered the full version of this approach, it immediately struck me as hitting all the right notes. Figure 10.5 shows the model itself, at headline level (it's expanded later, on pages 240–242).

This handles some important points beautifully. It engages with purpose questions of *intrinsic motivation*: why do people really do what they do? Do people work more happily and productively when they're doing fulfilling work? (Yes!) And what is the order of priorities for a healthy culture? This latter question is where the model scores highly, because the five elements are ranked in a hierarchy – unlike Maslow, this one ranks from top to bottom.

Clients

To be a viable business, a firm first has to win and keep **clients**, by looking after their needs. Not, by the way, to do absolutely anything a client asks – some clients might ask for inappropriate favours, for example – but for the firm to service each client to the best of its ability, using the following factors.

People

As a priority, find good **people**; look after them. See them as 'human capital' whose skills and careers the firm should invest in (that of itself isn't unusual); more than that, see your firm as *loyal* to employees. Interview carefully each 'regretted leaver' (anyone leaving, who the firm didn't want to go) and *ask not why the employee has shown disloyalty by leaving, but why the firm was insufficiently loyal to the person's career* that they had decided to leave. This inverts the usual, lazy habit, widespread in the industry, that when (even the best) people leave, we make excuses about why it didn't matter. Support this with a vigorous culture of self-directed learning, which strongly motivates loyalty.

Culture

Culture is about how people take risks, in large part, but this means judging the risks by their long-term benefits to building enduring business value, rather than by their short-term cash returns. Enfolded into this is the conduct (and 'social licence') question of thinking about wider consequences of one's risk-taking actions.

Society and the economy

Maybe surprisingly, next, participating in **society and the economy**. For example, what are managers doing to expand their personal knowledge of how modern markets work? Do they get involved in the wider world outside the bank? Do they attend conferences, industry roundtable groups? Do they write blogs, publish think-pieces and white papers on topics of sector-wide interest (not just marketing materials)? Do they participate in forums (such as 'culture sprints') where the future of regulation is shaped? Do they attend parliamentary committee hearings?

Shareholders

Perhaps most surprising of all is who's in final place: **shareholders**/business owners. The point is: *if* we get those first four points right, *then* shareholders get their dividend. We don't run the firm *for* the shareholders; they simply participate, lending us capital so we can create wider economic benefits, which generate payback.

* * *

In a deeply conduct-regime-friendly way: employees' adherence to each of these five points is 'sponsored' personally by a nominated board director. By the way, this model anticipated that feature of SMR (senior manager personal accountability) by about a year when it was first introduced. It also features what we'd now call culture assessment questions to populate the framework; we'll return to those later.

Another application of a similar technique combining 'hierarchy of needs' with healthy culture and benign corporate outcomes is the Barrett Values Model. Figure 10.6 shows a summary graphic; our distinguished co-author Ruth Steinholtz explains further in Chapter 13.

FIGURE 10.6   Barrett Values Model

Contribution	7	**Living Purpose** Being of Service, Future Generations, Vision, Social Responsibility, Long-Term Perspective
Collaboration	6	**Cultivating Communities** Community Involvement, Partnership, Mentoring/Coaching, Employee Fulfillment
Alignment	5	**Authentic Expression** Openness, Creativity, Integrity, Passion, Trust, Honesty, Transparency
Evolution	4	**Courageously Evolving** Accountability, Transformation, Innovation, Continuous Learning, Autonomy, Empowerment, Agility
Performance	3	**Achieving Excellence** Quality, Results-Orientation, Competence, Self-Esteem, Productivity, Efficiency
Relationships	2	**Building Relationships** Customer Satisfaction, Connection, Respect, Listening, Open Communication
Viability	1	**Ensuring Stability** Financial Stability, Profit, Safety, Health

Time now to put the purpose models together with some culture assessment tools.

From framing purpose to measuring culture

Distilling the academic and regulatory literature down to half a page, this is, again, a simpler train of thought than you might have expected. It's a three-step sequence.

First, do the 'standing on the mountain top' self-questioning about your **purpose and goals**. (Sustainable long-term stewardship, economic infrastructure, and so on.)

Then start to assemble detailed **indicators** and assessment questions to inform these, and also more importantly to help you to answer the two headline questions:

- To what extent you are fulfilling your purpose (the purpose that you've identified you have)?
- How does your progress look – both its pace and extent – relative to your peers in the industry?

At this point, don't panic if you think you haven't yet got any indicators, or can't think what the right questions might be; we will cover all that in the final part of this chapter.

The final step in the sequence is, using the assembled indicators, to see how best to **make behaviours consistent with** purpose. In case that sounds a bit abstract, it really isn't: for a start, just consider how compensation and promotion affect people's behaviour. Is your firm's style to pay big cash bonuses for hit-and-run selling (and never mind after-sales care)? To promote the person who sells the most stuff, no matter what else they might have done? If so, time to think again. A simple example: one of the most powerful ways to focus the minds of those super-salespeople on better conduct is... to defer their promotion. If you haven't tried that, do. It works.

Culture-based questions of purpose

Moving towards the final, 'asking better questions' part of this chapter, we need to boil down Schein's iceberg and recast it as the 'culture paradigm' or 'culture web' (Figure 10.7). This prompts us to start asking better questions about all those levels of surface and sub-surface culture (the iceberg's 'artifacts', 'espoused values' and 'shared basic assumptions'). We'll see those questions in simple form shortly, following The Big Question that we need to ask about purpose.

'What sort of people are we here... really?'

'To see ourselves as others see us!/It would from many a blunder free us,' the poet Robert Burns wisely urged us.[21] If our culture quest is to result in a

FIGURE 10.7   Culture web

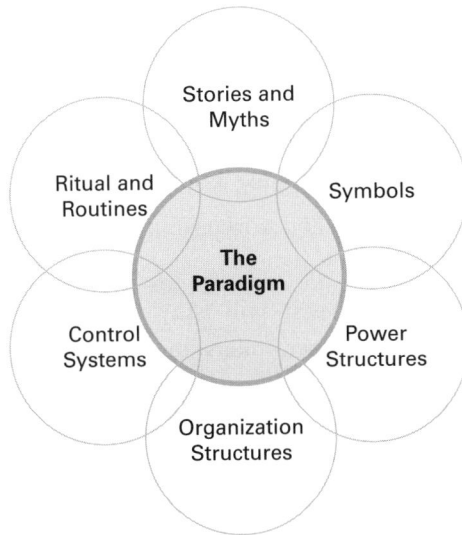

SOURCE Johnson-Scholes[20]

firm-wide understanding of what's 'acceptable and expected behaviour', it really helps if along the way we can acquire the habit of looking at ourselves and our firm from the outside in. It's no good me self-certifying to a regula-tor (or to anyone), 'Trust me, I'm an honest person'. As the world's leading behavioural statistician, Cambridge's Professor Sir David Spiegelhalter has pithily put it: 'Stop trying so hard to *look* trustworthy, and *earn* our trust'.[22]

Similarly, we should be serious about doing real assessment, not just going through the motions (so-called 'performative compliance'), by gather-ing external sources of information, not just talking to each other within the firm – although starting better internal conversations, based on questions raised in surroundings of psychological safety, is essential.

What good questions look like: the value of challenge

Writing on the need for psychological safety in firms, Professor Amy Edmondson has pointed out that once the firm achieves a 'safe space' for anyone to put a hand up and ask a question, the next most important thing is to make the questions as good as possible.[23] To her own question, 'Why ask better questions?', Prof Edmondson answers that a well-framed and effective question will:

- channel attention and focus enquiry;
- generate curiosity in the listener: it is thought-provoking, stimulating reflective conversation;
- bring to the surface any underlying assumptions;
- release energy, creativity, and forward movement that suggests new possibilities;
- have persistent meaning – it will 'stay around', evoking follow-on questions and revealing deeper understandings.

This helps establish a suitably positive frame of mind for the questions that follow.

Seven prompts to start the culture conversation

Looking back to our old friends the mountain-top question (Figure 10.2), the Schein 'iceberg' (Figure 10.1) and the Johnson-Scholes 'jellyfish' (Figure 10.7), we're now ready to roll with the opening set of culture assessment questions. Be warned: they look surprisingly basic – but that's the whole point. Edgar Schein himself, whose model it is, frankly says we should mention defining culture 'to frame the conversation' but then 'drop the word "culture"' and instead say 'Let's look at our history' [see 'stories' below] '...what we've become and how we've gotten to this place. Only then will we be able to understand the practice of culture, what gave rise to it, and what we may have to change.'[24]

Taking our cue from Schein, rather than fixate on defining 'culture' (which most staff would find an unnecessarily puzzling exercise), let's ask seven simple little clusters of questions (Figure 10.8).

Here they are in a practical sequence, with a brief note on how each informs culture assessment.

What are we here for?

At the core of the paradigm: the ultimate question of individual and collective purpose; we've looked above at principles-level example answers from two conduct regulators (along with Scrooge, Maslow and Ikigai) (pp 224–229).

FIGURE 10.8 Seven prompts for the culture conversation

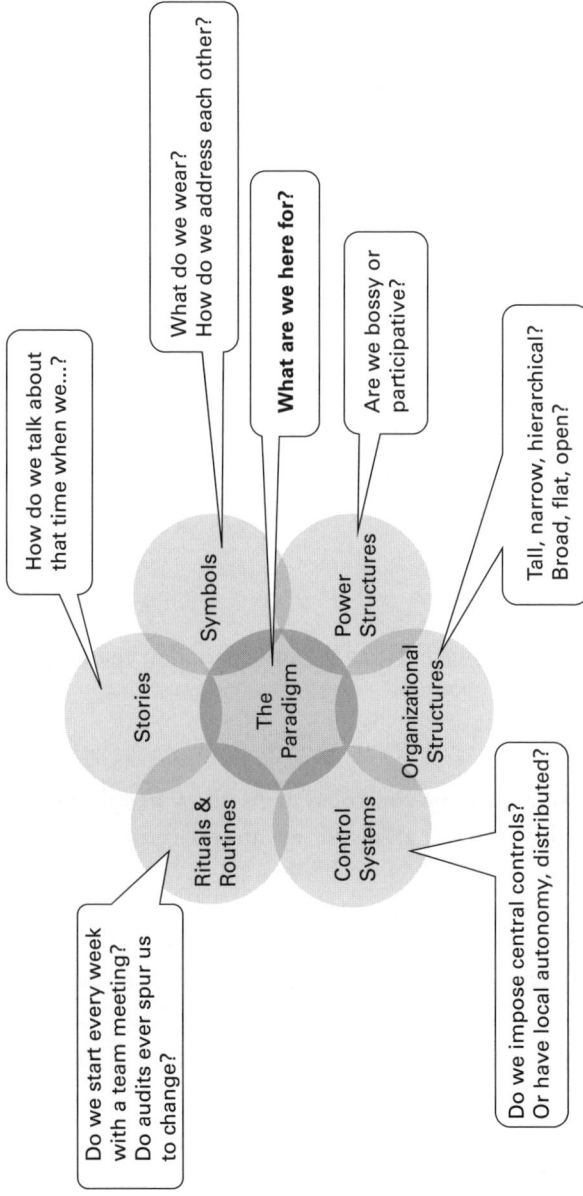

How do we talk about that time when we...?

What do we wear?
How do we address each other?

What are we here for?

Are we bossy or participative?

Tall, narrow, hierarchical? Broad, flat, open?

Stories

Symbols

The Paradigm

Power Structures

Rituals & Routines

Control Systems

Organizational Structures

Do we start every week with a team meeting? Do audits ever spur us to change?

Do we impose central controls? Or have local autonomy, distributed?

SOURCE Miles, after Schein, Johnson and Scholes

Now some day-to-day detail; do cross-refer this to our example material from real-life internal audit observations (see Chapter 8, pages 77–79, and Interlude 3, pages 308–311), to see what sort of 'tells' to look for.

What do we wear? And how do we address each other?

These 'symbols' are telling surface signals ('tells') of how people engage with one another in the workspace. They offer rich cultural cues, if we pay closer attention. Do people address each other formally/informally/deferentially/politely/jokily? How do they present themselves (what's 'acceptable' dress sense? Suit and tie? T-shirt and ripped jeans? Clean-shaven? Jewellery? Ink, piercings? etc)? Strong clues on 'the way we do things' – without a word of 'compliance' conversation.

Are people 'bossy' or participative?

Do people – especially managers – *really* want to discuss things, or just for others to shut up and do as they're told?

What's the hierarchy like?

Is our firm tall, narrow, dictatorial – or broad, flat, egalitarian?

How do we set about imposing controls?

As with hierarchy, do our control systems allow people local autonomy (eg to extend credit)? Or pull all decisions into the centre?

How bound are we by habits and routines?

'If it's Monday morning, must be time for our team housekeeping meeting' – why? Why then, and why meet with that frequency? Are you simply doing 'rituals of verification'[25] (go-through-the-motions, ineffective audit procedures)?

How do we explain to one another 'what just happened' (stories)?

You may think this is the most ridiculous of all the questions; actually, it's the single most effective of all of them. I have used this more than any other question in my work with firms: 'Tell me about a day when something went wrong, and what you did; what happened next?'. The power of the 'narrative research' method comes from the human animal's urge to makes sense of life experiences by *assembling them into stories*. Anything unusual happens, we share an anecdote about it. Less than two minutes after someone starts to tell me a story (about 'that day when...') I can identify, for example, whether they see themselves as having any agency (autonomy and control) in their work; whether they see their firm as overcoming challenges, or struggling to cope, and so on. It's an innocuous-looking question – that often yields the keys to the firm's culture.

Now let's revisit the regulatory version.

From the Question, to the Five Questions, to defining and measuring purpose

Headnote: This section will focus on the example of the UK model of conduct regulation; this model is widely regarded as a template for other jurisdictions (by conduct regulators in, for example, Ireland, Japan, Australia, Hong Kong and Singapore) (see Chapters 2 and 3).

The UK Financial Conduct Authority (FCA) publishes and regularly reviews sets of headline, principles-level Conduct Rules and Five Conduct Questions. These are intended to guide firms' progress in embedding 'exemplary conduct' and 'healthy culture' but their language is frankly rather legalistic and technocratic. Here they are in the form published in December 2020:[26,27]

Conduct Rules

Rule 1: You must act with integrity.

Rule 2: You must act with due skill, care and diligence.

Rule 3: You must be open and cooperative with the FCA, the PRA and other regulators.

Rule 4: You must pay due regard to the interests of customers and treat them fairly.

Rule 5: You must observe proper standards of market conduct.

Five Conduct Questions

Q1: What proactive steps do you take as a firm to identify the conduct risks inherent within this?

Q2: How do you encourage the individuals who work in front, middle, back office, control and support functions to feel and be responsible for managing the conduct of their business?

Q3: What support (broadly defined) does the firm put in place to enable those who work for it to improve the conduct of their business or function?

Q4: How do the board and ExCo (or appropriate senior management) gain oversight of the conduct of business within their organization and, equally importantly, how do they consider the conduct implications of the strategic decisions that they make?

Q5: Has the firm assessed whether there are any other activities that it undertakes that could undermine strategies put in place to improve conduct?

Though they're included here for ease of reference, we're not going to dwell on these formulations of the rules and questions, because they're rather dry and the FCA tweaks them each year. As we go to press (April 2021) it has announced plans to frame a sixth question, on **cognitive diversity**, a topic we've anticipated throughout this book. Instead, we'll frame culture assessment questions from a practical (literally), feet-on-the-floor standpoint: first, with some examples of the regulator's 'floor-walk' questions.

Culture assessment in action: example questions from regulator 'floor-walks'

As trailed earlier, one distinctive feature of the new culture assessments is that conduct regulators' case officers and inspectors are now much more likely to visit your firm (or drop in virtually, or invite you to 'tea with the regulator') to observe firsthand how you all work together. UK regulators have been testing 'floor-walk' questions within firms since early 2018. Here's a flavour of them (Table 10.1), raising five of the question topics most often encountered in firms. Again, as with the Schein questions, at first sight they seem disarmingly simple, but as you think about them, they may feel harder.

TABLE 10.1   The regulator's 'floor-walk' questions – and what they mean

Regulator's 'floor-walk' question	What it means
Tell me one of your values, then show me an example of some work you're personally doing today to put it into practice?	This is challenging the team to demonstrate understanding of 'values in action'. What do you do in reality, to make values more than just 'words on the wall'?
Why do you [as a (senior) manager] think you're competent for your role?	As in the *culture assessment approach*: What are you doing, beyond your job spec, to educate yourself as to how markets work, and be aware of the wider implications of the work you do?
When was the last time somebody in your team questioned a failing product or process? What happened to that person?	The punchiest form of the What Actually Happens test: Does anyone ever ask an intelligent challenge question and if so do you thank them, ignore them, fire them? A proxy test for the state of your challenge function, generally.
Show me a control that recently worked in practice to stop something bad happening.	Similarly: Show me how your controls work in practice, not just on paper; and that they're effective at stopping a local risk becoming a firm-wide one. Good if you can show a recent event of a control working to prevent a mishap.
In what ways do you find behavioural insights helpful?	Really just a test to see if you or any of your team has noticed that behavioural science now drives regulation. Any moderately intelligent answer (showing awareness of, say, bias effects) will give a positive signal.
(And an unspoken question: How's your attitude, as you reply to my question?)	Any good auditor is interested in whether you're really engaging with the process – or are you giving off the signal that you're simply trying to get rid of them?

SOURCE Miles/UK Finance

Starting the culture conversation at team level: humanize the Five Questions

To get your team used to the idea of working together as a source of cultural insight, you'll need to start a conversation about it. As prompts for that, here (see box) is a version of the Five Conduct Questions, in simpler language. This will get people thinking about firm-wide purpose and values and looking for which lagging/historic and leading/predictive indicators might give the clearest view of what customers, stakeholders, and employees expect from you.

FIVE CONDUCT QUESTIONS, PLAINLY PUT

1 What do I do to check for people behaving badly in our business?

2 How do we (managers) encourage each person to feel and be responsible for treating people well?

3 How does the firm give each of us support safely to put a hand up to call out abuses?

4 How do we (managers) look at behaviour and think about how our decisions affect the wider world?

5 Am I happy to call out anything I see that undermines anyone who's trying to encourage good behaviour?

Culture dashboard design basics: two templates

Working onwards from the 'five simple questions' above, before getting into detail on a conduct or culture dashboard, start thinking of the task as reporting on the state of your firm's contest between 'exemplary' and 'misconduct'. That's rather how the regulator (informally) conceives it. How far along a road are you, from 'careless/ignorant' towards 'exemplary', and what's your rate of progress? How's your progress relative to your peer group, and relative to customers'/clients' latest expectations? (And when did you last check what these are?)

At a headline level, then, we're looking for evidence of your firm's people doing the right thing (even if they do it intuitively rather than consciously) and of people doing the wrong thing (which may be out of ignorance, confusion, or malice). Observe the action first – remember we want to be 'relentlessly empirical': to look for What Actually Happens. Identifying the intent behind the action is harder, will very likely take longer and will almost certainly encounter various obstacles such as response effects, gaming of the test, and outright obstruction by cynical factions and anyone who's keen to hide their misdeeds.

As a simple starting premise, therefore, divide your report into 'exemplars' [E] (on the left in Figure 10.9) and 'misconducts' [M] (on the right). You might prefer to use plainer language for your working version, such as 'virtues and vices'. Setting out and then unpacking four example indicator groups, in opposing pairs.

FIGURE 10.9 Preliminary sketches for a culture dashboard (1): gathering example indicators

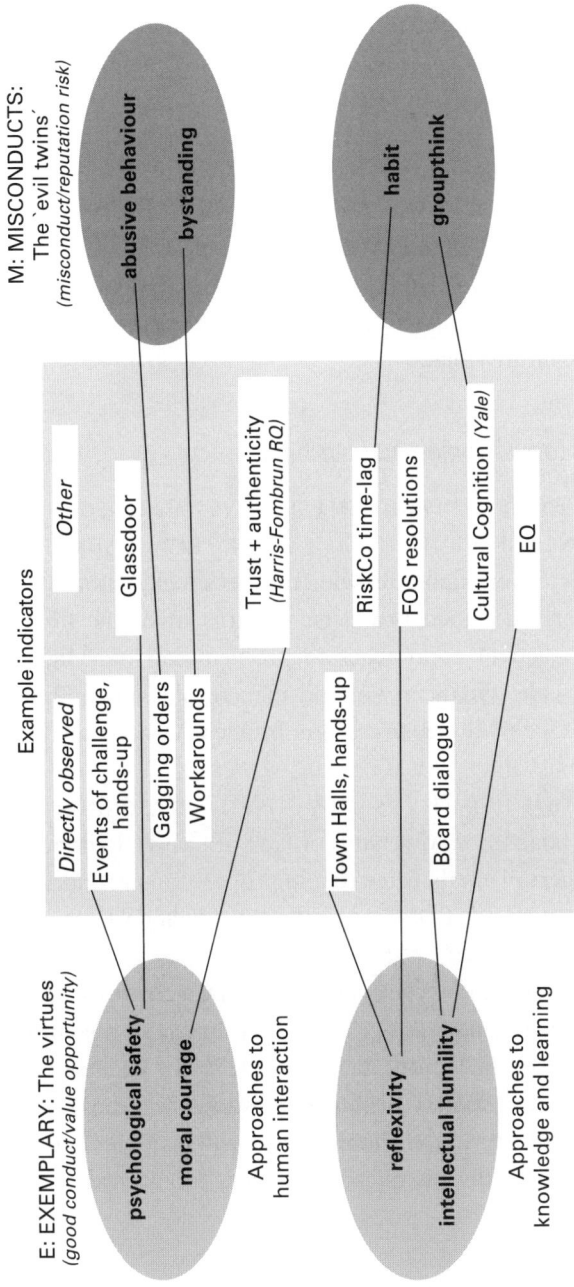

M: MISCONDUCTS:
The 'evil twins'
(misconduct/reputation risk)

abusive behaviour

bystanding

habit

groupthink

Example indicators

Other

Glassdoor

Trust + authenticity
(Harris-Fombrun RQ)

RiskCo time-lag

FOS resolutions

Cultural Cognition (Yale)

EQ

Directly observed

Events of challenge,
hands-up

Gagging orders

Workarounds

Town Halls, hands-up

Board dialogue

E: EXEMPLARY: The virtues
(good conduct/value opportunity)

psychological safety

moral courage

Approaches to
human interaction

reflexivity

intellectual humility

Approaches to
knowledge and learning

SOURCE Miles, UK Finance/CISI 2021

Approaches to human interaction

[E] PSYCHOLOGICAL SAFETY VS [M] ABUSIVE BEHAVIOUR

Possible 'as found' indicators: events/non-events of 'hands-up' challenge; good/poor reviews on Glassdoor; instances of aggressive gagging orders (injunctions) against past/present staff.

Possible higher indicators: Harris-Fombrun Authenticity score;[28] BSB industry survey recognition.

[E] MORAL COURAGE VS [M] BYSTANDING

'As founds': any senior manager saying 'I was wrong'; absence/presence of workarounds. Highers: Ivey Leadership Character Assessment (as trialled by the FCA);[29] CultureScope.

Approaches to knowledge and learning

[E] COGNITIVE DIVERSITY AND REFLEXIVITY VS [M] STEREOTYPING ('PERFORMANCE ATTRIBUTION BIAS'), HABITS, LAZY ASSUMPTIONS

'As founds': recovery time following market shock; withdrawal and replacement of poorly designed products; patterns of online browser use; wide range of (collective) approaches to problem solving. Highers: Emotional Intelligence scale; Financial Ombudsman resolutions finding against your firm; Active Open-Mindedness score; Implicit Association Test

[E] INTELLECTUAL HUMILITY VS [M] MOTIVATED REASONING, GROUPTHINK

'As founds': boardroom diversity (or lack of); 'town hall' meetings at which senior managers properly listen to and properly answer questions; quality of board dialogue and NED/other challenge. Highers: Dunning-Kruger (self-delusion) test; 'Cultural Cognition' test.

Now, keeping in mind the conceptual approach above, alongside that we can start to frame and use questions that attach to the culture assessment model introduced in Figure 10.5, page 227. For each of the five purpose entities, there are several headline questions we can pose straightaway (Figure 10.10). Later in the chapter, there will be plenty more questions.

For all points below, the question frame is 'Do we always...? And how do we know that?':

For our **customers/clients**, do we:

☐ Place clients at the heart of business?

☐ Build long-lasting relationships?

FIGURE 10.10   Preliminary sketches for a culture dashboard (2): five purposes

Clients	Place clients at the heart; build long-term relationships Deliver valued quality to clients Direct resources efficiently
Our people	Value diversity and merit Attract and raise talent; invest in careers Share common purpose
Culture (conduct, risk)	Don't harm our clients, reputation or markets Account for actions Acknowledge good conduct; challenge misbehaviour Learn from failures
Society, Economy	Acknowledge wider economic role: capital flow and investment Consider society, ethics and environment Engage positively with communities, sector initiatives
Firm, Investors	Create sustainable profitability Balance: optimise returns vs prudently manage resources Innovate; support good thinking

☐ Deliver valued quality?

☐ Direct our resources efficiently?

For all **our people,** do we:

☐ Value merit and diversity of all kinds?

☐ Attract and raise talent?

☐ Invest in careers?

☐ Share common purpose?

Considering our **culture** of risk-taking and general conduct, do we:

☐ Not harm our clients, reputation or markets?

☐ Account for our own individual and team actions?

☐ Acknowledge exemplary conduct?

☐ Challenge any misbehaviour?

☐ Learn from mistakes and failures?

For the firm within our **society and economy**, do we:

☐ Acknowledge our wider economic role as an enabler (of capital flows/investment in enterprise/cash transmission/protection through insurance, etc as appropriate)?

☐ Be considerate of social, ethical and environmental concerns?

☐ Engage positively with sector initiatives (attending or convening forums with regulators, industry interest groups, parliamentarians; publish think-pieces; outreach to vulnerable people, community, etc)?

Respecting the **owners** of our firm/**our investors**: *if* we are succeeding in all the above four points, do we:

☐ Create sustainable profitable business?

☐ Balance optimizing returns against prudently managing resources?

☐ Innovate?

☐ Support good quality in thinking and decision-making?

Having assembled two initial frames, we can now turn to how to populate the space raised by the questions, with answers validated by robust indicators. Let's see some examples.

The MI (management information) sources we have and the MI we need: finding better indicators

To help get started compiling indicators for culture, Tables 10.2 and 10.3 show two example sets of indicators: Set A, which many firms already use, and Set B, which various conduct regulators say they'd like to see used, though we might describe them collectively as 'aspirational'.

Some indicators you (maybe) have

TABLE 10.2   Indicator Set A: 'Found indicators'/'MIs we have, and are using'

Type	Indicator name	Typical data sources
Staff engagement	Mandatory training	Attendance, completion, adherence to deadlines
	Trust in leadership	Staff surveys, 360-degree reviews, 'back to the floors'

(continued)

TABLE 10.2   (Continued)

Type	Indicator name	Typical data sources
	Retention	Staff turnover; %age 'regretted leavers'; exit interviews
Service quality	Complaints responsiveness	Per-product complaints, conduct complaints, response times, resolved rates
	Customer/client satisfaction	Repeat business; revenues per client; timely settlement
	Retention	%age 'user-driven account closures'; cited reasons
	Communication	User feedback on charges (and rationale for them)

Indicators you'd like to have

To populate these indicator categories (Table 10.3), we finally need to turn to the topic of asking the right questions (pages 244–246). Until now, regulators' framing of formal conduct audit questions has been formulaic (as with the Five Conduct Questions). Based on the floor-walk examples above, expect future questions to be qualitative. The final section of this chapter offers some 'basic question and better question' examples.

TABLE 10.3   Indicator Set B: 'The MI we need'/aspirational and experimental

Type	Indicator name	Typical data sources, tests
Staff engagement	Psychological safety	Instances of hands-up, courageous decision-making, innovative (challenge) thinking
Purpose	Social licence (gap)	Consistency of investing in 'human capital'; stakeholder tolerance ('behavioural lens' test); 'family and friends' test
Problem solving	Cognitive diversity	Multi-diversity (gender, ethnicity, social origin, sexuality, neurotype, etc)
Reflexivity	Active open-mindedness	Active open-mindedness test; speed to market of competitive new products; absence of obsolete/failed products

(continued)

TABLE 10.3   (Continued)

Type	Indicator name	Typical data sources, tests
Trustworthiness	Authenticity	Externally perceived 'rhetoric gap' (what you say vs what you actually do); position relative to subsector benchmarks (reputation, trusted, etc)
Transparency	Excessive complexity	Plain-language tests on Terms of Business; product useability testing with customers
Leadership	Leadership character	Moral courage; emotional intelligence; tests for overconfidence (Dunning-Kruger, Motivated Reasoning)
Product fitness	Excessive margins	'Outlier' products with excessive profits or sales commissions; (surveyed) customer ignorance of real costs/benefits

Basic questions, better questions

In the early days of the Senior Managers Regime (circa 2016), the regulator would ask some rather dry, compliance-y, abstract-sounding questions. Since then, the sector has had much practice (with regulators and this author) at framing more intelligent, qualitatively probing questions. As we embark on this, remember Amy Edmondson's characteristics of a good question (pages 231–232). Generally, if a question could be answered by a simple box-tick yes or no, it won't be a decent qualitative probe. In Table 10.4 are seven questions in their original regulatory audit form, which you may be used to, from before the start of culture assessment. On the right is the same question topic, but reframed into a more culture-assessing probe.

TABLE 10.4   Conventional audit vs culture audit questions

Old audit question	Culture assessment question
Is the firm's risk culture aligned with its values, and clearly communicated?	How do we objectively measure the gap between the values and culture we claim to have, and actual behaviours happening at each level? (Board, managers, front line?)

(continued)

TABLE 10.4   (Continued)

Old audit question	Culture assessment question
Does the firm have a proactive culture of reporting risk governance breaches?	When was the last time anyone here reported a breach? How did we react when they did?
Do the firm's staff understand that they need to be conduct-compliant?	To what extent do all staff understand that their personal good conduct is what keeps customers bringing in business, and our owners and regulators happy?
Where a product's sales grow rapidly, is there evidence of skewed incentives or excessive risk-taking?	When we design a product or plan a sales push, do we consider how to identify and measure perverse incentive effects?
Do front office staff understand that as first line of defence, they are responsible for all aspects of risk?	How far do front office staff *care* that they are responsible for their risk-taking?
Does the firm weigh up 'conduct risk appetite' in its planning and risk analysis?	How do we define and report what stakeholders view as 'expected good behaviour', right now?
To confirm board and other expertise, is the firm up to date with senior manager attestations?	Who challenges leaders' claims to competence? Can we independently verify that every board member and senior manager has the expertise that the regulator now expects to see? How do we monitor that nobody over-reaches their actual expertise?

SOURCE Miles/UK Finance

Conclusion

Keeping in mind a clear (and socially wider) sense of purpose, it's possible to start to compile a culture assessment framework with the help of the right headings, indicators and questions. With more thoughtful questions, the firm gets a sharper focus on gaps between what we'd *like* to happen (and perhaps what we'd prefer to believe is happening), and what *actually* happens. In the next chapter we'll see how the regulator has wrestled with that question. Let's leave the 'better MI' topic with a tough set of questions based, once again, on the author's re-analysis of real, prototype, culture assessment questions that regulators pre-tested during 2019–20.

Rather than just asking, 'Are we culture-compliant?', ask instead:

- What motivates our people? Do we really know? Have we really challenged how or why we do things?

- How do we track changes in stakeholder expectations of 'good behaviour? What are their latest concerns?

- How do we recognize 'exemplary conduct' when we see it? How do we report it?

- What's the personal expertise of each senior manager here? Who objectively validates that?

- How do we measure objectively all our peoples' actual behaviours? How familiar are we with our conduct and culture metrics and the assumptions behind these?

- What did we actually do in response to any hands-up challenges from staff, regulatory questions, or customer complaints?

- What does each senior manager personally know about practical conduct steps we're taking?

- How do we demonstrate, in practice, our care for every customer?

Notes

1 Prof Alessandra Capezio, Australian National University (ANU) (2019), Banks using ineffective tools to combat unethical behaviour, ANU paper, also quoted in *Australian Financial Review*, 8 May 2019, afr.com/companies/financial-services/bank-risk-strategies-like-hitting-a-nail-with-a-cucumber-20190507-p51kwf (archived at https://perma.cc/5B6C-LFKK)

2 Prof Alessandra Capezio, Australian National University (ANU) (2019), Banks using ineffective tools to combat unethical behaviour, ANU paper, also quoted in *Australian Financial Review*, 8 May 2019, afr.com/companies/financial-services/bank-risk-strategies-like-hitting-a-nail-with-a-cucumber-20190507-p51kwf (archived at https://perma.cc/RYC2-QLP4)

3 FCA (2016) Behaviour and compliance in organisations, fca.org.uk/publication/occasional-papers/op16-24.pdf (archived at https://perma.cc/2C3B-DAJ3)

4 Sykes, G and Matza, D (1957) Techniques of neutralization: a theory of delinquency, *American Sociological Review,* 22 (6), jstor.org/stable/2089195?seq=1 (archived at https://perma.cc/AG77-AEX9); Baron-Cohen, S (2011), *Zero Degrees of Empathy: A new theory of human cruelty*, Allen Lane

5   Marc Teasdale, FCA Director of Wholesale Supervision (2020), speech to The Investment Association's Culture in Investment Management Forum, September, fca.org.uk/news/speeches/regulatory-perspective-drivers-culture-and-role-purpose-and-governance (archived at https://perma.cc/VZ2H-MMPE)

6   Jonathan Davidson, FCA Executive Director of Supervision (2020) The Business of Social Purpose, speech to Culture and Conduct Forum of the Financial Services Industry, 26 November

7   Marc Teasdale, FCA Director of Wholesale Supervision (2020), speech to The Investment Association's Culture in Investment Management Forum, September, fca.org.uk/news/speeches/regulatory-perspective-drivers-culture-and-role-purpose-and-governance (archived at https://perma.cc/LXV4-YGNY)

8   Jonathan Davidson, FCA Executive Director of Supervision (2020) The Business of Social Purpose, speech to Culture and Conduct Forum of the Financial Services Industry, 26 November

9   Jonathan Davidson, FCA Executive Director of Supervision (2020) The Business of Social Purpose, speech to Culture and Conduct Forum of the Financial Services Industry, 26 November

10 Jonathan Davidson, FCA Executive Director of Supervision (2020) The Business of Social Purpose, speech to Culture and Conduct Forum of the Financial Services Industry, 26 November

11 Jonathan Davidson, FCA Executive Director of Supervision (2020) The Business of Social Purpose, speech to Culture and Conduct Forum of the Financial Services Industry, 26 November

12 Chartered Institute for Securities and Investment (2021) Jonathan Davidson, FCA and Roger Miles, CISI, Ask the experts: Culture Assessments, *CISI Review*, cisi.org/cisiweb2/cisi-news/ (archived at https://perma.cc/NM3U-LSQL)

13 FCA (2020) Objectives, fca.org.uk/markets (archived at https://perma.cc/4GGC-7ZKS)

14 FCA (2020) Objectives, fca.org.uk/markets (archived at https://perma.cc/YWM7-PE4C)

15 Business Roundtable (2019) Purpose of a Corporation, businessroundtable.org/business-roundtable-redefines-the-purpose-of-a-corporation-to-promote-an-economy-that-serves-all-americans (archived at https://perma.cc/T34L-CEW4)

16 Maslow, A H (1943) A theory of human motivation, *Psychological Review*, 50 (4), pp 370–96, doi.apa.org/doiLanding?doi=10.1037%2Fh0054346 (archived at https://perma.cc/WKV6-9G4B)

17 Kumano, M (2018) On the concept of well-being in Japan: feeling Shiawase as hedonic well-being and feeling Ikigai as eudaimonic well-being, *Journal of Applied Research in Quality of Life*, 13 (2), 419–33 https://link.springer.com/article/10.1007/s11482-017-9532-9 (archived at https://perma.cc/ZP23-VKTY)

18 Kumano, M (2018) On the concept of well-being in Japan: feeling Shiawase as hedonic well-being and feeling Ikigai as eudaimonic well-being, *Journal of Applied Research in Quality of Life*, **13** (2), 419–33 https://link.springer.com/article/10.1007/s11482-017-9532-9 (archived at https://perma.cc/ZP23-VKTY)

19 Marlow, D E, Vluru LLC, linkedin.com/in/davidemarlow/ (archived at https://perma.cc/657U-M6B9)

20 see for example Johnson, G, Scholes, K and Whittington, R (2007) *Exploring Corporate Strategy*, FT-Prentice-Hall, London

21 Burns, R (1786) To A Louse, On Seeing One on a Lady's Bonnet at Church [In the original Scottish dialect: 'O wad some Pow'r the giftie gie us/ To see oursels as ithers see us! / It wad frae mony a blunder free us']

22 David Spiegelhalter (2020) Those who tell us what to do during the pandemic must earn our trust, The Guardian, 26 November, theguardian.com/commentisfree/2020/nov/26/pandemic-earn-trust-facts-vital-covid (archived at https://perma.cc/4KQG-SA24)

23 Edmondson, A (2019) *The Fearless Organization*, Wiley

24 Duke University (2020) Culture shift with Ed and Peter Schein, interview on https://dialoguereview.com/culture-shift-with-ed-and-peter-schein/ (archived at https://perma.cc/X3CR-PRVP), December

25 Power, M (1999) *The Audit Society: Rituals of verification*, OUP, oxford. universitypressscholarship.com/view/10.1093/acprof:oso/9780198296034.001.0001/acprof-9780198296034 (archived at https://perma.cc/LXJ8-N2C2)

26 FCA (2020) Handbook and Code of Conduct: The Individual Conduct Rules, paragraphs 2.1.1–2.1.5, handbook.fca.org.uk/handbook/COCON.pdf (archived at https://perma.cc/QM4N-7BEC)

27 FCA (2020) 'Messages from the Engine Room': 5 Conduct Questions. Industry Feedback for 2019/20 Wholesale Banking Supervision, fca.org.uk/publication/market-studies/5-conduct-questions-industry-feedback-2019-20.pdf (archived at https://perma.cc/VW29-J55Q)

28 Fombrun, C (1995) *Reputation: Realizing Value from the Corporate Image*, Harvard Business School Press

29 Crossan, M et al (2016) *Developing Leadership Character*, Routledge, New York; example assessment tool at www.ivey.uwo.ca/leadership/research-resources/leader-character-framework/ (archived at https://perma.cc/ERC6-9XNR)

Interlude Two
Case example: culture
rating in a retail bank

ANON

Context

Following the financial crash in 2008, retail banks had little choice but to revisit their previous understanding of why they were in business, what the value was for them being in business, and what it was that they added to society. In the years that followed, as was the case with many retail banks, various questions, interventions and industry reviews caused firms to consider their 'purpose' and the drivers of the behaviours that made each firm unique.

The financial crash left many banks' staff feeling embarrassed socially. If out and about with friends and family, few would voluntarily admit that they worked in banking, let alone state which bank they actually worked for. The shame that has followed many of these colleagues has shaped much of what the industry did during the 2010s, with efforts to rebuild those levels of trust that our communities had in banks pre-crisis and their stated ambitions in driving great customer outcomes as a primary driver to demonstrating a duty of care in how these ambitions are delivered.

'How do we go about restoring pride in our work?'

After much deliberation and research, and very much in line with the UK Financial Conduct Authority (FCA)'s publication (DP20/1[1]) on exactly this topic, at our retail bank we came to the conclusion that it all starts with Purpose: establishing what that is and having everyone truly buy into your company purpose. By way of example, Barclays has outlined their purpose as '*Creating opportunities to rise*', whilst HSBC has shared theirs as '*Together we thrive*'.

If we can truly deliver on our purpose, looking out for and enabling all those around us with pride, inclusion, diversity, psychological safety, a sound risk culture and positive can-do mindset, a healthy and fully functional culture starts to follow. It's generally now recognized that embedding a strong organizational/risk culture is an ongoing and iterative process that needs continued positive nurturing, enhancement and reinforcement. As the FCA's Culture Essays note, culture change is something that happens in small steps every day; not with a big bang, but with small fires that grow over time.[2]

The purpose of this case study is to examine a few of the 'small fires' which we tackled in an effort to drive transformational culture change, with reference to three sets of key indicators:

1 connecting to your purpose and your role in society;

2 psychological safety;

3 inclusion and diversity.

Connecting to your purpose and your role in society

The benefits of having a company purpose or mission are well documented.[3] How many of us, though, can actually say 'that's why I go to work, that's what I help us to achieve, that's what helps me make the right decisions, every day', etc?

Many firms publicize their strap lines or company purposes. Yet if you ask different people within an organization, 'What's your company purpose?' or 'What are you here to do every day?' you will get different answers. Leaders become frustrated by this discrepancy, yet fail to grasp that a programme to improve culture, or embed 'exemplary conduct', is not simply about agreeing a strap line, telling people about it repeatedly and then expecting them somehow to spontaneously believe it.

Our first step was to identify the progressive components of embedding purpose. Initially, it was around creating our **awareness,** then following this up with highly participative discussions throughout the bank to ensure everyone could **understand** what it means to them personally and in their teams. Our third step was, working collegiately (with colleagues), to test 'What Actually Happens': how far people truly **believe** the company purpose. Our final step was to ensure that across the bank, every member of staff could **demonstrate** how we all live that purpose through their day-to-day bank activities.

From 2018 we measured our progress against each of these steps, as well as collectively, combining four metrics to form a 'culture embedding' score. This showed an 8 per cent improvement over the first two years. Data gathering included internal surveys to ensure that messages were indeed landing – again, not simply repeating the same words each time and expecting it all to fall into place. As a team manager you must take time to communicate (meaning, discuss interactively) your purpose and explain how the role of each member of your team helps the delivery of the purpose. Then 'belief' and 'demonstration' follow, with staff members gradually bringing our company purpose to life by demonstrating it in all that they do.

At an employee level, we found that it was essential to start with a strong foundation; that every staff member's annual goals or objectives were aligned with our central purpose and that they understood exactly how this alignment works for them personally. In the course of the year, performance achievement is measured according to how staff members achieve those goals and that the behaviours they demonstrate as they pursue their goals are in keeping with the bank's values and moral compass.

As the bank set about entrenching its redefined purpose, we began to see how well this purpose statement resonated with colleagues throughout the bank. As staff members' views were surveyed, many felt that a purpose statement which included a focus on customers or communities was obvious, 'because we are a bank and that's what banks are here to do', but the inclusion of our people in the purpose statement was less expected but much welcomed. This reframing made a difference in employee perceptions and observed service practices (anecdotally at first, but later evidenced through the I&D index), linking us together as a team, helping us to remember to look out for each other and to ensure great outcomes for customers.

After three years, we could see more clearly the gap between our own culture embedding scores and related external benchmarks close, sustaining an overall 8 per cent increase over the period, bringing us in line with retail benchmarks.

Covid-19 tests and reaffirms our community purpose

During the Covid-19 lockdown, we saw signs that the newly heightened community awareness during the virus crisis was stimulating a rise in our perceptions of 'Shared Purpose'. Although this factor has been regularly surveyed by the Banking Standards Board since 2016, it has remained stubbornly stagnant. This left us wondering whether colleagues were feeling that their survey responses to an external organization are more confidential and less attributable to specific individuals, resulting in external surveys yielding less positive results than those we conducted internally. But, as the whole world quickly became far more agile in responding to a universal challenge, along with many other retail banks similarly tested by public demand, our bank has truly seen its purpose coming to life with a new vitality. This gives us cause to look forward to future external surveys, with the promise that experiences during the pandemic have deepened colleagues' understanding of the real value and meaning of 'Shared Purpose'.

The Covid-19 crisis has proved both an 'abrupt and brutal audit'[4] test of our social commitment and a 'reification moment'[5] – when suddenly, through the furnace of crisis, previously abstract-seeming topics become the focus of real, everyday patterns of behaviours. As noted earlier, everything starts with senior leadership demonstrating what it truly means to live our purpose. We as a bank have done exactly this for our customers through a number of interventions (mortgage and loan payment breaks, business loans, charitable donations and more), and also for our people (job security, well-being support). However, the truly impressive cultural transformation has been seeing how staff members across the bank have risen to the crisis, taking it upon themselves to live our purpose in their own unique way by volunteering in the community, helping each other's well-being or offering to take on an extra role for a few weeks to help out struggling teams. There have been so many examples of how both the bank and staff members took the lead, bringing our purpose to life and making so many of us proud to say that we work for our bank.

Psychological safety

We see psychological safety, the extent to which 'people feel secure at work, in teams they belong to, with colleagues and leaders they trust',[6] as the foundation of a strong culture of employee engagement and performance. As the FCA reminds us,[7] healthy cultures are both purposeful and safe; for a culture to be healthy, leaders at all levels need to foster an environment in which employees feel comfortable to express their opinions and are listened to when they do so. Without the backing of psychological safety and an actively inclusive culture, the value of diversity would be lost.

Our bank realized early on that addressing psychological safety explicitly was a new challenge within the business. We scoped the extent of this challenge through both our own internal surveys and reviews and by external surveys. These showed us that the challenge of widely informed decision-making was in its infancy; that a well-intended historic culture of being conservative, polite and hierarchical made challenge and transformation difficult; and that without psychological safety, there would not be any bottom-up challenge, leaving the bank at risk of groupthink.

We set up a working group to define 'what good looks like' in terms of psychological safety, ensuring that purpose, values and culture were connected into any measure of psychological safety, as core metrics across the bank. We ran research into global best practice and a strategy developed for the bank which explicitly committed to foster a culture of psychological safety: to encourage colleagues to share opinions, challenge and speak up without fear of any negative consequences. We addressed psychological safety as a headline topic at bank-wide roadshows for people managers, at leadership events and as a part of a dedicated skills training programme for all people managers. We track related scores annually, through both internal sentiment surveys (which found a 9 per cent increase over the initial two-year period, against specific questions) and external benchmarking through our rolling participation in the Banking Standards Board Survey[8] (which, as discussed above, we found remained stubbornly flat during the first three years of the initiative).

Generally speaking, psychological safety is more of a mindset than a behaviour, although the existence of psychological safety can also be revealed by how people adapt their own behaviour (for example, in an instance where someone might manoeuvre to avoid having to work with a 'difficult' boss/person). We continually look for new ways and channels to reinforce it and, more recently, have published a set of frameworks to aid psychological safety in tackling projects or specific tasks, to enable it to become a more widely used term and expectation, with managers explicitly communicating a desire to create an environment where everyone feels able to express an opinion without fear or detriment. The bank has worked hard to promote an environment of open communication and effective challenge, in which decision-making processes encourage a range of views, allow for testing of current practices, stimulate a positive, critical attitude among employees, and promote an environment of open and constructive engagement. Within this we also consider diversity: how far colleagues feel that they can bring their whole selves to work without fear of detriment or judgement.

All the while, we test ourselves to assess achievement against industry benchmarks. Although staff results in this area are improving, we are realistic in noting that a greater rate of progress is required to meet and eventually exceed external benchmarks and industry averages. Effective challenge across all layers of the bank remains a priority, with a conscious effort to improve related behaviours, demonstrated through initiatives such as a new meeting methodology framework that encourages openness and challenge at all parts of the decision-making process. As an added step towards embedding a healthy culture of challenging assumptions, the pace of transformation and open engagement, line managers with 20 or more responses will also receive online access to their teams' internal survey results. The purpose of doing this is to allow teams the opportunity to review and discuss their own progress, comparing their own results to the rest of the organization and related benchmarks. This process of discussion and review has been very beneficial in creating space for dialogue around constructive change, understanding the drivers of their scores and settling on what can be done at a team level to resolve any applicable subjects.

Alongside purpose, the Covid-19 pandemic has had a direct impact on the priority of elements in a hierarchy of needs (see Chapter 10) with an emphasis on psychological safety. Covid-19 has raised profound questions around the nature and expression of business purpose in the community and of how people interact; there are many areas where psychological safety will play a central role now. At a time of turmoil we remember the importance of healthy cultures being purposeful as well as safe: in 2020 and in years to come, how many organizations can positively say that they have supported their employees in these areas? This is something that all of us in the financial sector should be striving for – real belief in our purpose, supported by the ability to deliver in a psychologically safe environment.

BANKING STANDARDS BOARD (BSB) PSYCHOLOGICAL SAFETY DEEP DIVE

Our bank has been a member of the Banking Standards Board since 2016 when it ran its first industry survey. The annual assessment examines the extent to which characteristics that the BSB would expect to be associated with any type of good organizational culture, are demonstrated by and within banks. In 2020, over the four years that the BSB has been open for membership, they have seen member firms across the banking sector invest considerable time and resources in efforts to understand and manage their cultures.

Speaking up, in the context of the BSB's work, is about much more than whistleblowing. When they talk about speaking up, they refer to the readiness of employees to speak about, question or challenge something about which they feel uncomfortable, concerned or unsure at work. Doing so requires respondents to trust their own judgement and to take the risk of questioning decisions, actions or accepted norms. They report that this is not easy in any environment, and can be particularly difficult in the workplace. It is, however, precisely in the workplace that speaking up, questioning and challenge is vital, not only to prevent or expose bad behaviour and to catch and remedy mistakes, but to foster innovation and continuous improvement.

The BSB use three key questions each year to track trends on this topic:

- In my experience, people in my organization do not get defensive when their views are challenged by colleagues.
- If I raised a concern about the way that we work, I would be worried about the negative consequences for me.
- I feel comfortable challenging a decision made by my manager.

Since 2019 the BSB has expanded its questioning in this area, delving to understand whether people felt listened to; whether people who wanted to speak up had actually done so and reasons why they didn't if they chose not to speak up; the reasons for wanting to speak up and the preferred channels for speaking up.

The additional insight and understanding that this has provided has been hugely beneficial for us in understanding things like the link between fear and futility which prevents people from speaking up, as well as some of the anecdotal differences in people choosing to speak up or not.

In addition to the insightful psychological safety information the BSB is able to provide, the bank also uses a number of specific BSB questions to inform and track the embedding of risk management as part of its annual Risk Culture Assessment. The BSB questions (in addition to six internal surveying questions which speak to psychological safety, risk identification, lessons learned, clarity of responsibility, capability and manager behaviours) are:

- People in my organization are truly open to review and feedback from external sources.

- People in my organization do not get defensive when their views are challenged by colleagues.

- If I raised a concern about the way we work, I would be worried about the negative consequences for me.

- I am confident in the ability of people in my area to identify risks.

- In my experience, people in my organization are good at dealing with issues before they become major problems.

- I have observed improvements in the way we do things based on lessons learnt.

- There is no conflict between my organization's stated values and how we do business.

Inclusion and diversity

We know from the benefit of hindsight[9] that it is often lack of cognitive diversity at the helm of governments and business institutions that sows the seeds for crisis, whether weak signals of the impending fall of a government at a general election, or the complacency of value-at-risk modelling that paved the way for the 2008 financial crash, or the collective deafness to the lessons of SARS, MERS and Ebola, which left the world's governments unprepared for the Covid-19 stresses.

More specifically it was a lack of diversity of intellect, abruptly revealed in the failure of assumptions about risk models, liquidity, and 'self-correcting' pricing,[10] that contributed significantly to the depth and the severity of the 2008 financial crisis.[11] Yet more than a decade on, in 2021 many institutions still encounter (and fail to recognize) the related problems: groupthink, intellectual arrogance, expert bias, over-confidence, motivated reasoning and cultural cognition; 'bystanding' and insufficient challenge amid a culture of fear or complacency; continued over-reliance on legacy reporting systems and weak controls; and risk assessments that use narrow models, self-reporting, or other fragile assumptions. More broadly, many firms still just fail to comprehend the central significance of culture, with symptoms such as a continuing lack of diversity at the most senior levels. The new regulatory agenda of Culture Audit asks banks and other financial firms to reach beyond a single dimension of diversity: it needs to be at all levels and many dimensions (such as gender, ethnic, social, cognitive, sexuality and neurotype) for the benefits of diversity and inclusion to truly be felt.

As the conduct regulator also reminds us, diversity of thought and perspectives stimulates innovative ideas and helps to solve complex problems by bringing fresh perspectives and solutions.[12] We are challenged to move beyond simply building a psychologically safe environment and promoting greater diversity in the workforce, to look for and measure the business and social benefits that these bring: resilience, retained value and more productive staff who stay with us longer. Like other organizations, our bank has started to move past its old assumptions about recruitment and advancement – the old preferences for cultural fit (hiring 'people like us') – to reconsider how we may overcome a structural, industry-wide bias that has for too long blocked many promising people from moving into senior roles.

Over three years, the bank has made and continues to make a concerted effort to transform its culture and ways of working, by cultivating a welcoming, inclusive environment where every colleague feels that they are made welcome, feels psychologically safe to contribute, can challenge and fulfil their potential – where every colleague can flourish. We have underpinned this transformation effort with six Inclusion and Diversity networks, all of which are colleague-led:

- Accessibility: its purpose is to enable customers, colleagues and communities to thrive from the perspective of Accessibility and Disability Inclusion.
- Gender Balance: its purpose is to enable colleagues to network, learn together, and to support the organization's progress in relation to gender balance.
- With Pride: its purpose is to drive representation and inclusion of the LGBT+ community, promote bringing your whole self to work, and increase visibility across locations, regions and mediums.
- Intergenerational: its purpose is to promote greater understanding, appreciation, and engagement among colleagues of all generations.
- Multicultural: its purpose is to raise awareness and leverage the power of cultural and ethnic diversity among our workforce and communities.
- Parents and Carers: its purpose is to provide support, guidance and resources about balancing parenting and caring responsibilities.

The aggregate internally measured I&D index saw a 4 per cent increase in its first two years, with the greatest improvement observed (+8 per cent) in the question as to whether the bank values having a diverse workforce. The remaining four questions that drive this metric relate to respecting different opinions when making decisions, staff members sharing their opinion without fear of negative consequences, being themselves without fear of judgement, and clarity of the behaviours expected of staff at work. These improvements have been sustained by the six networks, the goals for which are aligned to the overall Inclusion and Diversity strategy, which comprises four core objectives (below) with examples of previous-year progress review included:

- **Increasing workforce diversity**
  The bank is making identifiable practical progress through:
  - ensuring that all advertised roles have a 50/50 male/female ratio throughout the recruitment process;
  - progress towards achieving the Women in Finance Charter 2021 target of 38 per cent women in leadership roles;[13]
  - supporting cognitive diversity through the removal of the minimum degree education requirement.

- **Fostering an inclusive experience for colleagues** such as by hosting a continuing series of I&D events (aligned with our 'six networks'), designed to address/raise awareness and celebrate those factors most pertinent to all colleagues, helping the bank evolve into a firm that truly values having a diverse workforce, as demonstrated by the 8 per cent increase in this area.

- **Financial well-being and accessibility:**
  - Launching an employee assistance programme.
  - Realizing that financial literacy was intrinsically linked to financial well-being, we launched a range of support initiatives to help colleagues obtain a better understanding of their own financial situations. We also made various banking products available to colleagues, including savings, personal loans, foreign currency and current account offers for all colleagues.
  - Developing a further range of offerings for subsequent launch, such as mortgages and mobile banking.

- **Strengthening I&D accountability:**

  – Empowering colleagues to take a more active role in helping to shape the I&D agenda. As the networks are colleague led, colleagues are empowered to identify and lead the delivery of specific actions in support of each network. For example, arranging learning lunches on particular topics, hosting motivational talks, the 'My Story' series where colleagues are encouraged to share their own journeys and how they came to be with the bank, participation in various Pride events each summer, etc.

  – We introduced a mandatory performance goal for all leaders, which outlines the expectation that they actively promote policies, practices and behaviours that are inclusive, drive diversity in the organization and support the bank's overall I&D strategy. The Executive Committee subsequently nominated a (SMF) sponsor supporting the further development of each of the six networks.

Conclusion

Through our efforts, we have found that culture transformation works best when everyone is involved, and as an ongoing, iterative process. To borrow the FCA's metaphor, it's more akin to setting a large number of smaller fires than expecting a big bang.

Given the complexity of human dynamics, even with the new generation of culture indicators, as shared by UK Finance's Conduct & Culture Academy and others coming forward, I see it as unlikely that there will ever be a magic wand for instant, radical cultural change. A firm's behaviour and efforts to root out non-financial misconduct whilst promoting exemplary conduct in all respects, can only change for the better if every person within the firm chooses to 'get on board' for that change, rather than seeing it as imposed (or indeed, finding it *de facto* imposed).

The firm will prosper as long as all staff experience the culture programme as a destination that entails a journey – and a long one at that, where we must expect a few bumps and detours along the road (for eg change in business strategy or leadership, impacts of cost programmes and organizational re-design on morale, the time it takes to shift deeply entrenched mindsets). But it's a deeply satisfying journey: remember to stop every so often and look back at how far you've come.

Notes

1 Financial Conduct Authority, Discussion Paper 20/1 at www.fca.org.uk (archived at https://perma.cc/2NL8-GF9Y)

2 Financial Conduct Authority, Discussion Paper 20/1 at www.fca.org.uk (archived at https://perma.cc/2NL8-GF9Y)

3 Financial Conduct Authority, Occasional Paper 24, at https://www.fca.org.uk/publication/occasional-papers/op16-24.pdf (archived at https://perma.cc/7F2W-L9AV)

4 Lagadec, Patrick (1991) *Preventing Chaos in a Crisis: Strategies for prevention, control, and damage limitation*, McGraw-Hill

5 Miles, Roger (2017) *Conduct Risk Management: Using a behavioural approach to protect your board and financial services business*, Kogan Page

6 Edmondson, Amy (2018) *The Fearless Organization*, Wiley

7 Financial Conduct Authority, Discussion Paper 20/1 at www.fca.org.uk (archived at https://perma.cc/2NL8-GF9Y)

8 Banking Standards Board (BSB) annual assessments, available at https://bankingstandardsboard.org.uk/bsb-assessment-results-2019/ (archived at https://perma.cc/DHJ7-M2A3)

9 Syed, Matthew (2019) *Rebel Ideas: The power of diverse thinking*, John Murray Press

10 Kay, John and King, Mervyn (2020) *Radical Uncertainty*, Bridge Street Press, London

11 Haldane, Andrew G (2017) Rethinking Financial Stability (speech to BIS Conference, Washington, 12 October 2017) (Bank of England, London), www.bis.org/review/r171013f.pdf (archived at https://perma.cc/ZVU4-ZPG5)

12 FCA Discussion Paper 18/2 at www.fca.org.uk (archived at https://perma.cc/2NL8-GF9Y)

13 HM Treasury, Women In Finance Charter, accessed December 2020 at www.womeninfinance.org.uk/ (archived at https://perma.cc/57NJ-L458)

11

Interventions and enforcements

How regulators have responded to a 'culture crisis'

RACHEL WOLCOTT

Preview

This chapter looks at how regulators have approached mandating firms' transformation of conduct and culture. It contrasts the United Kingdom's claimed leadership experience with the Netherlands and the United States, which have their own distinctive culture initiatives.

It will consider critically how regulators have changed the nature of their interventions during the years since the 2008 financial crisis, as they seek to bring about behaviour change in financial service firms. Whether regulators have punished, collaborated, nudged, coached, or simply ignored problems, how far have any of these different approaches succeeded in getting firms to adopt measured good behaviour as corporate policy? And could the strongest argument in favour of culture assessment be nothing to do with regulators at all?

THEMES AND CONCEPTS IN THIS CHAPTER

accountability – Banker's Oath – codes of conduct – culture assessment – culture iceberg model – culture transformation agenda – derivatives market – 'exemplary conduct' vs misconduct – groupthink – market abuse – non-financial misconduct – nudge approach – proprietary trading ('casino banking') – reference rate/ LIBOR-fixing – regulatory reform – rhetoric gap – rules and questions of conduct formalized – self-regulation ('government-sponsored voluntary regulation'/GSVR) – senior manager personal accountability – Senior Managers & Certification Regime (SMCR) – 'sludge' vs 'nudge' – systemic rule-gaming – 'treating customers fairly' (TCF regime) – Volcker Rule – whistleblowing

First wave of reforms: the major legislation

Poor conduct has been seen by many observers as the overarching cause of the 2008 financial crisis, which prompted a series of reforms to prevent a repeat. Previous, discredited regulation had included a strong element of industry self-regulation through '"pledges" made between businesses and the government'[1] (so-called government-sponsored voluntary regulation model, or GSVR; see page 41). An early collective regulatory response came in September 2009, when the G20 group of countries set out a vision for reforms to 'to turn the page on an era of irresponsibility'.[2] In the United States, the first wave of reforms came with the Dodd Frank Wall Street Reform and Consumer Protection Act (DFA), aimed at increasing transparency in derivatives markets and preventing so-called casino behaviour on banks' trading desks. It also launched the Consumer Finance Protection Bureau (CFPB) aimed at protecting consumers from some of the banks' most exploitative behaviour. Controversial from the outset, CFPB is still in 2020 under attack from financial services firms and conservative lawmakers.

The European policy and legislative response has been similar. The European Market Infrastructure Regulation (EMIR) brought in new reporting, clearing, and risk mitigation (clearing) requirements for derivatives contracts. The aim was to force the derivatives market – whose activities had triggered the 2008 global financial crisis (GFC) – to become more transparent and safe as well as accountable for its activity. Further reforms came through the EU's Markets in Financial Instruments Directive II (MiFID II) redraft which introduced changes to capital markets activities aimed at increasing price transparency, eliminating inducements and reducing financial products mis-selling while increasing transparency on costs and fees. MiFID II also brought in new governance standards for firms' boards and senior management.

The UK also introduced a new Bribery Act in 2010, the first reform to bribery laws in almost a century. The UK's new behavioural regulator, the Financial Conduct Authority (FCA) introduced the Senior Managers and Certification Regime (SMR) in March 2016, rules meant to hold senior managers accountable for their own actions and those who report to them. Meanwhile the European Union introduced Market Abuse Regulation in July 2016 which strengthened and expanded previous laws against market manipulation and insider dealing.

These legislative reforms intended to stamp out some of the conduct that caused the financial crisis – and should have. Firms' compliance operations ballooned in response as more people and IT systems were brought into implement a massive new rulebook. One regulatory monitoring firm found that 204,469 pages, or 60 million words, of rules had been generated by regulators worldwide to address systemic and to a lesser extent conduct weaknesses exposed by the crisis.[3]

Reforms not working?

Yet the reforms took years to implement. DFA was first to come into force, rolled out incrementally starting in 2010, and elements such as the Volcker Rule soon came under attack (see box) as the banking lobby fought hard against its provisions. EMIR was not applied until 2014 and MiFID II did not launch until January 2018 – almost 10 years after the financial crisis. Banks managed to delay implementation of the Volcker rule until 21 July 2015. It came under renewed pressure in 2020 when the US Federal Reserve sought to roll back rules that limit bank investment in venture capital and securitized loans.

THE VOLCKER RULE

Named after the former United States Federal Reserve Bank chairman, Paul Volcker, this legislation was aimed at curbing banks' unfettered risk taking by dramatically reducing their ability to conduct proprietary trading – colloquially known as casino banking.

The MiFID II reforms are themselves already under review, in accordance with its built-in review mechanism, re-examining consumer protection rules, and firms' lack of implementation of transparency requirements. With a poor design, EMIR was difficult for firms to implement and has not yet enhanced transparency. The European Securities and Markets Authority (ESMA) has not reported meaningful insights into derivatives market activity, as there is insufficient trade reporting data.

New approaches to a continuing conduct crisis

Meanwhile, events of misconduct have continued in financial markets, suggesting few lessons learned post-2008, despite firms paying multi-billion-pound/dollar fines after (for example) scandals of LIBOR reference rate rigging, foreign exchange market manipulation, and mis-selling of payment protection insurance (PPI).

LIBOR RIGGING

Manipulation of the London Interbank Overnight Rate (LIBOR) is possibly the biggest single banking scandal in history not just in terms of fines, but also in the number of banks and inter-dealer brokers involved in the multi-jurisdictional conspiracy to 'rig' the key benchmark interest rates.[4] Rate rigging was collusive behaviour whereby those bank employees tasked with submitting their cost of borrowing to the benchmark administrator would provide figures to benefit derivatives traders, instead of submitting the rates the bank would actually pay to borrow money. It is thought LIBOR rigging started in 2003 and the practice was first brought to light in 2008, during the financial crisis. The international process to wean financial markets off LIBOR and onto new risk-free rates is ongoing and expected to last until at least 2023.[5]

PPI

Payment Protection Insurance was designed to cover repayments in circumstances where a customer was unable to make them, for example in cases of redundancy or being unable to work due to an accident, illness, disability or death. As many as 64 million PPI policies were sold in the UK, mostly between 1990 and 2010, but some as far back as the 1970s. The UK Financial Conduct Authority (FCA) found most of these policies were mis-sold.[6]

Bank cultures where treating customers fairly, following the spirit of the law and not just the letter, psychological safety and cognitive diversity are at the core, remain elusive. Seeing clearly that rule changes alone would not promote ethical cultures and good conduct, some regulators, most notably the Dutch central bank (DNB) and the UK Financial Conduct Authority

(FCA) have turned to a cultural transformation agenda. This approach has attempted to educate firms about good culture and to introduce behavioural science into thinking about providing products and services to customers. In the UK, at least, this change in approach has led to fines against firms dropping dramatically, as fines against individuals rise.

Regulators have applied a nudge approach to launch the cultural transformation programme. Fines are now rarer in the UK. A firm must be a repeat offender or commit a fairly egregious mistake before the FCA slaps them with a fine.

'Nudging' (aka 'choice architecture') is the regulatory design practice of influencing choice by changing the manner in which options are presented to people. For example, changing a consumer choice from opt-in to opt-out may improve customer outcomes. Popularized by the bestselling political and behavioural science book, *Nudge*.[7]

The UK approach: a Conduct Authority to police conduct and culture

The UK's old Financial Services Authority (FSA) was reborn as the Financial Conduct Authority (FCA) in 2013. With 'Conduct' firmly at its core, work began to hold individuals – particularly firms' senior managers – accountable for actions that resulted in firms failing or treating customers unfairly.

Partly this initiative responded to the legacy of public frustration following the event of senior managers – notably certain high-profile leaders such as Fred Goodwin, the Royal Bank of Scotland's (RBS) former chief executive – walking away from the banks whose collapse they had presided over (in 2008), with big pension pots and seemingly zero accountability. Why was it so difficult to hold bankers to account for bad decisions and misconduct they never seemed to know was happening?

As we have seen, the UK's FCA and later other regulators introduced new principles, rules and policy objectives aimed at achieving senior manager accountability, better outcomes for consumers and better cultures that would naturally feature good conduct. Its new tools ranged from remuneration clawbacks, to regulatory references, to industry engagement initiatives such as the Five Conduct Questions, to softer diplomacy such as thought leadership essays and 'Insight' articles.

The FCA has come to view good conduct and healthy firm cultures as prerequisites to the fair and efficient functioning of wholesale markets, fair treatment of customers and as a deterrent to market abuse. The underlying argument is: good conduct risk identification, awareness and management will prevent the recurrence of all the bad things banks have done since 2008. Julia Hoggett, the FCA's director of market oversight, set out an explicit link between forward-looking conduct initiatives and the prevention of market abuse:

> A regulatory system that relies on controls that work by detecting when an event has happened, will never be as effective as a system that also helps ensure that misconduct does not happen in the first place... [challenging] the risks and issues posed by market abuse.[8]

Rules to enforce senior manager accountability

The Senior Managers and Certification Regime (SMCR, or SMR) was perhaps the FCA's biggest 'statement' rule change, holding executives personally to account. It was introduced to the UK's top-flight banks in 2016 and across solo-regulated firms in 2018–20, replacing the Approved Persons Regime (APR).

Its avowed aims are 'to reduce harm to consumers and [to] strengthen market integrity by creating a system that enables firms and regulators to hold people to account', by

- encouraging staff to take personal responsibility for their actions;
- improving conduct at all levels;
- making sure firms and staff clearly understand and can show who does what.[9]

The Conduct agenda and tools drive increased accountability, with individuals taking responsibility for their actions and decisions. This has in turn also increased senior managers' and other employees' regulatory and legal risk: senior managers are required to report misconduct to the regulator. Actual or suspected breaches of the conduct rules by those subject to the SMCR must be reported within seven days of discovery. Serious breaches of the conduct rules by any employee covered by them must be reported immediately.

SMCR sets out a range of Senior Management Function (SMF) holder designations, from SMF 1 (a chief executive) to SMF 17 (a money laundering reporting officer). SMFs have prescribed responsibilities and must produce and attest to a statement of responsibilities. These 'mapped responsibilities' aimed to hold SMFs and certified persons accountable for those employees reporting to them and for the business lines they oversee. No one wanted another repeat of the often-cited excuse, 'I had no idea what was going on in my own business'.

SMCR aims to make it easier for the FCA and PRA to act directly against senior executives when things have gone wrong in parts of the business for which they are responsible, even if the regulator cannot demonstrate that they have been personally involved in, or even aware of, the wrongdoing.

After SMCR: a few investigations, very few enforcements

Before SMCR's rollout, lawyers helping firms prepare for it expected the FCA to act quickly to produce a high-profile 'senior scalp' to hold to account.[10] No senior scalps have materialized. The FCA says it has investigated a number of SMFs and certified persons but that as of the start of 2021, no senior manager has faced enforcement action (fine, ban) specifically for failing to fulfil their SMCR governance obligations.

Parliamentarians such as Baroness Susan Kramer have expressed frustration that the 'softly, softly' approach to altering culture hasn't worked: SMCR 'sounds strong and positive... it has not been used. That is a real failure'.[11] Business heads seem unafraid that SMCR might harm, or end, their careers because the regulator appears not to use it.

CASE EXAMPLE 1

SMCR enforcement: a bank chief executive and a whistleblower

On 11 May 2018, the FCA and PRA jointly fined James 'Jes' Staley, chief executive of Barclays Group, a total of £642,430. An FCA press release heralded the case as the first brought under the Senior Managers Regime.[12] Staley had twice tried to identify a whistleblower who had sent an anonymous letter to the bank's board in June 2016. The letter contained various allegations, some of which concerned Staley. Regulators concluded that given his conflict, Staley should have maintained an appropriate distance; he should not have taken steps to identify the author.

The FCA/PRA investigation concluded Staley's conduct to be a breach of 'Individual Conduct Rule 2' – requirement to act with due skill, care and diligence – but not a breach of 'Individual Conduct Rule 1' which requires SMFs to act with integrity. Staley was not, in fact, sanctioned under SMCR, but under the Conduct of Business rules for his own actions, not those of direct reports or other subordinates. The FCA ruled that 'Staley should have explicitly consulted fully with those with expertise and responsibility for whistleblowing in Barclays and sought express confirmation from them that what he wanted to do was permissible. He failed to do this.'

The investigation found that Staley had made serious errors of judgement and both regulators viewed his misconduct as sufficiently serious for each to impose a penalty of 10 per cent of Staley's relevant annual income. In addition, the bank's whistleblowing systems and controls were required to submit to enhanced regulatory monitoring and scrutiny. The bank was required to report annually to the FCA and PRA, including any whistleblowing cases involving allegations made against its senior managers and any cases where the bank has sought to identify any anonymous whistleblowers.

Public opinion was deeply underwhelmed. In many people's eyes Staley was receiving a token reprimand and the £642,430 fine, though personal rather than against the firm, was unlikely to harm such a wealthy man. Regulators had built up SMCR as a robust tool that would finally enable them to hold senior individuals to account, yet their judgement on Staley seemed to fail to meet the public expectations created; no senior scalp, as Staley remained in post. Although the Barclays board had also held back his bonus, many had expected, or hoped, that regulators would enforce his removal.

Defending its response, the FCA commented that the regulatory action taken was 'timely, and robust, and demonstrated the seriousness with which we take senior management conduct'.[13]

CASE EXAMPLE 2
SMCR enforcement: a senior manager fare-dodger

In December 2014, 18 months before SMCR's rollout to tier-one UK financial institutions, the FCA banned Jonathan Burrows, a former managing director at BlackRock, from working in the financial services sector. Burrows had been stopped by railway revenue enforcers in 2013 and found to have exploited a loophole in the system that meant he avoided paying for his daily commute. Burrows reached an out-of-court settlement with Southeastern Trains totalling nearly £43,000, implying years of fare dodging.

Tracey McDermott, at the time FCA director of enforcement and financial crime, said Burrows' conduct fell short of what was expected: 'Approved persons must act with honesty and integrity at all times and, where they do not, we will take action'.[14] The FCA ruling said Burrows, who held an 'approved person' (regulator-cleared) customer-facing role, had admitted to evading paying his train fare, knowing he was breaking the law.

The Burrows case was held up as an early signal of the FCA's seriousness about senior managers' integrity and why a 'fit and proper' test was vital; was this a sign of things to come?

As the Jes Staley case (above) showed, no, it was not. The *Financial Times* published comments from an FCA press officer that the point of the rules is 'much like speeding cameras... is not necessarily fines but that their mere existence alters behaviour'; that SMCR is not primarily about enforcement but 'to encourage firms and their staff to take greater responsibility for their actions'. Its aim was 'encouraging senior management to exercise greater responsibility... improving firms' culture.'[15]

Cultural transformation as a policy objective: testing the limits of 'nudging'?

Cultural transformation of financial services firms has been FCA policy since at least 2017 when it began to emphasize culture more than conduct risk, which had been its focus previously. The FCA has launched a series of initiatives encouraging senior managers to look to change their firms' culture, improving customer outcomes, reducing misconduct and increasing workplace psychological safety. It's a sector-wide exercise in practical 'nudging' – as with *Nudge* author Richard Thaler's 'good signage' effect, guiding financial sector staff towards making better choices about behaviour, so driving positive transformation in culture.

The FCA's also published two volumes of essays (discussion papers), launching a 'culture conversation' in 2018 and advocating 'purposeful cultures' in 2020.[16]

The five high-level conduct rules and five conduct questions (see Chapter 10, pages 235–236) are complemented by four conduct rules specific to senior managers (FCA Handbook, Code of Conduct section COCON 2.2):[17]

- SC1: You must take reasonable steps to ensure that the business of the firm for which you are responsible is controlled effectively.

- SC2: You must take reasonable steps to ensure that the business of the firm for which you are responsible complies with the relevant requirements and standards of the regulatory system.

- SC3: You must take reasonable steps to ensure that any delegation of your responsibilities is to an appropriate person and that you oversee the discharge of the delegated responsibility effectively.

- SC4: You must disclose appropriately any information of which the FCA or PRA would reasonably expect notice.

With these three sets of enjoinders, the FCA urges senior managers and all financial sector workers to think about how to apply the rules and questions in practice to all aspects of their business. It could be summarized as, 'How is your behaviour impacting outcomes?' The FCA has been checking to see whether firms are asking these questions and what they have learned from the answers, with annual conduct meetings for the largest firms, to understand how the firm has considered the Five Questions and the steps being taken to improve conduct in the firm. The results of these reviews are published periodically, the latest currently being 2020's *Messages from the Engine Room*, which exclusively interviewed middle managers to discover how far firms were progressing beyond the early utopianism of 'tone at the top'.[18] In a speech in 2019, the FCA's market oversight director Julia Hoggett set out the intended scope of the five questions, as an approach 'sufficiently broad-and principles-based that it can apply to almost every manifestation of conduct risk'.[19]

The FCA views the five conduct questions, then, as a framework that all firms can use to identify conduct risk, to empower staff to be responsible for managing that risk, reducing misconduct and transforming culture in the process. The FCA envisions staff automatically using the five conduct questions as part of their working life, like a check list.

The industry body UK Finance encourages practitioners to adopt and use its own plain-language version of the Five Questions (see Chapter 10, page 238). The hope is that by eliminating regulatory jargon and recasting the questions as everyday moral challenges, they will become routinely used to prompt 'conduct conversations' in firms' team meetings.

More nudges: culture sprints and webinars

In 2018 the FCA launched a 'CultureSprint' live discussion forum and webinars to encourage financial services firms to improve workplace culture and overall behaviour. Hosted by Jonathan Davidson, executive director of supervision for retail and authorizations, these forums aimed to open up a crowdsourcing approach that could yield new solutions, especially to improve psychological safety so that employees could speak up, be listened to by management, and solve problems more sociably. One of the FCA's own participants, Olivia Fahy, a culture assessment specialist, commented that the 2008 financial crisis still leaves unresolved issues from 'cultures where people felt they couldn't call out poor behaviour, poor conduct. If people had felt safer in their environment... those failures could have been lessened.'[20]

The FCA advertised the CultureSprint as bringing together expert perspectives in a multi-disciplinary forum, inviting academics, behavioural scientists, representatives from consumer groups, industry representatives and other subject matter experts. All would be encouraged to collaborate in teams to develop experiments targeted at creating a sustainable, psychologically safe environment during 'moments that matter' to employees.

Some practitioners have questioned CultureSprint's lack of structure and clarity,[21] as harking back to pre-FSA (1990s) self-regulation (see 'GSVR' above), and that newly appointed culture and conduct officers may 'window dress' instead of solving tough problems. Firms are conscious of having made 'paper promises' on culture, not delivered. In one case literally: one winning proposal from CultureSprint was to place leaflets in firms' meeting rooms, reminding people to 'listen first sometimes'. As explored elsewhere in this book, behavioural experts are sceptical of slogan solutions such as posters and leaflets; a far stronger determinant of tone and culture at a firm is how leaders are seen to behave.

Policy on culture and vulnerable customers

In 2019 the FCA made firms' treatment of vulnerable customers a key policy objective, publishing Guidance Consultation (GC 19/3) ideas for where firms could improve. Andrew Bailey (then FCA chief executive; from 2020, Bank of England governor) pointed to fair treatment of vulnerable customers as a priority. The regulator sees firms' treatment of vulnerable customers as a strong 'tell' (proxy indicator) for the state of their risk cultures, engagement with and respect for conduct rules.

Fair treatment of vulnerable consumers is to be embedded in firms' culture, focusing people, products, services and processes towards this outcome. Everyone in financial services is to be responsible for a culture of fair treatment; leaders must 'manage the drivers of behaviour in their firms to create and maintain cultures which reduce the potential for harm, particularly with respect to vulnerable consumers.'[22]

CASE EXAMPLE 3

Enforcement against a car finance provider

The FCA's guidance consultation on vulnerable customers remained open at time of writing in Q4/2020, but in February 2020 it levied a £2.77 million fine on Moneybarn Ltd, a car finance firm, for not treating customers fairly (April 2014–October 2017) when they fell behind with loan repayments while in financial difficulties. The FCA emphasized the vulnerability theme in its final notice. Announcing the fine, Mark Steward, the FCA's executive director of enforcement and market oversight, noted that Moneybarn:

> did not give its customers, many of whom were vulnerable, the chance to clear their arrears over a realistic and sustainable period. It also did not communicate clearly to customers, in financial difficulty, their options for exiting their loans and the associated financial implications, resulting in many incurring higher termination costs. These were serious breaches.

As a used vehicle finance provider predominantly to customers unable to meet mainstream lenders' lending criteria, Moneybarn had an unusually high number of vulnerable customers on its books. The FCA saw in these customers an 'increased risk of financial vulnerability', with weak credit histories after 'adverse life events' and at greater risk of 'suffering detriment if they fall into arrears'.

Moneybarn voluntarily paid more than £30 million in redress to over 5,000 customers. The FCA gave Moneybarn credit for this redress in assessing the size of the penalty imposed, accepting that whilst Moneybarn had 'made considerable efforts and promptly took action to improve its forbearance and termination processes and practices', its earlier conduct had failed to meet regulatory expectations.[23]

The Moneybarn fine sent a clear signal: failing to treat customers fairly, especially vulnerable ones, is a 'serious breach' – conduct that falls short of regulatory requirements.

A second signal was that Moneybarn's voluntary redress scheme was seen as a mitigating factor. The FCA's Final Notices on enforcements alert firms to 'expected conduct and culture'. In this case, 'exemplary' practice is to act quickly to right wrongs and compensate any unfairly treated customers.[24]

Surveys reveal stalled culture programmes

Industry surveys published Q4/2019 and Q1/2020 (pre Covid-19) showed culture change programmes and related diversity initiatives making little headway, highlighting the limits of UK regulators' nudge approach.

CFA UK's 2019 annual diversity survey found 51 per cent of investment professionals believe their firms could be doing more to improve the culture of their organizations, with almost 60 per cent reporting they had received no diversity and inclusion training from their employers. Regulatory expectations were clear on this, noted the survey analysis.[25]

Since 2016, the UK's Banking Standards Board (BSB) has published an annual 'assessment' survey of bank employees' sentiment around cultural concerns.[26] Its 2020 edition (data collected in 2019) reported no significant year-on-year improvement and that since early gains in 2017, the industry's overall engagement in culture has flatlined. BSB expressed disappointment at this lack of progress, given the background of firms investing in culture transformation programmes. Despite 'pockets of improvement', culture indicators at smaller banks had declined during 2019, it noted: 'Actions taken by firms may take time to show results; culture change rarely happens quickly or in a straight line. Or, of course, none of this may be the case.'[27]

A worrying 34 per cent of BSB-surveyed employees reported not believing the senior managers at their firm would take responsibility if something went wrong at their bank. Thirteen per cent had witnessed individuals being rewarded for unethical behaviour; one in four employees reported working at their firm adversely affected their health and well-being (consistently, 2016–20); 37 per cent routinely slept for six or fewer hours each night.

NON-FINANCIAL MISCONDUCT

'Non-financial misconduct is misconduct, plain and simple,'[28] says the FCA. The call to engage with diversity and inclusion resonates still stronger as we move on through the 2020s, grappling with a range of culture-related themes including purpose-driven culture, cognitive diversity (to replace groupthink) and psychological safety.

Firms' efforts in diversity and inclusion tell the regulator's assessors a lot about their culture. The new emphasis on 'non-financial' shows regulator's policy move towards considering a firm's culture as a sum of all its behaviour, on- and off-campus, and not only its products and services. Abusive behaviour within teams, for example, is now clearly seen as a proxy indicator or 'tell' for every form of misconduct: how firms handle non-financial misconduct, including alleged sexual misconduct, informs the regulator's culture assessment of the whole firm just as much as how they respond to 'traditional' abuses (insider dealing, market manipulation, and so on).[29]

Regulator identifies key common indicator for 'a healthy culture'

As a principles-based regulator the FCA has long resisted a prescriptive approach to conduct and culture. It does not want to tell firms how to do culture, but rather firms should come to their own conclusions about what a good culture is for them. The problem is that many firms continue to regard culture change, SMCR and conduct risk management as regulatory change programmes to be implemented in the same way they might approach any new set of rules. Some firms will do a good job, implementing changes not because they are required, but because they can see the benefits. Others will simply comply.

Since 2018, the FCA has pointed to psychological safety as a core indicator of a firm's culture, and is looking to assess this from 2021 onwards. Jonathan Davidson, executive director of supervision for retail and authorizations, commented in an FCA webinar in 2018 that whilst there is 'no one-size-fits-all culture for organizations', one positive factor that is common to all firms with a healthy culture is 'a culture of psychological safety'.

UK outlook: as yet, no cause for optimism

There is, ironically, another big drag on cultural transformation in the form of a collective perception bias: firms' naïve optimism. In research conversations among many firms, I have noted a common belief that their culture has been good all along and that no change is needed. Marketing materials are full of nostalgia-tinted claims to a track record of stellar customer service, energetic funding of small and medium businesses, and generally being a motor for economic growth. There is also a continued denial mindset belief that any bad behaviour that caused the 2008 financial crisis, or reference rate-fixing of LIBOR/foreign exchange/precious metal markets (take your pick of scandals) were either a local aberration or 'legacy' behaviours, since eliminated. And yet, as we see throughout this book, the scandals continue.

Firms tell me they're getting back to core values, that anyone responsible for 'legacy misconduct' has been fired, and that therefore culture has trended back to the claimed, rosy-tinted norm. As research gathered in this chapter shows, these claims don't stand up to objective scrutiny. Firms' own, often crude prototype indicators, as well as external surveys comparing trustworthiness across multiple sectors,[30] point to significant numbers of customers determinedly disliking their financial providers.

Another mass self-deception is firms' persistent, default tendency to make culture change a 'tone from the top' slogan-driven exercise. When firms proclaim values and behaviours that put customers at the centre of everything they do, customers (and staff) expect to see that. Sloganeering demoralizes employees, who see it for what it is, with knock-on damage to customer service.

A case example shows how these elements are linked. UK bank RBS was mandated to review its retail advice practices following serious abuses. Employees working on the bank's resulting 'Project Amethyst' criticized its asymmetric 'YES Check' programme. Its design in theory stepped employees through making conduct-positive decisions to ensure good customer outcomes. Whistleblowers who worked on the project claimed managers told them to rote-learn a frictionless path through the YES Check, threatening spot checks and punishments for those unable to recall it. More perversely still, employees were actively discouraged from using YES Check to improve decision-making within Project Amethyst itself.[31]

SLUDGING, NOT NUDGING

Financial services firms' 'sludge' habit continues to produce poor outcomes for the full spectrum of customers, and in some cases for firms themselves. In a July 2019 feedback statement the regulator defined sludge as 'practices that appear intentionally designed to discourage behaviour which is in the consumers' best interests'.[32]

As Richard Thaler, one of the original architects of *Nudge* explains, sludge (or ill-intended nudging) can take two forms: 'It can discourage behaviour that is in a person's best interest such as claiming a rebate or tax credit, and it can encourage self-defeating behaviour such as investing in a deal that is too good to be true.'[33] Thaler is the co-author, with Cass Sunstein, of the popular manifesto *Nudge* (2008), in which behavioural economics tools solve some of society's more intractable problems. A nudge is a 'decision frame' that's meant to encourage beneficial behaviour. A 'sludge' is essentially its evil twin: a nudge-like process that's actually designed to deliver bad choices or prevent good ones.

Sludge has long been a feature of financial sector redress schemes. Project Amethyst's whistleblowers claimed that its methods were designed to minimize redress paid to customers given unsuitable advice, achieving this outcome through improper procedures. In 'systemic rule-games', remediation systems may be designed such that no customer will receive a positive outcome – much like the rigged casino where 'the house always wins'. This game of compliance[34] entails re-framing of definitions of the underlying offences and misconduct to reduce the number of eligible claimants. In other incidents:

- Lloyds Banking Group and Clydesdale Bank were both fined in 2015[35,36] for wrongly rejecting too many payment protection insurance (PPI) compensation claims.

- UK banks' interest rate-hedging product redress schemes were similarly criticized. In this case, claimants argued schemes' eligibility criteria were purposefully defined narrowly to exclude many of the bigger claims.[37]

Meanwhile in the Netherlands: psychologists in the boardroom

The Dutch central bank, De Nederlandsche Bank (DNB) is the regulator with the most experience incorporating behavioural and cultural observations into its supervisory programme. It draws on a deep Dutch research tradition of bringing scientific social observations into legislative drafting.[38] In 2011 DNB began explicitly observing behaviour and culture at supervised institutions. Famously it introduced psychologists into banks' board meetings to observe the group dynamic and how directors' behaviour influenced decision-making and firm cultures.

DNB has maintained a behaviour analysis team since 2010. (See 'culture iceberg model', Chapter 10).[39] 'I was rather taken with [DNB] 'iceberg' and have been wondering whether one of the British banks might like to volunteer to be a guinea-pig for the Dutch treatment,' Sam Woods, chief executive of the UK's Prudential Regulation Authority, told central bankers in Basel in 2019, having met DNB's behavioural team. He noted that DNB's approach offered genuine thought leadership.

While the DNB approach has been lauded by the International Monetary Authority (IMF) and admired by fellow central bankers, other regulators have been slow to emulate it, even as they express their admiration. There may be some anxiety, in boardrooms of both firms and regulators, as to what the clinical eye might reveal. In the UK, by contrast, the FCA had abandoned a planned Culture Thematic Review (announced in 2015, then withdrawn) – possibly why UK progress has been relatively sedate.

The DNB views culture assessment and change as a long-term project, aimed not only at symptoms or quick fixes, but building sustained change.[40] Like the UK FCA, the DNB does not prescribe one particular culture but sees culture as a prime responsibility of the board, saying that a prescribed 'good culture' may hinder diversity in business models, strategies and corporate cultures. However, it's not a 'culture-neutral' view: DNB 'knows bad culture when it sees it' and says it will act decisively where there's evidence of a culture that induces irresponsible or unsound behaviour.

Between 2015 and 2020 the DNB conducted 54 supervisory culture assessments, identifying 34 of these as showing fundamental risks in the area of behaviour and culture, intervening in 63 per cent of those cases. It found that executive and supervisory directors recognized the importance of culture and behaviour, yet their actions do not always effect 'desired changes'. Firms' senior managers were found to be poorly aware of their own strategy and core values, tending towards consensus and excessive optimism (signs of groupthink) and making decisions based exclusively on procedures and models. DNB observed that:

- most management boards lack sufficient expertise in behaviour and culture;

- the intention behind a desired change is not always convincing;

- proposed measures may be insufficiently drastic or implemented, so envisaged behavioural change fails to materialize;

- leaders do not sufficiently abide by the values that they endorse.

Financial firms' leaders and supervisory boards need to make more of an effort to improve and complete their cultural transformations, says DNB, and to appreciate the effect their own behaviour has on their firms' cultures. Meaningful change is about more than a branding or messaging exercise. Too often, DNB sees firms 'reluctant to effectuate changes all the way to the core of their business operations and culture'; changes may thus remain only 'instrumental or superficial and consequently do not lead to sustainable and genuinely different behaviour.'

Dutch Bankers' Oath

Another uniquely Dutch contribution to regulated behaviour, also not yet fully replicated (let alone enforced) elsewhere, is the Bankers' Oath (detailed in Chapter 5), a code of conduct meant to foster ethical behaviour. The Netherlands' Tuchtrecht Banken (FBEE) was established in 2015 by the banking trade body Nederlandse Vereniging van Banken (NVB), responding to the financial crisis; NVB has since 2016 administered the Bankers' Oath to 90,000 bank employees.

The oath is obligatory and legally binding. Those who break it face legal sanctions ranging from reprimands to severe fines, up to a maximum of €25,000, and/or a three-year moratorium on working anywhere in the Dutch banking industry. One aim of the oath is to empower bankers to stand up to and question demands made of them that seem potentially unethical. For example, if an employee's manager asks them to design or market a product that will make money for the bank, but disadvantage customers, the employee should refuse, citing the Banker's Oath.

After a banker has been sanctioned, the FBEE enters their details on a private register, where firms can check whether applicants have in the past violated the Code of Conduct or been professionally disqualified.[41]

The United States experience

As we go to press, with the start of a Democrat US Presidency we'd reasonably expect significant changes in policy around financial consumer protection and redress. Although US agencies and regulators still exact the highest fines against financial firms, post-2008, culture and behaviour have not featured strongly in the practical details of America's post-crisis regulatory response.

The New York Federal Reserve Bank has fronted the sole regulatory initiative aimed at governance and culture: a series of conferences and a webpage devoted to the subject.[42] Although there is much debate in institutional investment circles around a new socially conscious agenda to reset the balance between shareholder and wider stakeholder interests (see Chapter 6), in the regulatory sphere there has been little pressure towards, or uptake of, cultural transformation programmes. The following cases therefore represent rare instances of conduct-focused engagement.

US financial services have the same culture problems as many other countries. That was laid bare by the 2008 financial crisis and a quick glance at the US Securities and Exchanges Commission (SEC), Financial Industry Regulatory Authority (FINRA) or the Commodity Futures Trading Commission's (CFTC) long lists of enforcement actions will show little has changed. One case in particular stands out, however: case example 5 below. First though, a beleaguered consumer protection agency.

CASE EXAMPLE 4

A study in stasis: the US Consumer Financial Protection Bureau

Launched in 2011, the US Consumer Financial Protection Bureau (CFPB) was created under the DFA as a financial watchdog agency to regulate mortgages, student loans and other financial products. Its short, fraught history illustrates the high barrier to any conversation about cultural transformation in the US.

CFPB says it has provided $12 billion to 29 million consumers who fell victim to predatory lending, misleading credit card services and other financial products. Yet Republican lawmakers fought against it from its inception, arguing that the agency is an example of governmental overreach that curbs consumer choice and economic growth.

In March 2020 the CFPB's constitutionality was challenged in the Supreme Court by Selia Law, whom it had been investigating. Former CFPB director Richard Cordray noted with regret this challenge to the agency's independence:

> A law firm that we were investigating for possibly cheating its customers has mounted a challenge to block the investigation from proceeding. The Trump administration has sided with the law firm, contending that a government agency having a single director with some protection against removal by the president is a violation of our constitutional system of separation of powers.[43]

Selia Law did not get much pushback from Trump appointee Kathy Kraninger, the subsequent CFPB director. Kraninger wrote to Senator Mitch McConnell and US Representative Nancy Pelosi in September 2019 to inform them the bureau had determined that the agency gave her too much independence.[44] In June 2020, the Supreme Court ruled the 'restrictions on the removal of the CFPB director are unconstitutional'. The Court rejected Selia Law's argument that 'if the leadership structure is unconstitutional, the court should strike down the rest of the act creating the CFPB as well.'[45]

2021's advent of Democratic Presidency will (perhaps) reinvigorate CFPB and related enforcement.

CASE EXAMPLE 5

US enforcement against fraudulent cross-selling

Of all the bad behaviour during and post-2008, one firm, Wells Fargo, is uniquely distinctive for its intractable 18-year 'cross-selling scandal' and the number and scale of resulting enforcement actions.

In February 2020 Wells Fargo paid $3 billion and agreed to settle criminal charges and a civil action tied to a 14-year period (2002–2016) where employees opened millions of accounts in customers' names without their knowledge. They went on to open further accounts including credit cards and bill-paying programmes, creating fake personal identification numbers and forged signatures. Wells Fargo also admitted to charging mortgage customers unnecessary fees and forcing auto loan customers into buying superfluous insurance policies. (That misconduct was not included in the February 2020 settlement with the US Department of Justice.)

At the same time, the US securities regulator (SEC) charged Wells Fargo with misleading investors about the success of its core business strategy, at a time when it was opening fake accounts. Wells Fargo agreed to pay $500 million to settle the charges, to be returned to investors. The $500 million payment is part of a combined $3 billion settlement with the SEC and the Department of Justice.

The Office of the Comptroller of the Currency fined former Wells Fargo chief executive John Stumpf $17.5 million in January 2020. Carrie Tolstedt, Wells Fargo's former head of retail banking, contested her fine of $25 million. Criminal investigation of former Wells Fargo executives' individual roles in the sales practices scandal continued during 2020. Misconduct was attributed to a culture where branch employees were set unrealistically high sales targets which were raised year on year. In 2018, the Federal Reserve moved to restrict Wells Fargo from growing its business until it could prove having made changes to prevent bad behaviour.

Addressing incoming CEO Charles Scharf in early 2020, Maxine Waters, Democratic House Financial Services Committee Chair, said she was unsure he had a compelling plan for turning around the bank: 'While I wish you luck, it is clear to this Committee that the bank you inherited is essentially a lawless organization that has caused widespread harm to millions of consumers throughout the nation.'[46]

Conclusion

After contrasting regulators' initiatives in three jurisdictions, we might conclude that although these are three quite different regulatory styles at work, overall, regulators aren't exactly vigorous in challenging firms' apathy over culture change and persistent abuses. More than 12 years after the 2008 financial crisis, most regulated firms have yet to engage with culture reporting. The time for regulatory 'nudging' of culture is surely over: without more forceful demands for real change, any present momentum for culture transformation risks stalling entirely.

The US approach to culture engagement hitherto (admittedly during an aggressively pro-business Republican presidency) might kindly be described as 'polite curiosity'. The UK experience is bursting with good intentions but less evidently any wide improvement in outcomes, or aggressive prosecutions under new accountability rules. The Dutch experience represents a triumph of intellectual rigour and practical application of behavioural research but remains a beacon in the surrounding gloom.

Despite enormous fines in the earliest stages of Conduct regimes, firms would seem to need a more compelling argument than mere regulatory risk, if they are seriously to take up culture assessment techniques. Lack of an industry-wide road map, and senior leaders' apparent reticence to grasp the culture problem – if they see it at all – risks stalemate over culture transformation. New analytic technologies and other tools offer cause for optimism, possibly to re-engage senior leaders with culture as regulators ask: Why not use these to solve the problem? What kind of analysis are you doing? As long as firms stick to a widespread culture of 'boilerplate' purpose and values statements, average progress globally will remain glacial.

Ironic, then, that a more compelling argument is now emerging from the business side. As we'll see in Chapter 12, as reg techs and behaviourally literate designers develop more intelligent forms of culture assessment, supported by new technologies, these tools may vastly improve business resilience and responsiveness, re-motivating staff and customers.

Ever since the UK conduct regulator veered away from its planned sector-level Culture Thematic Review in 2016 – preferring 'thinking engagement' with each firm – it's been unclear how far agencies will push for enforceable standards of 'healthy culture'. Whether regulators have the will, and reflexivity, to place new culture audit technologies at the heart of their future engagement with firms, we may have to wait and see.

Notes

1 Decker, C and Hodges, C (2014) *Government-Sponsored Voluntary Regulation*, Oxford University Faculty of Law, www.law.ox.ac.uk/research-subject-groups/research-index/impact-index/government-sponsored-voluntary-regulation (archived at https://perma.cc/FH3T-GWUD)

2 G20, 2009 Pittsburgh Summit Communique, www.g20.utoronto.ca/2009/2009communique0925.html (archived at https://perma.cc/JX5U-A6HP)

3 Di Giammarino, P J (2020) RegTech 2.0: Winning in the decade ahead, *JWG*, https://jwg-it.eu/article/regtech-2-0-winning-in-the-decade-ahead-7-february/ (archived at https://perma.cc/4TFZ-JCVN)

 4 Council for Foreign Relations (2016) *Understanding the LIBOR Scandal.* Accessed at https://www.cfr.org/backgrounder/understanding-libor-scandal (archived at https://perma.cc/HN2X-XXRC)

 5 Wolcott, R (2020) U.S. dollar Libor given 18 more months; regulators seek to curb new lending, *Thomson Reuters Regulatory Intelligence*, 1 December

 6 FCA (2020) Payment protection insurance explained, https://www.fca.org.uk/ppi/ppi-explained (archived at https://perma.cc/7LBM-3K2P)

 7 Sunstein, C and Thaler, R (2009) *Nudge: Improving decisions about health, wealth and happiness,* Penguin

 8 Julia Hoggett, speech delivered in January 2019, www.fca.org.uk/news/speeches/market-abuse-requires-dynamic-response-changing-risk-profile (archived at https://perma.cc/8SX8-FU7V)

 9 See FCA's SMCR guidance in www.fca.org.uk/publication/policy/guide-for-fca-solo-regulated-firms.pdf (archived at https://perma.cc/R2AV-MRY8)

 10 Wolcott, R (2015) UK regulator refocuses enforcement on individuals; fines and investigations on rise, *Thomson Reuters Regulatory Intelligence*, 4 November

 11 Quoted in Lindsey Rogerson (2019) for Thomson Reuters Regulatory Intelligence: Banks no longer afraid of senior managers regime, UK lawmakers told, 12 September

 12 FCA (2018) FCA and PRA jointly fine Mr James Staley £642,430 and announce special requirements regarding whistleblowing systems and controls at Barclays, www.fca.org.uk/news/press-releases/fca-and-pra-jointly-fine-mr-james-staley-announce-special-requirements (archived at https://perma.cc/2RYS-6K5S)

 13 FCA (2018) Annual Public Meeting, https://fca.org.uk/publication/minutes/apm-2018-transcript.pdf (archived at https://perma.cc/D2SB-NP22)

 14 Quoted in Coyle, M (2014) # City fare dodger banned from industry by FCA, *Thomson Reuters Regulatory Intelligence*, 15 December

 15 Binham, C (2019) Net widens for UK's financial accountability rules, *Financial Times* 9 December, www.ft.com/content/119cf33e-19c0-11ea-97df-cc63de1d73f4 (archived at https://perma.cc/5AQR-XX5H)

 16 FCA (2018) Transforming Culture in Financial Services (DP 18/2); FCA (2020) Transforming Culture in Financial Services – driving purposeful cultures (DP 20/1)

 17 FCA Code of Conduct, www.handbook.fca.org.uk/handbook/COCON.pdf (archived at https://perma.cc/DMB5-QCD6)

 18 Quoted in Coyle, M (2014) # City fare dodger banned from industry by FCA, *Thomson Reuters Regulatory Intelligence*, 15 December

 19 Julia Hoggett, speech delivered in January 2019, www.fca.org.uk/news/speeches/market-abuse-requires-dynamic-response-changing-risk-profile (archived at https://perma.cc/8SX8-FU7V)

20 FCA (nd) CultureSprint video, www.fca.org.uk/events/culturesprint-supporting-and-empowering-managers-transform-culture (archived at https://perma.cc/75J7-QM5H)

21 Detailed in Wolcott, R (2019) UK regulator runs CultureSprints to improve finance workers' psychological safety, behaviour, *Thomson Reuters Regulatory Intelligence*

22 Detailed in Wolcott, R (2019) Treatment of vulnerable customers tells FCA much about culture, whether firms are meeting its standards, *Thomson Reuters Regulatory Intelligence*, 16 September

23 FCA (2020) Moneybarn final notice, https://www.fca.org.uk/publication/final-notices/moneybarn-limited-2020.pdf (archived at https://perma.cc/VM9S-5L9D)

24 FCA (2020) Final Notice on Moneybarn enforcement, www.fca.org.uk/news/press-releases/fca-fines-moneybarn-277m-unfair-treatment-customers-arrears (archived at https://perma.cc/7VX8-KBND)

25 Detailed in Rogerson, L (2019) SMCR roll-out: Half of investment professionals think their firms' efforts to improve culture and diversity have stalled, *TRRI*, 4 December

26 Banking Standards Board (2019) Assessment Results, https://bankingstandardsboard.org.uk/assessment-results-2019/ (archived at https://perma.cc/W9HA-L9FS)

27 Detailed in Rogerson, L (2019) SMCR roll-out: Half of investment professionals think their firms' efforts to improve culture and diversity have stalled, *TRRI*, 4 December

28 Christopher Woolard (2018) FCA interim chief executive and executive director of strategy and competition, speech to City of London, December, https://www.fca.org.uk/news/speeches/opening-and-speaking-out-diversity-financial-services-and-challenge-to-be-met (archived at https://perma.cc/NW5U-WFPF)

29 Christopher Woolard (2018) FCA interim chief executive and executive director of strategy and competition, speech to City of London, December, https://www.fca.org.uk/news/speeches/opening-and-speaking-out-diversity-financial-services-and-challenge-to-be-met (archived at https://perma.cc/NW5U-WFPF)

30 Such as Ipsos-MORI Veracity Index, https://www.ipsos.com/ipsos-mori/en-uk/ipsos-mori-veracity-index-2020-trust-in-professions (archived at https://perma.cc/HMW2-KLRM) – many other indicators are available

31 Wolcott, R (2020) UK FCA probes RBS's in-house investment advice review after receiving whistle-blower report, *Thomson Reuters Regulatory Intelligence*, 7 February

32 FCA Feedback Statement 19/4 (FS 19/4) Fair Pricing in Financial Services: Summary of Responses and Next Steps

33 Thaler, R (2018) Nudge, not sludge, *Science*, **361** (6401), pp 431

34 Miles, R (2014) Conduct risk: when compliance becomes a game, *Thomson Reuters Regulatory Intelligence*, https://legal.thomsonreuters.com/en/insights/white-papers/conduct-risk-when-compliance-becomes-a-game (archived at https://perma.cc/M2VT-7C5S)

35 FCA (2015) Lloyds Banking Group fined £117m for failing to handle PPI complaints fairly, www.fca.org.uk/news/press-releases/lloyds-banking-group-fined-£117m-failing-handle-ppi-complaints-fairly (archived at https://perma.cc/7ZFQ-ZUTP)

36 FCA (2015) Clydesdale Bank fined £20,678,300 for serious failings in PPI complaint handling, www.fca.org.uk/news/press-releases/clydesdale-bank-fined-£20678300-serious-failings-ppi-complaint-handling (archived at https://perma.cc/6MVA-S4MU)

37 Wolcott, R (2020) UK financial services' 'sludge' habit produces poor outcomes for all kinds of customers, even in crisis, *Thomson Reuters Regulatory Intelligence*, 27 March

38 For example 'Tafel Van Elf' assessment of public propensity to behave in compliance with stature laws: see De Tafel van Elf: Een wetenschappelijk ontwikkeld model die inzage geeft in de redenen waarom mensen de regels overtreden at https://decentrale.regelgeving.overheid.nl/cvdr/images/De%20Ronde%20Venen/i269534.pdf (archived at https://perma.cc/G8AW-TJKT)

39 Rogerson, L (2019) Top UK prudential regulator praises Dutch practice of having psychologists observe bank boards, *Thomson Reuters Regulatory Intelligence*, 13 March

40 De Nederlandsche Bank (Mirea Raaijmakers, editor) (2015) Supervision of Behaviour and Culture, https://www.dnb.nl/media/1gmkp1vk/supervision-of-behaviour-and-culture_tcm46-380398-1.pdf (archived at https://perma.cc/75WJ-SFB2)

41 Wolcott, R (2020) Dutch Foundation for Banking Ethics Enforcement handed down 79 bans in 2019, Thomson *Reuters Regulatory Intelligence*, 19 February

42 Federal Reserve Bank of New York (nd) Governance and culture reform www.newyorkfed.org/governance-and-culture-reform (archived at https://perma.cc/34M7-BS4N)

43 Comments reported in Cordray, R, (2020) Why the Supreme Court should protect the CFPB's independence, *The Atlantic*, theatlantic.com/ideas/archive/2020/03/why-court-should-protect-cfpbs-independence/608359/ (archived at https://perma.cc/WQ74-2RMB)

44 Higgins, T (2019) The head of the CFPB now believes that the financial regulator is unconstitutionally structured, *CNBC*, www.cnbc.com/2019/09/17/cfpb-head-tells-supreme-court-agency-is-unconstitutional.html (archived at https://perma.cc/G94R-JJQR)

45 Howe, A (2020) Opinion analysis: Court strikes down restrictions on removal of CFPB director but leaves bureau in place, *SCOTUSblog*, www.scotusblog. com/2020/06/opinion-analysis-court-strikes-down-restrictions-on-removal-of-cfpb-director-but-leaves-bureau-in-place/ (archived at https://perma.cc/F5ET-Y2RK)

46 Moise, I and Schroeder, P (2020) Wells Fargo CEO tells Congress bank has doubled down on regulatory issues, *Reuters*, 11 March

12

Intelligence gathering versus surveillance

Tried and failed methods; putting the latest research tools to work

RACHEL WOLCOTT

Introduction

Financial services firms have started using technology tools, adding to their use of supervisory 'reg tech', to gather intelligence about culture and conduct risks. Some aspire to embed findings into conduct risk frameworks and culture transformation programmes. This chapter will look at certain widely used but ultimately ineffective methods companies use to determine how their employees and customers view them.

Firms using surveillance tools may be tempted to assume that this is a way to protect culture and even foster good workplace behaviour. It is not. These monitoring methods give a distorted view of culture and are proven in some cases to reinforce poor practices. This chapter will also explore the risks associated with surveillance including data protection and privacy considerations, the ethical dimension as well as employees' rights and psychological safety.

By contrast, we'll then assess intelligence-led approaches and methods to explore whether there are better ways that firms can use technology to learn about their cultures and, most importantly, feed findings into conduct reporting frameworks and cultural transformation programmes.

THEMES AND CONCEPTS IN THIS CHAPTER

artificial intelligence and machine learning – 'bad actor' fallacy – criminally based approach to compliance – 'Dear CEO' letters – employee sentiment surveys, shortcomings of – establishing 'bad intent', difficulty of – false-positives problem – floor-walk test/direct observation – intelligence-gathering – predictive analytics – proxy indicators – psychological safety – 'reg tech' – 'rolling bad apples' – regulatory surveillance – 'silver bullet' fallacy – 'Stasi effect' – surveillance – trade surveillance approach

Tempting but dangerous 'supervision solutions'

Some regulated firms opt for artificial intelligence (AI) and machine learning (ML) powered surveillance systems and so-called people analytics to detect bad behaviour and punish employees. Yet there is little evidence that surveillance contributes 'lessons learned' for firms' shaping of conduct risk management or cultural transformation. As we'll see, use of surveillance tools to generate culture management information is dangerous. They not only have high potential for misuse, but increase staff disengagement and demotivation by implying mistrust at a systemic level.

Besides, surveillance technologies will not – at least in their current forms – yield positive insights suitable for required culture assessment indicators such as cognitive diversity or psychological safety. Because surveillance tends to be over-cautious, generating false positives, it reinforces a low-trust work environment and therefore a poor culture. Properly used, it may reveal financial misconduct such as insider dealing and identify possible indicators of poor culture such as sexist or racist language. However, AI tools' analysis of large amounts of structured and unstructured data collected through surveillance has been shown to be biased.[1]

The industry's move to systematize surveillance is going in the opposite direction to regulators' direct observation tests, a core tool of culture audit. Regulators promoting cultural transformation, notably the Dutch central bank (DNB) and the UK's Financial Conduct Authority and Prudential Regulation Authority (PRA), all use direct observation (informally, 'floor-walk tests') to examine culture and to coach firms to improve. Supervisors most of all want to see firms being proactive about solving problems and directly involving senior managers.

As a flavour of this, one former central bank supervisor said, in an interview for this chapter:

> Proactive problem solving was an indicator things were going well. All I wanted to see was that senior managers were taking ownership of problems. If I felt comfortable there were people who were competent and capable and willing to take accountability then I felt there was no point getting involved. Those firms that say 'It's all fine' or 'It's trivial' or 'We've got it all under control', then we thought, wait a minute, what else are you trivializing in your business?

Proxy behaviour and culture measurement tools: the classics

Across many industry sectors, job candidates have experienced that awkward moment in the interview process where a human resources manager hands them a personality test, asks for a urine sample or administers a non-verbal reasoning assessment. Employers have all kinds of voodoo magic (handwriting analysis being a personal favourite) to determine whether a job candidate is a good fit for their culture.

These are all ways companies seek to control culture, protect reputation and maintain the cultural status quo on the input side of the equation, but when deployed as tools to achieve this end, they are useless pseudoscience. Human resources departments and executive coaches love personality tests such as Briggs-Myers or Enneagram, which claim to identify personality types and provide 'a robust foundation for life-long personal development'. Psychologists, meanwhile, tend to reject these tests as unscientific and warn they may do individuals harm. Such 'personality type-based' tests are 'unscientific, do not validly nor reliably measure "personality", and could plausibly lead people to become inflexible learners with a fixed mindset',[2] notes psychologist Benjamin Hardy.

Personality tests could also reduce firms' cognitive diversity – a key indicator of 'healthy culture' – by excluding certain personality types, for example eliminating too many introverts at point of recruitment. Human resources departments should not rely on flaky behavioural measures in any case; regulators mandate firms to check job candidates' regulatory references to stop 'rolling bad apples'. They would like you to look at evidence, including records of directly observed behaviour, not a crystal ball or an online personality test.

'**Rolling bad apples**' are employees with poor conduct records who nevertheless manage to move from firm to firm unimpeded.

The UK Financial Conduct Authority's Senior Managers Regime (SMR) introduced regulatory references[3] which oblige firms to make sure senior managers and control function holders don't have a history of misconduct or behaviour that may cause harm. The Hong Kong Monetary Authority consulted on a similar programme in 2020.[4]

Firms use many similarly vague and inappropriate tools to measure conduct and culture, including net-promoter scores, engagement surveys and customer complaints. These approaches may gauge loosely self-identified sentiments, but they do not properly assess culture. These assessments can be biased in the questions they ask, failing the 'what actually happens' test (see 'floor-walk test' below) and measuring the outcomes of a culture rather than the behaviours that drive it. Firms also overlook or misinterpret data that might be useful, assessing culture over-optimistically and leaving conduct risk blind spots.

Are employee surveys sufficient?

Firms love surveys. They use them to gauge employee engagement, which is commonly (if wrongly) viewed as a good proxy for culture. They also use them to confirm customer satisfaction, considered another proxy for culture and conduct. Surveys can be useful, but all too many firms ask leading questions or ignore answers they dislike, as Frank Brown, a consultant at Bovill in London, observes:[5]

> Asking customers 'Hey what do you like about us? Would you like us to be better yes/no?' doesn't give you any meaningful data. Present people with wider and qualitative choices.

Firms make the same mistakes when they survey staff: self-reporting on sentiment is likely to induce a gamed response. Employees tend to supply positive answers because they do not feel secure enough to say what they really think. Others may believe their employer compares favourably with other firms, but (1) how do they really know? And (2) maybe the firm is just less bad than other employers.

Employee surveys are often a substitute for manager-to-employee and manager-to-senior manager engagement. They give firms specious satisfaction that feedback has been sought and received. The survey approach is particularly unsatisfactory when it comes to gauging employee well-being and psychological safety. The UK's FCA has highlighted both as indicators of good culture, and regularly lets firms know they are responsible for employees' mental health and safety as well as their physical well-being.[6] Still one in four UK financial services employees report poor mental health and/or 'negative impact on well-being' from their job.[7]

Employee surveys can reinforce the so-called 'middle management permafrost'[8] problem as one barrier to culture change at banks, among others;[9] that's one result of it being fairly uncommon in the United Kingdom to be trained as a manager. People tend to be put in roles but formalized management training across a wide range of skills, especially 'people skills', is not much evident in the Anglo-Saxon model. Managers need these soft people skills and the structure and framework around them.

There are of course surveys that seek to assess managerial effectiveness. However, in a poor culture with low psychological safety amongst staff, respondents will not answer honestly for fear of retribution. Effectiveness will also hinge on what questions are asked and what firms do with the responses received. Seeing little change, employees lose faith in the process, or note that assessments do not ask about issues that matter to them. Assessments may avoid focus on how managers treat staff and tend to benchmark them against economic targets. Employees judge managers differently. They will value empathy, accessibility, fairness and flexibility. These questions tend not to be asked.

Taking a different approach to assessing employee sentiment

Given the shortcomings of conventional techniques, some analysts have pursued a fresh approach to assessing employee engagement. Chief executive of London-based people analytics company Peakon, Phil Chambers, notes: 'It's not like employees don't want to be heard. Everybody wants to give their opinion.'[10] The Peakon platform gathers employee data in an opt-in fashion using surveys that can be distributed using mobile phones, Slack integration, emails or even on a factory kiosk.

These surveys are shorter, but more frequent than conventional formats. Instead of sending out 100 questions a year in a single survey, companies might ask three to four questions a week. It collects data on why employees skip questions (intelligibility, or other factors). Peakon keeps the raw data it collects to protect respondents or whistleblowers from being identified by their employer. Chambers explains:

> Anonymity is vital if you're going to ask people, 'Is it safe to speak up?', otherwise is someone in HR going to access the raw data, look you up? We don't allow clients access to the raw data [so they can't] put pressure on people.

Peakon can produce continuous demographics (gender, age, tenure, salary and department) and combined employee responses, then use machine learning to generate priorities for improving engagement.

What regulators are learning from direct observation: the new 'floor-walk test'

Financial regulators use technology to gather and analyse vast amounts of data to monitor prudential and conduct risk. European firms, for example, send millions of transaction reports a week to regulators who then use artificial intelligence or cloud-based analytics tools to scour them for signs of wrongdoing – such as market abuse. Since the latest round of transaction reporting rules were applied via the Markets in Financial Instruments Directive II in 2018 there have been only a handful of market abuse fines and court cases brought, however.[11]

Number crunching and surveillance will never be the only pathway to good culture. UK and Dutch regulators, recognizing this, gain great value and insight into firms' culture through direct observation: the so-called 'floor-walk test'.

A **floor-walk test** is nothing more than a supervisor arriving at a firm, meeting with staff in the course of their work at their desks, observing behaviour and using what they see to give another data point in their overall view of a firm. The supervisor may otherwise – or also – attend a board meeting or virtual team meeting; or invite individual employees to a real or virtual 'tea with the regulator' informal interview hosted from the regulator's own offices.

Interviewed for this chapter, one supervisor described direct observation as more of an art than a science:

> It's about triangulating lots of different sources to see where the truth is, somewhere in the middle. Sometimes regulators are good at making that judgement, sometimes not, because they have to look at bits they're not that competent in or are not their area of expertise.

Walking the floor gives the regulator a way to check senior managers' and non-executive directors' claims to know what is actually happening. A mismatch is a sign something could be wrong:

> It was remarkable how few [non-execs] had a good answer. A lot of them look at you and say we set the culture, it's all top down, what do you mean I need to know what's going on, on the ground?

Leaders need to know the attitude of people on the ground, the regulator told us; they'll supply anecdotal evidence, but many struggle to articulate what is happening in their firms. Some non-executives have not done the work and this is obvious to the regulator:

> The best ones can answer the questions. But there are still plenty who claim to be 'high and mighty', all-seeing and encompassing at board level, but not actually knowing what's going on.

Senior management and board members can send out as many employee surveys as they like, but these will not tell them that staff are not mis-selling products or giving customers incorrect information about what to do if there is fraud on their account. Artificial intelligence (AI) tools are equally unlikely to root out these direct indicators.

Regulators have by now worked out that proxy indictors – like net-promoter scores and employee engagement surveys – are not as useful as direct observation. On a floor-walk visit, a regulator can see for themselves whether senior management know what is happening in a branch or on the trading floor. If any member of staff cannot answer a simple question about 'what actually happens', this suggests they are struggling with culture (see Chapter 9).

Approaches to producing the new MI: culture tech, people analytics and surveillance

In the UK, some banks have started to look at new kinds of conduct risk indicators, metrics and measurement tools, in part because they acknowledge that they have not yet made the kind of cultural improvements anticipated by regulators. Banks are obligated to assess and root out conduct risk, too, hence the boom in surveillance technology and regulatory risk analytics. Firms want to avoid big fines and redress payments made on the back of benchmark-fixing and mis-selling scandals (see Chapter 11). They also want to show regulators they are doing something about conduct risk and trying to transform culture. Regulators, equally, like to see management information (MI) – facts and figures evidencing firms' efforts.

The quality, usefulness and honesty of firms' conduct risk and culture MI – the theme of this book – is difficult to understand based on publicly available information in annual reports, for example. Firms claim on the one hand to have cultures that put the customer first and tend to rate themselves highly as being good places to work. On the other hand, the small print in annual reports may tell a different story – untrusted by customers, facing huge litigation and conduct liabilities – with little commentary on what firms plan to do about it.

Other publicly available information, such as the event of a regulator's 'Dear CEO' letters, fines, complaints and skilled persons reviews (whereby the regulator orders a firm to hire an expert to assess and correct certain problem areas) paints a picture of an industry struggling to manage conduct risk – be it failing to safeguard client money or preventing money laundering or insider dealing.

'Dear CEO' letters: The UK Financial Conduct Authority and the UK Prudential Regulation Authority will periodically write to regulated firms' chief executives to inform them of specific poor practice and misconduct observed during routine supervisory work or other regulatory interventions. These letters come with the tacit expectation that firms will investigate and possibly remediate any similar conduct. They are sometimes viewed as a signal an enforcement action is imminent. Regulators will cite failure to heed such letters and other communications as an aggravating factor in enforcement actions that can sometimes lead to a fine being increased.

New technologies like artificial intelligence and machine learning have become the engines powering a dizzying array of conduct risk solutions, people analytics, and surveillance systems marketed as tools firms can use to learn more about what is actually happening on the ground. Some of these products can track employees' every mouse click and make big claims about being able to detect all kinds of behaviours including racism, sexism, harassment and inappropriate language. How firms are using these and to what end is less clear.

Broadly there are two kinds of tools being used to learn about conduct risk and culture. One is intelligence gathering and generating: tools that help firms understand where to look for conduct risk in their organizations or where certain behaviours might cause conduct risk to arise. The other approach is surveillance.

Surveillance is applied in various ways and can be intrusive, as when using data science, natural language processing and AI to establish an organization's baseline behaviour model from inputs like trade data and employee communications, then surveilling real-time trade data, electronic and spoken communications, social media, IT activity, keystrokes, mouse clicks, work times and place for patterns that deviate from that baseline. The idea is that a behaviour change (in the form of undue deviation from baseline or straying from an acceptability 'corridor') might indicate misconduct. Other systems use natural language processing to target specific regulated business lines; for example, attempting to pick up on traders using code words to disguise their plans to commit market abuse.

Surveillance systems' own level of intelligent engagement varies widely. Some surveillance vendors claim to be able to detect sexist and racist language; some will simply tell an employer how long a time an employee spends at (or not at) their desk.

Intelligence gathering and generating tools

Regulators give firms a lot of information about where they find systems and controls weaknesses that have the potential to translate into conduct risk and then regulatory action. If a regulator releases a thematic review on money laundering risks in the wholesale markets or a final notice and fine to a firm for failing to treat customers fairly, the regulators' findings will provide in both instances a road map for where firms ought to check, and check again for conduct risk.

In most cases, firms can gather a huge amount of information just from reading what the regulator has given them – which regulators actually expect them to do. Regulators like the UK FCA will cite their own work in final notices reminding firms how many times certain issues and failings were brought to their attention. Not heeding regulatory statements can be an exacerbating factor when calculating a fine.

However, ploughing through all this information, joining the dots and generating some management information pointing to potential systems and controls weaknesses remains a challenge for firms, who cite 'regulatory information overload' as a perennial problem. Intelligence-gathering and analytics tools can tell firms much about conduct and culture risks they face and point to where conduct risk frameworks and systems and controls should be revisited and possibly bolstered. We now list a few promising example tools.

Example approach 1: regulatory surveillance and analytics

One such tool is Dublin-based Corlytics' global regulatory enforcement database. It enables firms to generate conduct risk and culture-related intelligence by analysing enforcement trends, digging down into enforcement final notices, and then performing analysis to gain insight or make predictions about where regulatory interests are, where firms' systems and controls are and where those controls may be weak.

Corlytics monitors what the regulators are saying and doing. It ingests everything that conduct regulators publish globally, then tracks changes to regulations, enforcement cases going through, speeches, papers and press releases. It applies text analytics tools to the content ingest and then autogenerates content using artificial intelligence. Corlytics' tracker function follows how regulatory rules change over time and what influences those changes. It can, for example, pick up when academics and regulators begin to discuss a topic like climate change and show its evolution into new regulatory obligations. It can show users which regulators have the biggest influence in shaping policy. As John Byrne, Corlytics' chief executive says:[12] 'We can predict where conduct risk will arise; you have to monitor enforcement because enforcement is a huge driver of behaviour.' We might assume from this, he says, that regulators' frustration with poor culture in firms means that 'the only way the regulators can go about changing culture and behaviour is to have an emphasis on [various] types of enforcement.'

Enforcement action can tell firms a lot about behaviour and culture, says Byrne. Simply put, enforcement action is an outcome of poor culture, not a few bad actors working alone. Analysing enforcement actions will tell you a lot more about firms' culture than their public values and purpose statements.

The final notices and judgements that follow enforcement actions are a bank-by-bank guide to poor culture and conduct risk. Technology like Corlytics can help firms see where their peers are making the same mistakes, how often regulators pick up on the poor behaviour and how much it costs them in fines, disgorgement and compensation.

Byrne cites the 'Princelings scandal' as an example of enforcement action driven by poor culture. A number of investment banks were fined in the United States for Foreign Corrupt Practices Act (FCPA) breaches after law enforcement and regulators concluded banks' preferential hiring of Chinese officials' children – the Princelings – to gain investment banking mandates like initial public offerings was bribery.

'The mood of the investment banks at the time was: "It looks like we can't do this anymore to get mandates. If we do this, we're going to get caught." Enforcement works in banking because the underlying culture is poor,' said Byrne. He argues the root cause behind the Princelings scandal was cultural: banks' conscious decision to bypass recruitment procedures to buy influence and make money.

In the UK, senior managers are using Corlytics' tools to assess their personal conduct risk exposure. After the introduction of SMR in 2016, consequences of misconduct for the individual senior manager could be career ending:

> People are now saying, 'Is there is a personal consequence to me because of SMR?'; there's a demand for [our kind of] analysis of new regulations and what it means for the senior managers' SMR responsibilities, their personal accountability.

Example approach 2: predictive power

iPsychtec's CultureScope (methodology detailed in Chapter 14), is a behavioural measurement tool that gauges 'how both the individual and the organization behave across 15 critical behavioural dimensions using a cloud-based platform'.[13] CultureScope asks employees questions in a survey format designed to learn about behaviour. It is not your run-of-the-mill organizational health index work. Its methods are grounded firmly in behavioural science and designed by behavioural scientists, not management consultants.

CultureScope takes a distinctive approach. It can, for example, collect behavioural data from employees and use that information to map whether their responses match with the behaviours and values the firm has set out in conduct, culture and values statements. It can also show which behaviours are manifesting and which are not. That allows firms to predict where the next conduct problem will be: 'accidents waiting to happen'. It identifies where improvements are needed in a specific and precise way. It also can show how the adoption of certain behaviours together can improve culture and conduct outcomes.

CultureScope also shows firms how to connect culture and strategy: to build their own value statements, to see how they behave and whether there is a correlation between culture metrics, a firm's values, and outcomes. This approach is exactly what regulators want firms to do – to allow good culture to drive their strategy.

Behavioural-based metrics and analytic tools like CultureScope have been used by banks including HSBC, who used it to improve outcomes around various challenges including financial crime and insufficient 'speaking up' about problems. UK Finance also uses the tool as an exemplar at its Conduct Academy, to demonstrate how a consistent approach to culture assessment is achievable.

Surveillance: shortcomings of a criminally based approach to compliance

Conduct regulators are keen to promote 'exemplary conduct'. Yet the need to catch 'bad actors' persistently pulls the debate away from positive coaching and back towards enforcement. Whenever discussion turns to surveillance tools as a means to track behaviour or catch out bad actors, someone nearly always mentions casually but pointedly the Stasi – the former German Democratic Republic's intelligence service. That 'Stasi' has become a common nickname for workplace surveillance indicates just how toxic its use is perceived to be.

Reuters expert commentator Henry Engler identifies the corrosive effect of financial services' use of surveillance as a 'criminally based approach to compliance' associated with the 'Stasi mindset'.[14] It suggests to the employee that 'they are not trusted; that there is a need to watch their every move for fear they will do something that that harms the organization.' Surveilled individuals know they're being watched and find ways to circumvent this:

Widespread monitoring can lead to behaviours that are at odds with the values of open, democratic societies; increase in monitoring can actually increase misbehaviour, not decrease it.

Evidently, monitoring increases employee stress. There was a big uptick in the use of monitoring solutions amongst companies seeking to manage employee productivity during the Covid-19 crisis when many were forced to allow employees to work from home. Peakon's Chambers says that surveilled staff 'feel they're not trusted to be productive working from home even though they've been forced into this situation.' That feeling is then 'exacerbated by employers installing monitoring solutions, which explicitly says, "we don't trust you".' The conclusion is clear: 'People need to be able to decide some of how to do their job in the best way without feeling like they're being spied on; companies [using monitoring] depress any sense of autonomy... resulting in a decrease in engagement.' Ironically, by installing surveillance with at least a partial aim of increasing productivity, firms are ultimately decreasing it.

Firms try to blame bad actors and rogues

Surveillance perpetuates firms' common, optimistic and wrong assumption that their cultures are essentially fine and that the only problem is a few outlier 'bad actors'. Influenced in part by the US legal system culture of 'black letter law' certainty, surveillance tends to reinforce an unhelpfully simplistic zero-tolerance, black-and-white approach to behaviour and culture. What behaviours does it seek to detect in this way, that may be amenable to firm-wide cultural analysis and improvement? Many current surveillance tools prioritize tracking of whether an employee is at a desk interacting with a computer; yet another push-button solution to what is a people problem.

Surveillance has increasingly been turned on employees to find out everything about their behaviour. Facial recognition software is used in the recruitment process and closed-circuit television monitoring features in almost every workplace. Employers can track employees' every email, phone call, instant message, social media account – every mouse click. These systems pose as productivity optimization tools, but what they really do is encourage presenteeism by terrorizing employees. Eroding workplace psychological safety, surveillance maintains a low-trust work environment that will de-emphasize exactly the kind of cultural traits that employers ought to be nurturing, such as cognitive diversity and collaboration. Neuroscience-based employee well-being platform Helix Resilience's research lead, psychiatrist and chief executive Dr Stephen Pereira, observes that surveillance creates the impression that firms 'don't know how to govern, how to measure work output and function. It's taking micromanagement to a new level; the worst example of how an organization can interact with its employees.'[15]

A push-back has already begun. Employee surveillance systems may breach data privacy laws and have been ruled to infringe upon employees' rights to a private life in the workplace. The UK's Information Commissioner's Office (ICO) has investigated whether a high street bank's use of desk-based surveillance breached the General Data Protection Regulation (GDPR). As the ICO told Reuters:

> People expect that they can keep their personal lives private and that they are also entitled to a degree of privacy in the workplace. If organizations wish to monitor their employees, they should be clear about its purpose and that it brings real benefits. Organizations also need to make employees aware of the nature, extent and reasons for any monitoring.[16]

A 2017 European Court of Human Rights ruling bolstered the rights of employees to have a significant degree of privacy when sending and receiving workplace emails.[17] The Strasbourg appeal court decision forced employers to give more explicit warnings to staff if they want to monitor internet use. The case, which related to a Romanian engineer who was sacked in 2007 for exchanging messages on an office account about his sexual health with his fiancée, set a legal precedent across Europe.

Surely trade surveillance is acceptable...?

Some surveillance is of course mandated by regulators. So-called 'trade surveillance' is routinely present to detect forms of improper trading behaviour involved in committing market manipulation and abuse. These systems are set up to monitor for certain prescribed trading behaviours and patterns as set by the regulators, but the more progressive idea is for firms to scan continuously for new patterns of abuse by examining any and every new 'deviation' in behaviour. Some surveillance systems claim they can detect behavioural changes that indicate market abuse, insider dealing or other misconduct. These systems use AI and machine learning (ML) techniques such as natural language processing (NLP) to consume data from trading systems to generate alerts on behaviour pattern changes that may or may not indicate misconduct.

Trade surveillance systems typically generate a large volume of alerts, many of which are false positives which need to be checked by an analyst. This creates cognitive overload, as firms' analysts accrue backlogs of material to review, and data goes 'stale'.

Even the most advanced trade surveillance systems can be gamed, and even used to commit market abuse. Some firms buy the systems, plug them in, then adjust the parameters so that they find nothing 'inconvenient'; a UK firm was fined for not installing and calibrating its trade surveillance system correctly.[18] Perhaps the easiest way to subvert trade surveillance remains one of the oldest: to go outside the system. Many traders continue to use unmonitored encrypted messaging apps to communicate and collude on trades.

Trade surveillance systems are not a panacea; higher intelligence is required. Time for a third approach.

Example approach 3: looking for intent

Many of the top-tier investment banks now use AI- and NLP-powered surveillance platforms, of which perhaps the most intelligent is Digital Reasoning, led by Tim Estes, co-chief executive.[19] It offers a unified instant messaging, email, social and voice surveillance that connects to all employee communications sources. It comes with out-of-the-box policies for regulatory and corporate compliance including market and employee conduct, complaints, recommendations, mis-selling and suitability. As Estes states, the tool 'reads' emails, chat threads and voice conversations, looking to 'find behavioural patterns in that based on what people are saying; the language they're using... can be evidence of an intention.'[20]

This new surveillance technology replaces 'key word list' solutions that flagged specific language used in previous instances of misconduct. As it turned out, people had quickly learned to game those systems with simple workarounds, such as spelling 'fixing' as 'f1xing'. Digital Reasoning's pattern-seeking is intuitive enough to flag non-exact matches and look at context to detect potential misconduct.

This can also identify people's current frame of mind, such as: Is this person disgruntled? If their language indicates disquiet over compensation, do they then progress from disgruntled to secrecy and collusion? The model sees whether the language that person uses in trading or deal-making suggests they are trying to act dishonestly for outside profits that would make up for their belief their compensation is too low. It can highlight a chain of behaviours: predisposition signals, behavioural or activity signals and a decision point.

Once someone begins to execute market abuse, for example, they will shift to non-surveilled channels: face-to-face, an encrypted messaging app or something else. While the wrongdoing might be executed outside surveillance, Estes says it can still be picked up on surveilled channels. 'One of the remarkable things is after the fact, if they think they've succeeded, they still are either worried or they get arrogant: boasting on the one hand, or cover-up secrecy language on the other.'

However, even this advanced technology is not 100 per cent accurate, as language has 'high subtlety': natural language processing 'might deliver 95 per cent accuracy, [but] the idea that you can go into a deep domain area and nail secrecy language better than 50 per cent is pretty much not going to happen,' said Estes.

Besides, it is not a straight-line assumption that a misconduct offence has taken place. Firms cannot haul someone in for a meeting to make accusations of misconduct if a computer says they merely used language indicating a disgruntled mood. Firms need to have analysts in place working to a framework that considers multiple messages and social interactions to see if there is a substantive pattern that justifies an intervention. Language 'tells' are not always egregiously obvious, says Estes; more often, a possible pattern of words may appear 'sort of interesting, and you want to kind of dig in and see if [the initial alert] justifies something.'

He cautions against wide application of surveillance to measure firm-wide culture:

> There's a real fine line between individual privacy and sensitive listening. Listening to everything, that's the definition of Big Brother; it would get a lot of rejection, particularly in Europe, of the application... to culture [assessment].

Digital Reasoning seeks to 'protect what matters', according to its own mission statement. It looks to apply NLP and automation to protect 'people's time, customers' best interests' as well as protecting them from fraud. For example, another of its applications, Patient Intelligence,[21] is designed to augment cancer care workflow. Every step in the cancer diagnosis, treatment, navigation, documentation and follow-up process is enhanced by the software working invisibly behind the scenes. The idea is to reduce or eliminate missed appointments so the risk-critical data points are seen in time to make effective care decisions.

If this technology is to be used to shape culture in financial firms, it needs to be implemented carefully by an experienced company. In Estes' view, 'If you have the wrong player to get into this, it will get exploited and abused. It will poison the well on the goodness [it might bring] which is essentially shaping culture and acting as a steward over the values of the company.'

Conclusion: indicators through technology?
Sorry – no silver bullet available

We've compared and contrasted surveillance, direct observation and intelligence-gathering approaches. While some metrics are clearly better than others, there is no silver bullet, one-size-fits-all approach to culture audit. Culture audit and transformation is not a number-crunching exercise to be completed in 20 seconds using cloud computing.

It's clear that there can be a productive technology-led data-gathering element, which could help firms determine some starting points for further work and investigation. Yet an overreliance on surveillance could hinder firms' culture and conduct work by incubating fear and mistrust in the workplace and replacing meaningful employee engagement. Current surveillance tools remain prone to 'false positive' misfires – alerts to misconduct that simply is not there.

Firms cannot start a conduct conversation with 'The computer told me...'. It remains essential that intelligence is gathered sentiently, on a human-to-human basis. Conduct regulators are already doing this. In-house culture auditors of the future will find their eyes and perhaps even more importantly their ears are the best intelligence-gathering tools they have.

Notes

1 See for example Smith, R E (2019) *Rage Inside The Machine,* Bloomsbury, London

2 Hardy, B (2020) Two reasons personality tests like Myers-Briggs could be harmful, *Psychology Today,* 6 April, psychologytoday.com/us/blog/quantum-leaps/202004/two-reasons-personality-tests-myers-briggs-could-be-harmful (archived at https://perma.cc/T43B-R3HB)

3 FCA (nd) Regulatory references, https://www.handbook.fca.org.uk/handbook/SYSC/22.pdf (archived at https://perma.cc/N7F9-MYV6)

4 Hong Kong Monetary Authority (2020) Consultation paper on implementation of mandatory reference checking scheme to address the 'rolling bad apples', phenomenon https://www.hkma.gov.hk/media/eng/regulatory-resources/consultations/Enclosure_20200508.pdf (archived at https://perma.cc/AG2K-5DGW)

5 Interviewed for this chapter

6 See FCA Insight papers on psychological safety, for example fca.org.uk/insight/psychological-safety-secret-effective-teams (archived at https://perma.cc/Z3Q6-CFS8)

7 Banking Standards Board (BSB) (2019) Assessment Survey result: 25% of financial sector employees agree/strongly agree that their job 'has a negative impact on my health or well-being', bankingstandardsboard.org.uk/assessment-results-2019/resilience/ (archived at https://perma.cc/XS6P-KCRP)

8 FCA (2018) Transforming Culture in Financial Services, DP 18/2

9 FCA (2020) Messages from the Engine Room: Industry Feedback on 5 Conduct Questions, September

10 Interviewed for this chapter

11 Wolcott, R (2019) EU regulators' high-tech market abuse monitoring has not yielded across-the-board results, *Reuters*, 4 December

12 Interviewed for this chapter

13 https://ipsychtec.com/ (archived at https://perma.cc/YKN3-ZGGM)

14 Engler, H (2018) *A Behavioral Science Approach for Building Trust from the Bottom Up*, Palgrave MacMillan

15 Helix Research (2020) Employee wellbeing during Covid-19, https://helixresilience.com/blog/news-research/new-research-employee-wellbeing-during-covid-19 (archived at https://perma.cc/8A32-WBG6)

16 Singh, K (2020) Barclays being probed by UK privacy watchdog on accusations of spying on staff, https://uk.reuters.com/article/us-barclays-surveillance-probe-privacy/barclays-being-probed-by-uk-privacy-watchdog-on-accusations-of-spying-on-staff-idUKKCN25500P (archived at https://perma.cc/GJ4F-A2CJ)

17 Barbescu v Romania, see https://www.theguardian.com/law/2017/sep/05/romanian-chat-messages-read-by-employer-had-privacy-breached-court-rules (archived at https://perma.cc/J5CP-EXCX)

18 FCA (2019) Upper Tribunal publishes decision on Linear Investments Limited in relation to penalty imposed by FCA, https://www.fca.org.uk/news/press-releases/upper-tribunal-publishes-decision-on-linear-investments-limited-in-relation-to-penalty-imposed-by-fca (archived at https://perma.cc/THA8-3Z7R)

19 https://digitalreasoning.com/conduct-surveillance-2/ (archived at https://perma.cc/5DDM-SLPQ)

20 Interviewed for this chapter

21 https://digitalreasoning.com/patient-intelligence-2/ (archived at https://perma.cc/2DQN-2JVY)

Interlude Three
A sector-wide group seeks culture 'tells'

(Observing indications of good and poor conduct)

JULIE AMPADU

Introduction: why we do this

Conduct regulators have been trying hard since before 2000 to beam out a consistent message about expectations of firms' culture and behaviour. In their own way, each of the regulator's policy initiatives – the Principles for Businesses, Treating Customers Fairly and now Five Conduct Questions – has attempted to make the same point: that a box-ticking, compliance-driven approach isn't of itself evidence of a positive culture. Even complying under the latest (2020) iteration of the Senior Managers Regime doesn't automatically mean you think properly about culture and behaviour, as long as your firm persists in perceiving that regime as 'just another compliance exercise'.

In Q1/2020, as a Director of the Association of Professional Compliance Consultants (APCC), I set up a Working Group on Culture to support compliance consultants' advice to firms in:

- understanding 'culture';
- recognizing what is expected of them by conduct regulators;
- providing guidance on how to evidence firms' cultures.

Through this professional network, in Q2/2020 our working group surveyed 500 compliance professionals who work with several thousand authorized and regulated firms within the UK. Through working group members the APCC also enjoys access to other professional groups including CISI, UK Finance, and The Conduct Academy, on their respective Culture initiatives and informal Culture research among their own members.

Since the onset of the conduct regime's behavioural approach to regulation in 2013, reflecting a change across the industry, the role of compliance consultants has graduated from box ticker to trusted advisor, now supporting firms with business, cultural and behavioural matters as well as conventional compliance reporting. Hence we build up a relationship with client firms, getting to know each firm's people and inner workings and consequently their cultures.

The APCC survey asked compliance specialists to give 'what actually happens' examples of good and poor culture from their dealings with FCA-authorized firms. Findings were representative of our collective experiences and ranged widely from the very good to the very poor. Tellingly, they resonated with earlier, anecdotal research the APCC had done among regulated firms in 2006, a time when many of them believed that the Treating Customers Fairly (TCF) regime meant that they would have to create a whole new customer-centric control framework. As the 2020 survey proves, once again there's apprehension about being expected to 'drop everything' and start again. Of course, that's not the case. Just as when TCF was implemented in 2006, many firms were already able to demonstrate good conduct but they just didn't realize it; the 2020 survey findings seem to repeat that narrative.

In offering this short debrief, the APCC is keen to point to factors that conduct regulators say they are looking for: firms' exemplary behaviour, not just their misconduct in whatever form. We share below examples of good culture that are easy for any firm to replicate – and that they may well be doing already, without thinking about it. It was heartening to see rising awareness of, for example, psychological safety as an indicator of good culture. This suggests that at least at an intuitive level – if not yet formally – firms have begun to 'get it' about the regulatory agenda for culture.

The APCC survey also reminded us of how much pressure boards of firms now feel under to demonstrate competence and performance, individually and collectively. Some respondents noted good evidence of board decision-making, 'reasonable steps' and performance reviews; others pointed to boards whose minutes gave no sign of challenge, or rationale for decisions, or evidence of any thought given to their own competence or performance.

It's encouraging to some that firms are beginning to start their sales-side 'culture conversation'. For the firm that introduced coffee and doughnuts, with great success (see detailed responses below), one might ask why it took this new format – with added friendly non-executive director – to open the door to those conversations. How many employees had been feeling, and maybe in other firms still feel, unable to ask a question in a safe environment with their usual executive team?

Keeping it real: culture is about what actually happens – as when pandemic strikes

When we talk about 'culture', it can tend to sound grand and a bit abstract. What some firms don't yet seem to get the hang of is that it's the little things that can have extraordinary influence on people. And those things have, I'm afraid, nothing to do with 'just being compliant'.

As the regulator foresaw back in June 2020,[1] Covid-19 has provided us with a behavioural experiment and a test of culture. It so happened that the APCC survey of culture went out in April 2020, when firms had shifted quickly to remote working. Firms were already showing high levels of reflexivity: for example, one firm immediately encouraged staff to talk rather than email, nudging people to call one another for a quick chat to ask, 'how are things going?', giving the opportunity for others to open up in ways they might not normally do.

We have seen that disruption caused by Covid-19 has brought out positive, pastoral and leadership skills we didn't know that people had, even if the crisis also struck firms as an 'abrupt and brutal audit', especially for those unable to adapt and take their teams with them into the new normal. Leaders in some firms have sought new knowledge and new skills. There were many examples of the regulator's sought-after quality of 'reflexivity' – adapting positively to market disruption. Mental health, employee well-being and vulnerability became staple features on board agendas. People learned to be alert for and supportive in cases of mental ill-health, domestic abuse, anxiety and bereavement. I'd like to think that in each firm where this change of attitude has happened, culture as a whole has taken a turn for the better.

Meanwhile on the darker side, a few (let's call them) 20th-century attitudes survive. In an age when the average employee is now a millennial – that is, the workforce median birth date is now after 31 December 1981; people who turned 18 at or after 2000 – we'd like to think that bullying, blame culture and fear of reprisal from senior management are no longer routine. Yet the survey shows that some dinosaur attitudes have not yet disappeared.

In common with most of the authors of this book, as a trusted advisor visiting many businesses of different types, sizes and sectors, I've found myself developing a sixth sense that intuits their culture. Within two minutes of entering a firm, even without any formal audit conversation with a senior manager or review of a compliance document, one 'reads the signs' and can already form a strong first impression.

> One striking example lingers in my memory. I'd arrived at a private bank for the first time and, while being shown to my working space, saw a former colleague; we'd worked together in another firm some years before. As she waved 'hi' and smiled to me, I called cheerfully over to her – only to see her frown and place a finger to her lips to 'shush' me. At which point something struck me as strange: the entire office of more than 60 staff was completely silent. Moments later, I was told that no speaking was allowed. As you might guess, this closed mindset was clearly reflected within the files I reviewed – and of course, the firm's culture.

The APCC survey found many more firms seem to be really engaging with culture and trying to find a better way forward. Enjoy this selection of our findings of (mainly informal) 'tells' for good and poor culture. No doubt you'll have your own to add to the list we have started for you.

Survey findings: extracts

THE GOOD: Some observed 'tells' for exemplary culture

Is information shared?

- 'Extremely detailed management information relating to complaints (who, why, what) and however they have been resolved. Tracking information to make sure mistakes weren't repeated.'
- 'Open meetings, town halls and "ask a NED" sessions where *any* question is allowed.'
- 'Detailed MI on complaints and how they were resolved.'

Giving (and taking) responsibility:

- 'Positive encouragements to take on responsibility with an "it's okay to make mistakes and learn from them" attitude, giving confidence to junior staff.'

- 'Encouraging people to take responsibility whilst allowing them to make mistakes and learn from them.'
- 'Giving discretion to make small compensatory payments.'
- 'Giving individuals recognition and promoting from within.'

Leadership and senior manager visibility

- 'We bring a non-executive director into the business once each month, with an open door to all employees, offering confidential conversation, hot coffee and doughnuts. At the first attempt the employee queue went all the way down through the centre of the office (and this wasn't just for the doughnuts). It was a roaring success.'
- 'Reverse mentoring.'
- 'Senior managers walk about, or join Zoom meetings, in person instead of emailing. People are used to having a quick update chat on "How's it going? Any challenges today?" So they talk about what's really happening, and don't have to wait for a full risk assessment to spot any problems.'

Welfare and other positive signals

- 'Giving time for "Team reading days" so people can pursue personal interests.'
- 'Good office facilities for staff, with well-kept public areas.'
- 'Encouraging personal development, with self-directed learning funded by the firm.'
- 'Mental health awareness, communication and support.'
- 'Celebrating good teamwork and publicly recognizing when staff support one another.'
- 'Internal reflection in teams on "How is our work making a positive difference to peoples' lives?"'

THE BAD AND THE UGLY: Some observed 'tells' for dysfunctional culture

Is information shared?

- 'Doing a staff survey, then not sharing its results with staff – or indeed sharing any other management information with them.'
- 'Analysis paralysis and "terror of the template".'

Challenge – or lack of/resistance to it

- 'A mortgage broker who had a "cheque book" mentality to complaints. They thought they were being fair to customers by writing out a cheque in compensation without ever getting to the bottom of why something had gone wrong.'

- 'Stickiness. People resisting challenge, not being open to alternative ways of doing anything.'

- 'Shooting the messenger – calling anyone who asks questions "tiresome".'

- 'I've been hired to tick boxes. When I dared to challenge I was made redundant. I hear the new employee lasted eight months.'

Giving (and taking) responsibility

- 'A dominant chief executive and/or head of sales – in the boardroom and on the business floor.'

- 'People only ever admitting mistakes when forced to.'

- 'Betting that the ombudsman will find in our favour.'

- 'Too-long tenures on the board (executives *and* non-execs).'

Leadership, governance and senior manager (in)visibility

- 'Leaders invisible to employees; low levels of personal engagement.'

- 'Succession planning? No, we don't have that.'

- 'Secretive upper management; compliance staff, in particular, kept in the dark regarding important issues.'

- 'Reckless disregard for consequences of decisions made at a senior level.'

- 'Two bosses with different priorities.'

- 'An arrogant leadership style: "Do as I say, not as I do".'

'Asymmetric' rewards

- 'Incentives and remuneration being promised to employees for selling and making profit for the company; no rewards given for the quality of employee conduct with customers.'

- 'Pressure to meet over-ambitious "stretch" targets.'

- 'The things people do that get rewarded, aren't the things the firm wants them to be doing. They haven't aligned rewards with incentives, from executive remuneration downwards.'

- 'Promotion based on selling the most stuff (no matter what).'
- 'I do still see "rock stars": high-selling people can get away with breaches of ethics and conduct codes, as long as they're exceeding their commercial targets.'

The human factor: staff welfare… not so much

- 'Scruffy office (especially the public areas and the washrooms).'
- 'Conduct? No one ever talks about that.'
- 'High staff turnover; good people don't stay long.'

Exclusivity, abusive behaviour and other negative signs

- "Banter' as an excuse for racist and sexist comments.'
- 'Obvious gender pay gap.'
- 'Aggressive sales culture plus poor telephone manner.'
- 'Salespeople don't talk to compliance people.'
- '"Jollies" dressed up as training courses.'
- 'Myself (female) and my business partner (male) have been in meetings with clients. I will ask the questions, but all the answers will be directed towards my business partner and not to me. This doesn't happen so much in firms with a younger management team, but frequently happens during meetings with older generations of financial advisers.'
- 'Not much sign of positive change in diversity, by any measure: gender, social, or ethnic. And no one's ever heard of cognitive or neurotype diversity, so don't even ask!'
- 'A constant sense of rather forced formality; in the background in every conversation, there's that hierarchical attitude playing out.'
- 'Marketing that uses other companies' logos without permission.'
- 'Just paying for a fancy-looking standards certificate; what a scam.'

CASE STUDY
Exemplary Covid-19 response

A financial firm of around 300 employees has a CEO who, due to their busy schedule, can't routinely connect with everyone within the firm. Before Covid-19 hit, employees tended to know them from afar, rather than 'knowing' them. When the first lockdown began in the UK in March 2020, the firm had to furlough some of its employees and put others to work remotely. Until this point, the firm had been working really hard to create an inclusive and positive, healthy working environment for its employees – and it showed. The switch to remote working during Covid-19 presented a whole new challenge and it was far from clear that they'd cope. How would the firm be able to maintain any sense of leadership and team following the initial crisis mode, when so many employees were scared, confused and frustrated?

As it happened, very well.

Each morning, the CEO made themself available online to all employees. They ran a short daily meeting or sent an email, which covered topics from a business or regulatory update, to an item of news, a quiz or a joke; one morning they even brought one of their family pets to the Zoom call to meet everyone.

The new approach proved so popular and so useful that, at time of writing (Q4/2020) during the second UK national lockdown, these interactions now find the CEO engaging with their entire company. Regular take-up for these meetings is 80 per cent and employee surveys during milestone periods in lockdown show robust employee satisfaction. These individuals now know this senior manager, and that they're human – down to what their living room looks like, when they've had a bad night's sleep, and so on.

Conclusion

The 'tells' are usually there for all to see. If we approach culture assessment only from a viewpoint of formal reporting, this could blind us to the social signals out there. Frontline staff remain one of the best – if not *the* best – sources of early signals of whether controls are really working, managers are really accessible, and how decision-making plays out in practice. A firm can choose to ignore this source of free (and powerful) information, or embrace it. Formal staff surveys are only one element, and as noted elsewhere in this book (Chapters 10, 12) may be 'gamed' for various reasons such as by people looking to make a good impression, or avoiding conflict, or succumbing to a culture of fear.

Directly and objectively observing What Actually Happens on the frontline, as compliance consultants are uniquely well-placed to do, identifies sometimes unnoticed examples of excellent conduct but also the early 'weak signals' of trouble brewing. This survey has helped improve our collective consciousness and situational awareness; you're welcome to use its informal prompts as a starting point to sharpen observations within your own firm.

Note

1   Ewing, P et al (2020) Conduct, culture and Covid-19, *FCA Insight*, 10 June, www.fca.org.uk/insight/conduct-culture-and-covid-19 (archived at https://perma.cc/TS7B-7ZVU)

13

Putting respected research tools to work, example 1

Tools for cultural transformation: Barrett Analytics[1]

RUTH STEINHOLTZ

Values-driven organizations are the most successful organizations on the planet.

RICHARD BARRETT[2]

Not everything that can be counted counts, and not everything that counts can be counted.

ALBERT EINSTEIN (ATTRIBUTED)

Introduction

Given the growing focus on culture and conduct it is natural to want to measure and quantify 'culture' in order to be able to manage it. Indeed, in recent years there has been a proliferation of attempts to do that, particularly in the area of ethics and integrity. At the same time it is widely, but wrongly, believed that culture cannot be measured at all because it is such a vague concept. There are also many definitions of culture and many instruments that claim to measure culture when in fact they are measuring limited aspects of culture or organizational effectiveness. Academic research separates organizational culture from organizational identity; a distinction that is relevant here. Organizational identity generally focuses on 'what members believe and understand about who they are as an organization'.[3]

Here, we will focus on the broader concept of organizational culture. The widely respected expert on this topic, Edgar Schein's most recent definition, is that 'cultures are learned patterns of beliefs, values, assumptions and behavioural norms that manifest themselves at different levels of observability.'[4] Schein's earlier (2010) model[5] is easy to work with (see pages 221–222): it states that culture consists of three interrelated layers:

1 underlying assumptions and beliefs (conscious or unconscious);

2 norms and values about appropriate attitudes and behaviours (that may be espoused or real); and

3 artifacts that may reflect these (eg symbols and language).

Culture and identity are of course interrelated, but they are not the same.

THEMES AND CONCEPTS IN THIS CHAPTER

agenda for culture transformation – balanced values and behaviours – Barrett culture model, assessment and transformation tools – benchmarking of culture – business value benefits of culture reporting – cultural entropy (rating 'aligned vs misaligned') – desired vs current culture – employee engagement – norms and values – organizational culture-consciousness – organizational culture and identity – personal values vs collective (firm-wide) values – 'regulator-friendly' culture scoring – Schein culture model – starting a firm-wide 'culture conversation' – underlying assumptions and beliefs

---

We will now consider and explore one cultural measuring system in light of this model, to understand which aspects of culture it enables us to measure.

A Barrett Cultural Values Assessment (CVA) helps people to make sense of all aspects of their firm's culture, serving as the basis for the dialogue required to identify areas of risk, strength and opportunities for change. A CVA identifies the 'norms and values' that are operating in their organization, and the conversation it involves goes to a deeper level, to the 'underlying assumptions and beliefs' that may be driving behaviour. Over time, a series of CVAs provide evidence of cultural evolution. This evidence of culture change is valuable both for tracking progress internally and reporting on it, with proof, to regulators.

One of the important features that Barrett measures is the amount of dysfunction in an organization, known as 'cultural entropy'. By indicating culture risk in relation to employee engagement, this factor helps us to target our change efforts where they are needed most.

In the quarter-century since the values measuring system that later became known as the Cultural Transformation Tools® ('CTT' or the 'Barrett Analytics') were first introduced (1997) they have been used by over 8,000 organizations of all types in more than 90 countries. It would be a stretch to call them one of the 'latest' tools, and that is one of their strengths: they have been used by many organizations.

As we will see, the Barrett Model on which these tools are based, with their related analyses and dialogue tools, is unique in its ability to involve the entire organization and in the power of the insights and action that emerge. The potential for use in building an effective ethical culture is clear. Perhaps the best argument for adding the tools to the organizational arsenal is that they identify areas for improvement to drive towards a stronger business – that is, higher operational as well as ethical performance. They are also highly engaging: the data and insights they provide can be shared as a basis for increasing trust internally as well as with external stakeholders.

The Barrett Model

The Barrett Analytics are based on the Seven Levels or Barrett Model developed by Richard Barrett, originally derived from Abraham Maslow's hierarchy of needs (see pages 225–226). Despite its having been developed in reference to individuals, Barrett realized that Maslow's model could be used in an organizational context. The seven levels refer to the seven levels of 'consciousness' or focus that comprise the full spectrum needed for sustainable success (Figure 13.1).

The first three levels form the Foundation: the basic needs of a business – viability and stability, employee and customer satisfaction and performance. Level 4 is focused on adaptability and change, continuous improvement and evolution. The values and behaviours of Level 4 power the shift from basic or deficiency needs and more rigid structures to a focus on alignment, collaboration and contribution to a higher purpose illustrated by Levels 5, 6 and 7. The Barrett Model is based on the notion that the most successful organizations will operate from all seven levels ('full-spectrum') and have a balance of values and behaviours in the Foundation (Levels 1–3) and Purpose (Levels 5–7) areas as well as characteristics that foster growth and change at Level 4.

FIGURE 13.1   The Barrett Model of Culture[6]

Contribution	7	**Living Purpose** Being of Service, Future Generations, Vision, Social Responsibility, Long-Term Perspective
Collaboration	6	**Cultivating Communities** Community Involvement, Partnership, Mentoring/Coaching, Employee Fulfillment
Alignment	5	**Authentic Expression** Openness, Creativity, Integrity, Passion, Trust, Honesty, Transparency
Evolution	4	**Courageously Evolving** Accountability, Transformation, Innovation, Continuous Learning, Autonomy, Empowerment, Agility
Performance	3	**Achieving Excellence** Quality, Results-Orientation, Competence, Self-Esteem, Productivity, Efficiency
Relationships	2	**Building Relationships** Customer Satisfaction, Connection, Respect, Listening, Open Communication
Viability	1	**Ensuring Stability** Financial Stability, Profit, Safety, Health

After constructing the model, Barrett found that specific values could be attributed to each level and that by measuring these you could determine which levels of consciousness the organization was operating from. Subsequently the Barrett Values Centre fine-tuned the measuring system and recently made small changes to simplify the descriptions of the levels.

Benefits for culture reporting and creating business value

Firms can use CVAs in many ways to measure culture and create value for the business. It may seem obvious, but the main reason for measuring culture is to enable leaders to manage it armed with actual data. Most cultural transformation efforts don't achieve lasting success, often because they lack information about the causes of the issues holding the organization back. Measurement for the sake of measurement alone is meaningless. If you want to change behaviour, you must seek the causes and cures for dysfunction as well as the unique strengths of the organization and its people.

The Barrett tools benefit cultural measurement, change and reporting in many ways. For a start, they do not prescribe any specific or ideal culture and measure the organization against that ideal. Instead, they are a framework for measuring the current culture, or 'what is', and the desired culture, 'what we think will help us achieve high performance' in our particular set of circumstances, knowing what motivates and matters to our people. The data can be collected and analysed in different ways, ie by location, position, business unit or country. Leaders can identify the current and desired values and culture(s) without an externally dictated model of what good looks like.

Independent research confirms[7] that CVA is an agile tool connecting culture with organizational sense-making. It points to CVA as an appropriate tool to grasp culture understood as a 'dynamic and collective process of sense-making'.[8]

An approach that's easy to deploy, clearly analysed

The cultural values assessment (CVA) is easily rolled out through a weblink sent to all participants, usually all employees. After choosing their language and indicating demographic status (business unit, location, language, position, etc. depending on how leaders wish to be able to analyse the data) participants answer three questions. They are given a list of approximately 80 to 100 values and behaviours for each question and asked to choose:

- their top 10 personal values;
- the top 10 values they experience in their organization currently; and
- the top 10 values they believe would drive their organization to reach its full potential.

The assessment is usually left open for two to three weeks. The Barrett Values Centre aggregates and analyses the results and issues a report within a week to the in-house (or external advisor) certified consultant, for further analysis in preparation for the next stage: sponsor.

Customized values template

The template of each cultural assessment may be tailored to the specific language and values and behaviours used in that particular business. The ability to customize, which was discussed with psychometricians when the tool was first developed, greatly enhances the utility of the results for the sponsor firm. Tailoring to the individual organization makes sense, as these tools are primarily a means of measuring, monitoring and changing organizational culture, not an external benchmarking tool. Having said that, due to the length of time and number of organizations of all types that have used the tools, there are now various industry compilations that can be referred to for comparison purposes.

The assessment report presents the data in several formats. The main format shows the top 10 personal values, current culture values and desired culture values, including both positive and potentially limiting values (Figures 13.2 and 13.3). Other formats illustrate the values that increase the most between the current and desired culture; a focus on potentially limiting values; and plot of the percentage of values at each level and in the Foundation, Evolution and Purpose areas.

The assessment results then form the basis for a series of workshops and dialogues that offer a wide group of employees the opportunity to participate and contribute. These conversations focus on making sense of what is happening in the organization. Some organizations use the CVA to identify their core values, or to ascertain whether those values are espoused rather than real: 'Are we "walking the talk"?'

The very process of discussing and debating creates a common language about values and culture and enables a firm to explore otherwise difficult subjects. Since the results can be analysed in demographic cuts all the way from the department to larger groups to the entire organization they reveal sub-cultures and areas of higher or lower culture risk. This in turn means that the firm can (re)deploy resources where needed and target them towards removing any blockages or resolving issues adversely affecting conduct. Extensive experience with individuals from all levels and functions proves that the information is understandable and usable in any milieu.

Other benefits, including the reliability of a robustly grounded method, are set out in the following section.

FIGURE 13.2   Overall Group Results – Misaligned example – 1,403 participants

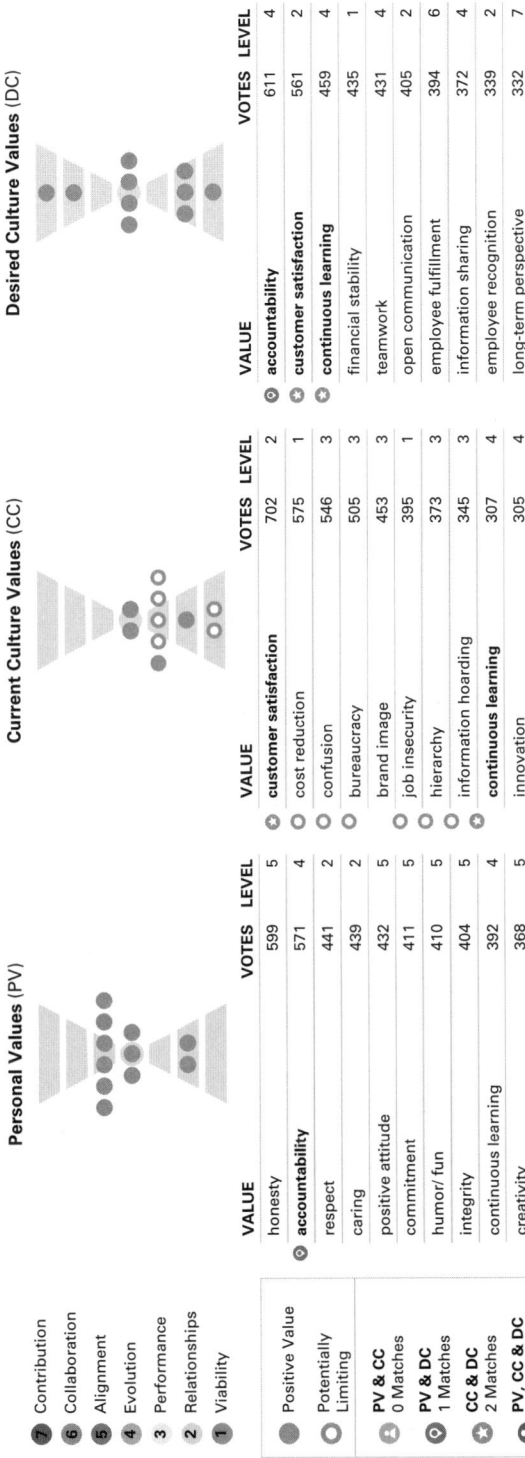

- 7 Contribution
- 6 Collaboration
- 5 Alignment
- 4 Evolution
- 3 Performance
- 2 Relationships
- 1 Viability

Personal Values (PV)

VALUE	VOTES	LEVEL
honesty	599	5
accountability	571	4
respect	441	2
caring	439	2
positive attitude	432	5
commitment	411	5
humor/ fun	410	5
integrity	404	5
continuous learning	392	4
creativity	368	5

Current Culture Values (CC)

VALUE	VOTES	LEVEL
customer satisfaction	702	2
cost reduction	575	1
confusion	546	3
bureaucracy	505	3
brand image	453	3
job insecurity	395	1
hierarchy	373	3
information hoarding	345	3
continuous learning	307	4
innovation	305	4

Desired Culture Values (DC)

VALUE	VOTES	LEVEL
accountability	611	4
customer satisfaction	561	2
continuous learning	459	4
financial stability	435	1
teamwork	431	4
open communication	405	2
employee fulfillment	394	6
information sharing	372	4
employee recognition	339	2
long-term perspective	332	7

Legend:
- Positive Value
- Potentially Limiting
- PV & CC 0 Matches
- PV & DC 1 Matches
- CC & DC 2 Matches
- PV, CC & DC 0 Matches

SOURCE Barrett Values Centre

FIGURE 13.3 Overall Group Results – Aligned example – 521 participants

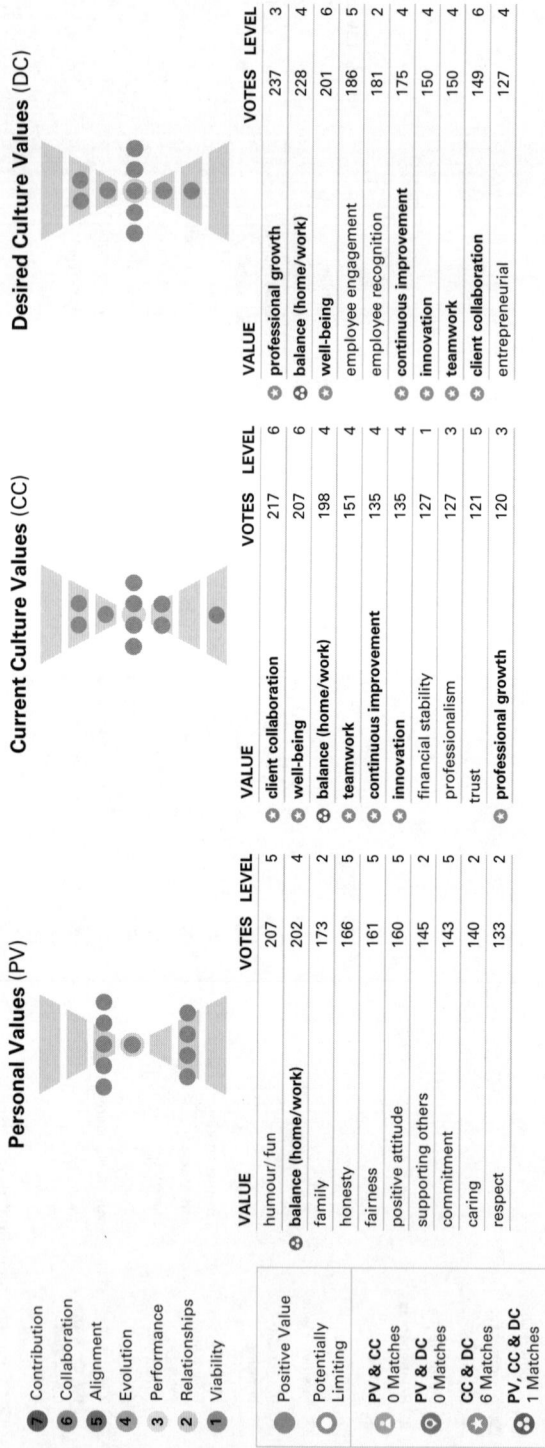

	Level
7	Contribution
6	Collaboration
5	Alignment
4	Evolution
3	Performance
2	Relationships
1	Viability

Personal Values (PV)

VALUE	VOTES	LEVEL
humour/ fun	207	5
balance (home/work)	202	4
family	173	2
honesty	166	5
fairness	161	5
positive attitude	160	5
supporting others	145	2
commitment	143	5
caring	140	2
respect	133	2

Current Culture Values (CC)

VALUE	VOTES	LEVEL
client collaboration	217	6
well-being	207	6
balance (home/work)	198	4
teamwork	151	4
continuous improvement	135	4
innovation	135	4
financial stability	127	1
professionalism	127	3
trust	121	5
professional growth	120	3

Desired Culture Values (DC)

VALUE	VOTES	LEVEL
professional growth	237	3
balance (home/work)	228	4
well-being	201	6
employee engagement	186	5
employee recognition	181	2
continuous improvement	175	4
innovation	150	4
teamwork	150	4
client collaboration	149	6
entrepreneurial	127	4

Legend:
- Positive Value
- Potentially Limiting
- PV & CC — 0 Matches
- PV & DC — 0 Matches
- CC & DC — 6 Matches
- PV, CC & DC — 1 Matches

SOURCE Barrett Values Centre

Measuring cultural health vs culture risk
and other drivers of behaviour

A CVA can measure and compare important characteristics such as alignment between the personal values of the workforce and the current culture. This illustrates employees' ability to 'bring their full selves to work'.

Matches between current and desired culture values indicate participants' view of the organization's direction of travel, which illustrates the gap between the culture we have and the one we would like to have. The amount of cultural risk in the organization or 'cultural entropy' is revealed through potentially limiting values (see sidebar).

CULTURAL ENTROPY

Cultural risk arises from values that are likely to result from or represent dysfunction, fear, frustration and/or wasted energy in the system. The resulting 'cultural entropy' score is determined by measuring the number of votes for potentially limiting values in relation to all votes.

FIGURE 13.4   Employee engagement vs cultural entropy[9]

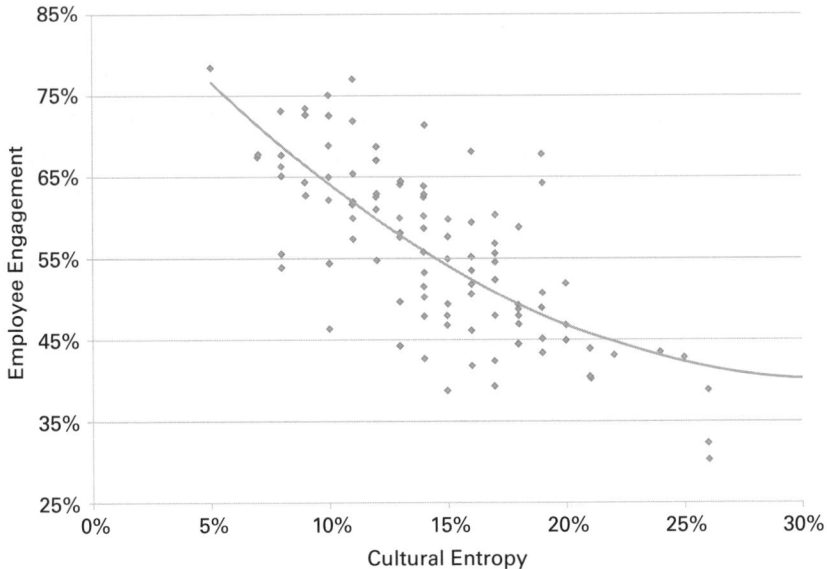

SOURCE Steinholtz-Barrett

Cultural entropy is a key measurement for conduct purposes, since a high reading will indicate low employee engagement and so a high risk of dysfunctional culture and unethical behaviour. Figure 13.4 shows an example of Barrett Model research on this topic.

Behavioural scientist Dan Ariely's 'fudge factor' provides the link:[10] as individuals we wish to feel good about ourselves ('benign self-image'). At the same time, we are often willing to cheat in order to gain an advantage for our family or ourselves. So our ability to cheat is limited by our ability to feel good about ourselves when we do so. In a dysfunctional culture, or one that tolerates unethical behaviour so long as it brings results, it will be easier to rationalize unethical behaviour. For example, if you feel you are not being treated fairly by your manager, you might feel justified in doing a bit of competitive contract trading as a 'side gig'. Disengaged employees are also less likely to speak up when they witness unethical behaviour by others.

A useful way to think of cultural entropy is as a measure of lack of psychological safety, of the level of fear, frustration and/or wasted energy. What are the (negative) values, beliefs and behaviours needed to survive in an organization that feels like that? The personal values and behaviours of leaders are also an important element driving this conduct. As Barrett says: 'Cultural risk is a function of the personal entropy of the current leaders and the institutional legacy of past leaders as embedded in the structures, systems, policies and procedures.'[11]

By exploring the data, leaders can determine where additional effort is required to address and avoid conduct risks, so it allows scarce resources to be deployed where most required. To understand conduct, cultural entropy is one of the most useful measures, though not the only one. The extent to which stated values are embedded in the culture is valuable information. The CVA is an excellent way to involve all employees and other stakeholders in identifying the best set of core values for their firm, to ensure that the values ultimately chosen have meaning and motivate everyone.

Highly motivated and engaged employees create more value for the organization. They will bring their discretionary effort to work. By creating a sense of belonging and shared values and opportunities for engaging employees' desire for meaning and purpose in their lives, leaders unleash potential that would go unexpressed in a demotivating atmosphere. There is an increasing amount of literature and research[12] on the relationship between values, purpose and culture that cannot and should not be ignored.

CVA (the Barrett Method) is not only an excellent way to measure culture but, used as part of a programme of conscious cultural evolution, it provides management information (MI) for reporting both on improving culture and conduct and a process for measuring and reporting progress. It adds value to the business by continuously and actively listening to the needs of stakeholders – especially employees.

Producing reports: why a conduct regulator would approve

The Barrett Method was originally created to support cultural transformation within organizations, not as a reporting tool, but has great value when used for conduct reporting. Notably, some firms already use the CVA tool to share culture scores externally, for example to show how culture is changing over time. Two case examples at the end of the chapter show how this can be done, and its value to the business.

Knowing conduct regulators and their agenda as we do, we see many reasons why a regulator would approve of firms using this model and the 'conduct conversations' that it enables:

- 'Behavioural regulators' including the Dutch central bank (DNB) are sending organizational psychologists into financial firms to observe meetings and interview staff one-to-one. They cannot see into all parts of the organization; a CVA provides the view from the employees' perspective. A CVA reassures staff as to norms and values, overcoming the possibility that the presence of observers may itself influence behaviour. In addition, employees might not be willing to be open with a regulator, a possibly 'truculent' response that has elements of a parent-child relationship.

- Financial institutions themselves should have reporting information that they can present to regulators; this shows that they are being proactive about managing their culture. Showing you're willing to share information regarding progress is a powerful way to build trust with regulators and other stakeholders.

- New insight, getting a picture of the intangible and invisible life of your firm. What are the aspirations and positive energy that are available but untapped? Where are there pockets of fear and negativity that undermine and hold the organization back from performing at its best?

- It is based on global human wisdom about how we as human beings develop and grow, and provides a language for us to understand the human dynamics at play in a particular individual, group and organization.

- It is a simply understood, yet rich source of information that offers the most profound picture of the human conditions in a particular culture.

- You can assess the whole 'ecosystem' of an organization, including for example clients, partners, suppliers and other potential stakeholders in the assessment.

- Findings can be reported in a summary Culture Score® that indicates how healthy and well functioning the firm's culture is, with a benchmark comparison if desired.

- Regulators and boards can be more confident that they have a true picture of the values and culture in the organization and the aspects of the culture that may need attention. If the organization is willing to share its results with the regulator, particularly over time, it will give the regulator a broad picture of the culture and can be the basis for creating trust between regulator and business.

- Accounting guidelines (FRC) require boards to assess culture using robust and reliable methods. The CVA cultural assessment tool has been in use for over 22 years and has been used by 8,000 organizations. It is easy to repeat periodically, providing the board with a realistic time-series view of the culture of the organization and how it is evolving.

- Other measurements do not consider the individual dimension, level of fear, and the common good values (Levels 6–7).

- Conduct regulators may look to use it themselves to understand how their own culture influences regulatory delivery and to more deeply understand the reporting information that firms are providing to them.

Setting an agenda for cultural change

Originally called the 'Cultural Transformation Tools', this method is all about evolutionary change, driving this in various ways:

- The results give business leaders (and all staff) an opportunity to talk about what needs to be talked about, so as to understand and improve collective culture and conduct.

- It displays the business's values as well as its potential blind spots and areas for improvement. It helps senior management to see the vital 'What Actually Happens' factor: what's really going on in the organization. Drawing on years of deep practical experience it also gives them the collective wisdom of many past problems solved in managing culture.

- It raises to view the values that are potentially limiting, offering the opportunity for leaders and employees to become aware of any unconscious fears that may hold them back from creating a trusting and well-functioning operation.

- It creates a common language in the organization (and with regulators potentially) that makes it easier to talk about culture, including the potentially limiting factors that need addressing.

- It identifies and reports on individual human motivation and its impact on the organizational culture.

- The addition of the personal values perspective provides an insight that allows leaders to guide the transformation with the level of understanding and sensitivity that many other tools ignore.

- It is an evolutionary model that offers the possibility to transform the focus from self-interest to common good behaviours and therefore drive sustainability into the business strategy.

How well does it work in practice? About the case examples

Case 1 (page 328): Old Mutual Group

Old Mutual Group used CVA in its contribution to the 2016 FRC Report, *Corporate Culture and the Role of Boards.*[13] The technique supported the firm's drive to put the customer back at the heart of its business.

Case 2 (page 329): Nedbank

Nedbank sought to transform its business when at a very low point. As is described in the case study, the new CEO realized that a set of values that would unite employees and help to create a 'High Performing Culture' was key. Over the years, Nedbank has made significant investment into keeping its culture journey on track and, as can be seen from its website, today it is a purpose-led organization. Today it is one of the largest banks in South Africa.

CASE EXAMPLE 1
Old Mutual Group

This is a historical case study that reflects the position up until a change in strategy. In March 2016, Old Mutual announced its plans to separate the group into four stand-alone businesses. Old Mutual brand subsidiaries were phased out in rebranding from 2016 onwards. At the time of the values assessment, Old Mutual was an international investment, savings, insurance and banking group in South Africa and Africa, the UK and the US.

Following the financial crisis in 2007/2008, Old Mutual decided to 'put the customer back at the heart of the business', and knew that values and culture would be crucial to this. The business set out its vision and strategy, made up of a customer promise – four values and six behaviours.

Sponsored by the board, the group's HR function led a review of the values (integrity, respect, accountability, and pushing beyond boundaries) to see if they were aligned to the new customer-centric vision. Employees felt the values were still relevant, but they were generic and help was needed to understand what they meant in practice.

Through interviews with the top 100 leaders, a survey of employees at all levels of the group and workshops with the executive committee, Old Mutual identified six guiding behaviours that described the values in practice in the context of the new customer-centric vision and strategy:

- Aim high and take your team with you.
- Customer first – they're the reason we're here.
- Treat the business like it's our own.
- Need to listen carefully and talk honestly.
- Own our decisions, decide and deliver.
- Win together and help others succeed.

Employees were regularly assessed against these behaviours. Performance management included compulsory 360-degree feedback for all leaders solely around the behaviours, and this feedback influenced individual performance scores which were linked to rewards.

Once the new behaviours had been introduced, Old Mutual looked to how it was going to measure progress with the required overall shift in culture and chose to use the Barrett Values survey across the group. Barrett differs from employee engagement surveys, as it starts with an individual's personal values, the values they perceive exist in the current organization, and the values they believe are needed to take the business forward. By identifying misalignment, the data is used to generate conversations and then actions.

The first survey in 2011 identified a number of areas of dysfunction and only two matches (of 10 possible) between existing and desired culture as described by the company's leadership group. Actions to address these areas included work to focus on the customer, changing the operating model to reduce bureaucracy, changing its product offering, and future scenario planning to reduce short-term focus. The result was that by 2015 the leadership group reported there were seven matches between existing and desired culture and a 'healthy' culture score. How culture is measured became central to how Old Mutual assessed and managed cultural risk.

CASE EXAMPLE 2
Nedbank

In 2003, South Africa's Nedbank had a new CEO with a vision 'to become Southern Africa's most highly rated and respected bank... by our staff, clients, shareholders, regulators and communities.' However, in order to be successful, the bank's leadership understood that the vision needed to be supported by a strong strategy and a uniting set of values. For a 'High Performing Culture', it was critical these values were adopted, accepted and lived by all employees, and seen to exist with top leadership.

The CEO launched Strategy, Values and Brand workshops with senior leadership to establish the direction and core values of the organization. Four of the core values were established during this process, and were aligned with their parent company's values.

For the final value, Nedbank's employees were encouraged to offer their input. The value cohesively chosen was 'people-centred', which reflected Nedbank's efforts to become more client driven and employee focused. As a part-owned member of the Old Mutual group of companies (see case study above), Nedbank shared certain core values. Its ultimate five values were: Accountability; Respect; Integrity; Pushing beyond boundaries; People-centred.

The 'Journey Back to the Top' was a three-year planning process which sought to address the immediate issues facing Nedbank while establishing measures to track the effectiveness of their initiatives. Priorities included breaking down silos within the organization through restructuring departments and the executive team, fostering transparency by promoting two-way communication between leadership and staff, and developing a fair and equitable environment which went beyond the laws required in South Africa.

Nedbank used regular Cultural Values Assessments to gauge the effectiveness of their various initiatives, using the assessment in conjunction with employee satisfaction surveys to listen to their employees. This pointed the organization in the right direction and with an understanding of what shifts in priorities might be needed to improve performance.

Outcomes

Nedbank measured culture change during 2005–10, including results from their annual Cultural Values Assessment as part of their corporate scorecard. The regular assessments of their culture allowed Nedbank to measure and monitor the evolution of their organization (Figure 13.5).

Each year the survey was offered to employees, the participation rate increased – from 20 per cent in the first year to 69 per cent in 2010. The entropy score fell from 25 per cent in 2005 to 13 per cent in 2009. The value matches from Current to Desired Culture rose from three to six. Nedbank staff surveys showed an overall improvement of 26 per cent over the same period. In 2010, Nedbank achieved an additional milestone when they reached their long-sought-after goal of a top Current Culture value at Level 5.

Changes to the organization were not just felt internally. Hard business gains were also achieved, as Nedbank realized their targets of 20 per cent return on equity and 55 per cent cost-to-income ratio. In 2009 they also had the highest shareholder return of all the 'Big Five' South African banks. Nedbank's great strides during this period can be attributed, at least in some part, to their focus on building a strong foundation of values within the organization.

FIGURE 13.5 Nedbank's cultural evolution 2005–10: CVA extracts

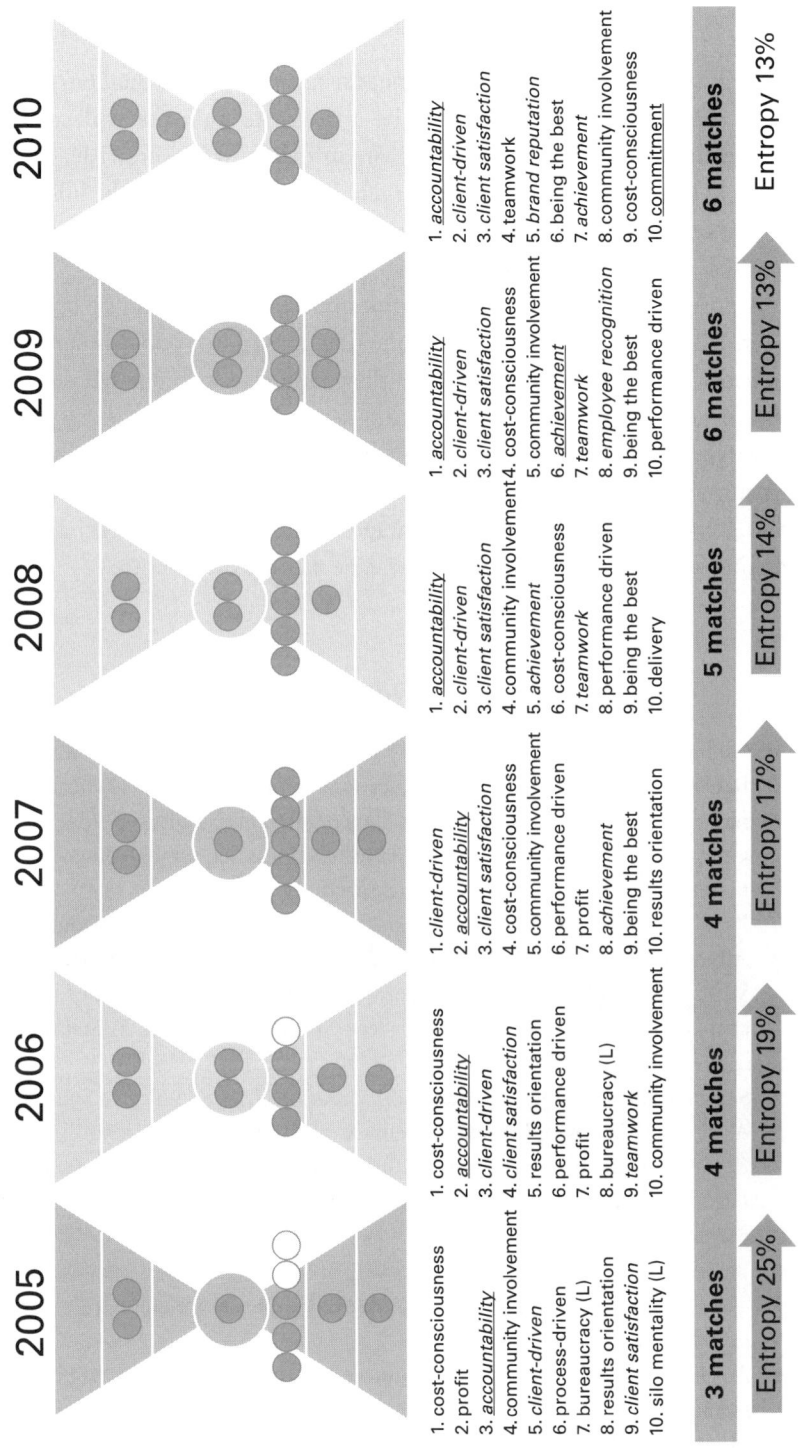

2005
1. cost-consciousness
2. profit
3. *accountability*
4. community involvement
5. *client-driven*
6. process-driven
7. bureaucracy (L)
8. results orientation
9. *client satisfaction*
10. silo mentality (L)

3 matches
Entropy 25%

2006
1. cost-consciousness
2. *accountability*
3. *client-driven*
4. *client satisfaction*
5. results orientation
6. performance driven
7. profit
8. bureaucracy (L)
9. *teamwork*
10. community involvement

4 matches
Entropy 19%

2007
1. *client-driven*
2. *accountability*
3. *client satisfaction*
4. cost-consciousness
5. community involvement
6. performance driven
7. profit
8. *achievement*
9. being the best
10. results orientation

4 matches
Entropy 17%

2008
1. *accountability*
2. *client-driven*
3. *client satisfaction*
4. community involvement
5. *achievement*
6. cost-consciousness
7. *teamwork*
8. performance driven
9. being the best
10. delivery

5 matches
Entropy 14%

2009
1. *accountability*
2. *client-driven*
3. *client satisfaction*
4. cost-consciousness
5. community involvement
6. *achievement*
7. *teamwork*
8. *employee recognition*
9. being the best
10. performance driven

6 matches
Entropy 13%

2010
1. *accountability*
2. *client-driven*
3. *client satisfaction*
4. teamwork
5. *brand reputation*
6. being the best
7. *achievement*
8. community involvement
9. cost-consciousness
10. *commitment*

6 matches
Entropy 13%

Conclusion

A big advantage of this method of measuring culture is its dual purpose. The main reason for the exercise will be a desire to gain the widest possible perspective on the culture(s) of the organization, to ensure risks are accurately assessed and solutions well targeted. The ability to use the information as part of a dialogue with regulators that supports trust building means it is an efficient use of resource.

An organization that is able to look honestly at itself and be open about its efforts to improve its culture is one that a regulator could generally trust to deal with any conduct matters as they arise. It is also one where employees are more likely to feel safe informing senior management of any problems they experience. Leaders are always surprised at the depth of insight in these three questions and the conversations they ignite. Because the underlying model is holistic, the other advantage is the way it supports leaders in making sense of what might otherwise be a confusing picture.

Notes

1   Author note: I would like to thank Phil Clothier and Tor Eneroth of the Barrett Values Centre for their inspirational work in the field of culture measurement, and Jordi del Bas Avellaneda, Research Fellow at the EU-Asia Global Business Research Center (EADA Business School, Barcelona) for his insights on organisational culture research.

2   Barrett, R (2017) *The Values-Driven Organization*, 2nd edition, Routledge

3   Albert & Whetten, 1985; Whetten, 2006 cited in Hatch, M, Schultz, M and Skov, A (2019) Organisational identity and culture in the context of managed change: transformation in the Carlsberg Group, 2009–2013, *Academy of Management Discoveries*, 1 (1) pp 58–90

4   Schein, E (2017) *Organizational Culture and Leadership*, Wiley & Sons, Inc, p 2

5   As cited in Chatman, J A and O'Reilly, C A (2016) Paradigm lost: Reinvigorating the study of organizational culture, *Research in Organizational Behavior*, http://dx.doi.org/10.1016/j.riob.2016.11.004 (archived at https://perma.cc/DWU7-VJAB)

6   Barrett Values Centre

7   The study is conducted by the EU-Asia Global Business Research Center at EADA Business School, Barcelona

8   A definition provided by Silvester, J, Anderson, N R and Patterson, F (1999) Organizational culture change: An inter-group attributional analysis, *Journal of Occupational and Organizational Psychology*, 72 (1), pp 1–23

9 Barrett Values Centre (2008) Research carried out in 163 organizations in Australia by Barrett with Hewitt Associates, accessed at www.valuescentre.com (archived at https://perma.cc/5UML-TE7G)

10 See Ariely's excellent and concise RSA briefing The Honest Truth about Dishonesty, www.youtube.com/results?search_query=dan+ariely+rsa+honest+truth+about (archived at https://perma.cc/5V46-PEQU)

11 Barrett, R (2017) *The Values-Driven Organization*, 2nd edition, Routledge

12 Mayer, C (2018) *Prosperity: When better business makes the greater good*, Oxford University Press

13 Financial Reporting Council (2016) Corporate Culture and the Role of Boards: Report of Observations, July, Appendix 1

14

Putting respected research tools to work, example 2

*Using the CultureScope 'combined analytic'
to deliver measurably better culture*

HANI NABEEL

THEMES AND CONCEPTS IN THIS CHAPTER

*avoiding change programme failure – behavioural change roadmap – doughnut
chart – individual and group propensity to change – persuasive design – regression
analysis – target (desired) behaviour – the 'ask' – the people vs the place*

Introduction

Is your organization one where people are expected to conform? Is it a place
where you're just expected to learn on the job? Is yours a culture where
you're encouraged to express yourself? Do long-standing employees behave
in different ways to new recruits? These are the kinds of insights that a scientific behavioural insights tool should answer.

While more and more aspects of commercial life can be measured and
tracked, for many firms culture remains cloudy and elusive. You recognize
good (and bad) organizational cultures when you come across them, as
when the UK parliamentary committee examining the collapse of British

multinational construction and facilities manager Carillion in 2018 (the country's largest ever trading liquidation) vividly described the company's culture of short-termism and lackadaisical executive oversight as 'rotten'.[1] Yet what is it precisely that makes an organization's culture good or poor?

Organizations have long relied on lagging qualitative and subjective measures (engagement surveys, sentiment surveys, individual interviews) when assessing current sentiments or opinions, which tend to rise and fall quickly in response to transient business choices. The resulting information only gives a partial view of what is really happening in the business. What if instead we could use a quantitative behavioural diagnostic and take a more predictive, insightful and actionable approach?

Such approaches now exist. One of them, CultureScope, quantifies the culture of an organization using advanced diagnostics, by assessing individual and organizational behaviours (how do I behave and what do I observe around me), linking these with organizations' outcomes to provide predictive analytics and actionable insights to drive the business forward, reduce risk and generate sustainable value. Its predictive analytics work in both directions; behaviours to outcomes and outcomes to behaviours. This tool measures within an organization 30 behavioural dimensions in 15 scalar pairs. The result draws contours of an organization's culture (Figure 14.1).

FIGURE 14.1   Example of CultureScope behavioural dimensions readout

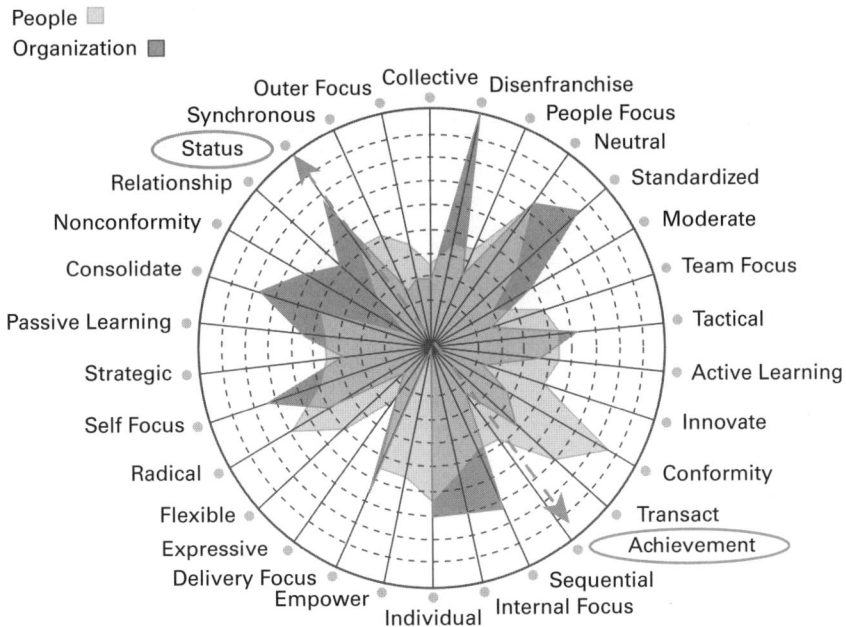

FIGURE 14.2 Example scalar pair term definitions

Left term	Description	Right term	Description
Collective	Goals are achieved through partnerships and alliances	**Individual**	Maintaining high individual performance and winning prevail over working relationships
Disenfranchise	The structure is hierarchical ensuring that leaders retain decision making	**Empower**	Decisions are delegated to lower levels with supportive guidance
People Focus	A working environment that focuses on people rather than purely on tasks and outputs	**Delivery Focus**	There is a clear focus on results and task outputs; employees are accountable for their own actions
Standardised	People value working within clear processes and systems	**Flexible**	People value variability and deal with each situation afresh
Active Learning	Active steps are taken to improve employee's skill sets and careers; employee growth and development is considered an integral part of the job	**Passive Learning**	On-the-job experience is seen as the best approach for learning and skill development
Achievement	People believe that you are what you do, and they define your worth accordingly. These cultures value performance independent of status	**Status**	People believe that you should be valued for your status. Power, title, and position matter in these cultures, and these roles define behaviour

One might well ask why it is useful to calibrate culture in this way. In summary, cultural factors evidently link to an organization's commercial well-being. Financial businesses, for example, need to have a culture where people feel free to speak up, so as to mitigate any risk of financial crime or of conduct that brings detriment to customers.

As an illustration of the definitions underlying the scalar pair indicators, Figure 14.2 shows a set of the scalar pairs found to be most relevant to a healthy 'hands-up' culture in one analysis.

What's the method?

This approach deploys five stages of behavioural insight (Figure 14.3) to track and drive change. These are:

1 Define: can you firm test any relevant current frameworks? Such frameworks could include organizational values, conduct risk, financial crime risk framework. This tool can create a behavioural factor map to represent the firm's specific framework. Having done so you can now set the objectives of the diagnostics and analytics and define the benchmark criteria, eg demographics data and the outcome-based management information that you want to include in the analysis.

2 Measure: design a communication plan to invite participation and launch the online behavioural diagnostic questionnaire.

3 Insights: once all the behavioural measurement data is collected, the firm can now analyse to what degree the targeted frameworks are enacted (behaved) – (do we do what we say we do?), reporting on the presence or absence of behaviours and where. And further understand how the presence or absence of the behaviours drive the outcome metrics. You can also design a predictive model by starting with an outcome-first approach and building a behavioural model through regression analyses.

4 Action: once the behavioural (actionable) insights are generated, you can design a specific intervention based on the workplace (this can include organizational design, reward management, processes, policies etc.) or the people (this can include classroom-based or online training/ development programmes targeting the intended behavioural change).

5 Validate: remeasure so you can examine to what degree your designed interventions have worked, and also relate the change to the targeted outcome metrics.

FIGURE 14.3   Five-step programme

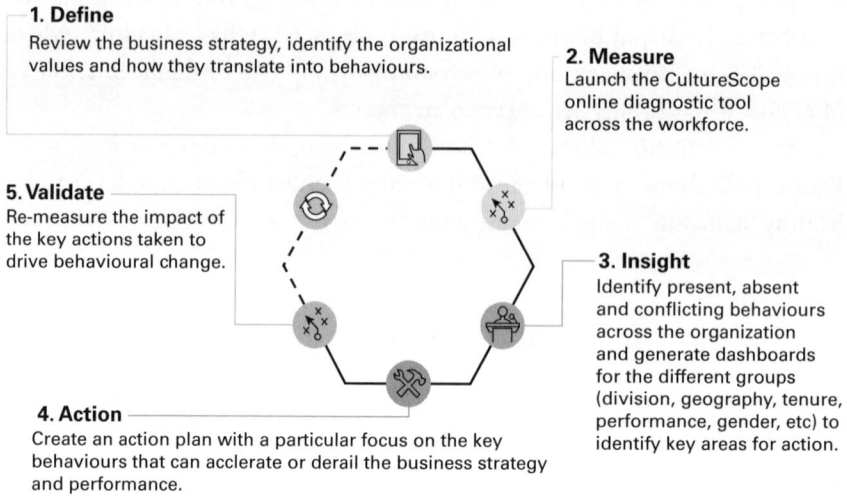

1. Define
Review the business strategy, identify the organizational
values and how they translate into behaviours.

2. Measure
Launch the CultureScope
online diagnostic tool
across the workforce.

5. Validate
Re-measure the impact of
the key actions taken to
drive behavioural change.

3. Insight
Identify present, absent
and conflicting behaviours
across the organization
and generate dashboards
for the different groups
(division, geography, tenure,
performance, gender, etc) to
identify key areas for action.

4. Action
Create an action plan with a particular focus on the key
behaviours that can acclerate or derail the business strategy
and performance.

Let's look at applying this culture diagnostic tool to setting an agenda for change and overcoming the common root causes of why change programmes fail.

Do your firm's programme leaders have what it really takes to make it happen?

The statistics have remained stubbornly negative for decades. Whether it is the bleaker 70 per cent of change programmes failing to achieve their objectives[2] or a more benign (if 20 years earlier) statistic of 50 per cent success for Forbes 1,000 companies,[3] the evidence suggests that change programmes may have barely an 'evens' (50 per cent) chance of succeeding.

Although change has become the norm, amid increased economic and social uncertainty and disruptive new technology, leaders and managers reasonably ask: 'Why are the odds stacked so heavily against change programmes succeeding?' The problem is not that organizations are incapable of launching change programmes. Why then do change programmes so often fail to land effectively, or to deliver the outcomes they were launched to deliver?

It's known that culture change programmes need a compelling purpose, must be supported by effective management processes, and must have clear commitment and support from the organization.[4] Yet despite this well-known wisdom, statistically change programmes remain less than 50 per cent likely to succeed against their own objectives. Hence there's a growing interest in exploring the application of behavioural psychology to improve these programmes' chances of success.[5] This is the focus of the tool discussed here. Although this is a relatively new field, we can now explore how combining behavioural psychology with data analytics addresses three of the root causes for why many change programmes fail.

Three reasons why change programmes fail

Change programmes often pursue a move towards 'exemplary' behaviour, with structures and processes interacting, reflecting also how teams interact with individuals, among themselves, with customers and with other external stakeholders.

Bearing this in mind, experience shows that change programmes fail for three behaviourally related reasons. Whilst these are not the only reasons for failure, they do point to the commonest blind spots in well-intended programmes. All three follow from a lack of knowledge about the organization's people and how the workplace influences employee behaviour.

A Harvard study (back in 2013) showed over 83,000 books on change management on Amazon;[6] we may safely assume that this number will continue to grow. Yet, despite all of that published wisdom, the statistics on the success of change programmes continue to disappoint. We believe that organizations can beat the odds of failure for change programmes by addressing three root causes driving that failure:

1 A lack of insight into the **employees** who are the true champions of change and have what it takes to be effective in delivering change programme objectives.

2 A lack of insight into the **size of the change task** – the 'ask' of employees and work teams – that their change programmes demand and how much the size of that ask varies across an organization.

3 A lack of **tools** and specifically a behavioural roadmap that enables them to promote shared learning through change and to understand where in the organization they are most likely to gain early traction with their change initiatives.

If change management is to deliver its important benefits of more consistent value, then as CultureScope data demonstrates, the thinking behind change management itself needs to change. Using applied behavioural analytics, success in change programmes is not only feasible in practice but also predictable.

TWO SETS OF CULTURE FACTORS: PEOPLE AND PLACE

Culture factor set: **'the people'**. When we talk here about the people, we mean the deep-seated behavioural profiles of employees at any level and in any location, including their appetite for personal change. Yet, few organizations have detailed insight and data on the behavioural profiles of their people and this includes the people they nominate or who offer themselves to be champions for a change programme.

   Culture factor set: **'the place'**. It is important to contrast 'the people' with insight on the place (our shorthand for the workplace) or, to be more accurate, the places that make up the organization. The question here is not the natural behavioural profiles of the people who occupy those places but how those places act to frame and influence employee behaviour. Social psychology research has shown that the place exerts a strong influence on how we behave, so strong that the place can override how a person would naturally behave outside that work context.[7]

Lack of data and insight into the place may result in misguided setting of common change objectives for the entire organization, on a 'too-easy assumption' that every business function, location, team and individual employee faces similar challenges. In reality, of course, firms are not so homogenous. A one-size-fits-all approach will misfire in at least two ways.

- the 'change gap' between current and targeted states may be small – some parts of the firm are already where they should be;
- conversely, in some parts of the firm the gap may be substantial, and even 'too much of an ask'.

Sizing the 'ask': a metric for employees' openness to change

Just how willing are employees to change their behaviours? To develop a metric for individuals' commitment to change, we used the data on the people – those deeply ingrained behaviours we all have as individuals – produced by the CultureScope tool. (We will come to the specific behaviours that drove that metric and what that metric offered a client business in a case example below.) Figure 14.4 shows how that metric distributed people's personal propensity for change, in far greater detail than the plain binary yes/no question formerly used by the firm.

FIGURE 14.4 Employees' predisposition to change

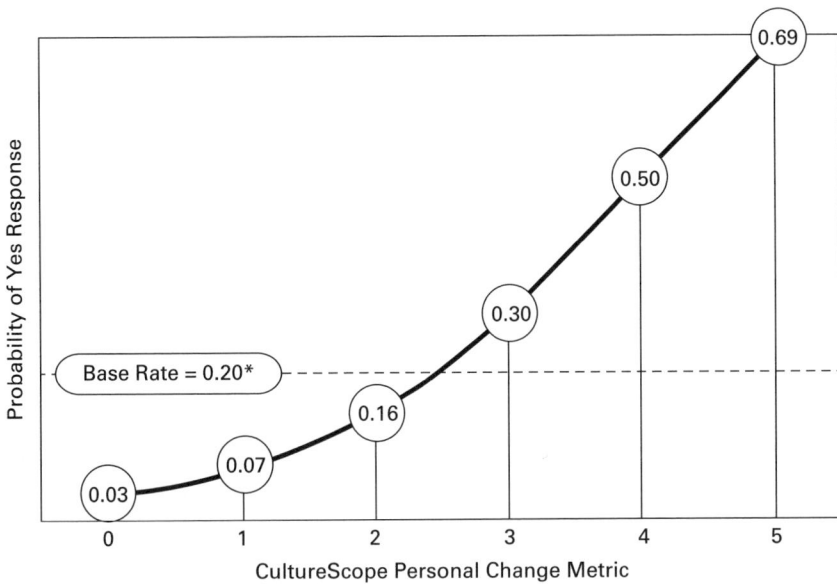

*20% of sample responded yes

The base rate (1 in 5 responsive employees, or '4:1 against') here masks an underlying metric that ranges widely from a very low disposition to personal change (0 on the horizontal axis) to a very high disposition to personal change (5 on that horizontal axis). Those who are highest on the underlying metric (5) are 23 times more likely to commit to behavioural change than those lowest on that underlying metric (0).

Here, 37 per cent of employees were identified as showing positive likelihoods of being able to change their own behaviours (3 and above on the metric). Yet odds of employees being predisposed to personal change were still 1.7:1 against – at least, a big improvement on 4:1 against. However, within those behavioural profiles the tool could identify both the strongest 'change champion' candidates *and* others who, with the right support, would soon embrace the change programme.

Profiling the behaviour that informs the 'ask' metric

In this case, modelling revealed eight behavioural factors that, together and either positively or negatively, drove that metric (Figure 14.5).[8]

FIGURE 14.5   Factors driving a predisposition for personal change

⬆ Personal Change Metric	⬇ Personal Change Metric
Expressive and more likely to voice an opinion	**_Neutral_** and less likely to voice a thought or opinion
Flexible and more likely to value the ability to work flexibly	**_Standardized_** and more likely to place importance on processes and systems
People Focus and more likely focus on people rather than just outputs	**_Delivery Focus_** and more likely to focus on outputs rather than people
Team Focus and more likely to value team working	**_Self Focus_** and more likely to value individualism and individual reward

Employees most likely to embrace behavioural change and commit to change programmes were those more likely to focus on the impacts of change on people and to incorporate goals into routine teamwork. They were also likely to adapt their approach to the demands of different situations and challenges, to share their opinions and views on how best to approach change and on whether change programmes were achieving their goals or not.

In contrast, those less likely to embrace behavioural change, or to commit to change programmes, were people who tended to focus on process for the sake of process rather than the impacts on other employees. They were preoccupied with what change programmes offered them as individuals and were also less likely to voice their opinions on whether or not change programmes were achieving their goals.

Putting the metric into practice

These detailed behavioural profiles offer greater scope for detailed data analysis, and qualitative insights for change programme leaders, to support change champions. The data analytics could offer further drill down – by employee segment (seniority, tenure, gender and age) and by business function, department, team and location – to identify where to find the most effective change champions. Behavioural profiles also reveal clearer qualitative questions such as: How can we promote employee voice[9] to flag issues and course correct as we go? How to reward team rather than individual successes? How do we best communicate to engage with the 'people' change as well as the 'place' improvements in process?

CRUNCHING THE NUMBERS

The question about disposition to change was framed as a closed binary (yes/no question). Logistic regression was used to identify which behavioural dimensions predicted whether employees were more likely to respond positively and with a yes.

Logistic regression models identify which of a set of non-binary and binary predictors are most strongly related to an outcome (such as, here, a yes response). Their results enable us to build metrics that measure how likely any given outcome is to occur (eg a yes response to the personal change question). Those metrics can then be used to predict how likely it is that each outcome will be observed. We tested several nested models to find the one that most reliably predicted employees' willingness to change behaviours. These strongest predictors formed the basis of the behavioural profile described in the main body of this piece.

Regarding 'model fit', if you're interested (and not all will be, I appreciate): using correlations and least squares regression models, two indicators of fit allied to those obtained from linear methods are available from logistic regression – Cox and Snell R^2 and Nagelkerke R^2. Taking the square root of these fit indices yields indicators that approximate the Multiple R obtained from linear regression or the correlation between two variables. The Multiple R's associated with our final model for predicting a yes response to the survey question from behavioural factors were 0.43 (Cox and Snell) and 0.53 (Nagelkerke). These confirm confidence in the correlation (predictive power) in our model as at or above the 75th percentile, a very sound basis for studying employee attitudes and intentions, as a means to identify and predict commitment to change programmes.[10]

Effective change means understanding the people *and* the place

Using behavioural diagnostics to guide change programmes makes them four times as likely to succeed.[11] Yet the diagnostics are not just useful for understanding the behaviours of employees; we need also to understand how the workplace influences employee behaviour. Work context provides a strong set of stimuli that frame the behaviour of employees. Employees tend to act to satisfy what they see as the expectations of the place even if those expectations go against how they would normally behave in non-work settings.

It makes sense to use a behavioural diagnostic tool to guide change programmes: to know where you are going, you need to know where you are starting from – and the starting point will vary across the firm. Desired behaviours may already exist, offering opportunities to jump-start change, sharing and diffusing 'exemplary' attitudes and experiences.

Actionable insight also requires a deep understanding of the business context. To gain that understanding, we start by running a series of workshops

FIGURE 14.6   Eight 'cluster levels' of employee engagement within the firm, ranked within three primary drivers of behaviour

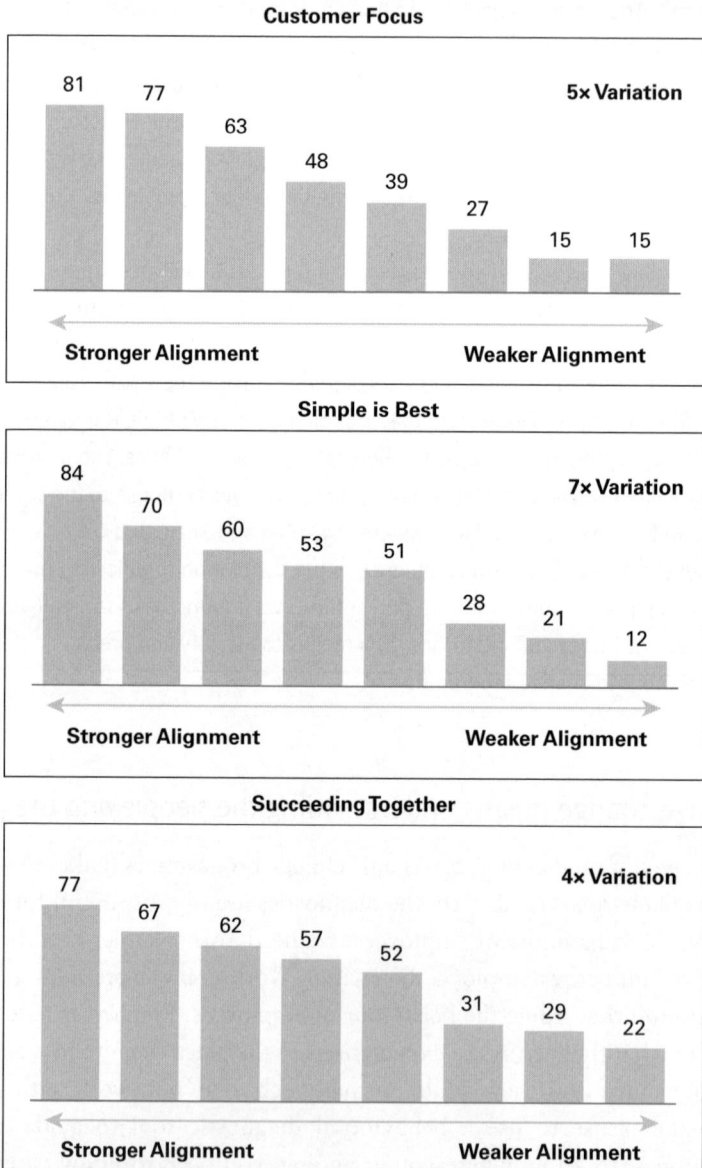

with senior managers, using a 30-factor taxonomy of behavioural factors.[12] While firms strive to promote consistent values and behaviours, we have found again and again that the 'place' (work context) may actually promote very different employee experiences depending on where employees work. In this example (see 'Crunching the numbers' box above for method) we found eight clusters from the data on how employees saw their workplace (Figure 14.6). With these we could see the varied range of starting points for different groups of employees in their change journey[13] (Figure 14.7).

Had this firm adopted a one-size-fits-all approach, it would have ignored the nuances in the cluster profiles and that all three factors act together to define the work context for any given employee. Looking at the differing profiles within the eight clusters we could see that the change programme would need a tailored approach reflecting each cluster's different starting points and needs; for example, some parts of the firm were already strongly aligned with the programme's goals and could be drawn on to support change elsewhere in the firm. We were then able to assess the extent of the 'ask' of each of the groups (1–8) to find which teams would be most or least engaged and how the firm would need to adapt its communication with each group accordingly (Figure 14.7).

Finally, we bring together behavioural diagnostics on the people and the place, combining these with 'persuasive design' to significantly improve the odds for the success of change programmes (Figure 14.8).

FIGURE 14.7 Ranking different 'clusters' starting-point alignment with the change programme

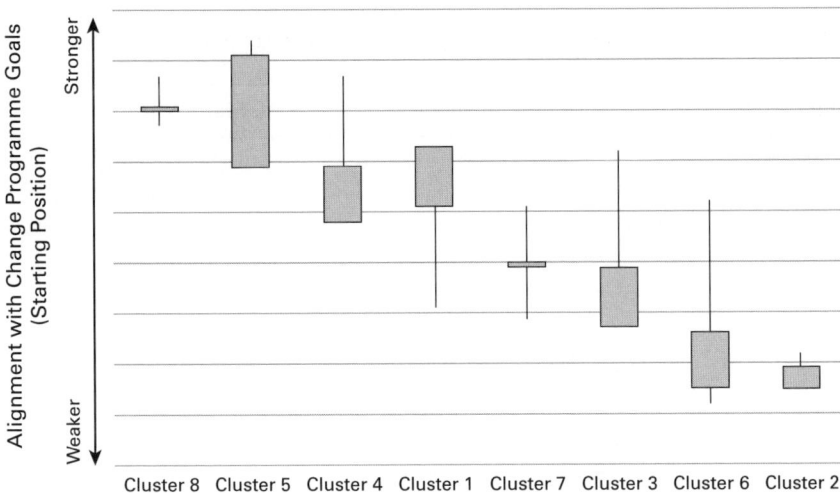

FIGURE 14.8　Force of each behavioural driver within each 'cluster' group

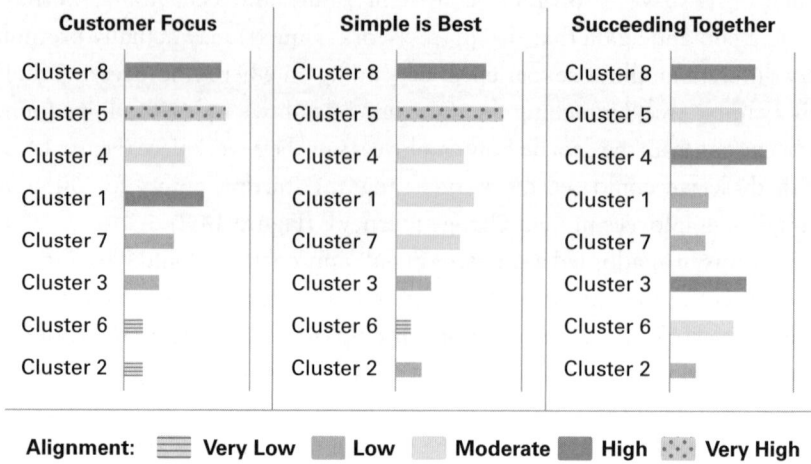

Making a behavioural roadmap to drive effective change

It's now, for the first time, possible for firms to use cultural diagnostics and behavioural analytics to ensure that change initiatives succeed, unlike the great majority of programmes in the past. We now know that behavioural analytics is a validated tool for enabling organizations to improve the odds that their change programmes will deliver.[14] Used properly, we can see the efficacy of behaviour measurement tools, such as in this before-and-after analysis of the impact of a targeted intervention for change (see Table 14.1).

TABLE 14.1　Assessed outcomes following a culture-measured intervention

Behaviours	Pre-intervention	Post-intervention
Collective – Goals are achieved through partnerships and alliances	Personal behaviours are supported. People observe the organisation working against collaboration. This could eventually deteriorate personal scores.	Personal behaviours remain supported, but now people observe the organisation being neutral towards collaboration.
People focus – A working environment that focuses on people rather than purely on tasks and outputs	People observe the working environment as centred on tasks and outputs. People are neutral.	People remain neutral, but now they observe the working environment as neutral rather than working against people focus.

(continued)

TABLE 14.1   (Continued)

Behaviours	Pre-intervention	Post-intervention
Team focus – Work is delivered through collaborating group efforts and team results are prioritised over individual results	People behaviours are neutral towards group effort as the way to work. They also observe the organisation as rewarding independence and individualism over group results.	People prefer to work in a manner where the focus is more on the team rather than the individual. They also observe work in the organisation being delivered through collaborating group efforts.
Innovate – New and creative ideas are pioneered. Intelligent risk taking is encouraged and praised	Personal behaviours are neutral. People observe the environment as inhibiting innovation, focusing more on tried and tested methods.	Personal behaviours haven't changed yet, but people observe the organisation working against innovation to a lesser extent.
Achievement – People believe that you are what you do, and they define your worth accordingly. These cultures value performance independent of status	People neither support nor work against this behaviour. They observe that in the organization status more often prevails over achievement.	People neither support nor work against this behaviour. They now observe that the organisation is neutral towards achievement.

FIGURE 14.9   Achieving change: motivation and ability determine success

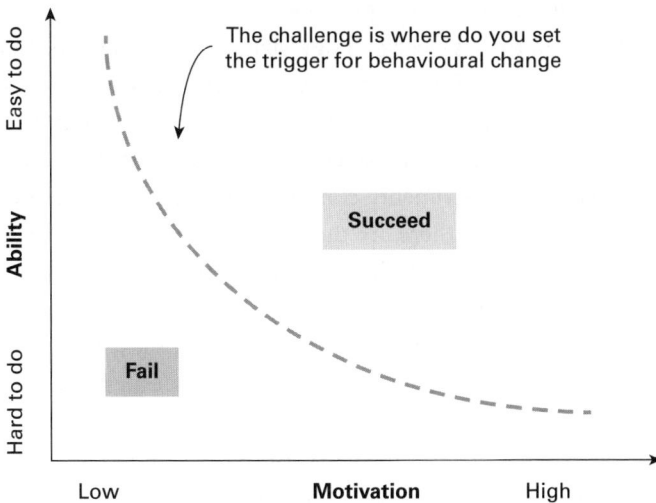

We'll see next how combined insight into the people and the place can help set out a behavioural roadmap for planned, fully managed change. This gives firms a surer method of implementing change and also promotes firm-wide learning, which greatly improves rates of achieving change programme goals.

A challenge has always been how to design any programme or intervention that makes it measurably more likely that people will adopt and sustain the desired 'good behaviour'. Enter a new method: persuasive design.

'Persuasive design' in change programmes

As with any change initiative, the first step is to identify the desired 'target behaviour'. This is no different to the first step in designing a change programme. Since success lies in changing people's behaviour and setting and reinforcing new norms for that behaviour, this in turn requires a clear, tangible, and commonly understood definition of the target behaviour. Various tools, including CultureScope, enable this.

Once the target behaviour is identified, persuasive design requires us to find out what might prevent people from behaving how we'd wish. Is it a lack of motivation? Are people unwilling or simply uninterested in adopting the target behaviour? Is it lack of ability? Do people lack the means or resources to adopt the target behaviour, or, correctly or not, see the target behaviour as 'beyond them' (too ambitious to be do-able)? Or is it a lack of a well-timed trigger to prompt performance of the behaviour; is the firm asking the wrong people at the wrong time to perform the target behaviour? These issues are summarized in Figure 14.9.

Persuasive design thinks clearly about 'sizing' the goals for people so that the goals improve motivation, promoting a common perception that they're achievable and worth achieving. Much of that effort is centred on how best to promote incremental learning, since this best drives durable behavioural change. Smaller-scale experiments conducted in targeted parts of the firm can help to identify where there are the strongest (and most willing) opportunities for learning. The resulting stronger work practices can then be diffused across the wider organization.[15]

The challenge is how to identify where in the firm these opportunities are strongest; this is where the behavioural road map comes into its own. To begin mapping, you need to know which employees are more likely to be more open to change and more likely to adopt the behaviours that a change programme seeks to promote. Next, you need to know where in the firm a 'big ask' is more likely to be achievable and where it isn't; diagnostics on the place will answer this.

FIGURE 14.10 Change programme feasibility (map grid)

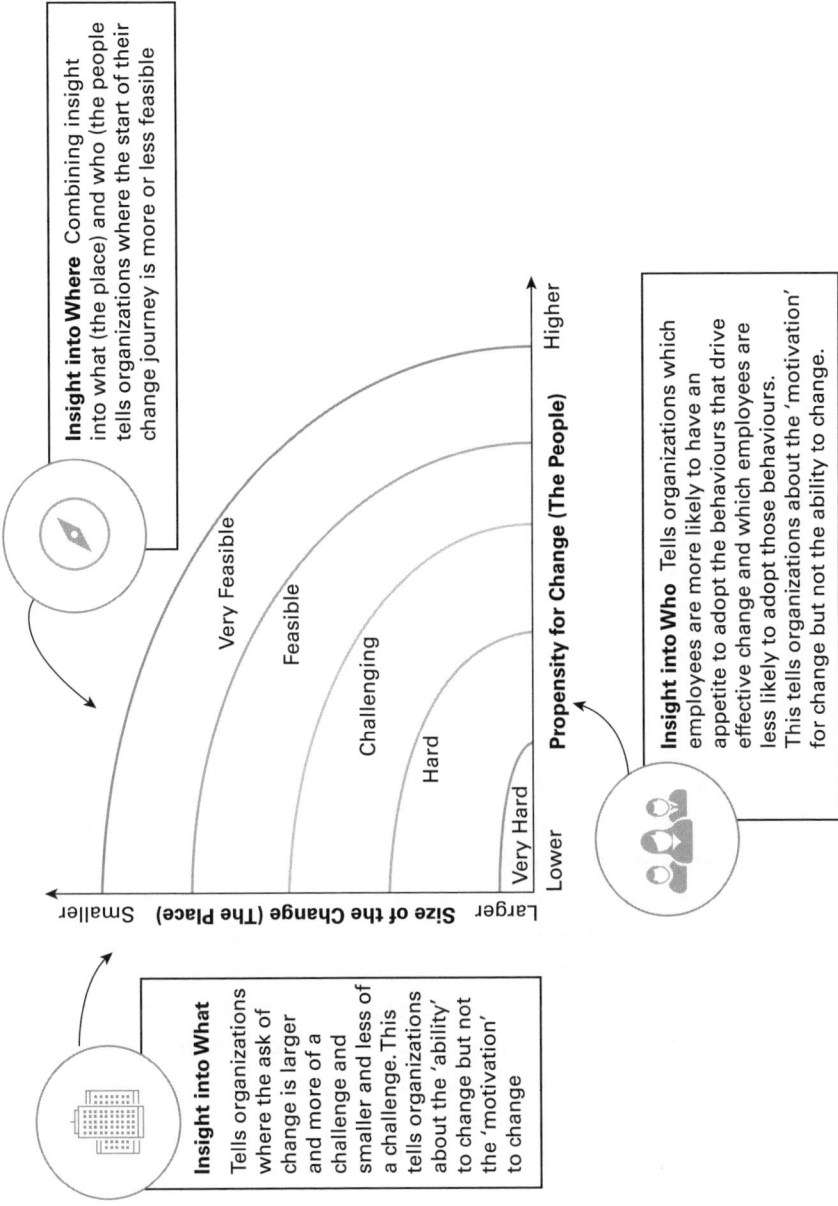

Insight into Where Combining insight into what (the place) and who (the people) tells organizations where the start of their change journey is more or less feasible

Size of the Change (The Place)

Larger — Smaller

Very Hard

Hard

Challenging

Feasible

Very Feasible

Propensity for Change (The People)

Lower — Higher

Insight into What
Tells organizations where the ask of change is larger and more of a challenge and smaller and less of a challenge. This tells organizations about the 'ability' to change but not the 'motivation' to change

Insight into Who Tells organizations which employees are more likely to have an appetite to adopt the behaviours that drive effective change and which employees are less likely to adopt those behaviours. This tells organizations about the 'motivation' for change but not the ability to change.

Conclusion

The final output, and business benefit, is that once we know where the opportunities for learning are strongest, we know where and when well-timed triggers will best initiate the firm's change journey.

Figure 14.10 summarizes how combining insight into the who (the people) and the what (the place) helps determine where opportunities to start the change journey lie in an organization. The question of where is answered in terms of where change is more or less feasible. Feasibility is driven taking into account the size of the ask from change across the organization and combining that insight with knowledge of the propensity of employees to engage positively with change.

By combining insight on the what (the place) and the who (the people), the behavioural roadmap gives firms a strong start at identifying where they are likely to see the strongest returns on any initiative for change.

A concluding case example below illustrates this tool in action.

CASE EXAMPLE
Putting a behavioural roadmap to work

A firm looking for learning-led transformation

Here's the starting position (Figure 14.11) for a firm where we'd mapped combined analytics on the people and the place. This enabled us to dig deeper into each cluster and segment by employee demographic to understand what membership of each cluster represents in terms of employee age, gender, tenure, job level, business function, work team and location.

The mapping told us that around 20 per cent or 1 in 5 of employees (Cluster 8) already showed strength in the behaviours the firm wanted to strengthen. Although this cluster ranks among the lowest for propensity for change, it still has scope for improvement. More importantly, it's a great potential resource for the firm to draw on, for others to learn from sharing how Cluster 8 is 'doing it right'.

Meanwhile Cluster 6 shows the highest propensity for change and it faces a large challenge in adopting the target behaviours. Whilst these employees might be willing, they would be unlikely to achieve the goals of the change programme any time soon. Not, then, the best place to start the programme.

Turning attention to the top-right clusters (5, 4 and 1) we see there are employees and parts of the firm where there is scope for improvement, where change is feasible and where the propensity for change is relatively strong. This is where a roadmap for change can most usefully start. And so to the final map (Figure 14.12).

FIGURE 14.11   Starting point for a change programme: mapping employee propensity to change

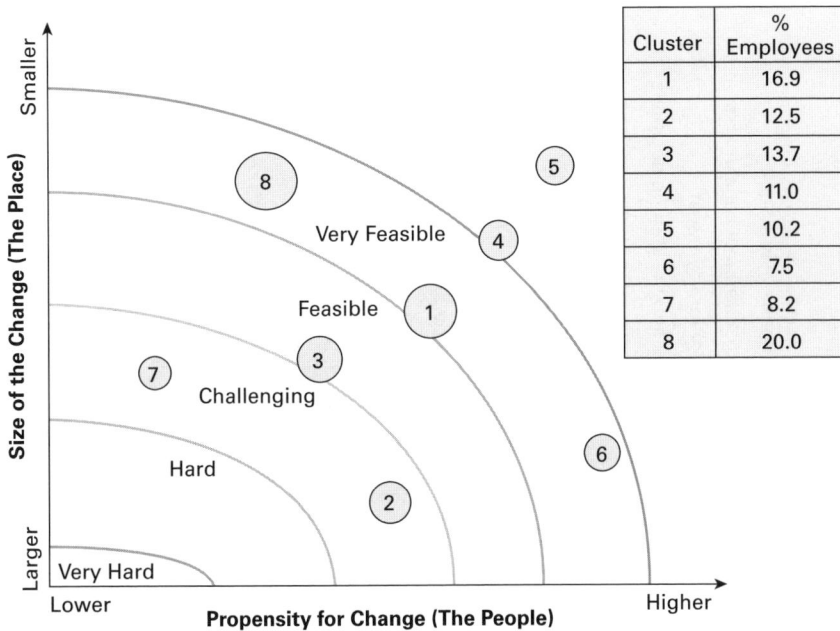

Cluster	% Employees
1	16.9
2	12.5
3	13.7
4	11.0
5	10.2
6	7.5
7	8.2
8	20.0

Here's what Figure 14.12 can tell us. First, the doughnut charts along the lower edge: these show internal benchmarks for each of three target behaviours drawn from original analytics on the place. The three Bs are behavioural markers for:

B1 = 'customer focus' factor.

B2 = 'simple is best' and 'desire to remove internal barriers to the firm's performance.

B3 = 'succeeding together' and 'aspiring to break down internal silos and promote shared commitment to achieving organizational goals'.

Our suggested direction of travel at the start of this firm's change journey centred on Cluster 5, Cluster 4 and Cluster 1. These represent employees and parts of the organization with a stronger propensity for change and where there is specific rather than general scope for strengthening target behaviours. These groups can share learning from their respective strengths to address target behaviours where a cluster is weaker. Iterating with and learning from these clusters offers a bridge to other parts of the organization as the change programme demonstrated that change is feasible, builds success stories and leverages shared learning across and beyond these clusters.

FIGURE 14.12   Behaviour change mapping tools

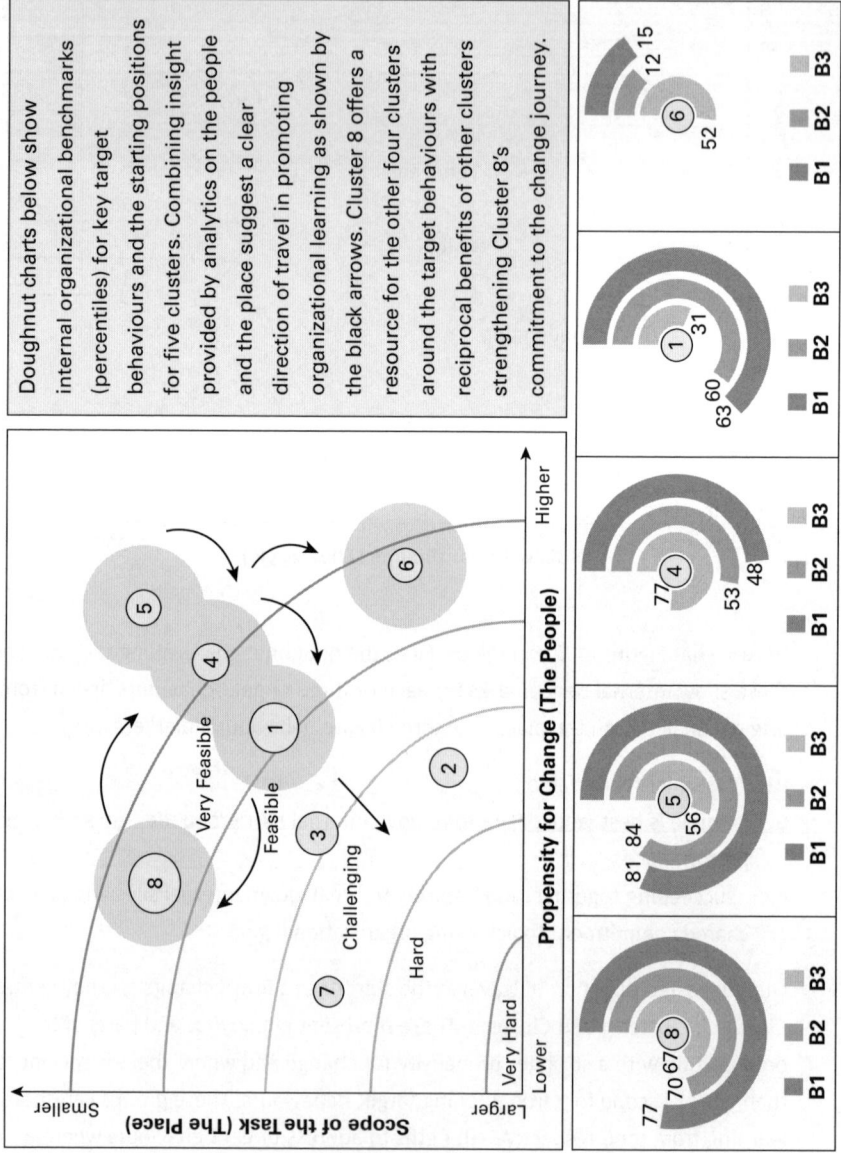

Doughnut charts below show internal organizational benchmarks (percentiles) for key target behaviours and the starting positions for five clusters. Combining insight provided by analytics on the people and the place suggest a clear direction of travel in promoting organizational learning as shown by the black arrows. Cluster 8 offers a resource for the other four clusters around the target behaviours with reciprocal benefits of other clusters strengthening Cluster 8's commitment to the change journey.

Notes

1   House of Commons (2018) Carillion (HC 769): Second Joint Report from the Business, Energy and Industrial Strategy and Work and Pensions Committees of Session 2017–19, https://publications.parliament.uk/pa/cm201719/cmselect/cmworpen/769/769.pdf (archived at https://perma.cc/4HBD-B8FR)

2   Ewenstein, B, Smith, W and Sologar, A (2015) Changing change management, McKinsey & Co.

3   Strebel, P (1996) Why do employees resist change? *Harvard Business Review*, May–June

4   Gleeson, B (2016) Leading change: 6 reasons change management strategies fail, *Forbes*, December

5   Lawson, E and Price, C (2003) The psychology of change management, *McKinsey Quarterly*, June

6   Ashkensas, R (2013) Change management needs to change, *Harvard Business Review*, April

7   For an example of how the impact of context such as the workplace is now being recognized in research on organizations see Johns, G (2006) The essential impact of context on organizational behaviour, *Academy of Management Review*, **31**, pp 386–408

8   These behavioural dimensions are consistent with broader research on the characteristics of people who are more open to personal change and more likely to commit to organizational change programmes. For an example of this research see Vakola, M, Tsaousis, I and Nikolaou, I (2004) The role of emotional intelligence and personality variables on attitudes towards organizational change, *Journal of Managerial Psychology*, **19**, pp 88–110

9   iPsychTech (2020) Gaining insight into employee voice through behavioural analytics: how behavioural analytics can be used to promote employee voice and address employee silence.

10   For details of benchmarks associated with different lines of organizational research, see Bosco, F A et al (2015) Correlational effect size benchmarks, *Journal of Applied Psychology*, **100**, pp 431–49

11   Keller, S and Schaninger, B (2019) Getting personal about change, *McKinsey Quarterly*, August. This paper shows that executives in organizations that use insights into the mindsets of employees to guide their change programmes are four times more likely to rate those programmes as successful.

12   These workshops follow the principles outlined by Kurt Lewin for action research with a specific focus on the 'Changing' aspect of change. That is, diagnosing the impetus for change and exploring and testing new models of behaviour.

13   The metrics shown in this paper are calibrated in percentiles using an internal benchmark based on client employee responses to the CultureScope behavioural diagnostic.

14   Keller and Schaninger (2019) ibid

15   Method also explored by UK Government's Behavioural Insights Team, see BIT's Update Report 2013–2015, www.behaviouralinsights.co.uk/wp-content/uploads/2015/07/BIT_Update-Report-Final-2013-2015.pdf (archived at https://perma.cc/84RV-7XK2)

15

What regulators really want: wrap-up and look ahead

ROGER MILES

Wrap-up introduction

Firms have been put on notice that 'purpose' (in a societal setting) is now the essential driver of acceptable conduct. We know that business can be productive and ethical – indeed, that the most productive and sustainable businesses *are* ethical,[1] as the UK's Conduct regulator reminds us: we must purposefully 'reduce potential harms'[2] that our business model creates.

Covid-19 is in one sense just the latest and largest example of how crisis imposes an 'abrupt and brutal audit [of our] every weakness'.[3] At the level of individual human risk perception, it has also provided what psychologists call a 'reification moment',[4] as previously abstract-seeming topics (like 'pandemic') burst in on everyday reality, forcing us to change our routine behaviour. As we recover from a global healthcare shock that has left many nations' budgets in worse shape than two world wars, those potential harms loom large in citizens' daily lives.

What's our industry now to do? Let us take stock of what we now know.

What does a conduct regulator really (really) want?

This is the number one question that firms bring to my workshop sessions. Research evidence in earlier chapters here, plus informal conversations with conduct regulators around the world, assure me that we may draw some robust summary conclusions as to 'what they (really) want', which is the following.

First, to **raise public trust in financial providers**. They want to see the firms delivering the best possible customer outcomes, and preventing harm. As politically sponsored organizations, regulatory agencies want to keep their sponsors happy, remembering also that those sponsors are only in power because a public vote put them there. What matters to a regulator is that your firm serves the public good, not just its own profit-seeking, and that it gives a better account of itself whilst doing so.

Second, to **see firms thinking for themselves**. Also showing evidence of how they're doing that, such as by welcoming challenge and improvement; by not 'box-ticking' or delegating away Conduct initiatives; by bringing the whole firm in on the 'culture conversation' – especially those tricksy 'managers in the middle'. Culture assessors will watch for how everyone in a firm is not just 'doing culture as compliance' but each *feeling* personally responsible for doing what's right, reconnecting with their own personal moral sense rather than 'leaving it outside the office door'. Healthy culture is massively more likely when each person is thoughtful about purpose ('why we're here').

Every conduct regulator also, if only privately, has three core beliefs:

- That **social purpose** matters, in any financial enterprise. Prosocial behaviour matters more than 'just making money'.

- That to prevent future crises we must **study human behaviour**, not just economic models. To prevent mis-selling and overconfidence, for example, we must all recognize and overcome certain cognitive biases.

- Finally, that by holding *each* practitioner **personally responsible**, we can improve behaviour industry-wide.

Conduct and culture: what lies ahead?

After five years of 'behavioural reporting', things are changing up a gear with the introduction of culture assessments in 2022. Firms will be expected to engage with new assessment tools – but this needn't be as daunting as it may seem.

Remember first that regulators just want finance to give a better account of itself to the public. Start by asking yourselves better questions, bearing in mind a few underlying shifts in emphasis of regulatory policy and practice:

- not fixating on punishing bad behaviour but looking to encourage exemplary conduct;

- 'tone at the top' still matters, but 'motivation in the middle' now matters more (albeit directors' behaviour at board meetings, the event of challenge in those meetings, and good risk governance from leadership downwards are also vital observational 'tells');

- towards forward-looking indicators, based more on delineating purpose than defining offences;

- new tools and techniques for culture assessment will overlay pre-existing conduct assessment frameworks;

- learning to ask better (more qualitatively searching) questions;

- more direct observation, with less reliance on in-house or third-party reported sentiment surveys; be ready to respond to in-person questions from a regulator's case officer walking the floor, dropping in on your Zoom meetings, inviting you in for a friendly cup of tea, or remotely surveilling you.

If your firm is using only financial reporting indicators, these will need augmenting with human factor MI. Start straightforwardly by grouping your knowledge sources on conduct and culture into 'misconduct' and 'exemplary' ('virtue' and 'vice') paired indicator sets, such as for psychological safety vs abusive behaviour; moral courage vs bystanding; diverse thinking vs tendency to stereotyping, and so on.

Use the plain-language reframe of the Five Conduct Questions (page 238) that every single employee can understand and work with, to prompt the start of a firm-wide 'conduct conversation'. This also prepares everyone for a conduct regulator's imminent appearance in person at anyone's desk, asking how your firm is putting those vaunted corporate values into everyday practice. You definitely don't want to be thinking about that for the first time as the regulator's culture assessor appears at your desk: start now.

The virus crisis, as well as regulators, prompted us collectively to measure how far there is – or could be more – diversity of thought to help stimulate innovative ideas by bringing fresh perspectives and solutions. Where thought diversity is lacking at senior levels, culture audits will prompt firms to reach beyond standard markers for diversity (gender, ethnicity, social, cognitive, sexuality and neurotype) to pursue complex cognitive diversity that transforms capacity for problem-solving. The more enlightened brands are already looking beyond 'mere compliance', to measure the business value uplift that profound diversity brings: resilience, higher retained earnings, happier customers and more productive staff who stay longer. Financial firms are starting to move past old assumptions about recruitment and advancement – such as deeply rooted preferences for cultural fit (hiring in-group 'people like us') – looking to remedy an inherent industry-wide bias that has for too long blocked many promising people from moving into senior roles.

There will be new 'cultural benchmarks', building on the pioneering work of industry groups such as the Banking Standards Board, the Institute of Internal Auditors, FICC-Financial Markets Standards Board, and commercial-side analytics such as Barrett, Starling, iPsychTec, Harris-Fombrun and Edelman.

Coming next: supervisory focus on 'cultural capital' and reputation risk

On the supervisory front, although the Dutch central bank (DNB) was of course always way ahead, others are now catching up. The Basel Committee has weighed in, since 2018 experimenting with monitoring reputation risk ('idiosyncratic risk capital', in BIS-speak) to test how far stakeholder opinion of a bank's business differs from the econometric view generated by conventional value-at-risk analysis. Central bankers in the UK, US and the Netherlands, have started alluding to commercial banks' 'cultural capital'.[5] In the near future, a bank will need to persuade capital supervisors that its Pillar 2 assumptions are correct, or risk a Pillar 2A capital add-on – an implicit indictment of the bank's non-financial performance. Yes, that's right: a capital charge on account of 'unhealthy culture'.

We think of all such new assessments as behaviour-at-risk indicators, challenging now less credible value-at-risk models. With a little help from this book, firms can begin to assemble a wide-ranging toolkit of indicators and potential benchmarks for culture; we'll start to see more of measures for psychological safety, cognitive diversity, reputation risk and plenty of other human-risk factors. All of which is strategically exciting, perhaps, but the other question everyone asks is: What should we do *now*? Let's deal with that shortly, but first, some call-backs to lessons learned in earlier chapters.

What we've learned: some call-backs

Over the last 357 pages we've discovered some strange and sometimes wonderful things. Here's a selection, to keep the flame burning:

- The new orthodoxy of 'wider purpose', social engagement, and 'bringing your whole self to work' is here to stay. More than half the workforce are now post-millennials, with millennial ethical values; they/we *really* care about ethics and treating everyone well – and not so much about the mono-linear pursuit of profit.

- Today, culture assessment; coming soon, capital charges against your 'reputation risk'. The regulatory ratchet continues to turn.

- There's a seething mass of 'vox populi risk' out there. The 'normal people' (who don't work in academic or financial risk analysis) very much want us to improve and exhibit our social conscience. Meanwhile, and otherwise, vox pop risk will hit you almost at random. It has already displaced brands, business leaders, and governments. Ignore it at your peril.

- Regulators have a quietly effective sanction against badly-behaved firms: 'the naughty step' (or more formally, the watchlist). Although who's on the list isn't published, each firm on the 'naughty step' will be told privately that they're on it, and exactly how they need to improve their behaviour before being allowed back into the playroom.

- Some naughty firms do a thing called sludging – it's the evil twin of 'nudging'; designing 'customer care/remediation' processes that are actually designed to drive people away rather than engage with them.

- Talking of evil twins, almost every positive conduct has a negative opposite indicator: for 'moral courage' it's 'bystanding'; for 'open-mindedness' it's 'groupthink', and so on. A simple starting point for your prototype culture balance sheet of exemplaries versus misconducts.

- Culture indicators can indeed be infuriating sometimes, as it's not always instantly obvious 'which way is up'. Sometimes it's not even a matter of 'up or down'. For example, 'simple courage' – you need to have enough of (ie be enterprising), not too little (timid), but also not too much (foolhardy).

- Some already-in-use approaches to culture tracking are a really bad idea – such as covertly surveilling staff in their homes (maybe no surprise there).

- Certain other already-in-use indicators are a waste of time. 'Conduct risk appetite', 'training attendance', 'net promoter score' and 'unconscious bias testing' are all popular in some quarters. They won't help the design of your culture scorecard one little bit. But by all means carry on using them if they give you a warm feeling.

- Far from being 'primitive', early mankind's tribal societies were socially wonderful in many ways, creating incredibly subtle social signals that enabled people to interact safely with strangers. Since then, these formerly useful signals have morphed into dangerous bias effects which lead people to negatively stereotype others, to bully and discriminate against 'out-groups', and to seek chat-room affirmation of their own darkest beliefs. We need to constantly watch out for the unwanted effects of our 'inner animal brain' at work.

- As a motivational mechanism to get people to feel good about and engaged with a positive firm-wide culture, 'conduct enforcement' is a complete non-starter (on the regulator side), as is 'conduct compliance training' (on the firm side). Rethink required on both sides.

- Attempts at culture control have historically produced some bizarre unintended consequences. Make sure your rationalization of 'culture assessment' leaves space to consider *irrational* (but predictable) responses to your oh-so-rationally designed questions.

- The world's regulators and supervision technologies are converging around core ideas of 'acceptable and expected conduct' including the tracking of psychological safety, cognitive diversity, morally courageous leadership, effective challenge, anti-bystanding, and more.

Simple, instant changes that will make a big difference

Knowing what you now know from this book, it's possible to tweak everyday work habits in a few simple ways that greatly improve a firm's preparedness for culture assessment.

Make **senior managers more evidently available** to all staff. (If they're already doing any of these things, fine, by the way – keep going.) Encourage them to walk the real or virtual floor: 'Management By Wandering About', holding status-neutral conversations; to tour different teams' meetings; to give town-hall question and answer sessions, with a firm emphasis on dialogue rather than broadcast.

Begin a rolling '**conduct conversation**', using this book's materials (such as Chapter 10). Try starting each team meeting with one of the plain language Five Questions (page 238), and/or ask anyone, in freestyle speech, to 'tell us about the time when…' (eg a day something went wrong, and what we did about it). Engage people in discussing 'how would we explain what we do, in terms that our friends and family would understand, without using any jargon?' You'll no doubt readily be able to think of many more such team-building exercises – do ask teams for their own ideas for these too, maybe offering prizes for the most engaging and imaginative suggestions.

Look in new places, including close at hand, to find **fresh sources of management information** (MI) about the firm's culture. Don't be hidebound by the weight of 'the MI that we have', or put off by the elaborate-looking solutions offered by reg techs and consultants. Some of these are excellent (we've looked at a few of the best in this book); some of them are worthless. Before parting with hard-won budget resources to buy in a solution, have you considered all the available sources that are already right in front of you? A firm's frontline, customer- or client-facing staff are its biggest, yet weirdly still most often overlooked source of free early warning signals that something might be wrong; it's all about working towards a culture that supports them putting a hand up to tell you about it.

There is lots of free but still valuable MI out there, first in the form of things we half-know about and need to look harder at – 'semi-structured knowledge' such as:

- How are people putting their training learnings into practice?
- What's Glassdoor saying about us?
- How many events of 'hands-up' do we get, each day/week/month?
- How many aggressive gagging orders has the legal department issued against departing employees (and was the same team manager involved each time?)?
- How often does any member of frontline staff see a senior manager?

Then there's even looser, but maybe even more valuable 'unstructured knowledge':

- Are there a lot of 'workarounds' of problems, rather than actual problem-solving?
- What are people talking about in their 'conversations in the (real or virtual) corridor'?
- What's the cultural 'feel' (interpersonal dynamic) in board meetings, team meetings?
- What do people want to talk about, that they don't?

Initiate your firm's **conversation with the regulator** yourself. Yes, take the initiative. (Otherwise, your firm risks always being on the back foot, or one move behind in the regulatory 'chess game'.) This can include attending industry forums – conferences and roundtables where regulators speak. You'll soon find yourself sharing a platform (literally) with a regulator – an experience that's routine and common to every single author of this book, by the way. As with your internal Management By Wandering About, the more informal the conversation, the better, at least to begin with.

Talking of **industry-level groups**, get involved with more of them. You can start small: write a blog or think-piece for your house journal. Then step it up a gear or two: write a white paper for an industry conference, or attend any worthwhile industry roundtable group (trade association working group, think-tank, academic research group, parliamentary working group). On your firm's behalf, respond to a piece of proposed regulation or draft legislation that affects you. Attend a peer group roundtable with people in other firms who do the same job as you – or set up your own, as one of my favourite clients did; now she's the Culture Queen of the City.

In case you're one of those people (like your editor here) who starts reading a book at the last chapter, the above points alone should provide enough ammunition for your first couple of months' programme, especially if you're a newly appointed culture team leader. Then, by all means, work through the main part of the book. Then try some of our recommended reads. Still hungry? Try following up all the original research sources cited in the footnotes. By that stage, you'll be about as knowledgeable as the authors, so maybe call us about co-authoring a chapter in the next instalment!

The final takeaway

On a slightly more reflective note: whilst by some measures the financial sector's 'human risk' scores are improving, we're under no illusions. There's a deficit of public trust that still runs deep. Covid-19 has perversely provided myriad opportunities at every level to show moral courage and make an exemplary response. In some financial firms' boardrooms, it's evident that the virus emergency provoked a recognition that this was indeed 'a chance to get things right, compared to the past'.[6]

How providers will be rated, which of them will forfeit their social licence, and indeed who will cease to have a long-term future, has never been such a hot topic among behavioural predictive analysts. It's fair to say, as we emerge into several kinds of new landscape, that the public interest is pretty high too. We'll see how carefully each financial firm has listened to the call to make and report a purposeful culture; and whether plainer, public versions of the same message have been listened to, either before a conduct regulator compels firms to, or market forces deliver a more 'abrupt and brutal' verdict.

Culture assessment is here, and is real. It will require your firm to ask better questions of itself, to know where to look for the required new reporting information, and to foster a work environment of positive engagement where it's safe to ask constructive challenge questions and to solve problems collaboratively. At ground level, keep it simple by bearing in mind what conduct regulators really want: to see all staff, across all regulated firms, thinking and speaking intelligently for themselves about what purpose and 'exemplary conduct' means to them. To see them applying both formal training and personal intuition to reflect on what 'good behaviour' is in daily practice. For all that we've just taken 100,000 words to consider the question, that's the answer in a nutshell, actually.

No reason now not to get started!

Notes

1 Sources include currently (Q1/2021) Edmondson, A (2019) *The Fearless Organization: Creating psychological safety in the workplace,* Wiley; Kiel, F (2015) *Return On Character,* Harvard Business Review Press; Sanderson, C A (2020) *The Bystander Effect: The psychology of courage and inaction,* William Collins

2 See eg FCA (2021) FCA clamps down on consumer investment harm, www.fca. org.uk/news/press-releases/fca-clamps-down-consumer-investment-harm (archived at https://perma.cc/T976-PE2B)

3 Lagadec, P (1993) *Preventing Chaos In a Crisis,* McGraw-Hill, p 84

4 The cognitive stress-point that occurs when a person realizes that a formerly notional threat or abstract worry is now real and physically present in their life. See Miles, R, *Conduct Risk Management: Using a behavioural approach to protect your board and financial services business,* pp 178–80, 262

5 Stiroh, K (Federal Reserve Bank of New York) (2021) The impact of the pandemic on cultural capital in the finance industry – speech to international capital supervisors group at 'Risk USA', www.bis.org/review/r201117a.pdf (archived at https://perma.cc/CTF5-US9N)

6 Woolard, C (2020) FCA, interviewed in *Financial Times,* 20 April

GLOSSARY

acceptable and expected conduct/behaviour *see norms*

action bias the way we often believe it's better to 'do something, anything' rather than do nothing.

affect behavioural science jargon for 'emotion', in a decision context; when we make a snap decision based on how we feel at that moment (anger, excitement, pain, love, fear, etc).

affective shock when your rational judgement is impaired because your feelings (anger, fight-or-flight, desire, anxiety, arousal, etc) overwhelm it.

agency/power (loss of) how far you have control over a situation you're in. Where there's 'limited agency', nothing much you do will change the outcome.

anchoring/'sticky bias' having made up one's mind, 'hanging on' to the first point that informed the decision and not reviewing it, even if the situation has changed. The first fact becomes the reference point for all subsequent judgements.

asymmetric incentives where the reward (such as to a salesperson) is out of scale with the product's benefit to the customer; as when selling a 20-year contract product delivers a huge 'front-end-loaded' sales commission in year 1.

asymmetry where key aspects of a transaction (knowledge, rewards, pricing) are badly out of balance, as when a customer's knowledge is far less than the salesperson's.

attestation a designated Senior Manager formally assuring the regulator, in a signed personal statement, that they're competent 'in role'.

audit ritual/ritual compliance how, after a while, executives tend to 'go through the motions' of checking information, seeking comfort in familiarity and not questioning underlying assumptions.[1]

availability bias deciding based on only information that comes to hand. For example, if we asked for three product brochures and only two arrived the next day, we might decide between the first two and not wait for the third.

behaviour-based regulation/conduct regulation new rules and sanctions aiming to prevent harms to customers and encourage 'exemplary' behaviour in financial firms. Based on concepts from *behavioural science*, notably *biases, psychological safety and cognitive diversity*; and management science of organizational *culture*.

behavioural economics how understandings from *behavioural science* help us to see and predict patterns in people's decision-making, especially when they're trading (buying, pricing, selling).

behavioural lens analytic tool revealing 'human risk' of people being unable or unwilling to engage with a given proposition or activity (a new enterprise or policy, behaviour change, consumer choice, external threat, etc).

behavioural science study observing 'what actually happens' as humans interact and respond to events. Often questions why observed behaviour confounds rational expectations, as humans behave *irrationally* much of the time; so uncovering patterns of bias (we tend to be *predictably irrational*) and social influences.

behaviour-at-risk the potential cost resulting from any things that your staff do (especially around customers) that cause *detriment* to customers, and/or undermine trust or value in your business. Requires real-time, dynamic observation to track rapid change. See also *conduct risk*.

benchmarks standard indicators agreed for use across a sector as set point 'norms', for example for the level of daily prices struck in a given marketplace. One major benchmark, the London Interbank Offered Rate (LIBOR), used to indicate each day the average interest rate that leading banks would charge to lend money to each other; this affected the price of many other products down the line, such as how much interest *normal people* had to pay on their home mortgages. Hence huge *vox populi* backlash when some bankers *rigged* LIBOR in the mid 2000s.

bias effects what happens after various systematic (non-random) errors in our thinking start to upset any attempt to make a logical, well-informed decision. Some biases are self-serving (such as *optimism*, which helps keep us alive). Others flow from evolutionary kinks in the ways that our brains deal with incoming information (see *cognitive bias*).

bias-correction see *de-biasing*

binary vs. scalar (view of assessment design) a binary question has only two possible answers, such as 'yes' or 'no'. This set-up forces a respondent to choose between two, perhaps over-simplified options. Real-life choice situations are more nuanced.

blame-shifting reports formatted such that anything going wrong is 'not your fault' but someone else's.

bounded rationality when perceiving risk and making decisions, we are 'blind to the limitations of our own understanding'.[2] Our ability to decide logically is limited ('bounded') by our capacity for thinking and *cognitive bias*.

box-ticking approaching a management task (such as compliance) as an unthinking routine to be completed, rather than series of real questions that need to be thought about intelligently. Also fosters an attitude that having 'made a mark on a piece of paper' displaces one's responsibility to resolve any present problems.

business culture the attitudes and beliefs that shape how employees of a commercial firm go about their work from day to day; in regulators' view, having a business model and practices rooted in the fair treatment of customers, and market integrity.

bystanding not intervening to fix a problem, because you believe, perhaps sincerely, that someone else will shortly be coming forwards to fix it.

capital adequacy/'regulatory capital' a form of cash buffer against business collapse, that banks are required by regulators to maintain. It is the minimum fraction of a bank's business value which the bank must hold ready on its own account (in 'liquid form') in order to be able to pay off its market obligations.

challenge function see *constructive challenge*

cherry-picking selective (usually favourable) reporting of information.

choice architecture/'nudging' regulatory design practice that seeks to influence choice by changing the manner in which options are presented to people. Popularized by pop-science book, *Nudge*.[3]

classical economics/neoclassical economics (as distinct from *behavioural economics*) field of study asserting that human decisions can be logically explained by (assumed) preference for 'resource maximizing' (profit-seeking, accumulating property). Behavioural science disagrees, because real people don't behave as classical models predict.

codes of practice, voluntary see *GSVR*

cognitive bias any systematic (non-random) error in thinking, that regularly makes our judgement deviate from what would be considered desirable as accepted norms, or correct in terms of formal logic.

cognitive diversity having in your firm people who bring different styles of thinking, information processing and perspectives, to improve collective problem-solving. Not a function of conventional 'diversity markers' (gender, ethnicity, social background/education, neurotype, etc) although it's a good sign if these markers are strongly present.

cognitive load (and overload) how much of your brain's processing capacity is taken up with handling new information or sensory stimuli. At overload point, your brain stops being able to make sense of all the incoming information; our brains have *bounded* capacity.

cognitive miser we ration our use of brain resources, just as we conserve our bodily energy, though this is mostly done unconsciously. We might think summarily of people as stereotypes, not their true personalities; or use *heuristics* to lighten the *cognitive load* that a decision needs, such as only using readily available information.

common goods the objective of many public policies of risk control: to promote activities that make life better for people.

conduct costs as a conduct regulated firm, all the money that you have to budget and spend to comply with conduct regulation and (perhaps) to recover after a prosecution for misconduct.

conduct regulation laws and rules prescribing acceptable and expected behaviour by financial service firms, setting out 'harms' that providers must prevent.

conduct risk subset of *behavioural risk*: potential cost resulting from employees or suppliers breaching conduct rules; or more generally, business loss following staff or supplier behaviour (especially towards customers) that undermines trust or value in the business or creates a 'disorderly market'. Includes managers' *inaction* failing to anticipate and overcome *biases* or *asymmetry* in transactions.

confirmation bias seeking or evaluating information in a way that fits with existing beliefs (e.g. looking for reasons to stay loyal to a brand and not consider an informed choice to change).

conflict of interest where for example a firm's business loyalties upset its good judgement; or an employee gains personal benefit from a task they're doing in an official capacity.

constructive challenge questioning why things are as they are, in a way that encourages a search for better alternatives. Not just saying 'This system isn't working' but 'How can we improve it?'

creative compliance when, to avoid an unwanted control, a practitioner manipulates a rule or report, to deflect its impact away from the regulator's intentions and towards the practitioner's own interests.

credit crunch in financial markets, a point in time where lenders realize that they may have taken on more business than they can manage, so they panic (*affective shock*) and stop extending credit to each other.

culture (organizational) shared values, assumptions, beliefs and ways of interacting within a firm; informally, 'the way we do things here'; 'what we do when no one's looking'; 'stories we tell, to make sense of why we do what we do'.

culture assessment/culture audit a regulator examining people's assumptions, norms, beliefs and actions at a firm, to see whether these align with the firm's claimed values and stated purpose; also, the firm pre-emptively examining these aspects of itself, to improve business value and to prepare for the regulator's visit.

cultural entropy a culture audit measure: how dysfunctional is the firm? It measures how much of the firm's collective energy is wasted on unproductive work, friction in processes, and other forms of frustration.

customer detriment see *detriment*

customer-centric in a business, always first considering what the customer needs.

data fallacy popular myth that 'the more information we have, the better decisions we will (automatically) make'; ignoring 'information overload' ('can't see the wood for the trees').

de-biasing/bias-correction regulatory suggestion that firms prevent customer purchases based on *cognitive biases* (such as *selective attention*), or the salesperson's biased presentation of choice (such as *framing*). In practice, difficult to achieve.

decision science research fields examining how humans take decisions. Includes neurology, cybernetics, social psychology, much of behavioural economics.

delusion (of adequacy), delusional see *Dunning-Kruger effect*

denial a *bias* state of being unwilling or unable to acknowledge a proximate threat to well-being, or the consequences of one's own bad behaviour.[4]

de-risking often crude response by firms to regulatory demands for better management of risk: such as by expelling customers or products with 'inconvenient' risk profiles.

derivatives a financial contract whose main value is realized if and when an expected event happens, such as needing a market price index to reach a certain level.

detriment, detrimental conduct regulators' term used to describe any harm suffered by customers as a result of their buying financial products.

dissonance in cognitive science, the gap between the reality of what's happening and how you explain to yourself what's happening, as you may prefer to interpret it; a discomforting clash that you might experience between your own thoughts, beliefs or attitudes, and a contrasting reality. A common response is to kid yourself that your misjudged view of things is still the 'right' one.

diversity see *cognitive diversity*

drivers of risk any activity or behaviour that makes it more likely you (or your firm) will incur some form of risk.

due skill and care legal test of the basic standard of acceptable behaviour in customer service; now overtaken by the tougher standard of not causing *detriment*

Dunning-Kruger effect when objectively measuring someone's (professional) ability and skill, a finding that they're unduly confident yet also unaware they lack the relevant competence.

dynamic sensing of risk (see also *situational awareness*) rare human intuitive faculty of locating a significant source of risk from among a mass of assorted incoming information or signals. Prevalent skillset in certain professions (test pilots, renal surgeons, the most successful entrepreneurs, submarine commanders) but regrettably not in most commercial boardrooms, whatever directors may claim (see *Dunning-Kruger effect*).

econometrics, econometric measures/models formalized decision tools, often based on mathematical probability, calculating risk in financial products. Gathering and arranging numbers into logical structures, it fallaciously assumes that (1) numbers and (2) money are effective *proxy indicators* for human behaviour. Why the world needed *behavioural economics*.

economic benefit getting more money as a result of doing something.

'Econs vs. Humans' debate academic spat between 'neoclassical' economists who advocate *econometrics* (*rational actor*, financial statistics) and new-wave behavioural economists who value the impacts of emotions (*affect*) and *biases*. See also *normal people.*[5]

emerging markets financial trading in a developing country which has not yet instituted the risk control standards common in developed markets; a setting where investment carries greater risk, but with potential for higher returns.

empathy-deficient having difficulty in understanding what other people may be thinking or needing. A familiar impairment in people with autistic spectrum disorders,[6] but also sometimes found as a form of sociopathic disorder in senior managers.

endowment effect a form of bias. For the customer: valuing a thing more the minute that you own it (and maybe because you spent so much on it in the first place); defending your purchase of something expensive. For salespeople: encouraging the customer to buy the most expensive option 'because it must be worth the extra cost'.

enforcement against inaction where a prosecutor takes action against a provider for *not* instituting a required risk control, such as for failing to set up a mandated framework for managing conduct risk.

enforced self-regulation see also *GSVR*: regulatory regime preceding *conduct regulation*, but discredited by the control failures of 2008; regulated firms had to self-report on their own compliance, with occasional enforcements by the regulator where non-compliance was suspected.

expert bias/expert problem excessive faith in one's own talents, knowledge, or skills, or in those of an expert who has been drafted in to give topical advice. (See also *delusion of adequacy/Dunning-Kruger effect*.) Commonly, someone who may or may not have expert knowledge in one field comes to believe that this qualifies them to have an expert opinion on other topics. Alarmingly common in corporate boardrooms and management consultancies.

external trust the extent to which people who *don't* work for you are willing to believe what you say.

fair outcomes what conduct regulators expect providers to achieve for customers; the opposite of *detriment*.

financial capability the limits on a customer's access to information, or their 'literacy' in understanding your financial product jargon.

fit and proper person regulatory requirement that a manager is free from suspicion on ethical grounds – no criminal record, nor court judgements for personal debt, for example.

formal organization vs. informal groups social theory contrasting how organizations claim they operate (with published forms of structured hierarchy, organizational charts, lines of reporting, and so on), as against 'what actually happens' thanks to the hidden influence of private, personal social links and values.

framing how you choose to acknowledge and describe a given risk or other phenomenon. Also, how you arrange the wording or illustration of any related choices to manage it, in such a way as to alter the 'natural' balance of attractiveness of each choice. The business of politics and regulation has been described as 'a framing contest':[7] leaders compete to 'capture the narrative'; whoever succeeds gets elected.

'friends and family test' see *'what actually happens'*

fundamental attribution error the *bias* mistake of assuming there's a simple cause, such as a single person's actions, that created a particular situation. Such as: 'the CEO made the bank fail'. Related problems: scapegoating, *stereotyping*. Popular tactic among media pundits and internet trolls.

gaming (of rules/compliance) misconduct attitude that sees rules and compliance obligations as a chance for creative 'rule-bending'; reinterpreting unclear rules in a way that favours the practitioner's needs.

global financial crisis (GFC) there have been several, but this is now generally taken to refer to the financial market crash of 2008 (unfolding 2007–9), following overheating of household mortgage markets, with associated *derivatives* and insurance; and widespread under-weighting of credit risk.

goodwill that element of the value of a business which is not accounted for by its physical assets alone; extra value (or 'share premium') in a firm, that reflects customers' preference to buy the brand, trusting the firm's general *reputation*.

granular regulation very detailed rules. A catch: more detailed rules create more 'loopholes' in between; granular isn't necessarily better.

'grey areas' aspects of firms' regulated activities that are not yet clearly defined by new regulations; such as what 'good behaviour' means in practice, where profitability and ethics diverge.

group norms see *norms*

groupthink where a group of (often senior, often expert, often highly intelligent) individuals makes an ill-judged collective decision with unexpected, disastrous consequences. Prevalent where there's strong internal social pressure; strict hierarchy; and new forms of external threat. See also *motivated reasoning*.

GSVR/government-sponsored voluntary regulation Policy-makers' jargon name for codes of practice and the like: industries' self-governing 'binding voluntary' initiatives that try to put off full regulation. Some industries have made progress using GSVRs in response to society's concerns (food producers reducing fat or salt content; retailers reducing plastic bag use). Still widely prevalent in finance, environment, public health, social policy and other fields.

harms see *detriment*

herding justifying that you're doing what other people are doing, because they're doing it as a form of *social proof*.

heuristics see *rules-of-thumb*

human risk any risk factors assignable to how the relevant people behave, rather than economic or environmental factors.

humility/intellectual humility see *metacognition*

illusory correlation we are attracted to the idea that some actions and events are connected, or dependent on one another, when in fact they aren't; so we search for meaning in places where there isn't any. Hence: horoscopes, 'omens', etc.

indicator anything that points to, shows or suggests the state or level of something. In neoclassical economics: a statistic used to point out trends in markets and nations' economies.

inertia (bias) see also *sticky*: human tendency not to want to change one's existing position or beliefs.

information asymmetry a 'knowledge skew': where one party has more or better information than the other, so compromising a decision and/or balance of power. Financial firms generally have far better information resources than their customers and regulators; fertile ground for exploiting of customers and 'gaming' of audits.

in-group a (typically small) group of people with a shared interest or identity, who use this identity as a way to exclude others – the 'out-group'.

input measure, not outcome measure see also *indicators*: when describing a project, listing all the resources that you put into it (time, money, knowhow) as a way to evade talking about what the project actually achieved. A favourite tactic of MPs, when quizzed about a failed intervention.

insider dealing illegally exploiting access to unpublished information to make unfair profit when trading in securities, typically in publicly listed company shares.

irrational behaviour we tend to just get on and do things without pausing to logically evaluate choices available, or even to gather available information (*bounded rationality*). Intuitively we tend to prefer pain-free, rapid gratification; to avoid any loss; and use expedient *rules-of-thumb*. This behaviour isn't random; it frequently occurs in *predictable* patterns (see *predictably irrational*).

legitimacy where a rule-maker or controller has a fair claim to broad support from the general public, and/or regulatees.

lines of sight (in compliance): managers having clearly defined responsibilities for overseeing certain aspects of the business; and for managers to see one another's responsibilities in the context of the whole enterprise.

loss-aversion the human feeling that you'd rather avoid the chance of a possible loss, than bet on an equal chance of a possible gain.[8]

manipulation/'rigging' deliberate attempt by a person or informal group to interfere with the free and fair operation of a financial market by introducing misleading information.

market abuse see also *insider trading* and *manipulation*: using unpublished or unverified information to distort the price-setting mechanism of financial instruments.

mental accounting people think of their own money as divided into 'different bits', according to where it came from, what they plan to spend it on, and what method of payment they use.

metacognition thinking about how you think; having critical awareness of your own learning, and the boundaries of your own knowledge and ignorance; being comfortable saying 'I don't know' (intellectual humility).

misselling, mis-selling where a financial provider profits from selling a product to a customer who gains little or no practical benefit from the purchase.

mission creep where a public policy, campaign, or control intervention gradually increases its remit, attempting to widen its influence over a community.

models-based (of a risk control or regulation) relying on numerical data and *econometric* assumptions, rather than observed behaviour.

moral courage the intuitive human quality of 'doing what's right', even in the face of strong opposition from *vested interests*. An important human resilience factor that's notably absent from risk reports.

motivated reasoning/cultural cognition where having a personal and/or institutional stake in the outcome derails your objective analysis of a choice to be made. For example, turkeys would be unlikely to argue in favour of Christmas (even if they had the means to do so).

'normal people'/social perception behavioural scientists' term for how non-expert people perceive the world around them, and in particular the risks in it.[9] 'Normal people' don't generally stop to fully evaluate a risk; they just press on, taking an intuitive view.

norms (current); norming the level of pro-social, 'good' behaviour that most of the population require; the re-setting of these levels from time to time.

'nudging' see *choice architecture*

ombudsman a government-appointed independent mediator who helps resolve disputes between customers and service providers in a given business sector.

operational risk the prospect of loss resulting from inadequate or failed procedures, employee activities, systems or policies; includes errors made by employees, frauds, hacking, and other forms of disruption to business.

optimism (bias) human tendency to overestimate how likely a good thing is to happen, and underestimate the chances of a bad experience.

overconfidence a *bias* effect: where your subjective confidence in your own judgements is greater than it should be, if you checked against an objective analysis of the situation. As in: 'Don't stop me, I know what I'm doing.'

over-extrapolating justifying making a long-term commitment on the basis only of short-term information. For example, taking out a 20-year mortgage because you've just received a pay rise.

overload/cognitive overload to have too much of a burden imposed (such as of work to do; or cognitively, too much information to have to understand). See *cognitive load*.

overselling selling a product in quantities such that most buyers won't benefit from buying it.

oversight failure not noticing that something's gone wrong.

perception of risk how our brains make sense of hazards, events or information about a risk, and how that conditions our response to them. Less about rational analysis, more often 'how it makes us feel'.

performance attribution bias attributing skills and personal qualities, or lack of these, to someone based on how 'like me/us, or unlike me/us' they are: 'He must be OK, he went to Oxford too.'

performative (compliance), performativity Looking busy! Such as by: creating a 'culture initiative' whose activities misdirect the regulator's attention away from the lack of any real progress.

personal liability (SMR) a senior manager's obligation, under conduct rules, to answer for the consequences of a control failure in any business activity they're responsible for.

perverse effects when what actually happens is the opposite of what the control measure was designed to achieve.

perverse incentives where systems of risk and reward (well-intended or otherwise) promote bad behaviour; as when big front-end cash commissions encourage sale of poor-value products.

post-rationalizing (hindsight bias) after the event, inventing an explanation for why you did what you did. (If you'd been asked back then, you wouldn't have had an answer.)

predictably irrational human nature! We don't always act logically; but so-called illogical behaviour isn't usually random. Our intuitive (non-logical) mind leads us to behave in illogical but still consistent patterns, which can be predicted.

predictive power when a scientific test of a present phenomenon is frequently repeated with consistent results, it becomes highly reliable; this suggests that testing what *has* happened may reliably tell us what's *going to* happen next: it has strong predictive power. Except, of course, that when underlying conditions change, even 'reliable' predictors fail.

preferences and beliefs categories of bias, which lead consumers to choose a product that may not suit their real needs. Salespeople should challenge these.

present bias giving more weight to payoffs that come 'now'.

priming if we have in mind (even subconsciously) something that recently made us happy, we're more likely to agree to make a purchase. Salespeople know this, and so go out of their way to make us cheerful at the exact point where we're about to decide to make a purchase.

projection bias the idea that the future will bring 'more of the same' that we've just experienced, and that our own tastes and preferences will remain the same in future.

pro-social doing things for the public benefit. The opposite of antisocial.

providers for the purposes of this book: any organization providing financial services and having this activity subject to regulation.

proxy indicator/'proxy' an indirect measure that its users claim is representative of 'what's happening', where there is no direct measure. Beware 'false proxies': see *input measures.*

psychological safety sensing that one may speak up with a question, idea or concern, or to note a mistake, without being punished or humiliated

public goods activities, products or services which benefit the well-being of the general public, with or without profit to whoever is providing them.

rational actor the imaginary person at the centre of classical economists' assumptions: someone who is assumed to value profit and personal gain above all other considerations. See also *rationality assumption.*

rational compliance/rational compliers (people) obeying the rules because this appears to offer a quieter life than risking breaking them.

rational maximizing see *rationality assumption*

rational non-compliers/rational calculators people who work out that it might be more profitable (and/or fun for them) to break a rule than to obey it. The opposite of *rational compliers.*

rationality assumption basic tenet of *classical economics*, that humans in market-oriented societies ('homo economicus') make logical, self-interested decisions looking to accumulate wealth and increase utility (value to themselves) of goods, services and relationships ('rational maximizing'). Actually, oops: real people often don't behave like this (see *behavioural* dimension).

rear-view regulation writing new rules that refer only to failures that have happened in the past, rather than taking account of imminent and future changes in the market that's being regulated.

recency (bias) making a decision based on only information we can remember as arriving most recently. This is why the final contestant on a TV talent show often wins the public vote – the audience recalls their performance more vividly.

reciprocity 'social rule' urging people to give back (reciprocate) any goodwill or kindness they have received from someone else; feeling obligated to return a favour. Why salespeople start by giving away 'free samples': to nudge the customer into feeling socially obliged to reciprocate by buying something.

reference-dependence lazy, or self-comforting, assumption of evaluating outcomes against a casually available reference point: 'Based on the last year-end figures, we're currently in good shape.'

reframing looking at a situation in a different way; rationalizing or describing it differently and so seeking to change its 'meaning', especially for anyone who's discomforted about it.

regret ('buyer's remorse') unwelcome emotional response in a person who has bought something, then finds the purchase has not satisfied them as they had expected it to.

regulatees any sector or group within it bound in common by a set of regulations.

regulatory assumptions things that the people who design regulations like to think are true, but which often aren't. Such as, that 'tone from the top' induces behaviour-change throughout a workforce (it doesn't).

regulatory capital see *capital adequacy*

regulatory capture where regulatees in a sector have sufficient power (political/economic) to dictate what they want regulators to do. These powerful interests typically co-opt their regulator's agents, strike 'control bargains', then disparage the regulator.

regulatory design how governments and regulatory agencies set about *framing* their instruments of control, identifying which forms of behaviour and other factors they deem most important to acknowledge, accept or reject, and seek to influence.

reputation risk (in supervisory jargon, 'idiosyncratic risk capital') potential loss of capital value, business good name and/or market access as the result of the firm's own neglect of *social licence*.

response effects/Goodhart's Law when filling in a questionnaire: second-guessing 'the expected answer'. Worst-case outcome (Goodhart) is where a regulated group 'games the indicators' so vigorously that the test itself is rendered useless.

responsible person a manager formally designated by the regulator as responsible for running a business function and/or its compliance with the rules.

'rigged' see *manipulation*

risk appetite at its simplest, the amount and type of risk that an organization is willing to take in order to meet its strategic objectives. Soon gets a lot more complex when boards start to evaluate it in terms of numbers and acceptable cut-off points.

risk cognition how people perceive risk and consider engaging with it; including how they form subjective impressions rather than making rational evaluations.

risk culture how an organization engages with risk-taking, including its attitude to risk and reward (risk appetite); employees' conduct with customers and between internal businesses; and its transparency in acknowledging and remediating any problems of risk control and customer care.

risk governance institutions, processes and mechanisms, often at senior management level, that make and implement decisions on acceptable risk-taking.

risk metrics any numerical measure of the characteristics of a risk; commonly, *econometric* analysis.

risk perception see *perception of risk*

risk-aware working encouraging everyone to use their intuition as a tool for everyday risk management; rewarding staff for reporting near-miss incidents and low-level customer dissatisfaction; promoting internal discussion about risk, rather than boxing risk into a technical 'silo'.

rogue trader a single criminally misbehaving person who uses a firm's marketing access and systems for money-making private dealings or high-value, risky 'unauthorized' trades putting the whole organization at risk.

rolling bad apples employees with poor conduct records who nevertheless manage to move from firm to firm unimpeded.

rules-of-thumb/heuristics simplifying decisions, often unconsciously, by replacing a difficult question with an easy one. ('Both these cars have lots of useful features. So, do I fancy owning the blue one more, or the red one?')

sanctions regulatory 'punishments' against wrongdoers, such as fines or suspension of trading licences.

satisficing doing the bare minimum of activity, just enough to qualify (as compliant, or whatever).

scalar see *binary*

Section 166 see *Skilled Person Review*

self-regulating see *GSVR*

self-reporting sending in to the regulator your own reports on how well you're complying with the rules; or events of breaking them.

Senior Managers [and Certification] Regime (SMR/SMCR/SM&CR/SIMR) UK financial regulators' initiative (2016–) to hold financial firms' senior managers personally accountable for defined business functions, and having to regularly attest their fitness and competence to do so. Similar regimes globally: see Chapter 2.

signal value of one initial incident, implying that it means we should expect more, similar and more severe incidents to follow.

situational awareness being intuitively familiar with the range of likely threats in a given setting (business or public). Much improved by having a high level of intuitive skill in *dynamic sensing*.

skilled and competent regulator's expected characteristics of providers' managers in general, and senior managers in particular.

Skilled Person Review (Section 166 notice) UK regulator's formal demand for an organization to open its records and senior personnel to close scrutiny by an outside appointed 'skilled person' inspector, on suspicion that an offence may have been committed.

social contract understanding between employees and their employer, or voters and their elected government, that their interests will be looked after by those in authority. Only implicit. Broken where trust is lost between the two sides.

social cues hints, or informal suggestions as a result of how other people are behaving, that something needs to change.

social licence/'licence to operate' the extent to which stakeholders refrain from criticizing an organization, so allowing the organization to exist and flourish. Social licence is not about stakeholders *supporting* the organization, just not criticizing it.

social proof/'informational social influence' noting and copying what other people do; such as because we want to avoid having to make a decision for ourselves, or as a quick way to confirm that our own behaviour is acceptable.

social purpose (of finance)/socially useful the function of a firm, beyond self-enrichment, to create *public goods*.

socially defined other people's opinion influencing yours; whether people think that something's acceptable. See also *social proof, social licence*.

sociopath see *empathy-deficient*

spotlight effect (bias) the way we tend to believe that we're noticed by others more than we really are.

stakeholders anyone with an interest in, and affected by, how an organization is getting on: owners, customers, staff, suppliers, regulators, local communities, governments, and so on.

steady-state assumption most regulation is designed to function optimally when the regulatee group is behaving itself. Of course, the time that most of us want regulation to work best is when the regulatees are *mis*behaving, but that's not how the assumption operates.

stereotyping judging a person according to your own (or others' commonly held) belief about 'what a person like that, is like'; such as 'that person's a librarian, so they must be an introvert'. See *cognitive diversity, performance attribution bias*

sticky bias/inertia 'playing it safe', sticking with what you know. Passing up good opportunities; buying only on a clear recommendation.

symbolic enforcement the regulatory enforcer making a big show of punishing one organization, as a way of signalling to others to be more careful.

tells/tell signs involuntary signals that we may give off, when under stress, that reveal the presence of an underlying anxiety, uncertainty as to a decision, or attempt to abuse a situation. A word borrowed from the world of professional poker-playing, where an uncontrolled 'tell' may lose a player the match.

three lines of defence a regulatory model for preventing harm. The first line is a firm's operational management, the second the firm's risk and compliance specialists, and the third its internal audit and board risk governance.

transparency allowing people, including colleagues and regulators, to see clearly into your operations and control systems; not hiding or obfuscating your systems and activities.

treating customers fairly ('TCF') historic UK regulatory initiative urging providers to keep their customers' best interests in mind at all times.

tribes/tribal network culture of staff, being loyal to informal close groups of associates (such as one's sales team, or 'mates' at work) rather than to the employer brand.

unintended consequence when your policy or control intervention actually starts people doing something you didn't want them to do, and possibly that the control was trying to prevent them from doing in the first place. Worst case, the intervention makes the original problem worse.

untouchables typically, middle and senior managers within a financial firm who believe that their high earnings for the firm exempt them from criticism or the need to comply with regulations.

vested interest having a strong personal or corporate motive to keep doing something because you benefit directly from it; as when 'dirty industries' resist new environmental controls.

volatility a measure of how much (and how rapidly) a trading price has varied over time.

voluntary code of practice see *GSVR*

vox populi risk business impacts resulting from fast-changing and increasingly volatile public opinion, notably public changes of mood that may rapidly redefine what is now 'acceptable and expected' behaviour. See also *behavioural lens, legitimacy, social licence*.

watchdogs informal name for regulators and other institutions guarding the public interest, such as ombudsman services, consumer advocacy groups, and even public prosecutors.

'What Actually Happens' examining why people behaved as they did, looking for explanations not from economic models but by directly observing and by asking any *normal people* who were involved for their perceptions. Also: the study of how groups of regulated people *actually* responded to a new control rather than what its originators *hoped* would happen. (See *formal vs. informal*)

whistleblowing (aka person of conscience report) where a current or former employee raises concerns about wrongdoing in their workplace. Regarded by many legislators as a vital safeguard to the public interest; whistleblowers' rights (including anonymity) are widely protected by laws governing 'public interest disclosures'.

Notes

1   Phrases used by Prof Mike Power (LSE) in Hutter, B and Power, M (2009) *Organizational Encounters with Risk*, Cambridge University Press

2   Professor Herbert Simon (1982) *Models of Bounded Rationality*, MIT Press, Cambridge, MA. See also definitions in Miles R et al, *Encyclopedia of Behavioral Science Concepts in LSE Behavioral Economics Guide* (annual), www.behavioraleconomics.com/resources/ (archived at https://perma.cc/ E8B7-UT3X)

3   Sunstein, C and Thaler, R (2009) *Nudge*, Yale University Press

4   See Sykes and Matza (in Recommended Reading list)

5   Camerer, C (2003) 'The behavioral challenge to economics: understanding normal people', Conference Series; [Proceedings], Federal Reserve Bank of Boston, vol. 48 (Jun), http://www.bostonfed.org/economic/conf/conf48/papers/ camerer.pdf (archived at https://perma.cc/3MFW-UHFC)

6   Baron-Cohen, S (2012) *Zero Degrees of Empathy*, Penguin

7   Kaplan, S (2008) Framing contests: strategy making under uncertainty, *Organization Science*, 19 (5) pp 729–752

8   Kahneman, D and Tversky, A (1979) Prospect Theory: An analysis of decision under risk, *Econometrica*, 47 (2) pp 263–91

9   Camerer, C (2003). 'The behavioral challenge to economics: understanding normal people', Conference Series; [Proceedings], Federal Reserve Bank of Boston, vol. 48 (Jun), http://www.bostonfed.org/economic/conf/conf48/papers/ camerer.pdf (archived at https://perma.cc/3MFW-UHFC)

RECOMMENDED READING
With authors' comments

Here's our personal selection of favourite reads that have influenced us, as pooled by all the authors of this book.

It introduces some of the best further reading if you're new to the subject. For the more experienced, there's also material to help develop your understanding of culture in firms, behavioural research and regulatory design. (If you're already a culture assessment pro and have zipped through this book, there are several hundred specialist citations at our chapter-ends throughout, to help you explore the field at a higher level.)

All of the titles in the following list have proved themselves to us, as offering accessible and enduring insights. That's why we add a couple of lines next to each one, to say what makes it worth a read. These are our own opinions, by the way, not an objective critique. Most of these titles are readable for general interest; a few get two stars as both good science *and* a really good read.

KEY, SUBJECT FOCUS [ ]

** – highly recommended

BE – behavioural economics

C – culture; how individuals relate to institutions

DR – design of regulations, policies and controls

F – financial crises and their aftermath

OB – organizational behaviour

P – psychology (social and cognitive) of risk, biases and risk perception

RM – risk modelling (theory and social history)

Adams, John (1995): *Risk* (UCL Press)

- [BE, C, P]: Why so many rules don't work. Read this if you're a designer of any kind of control. Great primer on risk culture – cool, irreverent, way ahead of its time.

Ariely, Dan:
(2009) *Predictably Irrational* (Harper Collins)

- [BE]: In daily life we blithely assume our choices are rational. They're often not. But our 'irrational' choices are not random: they're systematic and predictable. Discover why and how.

(2012) *The Honest Truth about Dishonesty* (Harper Collins)

- [BE]: We lie to everyone, especially ourselves, says Ariely. Good easy-read introduction to the Fudge Factor and other behavioural factors that lead us astray.

Barrett, Richard (2017): *The Values-Driven Organization: Cultural health and employee well-being as a pathway to sustainable performance*, 2nd ed (Routledge)

- [OB, P] Influential methodology for assessing culture (Barrett Model); building on Maslow's Hierarchy of Needs to create a holistic way of understanding and measuring culture, and many other things besides.

Bernstein, Peter L. (1996): *Against the Gods: The remarkable story of risk* (John Wiley & Sons, New York)

- [RM]: A robust social history of attempts to manage risk.

Blacker, Keith and McConnell, Patrick (2015): *People Risk Management* (Kogan Page)

- [OB, P, RM]: How humans subvert well-intended controls; how we can improve risk culture and decision-making to deal with that.

Camerer, Colin (2003): *The behavioral challenge to economics: understanding normal people* (Conference Series; [Proceedings], Federal Reserve Bank of Boston, vol. 48 (Jun))

- [BE]: Leading behavioural scientist calls classical economists' bluff for failing to see basic truths of human behaviour, and demolishes a stack of their assumptions as unfit for purpose.

Cialdini, Robert (2014): *Influence: Science and practice,* 5th ed (Pearson)

- [P]: Benign biases play to our underlying human needs – for reciprocity, reassurance, common good, and other factors. We can't 'de-bias', but we can learn to see and deal with them better.

Cox, Louis Anthony (Tony) (2008): *What's wrong with risk matrices? (Risk Analysis* **28** (2), pp 497–512)

- [DR, F, RM]: Why econometricians (including in HM Government) missed warnings signs of an approaching financial crisis.

De Becker, Gavin (2000): *The Gift of Fear* (Bloomsbury)

- [P]: How our intuition 'survival signals' give us robust early warnings of misbehaviour, in many forms – if only we'd learn how to recognize them.

de Botton, Alain (2000): *The Consolations of Philosophy* (Vintage International)

- [C]: Millennia of thought, in precis: how to reassess the world around us. Trenchant tools for thinking about and working through cultural questions and challenges.

De Nederlandsche Bank (DNB), ed. Mirea Raaijmakers, (2015): *Supervision of Behaviour and Culture:* at https://www.dnb.nl/media/1gmkp1vk/supervision-of-behaviour-and-culture_tcm46-380398-1.pdf

- [**, C, DR]: Masterwork on assessing financial firm culture from a capital supervisor's viewpoint.

Dekker, Sidney (2012): *Just Culture: Restoring trust and accountability* (Ashgate, UK)

- [DR]: Provoking thought in the financial sector: the relationship between consequences and transparency.

Diamond, Jared (2005): *Collapse: How societies choose to fail or succeed* (Penguin)

- [C, P, RM]: For 'societies' read 'cultures'. How they help or (through short-termism) harm various people and environments – repeatedly. Why a burn-and-pillage business model isn't sustainable; financial firms, note.

Dobelli, Rolf (2014): *The Art of Thinking Clearly: Better thinking, better decisions* (Sceptre)

- [**, P]: Million-selling, cheerful, short primer on bias effects. Hundreds of real-life examples, from laugh-out-loud to terrifying.

Duhigg, Charles (2013): *The Power of Habit: Why we do what we do and how to change* (Random House)

- [P]: With impressive brain-function research, explores the many ways habits shape our lives; and how to break destructive patterns of behaviour.

Dunbar, Robin (2016): *Human Evolution: Our brains and behaviour* (Oxford University Press)

- [C, OB, P]: Engaging tale of how we evolved as social animals. Find out how 'Dunbar's Number' predicts success or failure of any initiative.

Edmondson, Amy (2018): *The Fearless Organization: Creating psychological safety in the workplace* (Wiley/Harvard Business School)

- [C, OB, P]: We've personally seen this book on the desks of every one of the world's major conduct regulators during 2020. Enough said.

FICC Markets Standards Board (2018): *Behavioural cluster analysis: misconduct patterns in financial markets* (FICC), at https://fmsb.com/wp-content/uploads/2018/07/BCA_v32_1.pdf

- [F, OB, P]: Fascinating, disturbing, recurring story: 200+ years of financial wrongdoing, as multipally repeating patterns. The human animal is ingenious, adaptable… also often greedily dishonest, and gullible.

Financial Conduct Authority (UK-FCA) (Annual, 2013 onwards): *Risk Outlook* (www.fca.org)

- [BE, DR]: British conduct regulator's annual digests of research material they expect to inform their future activity. A free steer!

Gray, J L and Starke, F A (1998): *Organizational Behavior: Concepts and applications* (MacMillan, London)

- [OB]: Formal vs. informal: What accounts for the difference between the published version of the management structure and 'what actually happens'?

Helms-Mills, J (2003): *Making Sense of Organizational Change* (Routledge)

- [OB, C]: How to do sensemaking at strategic level; what happened when a big company tried a big change.

Hodges, Christopher and Steinholtz, Ruth (2017): *Ethical Business Practice and Regulation* (Bloomsbury, London)

- [**, DR]: Fascinating, readable, deep scholarship. A must-read if you care about improving regulatory design. How might we make better dialogues between regulators and regulatees, to improve outcomes for everyone? Deeply informed sector-wide case studies (including finance, aviation, food, healthcare) comparing different risk cultures and how varied approaches to regulatory dialogue helped or harmed 'public goods'. The financial sector emerges poorly.

Hofstede, Gert Jan (2010): *Cultures and Organizations* (McGraw-Hill)

- [OB, C]: Why organizations' attempts at cooperation fail, even when everyone present wants them to succeed. Cultural evolution, plus epic data analysis from World Values Survey.

Janis, Irving L (1972/1982): *Groupthink: Psychological studies of policy decisions and fiascoes* (Houghton Mifflin, New York)

- [OB, P]: A milestone. What drives elite groups' self-delusion that 'they know best what's good for the rest of us'; its catastrophic results.

Kahan, Dan M (2012): *Cultural cognition* in *Handbook of Risk Theory* (Yale/Springer): https://doi.org/10.1007/978-94-007-1433-5_28

- [C, P]: How communal-interest beliefs overtake facts as a basis for decision-making. Essential research. Next-level insight into 'groupthink' (aka 'motivated reasoning') and its massive costs to society.

Kahneman, Daniel H (2011): *Thinking, Fast and Slow* (Allen Lane)

- [**, BE, P]: Nobel laureate grandfather of modern behavioural science shows why we 'overestimate how much we understand', and how to overcome our cognitive flaws.

Kiel, Fred (2015): *Return on Character* (Harvard)

- Assessing, with big data, how leadership character drives organizational success or failure. Another big influence on how conduct regulators are designing culture assessments.

King, Anthony and Crewe, Ivor (2014): *The blunders of our governments* (Oneworld)

- [DR]: Disruptive effects of bias in policymaking. Vivid analysis of major policy misfires and their catastrophic cost to citizen-taxpayers.

Lewis, Michael (2011): *Boomerang: The disaster tour* (Allen Lane) (2012): *The Big Short* (Penguin)

- [**, F]: Wise, razor-sharp and darkly hilarious front-row dispatches from the 2008 financial crisis. Not coincidentally, Lewis has since become a big fan of Daniel Kahneman (see Kahneman, above).

McCormick, Roger; Stears, Christopher and Duarte, Tania (2016): *The Conduct Costs Project* (LSE-Cambridge University-CCP Research) (conductcosts.ccpresearchfoundation.com)

- [DR, F]: Unflinching study of catastrophic (largely self-inflicted) cost impact of conduct enforcements on banks.

McKay, Charles (1841, republished 1996): *Extraordinary popular delusions and the madness of crowds* (Harvard University/John Wiley & Sons, New York)

- [F, P]: Bravura social-history tour of 'crowd effects': investment bubbles, alchemy, and much more. 180 years ahead of its time. Finely observed, immense fun. (But not 'science', to be clear.)

McRaney, David (2012): *You Are Not So Smart* (Oneworld)

- [P]: Breezy tour of errors in human understanding; how to recognize and overcome your own bias-based delusions. Cognitive psychology, minus the boring bits; a great easy intro.

Merton, Robert K (1936): *The unanticipated consequences of purposive social action* (*American Sociological Review*, **1** (6) pp 894–904)

- [DR]: Why controls and policies fail. A political science landmark.

Miles, Roger (2017): *Conduct Risk Management: Using a behavioural approach to protect your board and financial services business* (Kogan Page)

- [all]: Companion volume to what you're reading now. Plain-speaking, popular guide to why conduct regulators do what they do, and where they're heading next. 'Behavioural lens' and other tools for predicting and averting misconduct.

Milgram, Stanley (1974): *Obedience to Authority* (Harper & Row)

- [P]: Controversial (and not now replicable) experiments showed how ordinary citizens will, for example, willingly electrocute others in the name of 'Compliance'.

Ordonez, L D et al (2009): *Goals Gone Wild* (Academy of Management Perspectives)

- [DR, OB]: Our go-to piece on the unintended side effects of traditional quantitative targets.

Perrow, Charles (1984, revised 1999): *Normal Accidents: Living with high-risk technologies* (Princeton UP)

- [DR]: Why no control is ever '100% safe'. Read, accept, discover what to do about it.

Phillips, Tom (2019): *Humans: A brief history…* (Wildfire)

- [OB, P]: Jolly, easy-read social history of biases and the unforeseen disasters that follow from them.

Pink, Daniel (2018): *Drive: The surprising truth about what motivates us* (Canongate)

- [OB, P]: Psychology of motivation, rebooted. Great starting point if you need to scope 'purposeful culture' in the firm.

Plato (399BCE / 2010): *The Last Days of Socrates* (Penguin Classics) Harold Tarrant (Introducer) Christopher Rowe (Translator)

- [C, P]: The ultimate in uncomfortable 'better questions' and equally tough answers. Psychological safety and safe speak-up – in ancient Athens.

Ravasi, D and Schultz, M (2006): *Responding to organizational identity threats: Exploring the role of organizational culture* (*Academy of Management Journal*, **49** (3), pp 433–58)

- [C, OB, P]: A favourite read of Ruth Steinholtz's; that's good enough for us.

Reinhart, Carmen M and Rogoff, Kenneth (2011): *This Time Is Different: Eight centuries of financial folly* (Princeton UP)

- [F, P]: In searing statistical detail: exactly how financial misconduct and over-optimism keep inevitably recurring. The lesson of history? We don't learn from history.

Robertson, Fiona (2020): *Rules of Belonging: Change your organisational culture* (Major Street)

- [OB]: Grounded firmly in practice, 'what actually happens' in organizations: how to change culture for the better.

Robson, David (2020): *The Intelligence Trap* (Hodder)

- [P]: Why smart people do dumb things: it's not just a little, but a lot of knowledge, that can be a dangerous thing. Anyone can have a cognitive failure, experts included – with grave consequences.

Samson, Alain (Ed.), with Miles, Roger (Co-Ed.) (Annual, from 2014 onwards): *The Behavioral Economics Guide* (LSE, at behavioraleconomics.com)

- [**, BE]: Annual digest of the latest thinking in behavioural economics, including glossary of key terms and concepts – like the one you're reading now – but we make the LSE one much bigger, 'cos it's more scientifically rigorous.

Schein, Edgar (2004, revised 2016): *Organizational Culture and Leadership* 5th ed (Wiley/Jossey Bass)

- [**OB, P]: Essential, timeless insights from 'the grandfather of organizational culture'. The most often cited work on culture, including now ubiquitous 'iceberg' and 'culture paradigm' templates (e.g. see De Nederlandsche Bank, above, globally admired supervision framework). Densely informative but worth at least a skim!

Schneier, Bruce (2012): *Liars and Outliers: Enabling the trust that society needs to thrive* (Wiley)

- [C, P]: How trust works, in modern hyperconnected society. Science probes the evolutionary roots of the group-based trust that defines humans' socialised risk-taking.

Sheedy, E and Griffin, B (2015): *Risk Governance, Cultures, Structures and Behaviour* (McQuarie University)

- [RD]: Landmark challenge to the 'new financial regulation', showing which behavioural factors actually matter most. Explodes regulators' lazy former assumptions (such as that 'tone at the top' changes sales-floor behaviour).

Slovic, Paul (with Finucane, Peters, MacGregor) (2004): *Risk as analysis and risk as feelings: Some thoughts about affect, reason, risk, and rationality* (*Risk Analysis*, **24** (2))

- [P, RM]: Watershed moment in the science of risk analysis. From this point on, we include 'affective' (emotion, mood, intuitive) factors in decision-making and we downgrade 'rational actor' explanations.

Smith, Robert Elliott (2019) *Rage Inside the Machine* (Bloomsbury Business)

- [DR, P, RM]: Steps to stop ourselves getting overwhelmed by 'baked-in biases' – AI controls that reflect their makers' prejudices, and internet echo-chamber bigotry. Tech star Rob Smith interrogates human 'pattern assumptions' and the assumption of 'value instead of values'.

Starling Trust (Stephen J Scott, ed.) (annual): *The Starling Compendium: Culture & Conduct Risk in the Banking Sector*, at https://starlingtrust.com/the-starling-compendium/

- [BE, C, DR]: The latest thinking from the heads of central banks, regulators, and financial firms, about what matters most in managing conduct and culture. Reliably readable and super-informed. How to stay ahead of the curve.

Steinholtz R with Nando, D (2014): *Performance Management for an Ethical Culture* (Institute of Business Ethics)

- [DR, OB]: If you're looking for ideas on performance management that support and don't undermine an ethical culture.

Sunstein, Cass, and Thaler, Richard (2009): *Nudge: Improving decisions about health, wealth and happiness* (Penguin)

- [**, BE, P]: Policymakers can manipulate citizens' behaviour towards doing 'the right thing' policywise – often at almost zero cost – by tweaking how choices are presented. Is this good, or alarming? You decide.

Sutherland, Rory (2019): *Alchemy: The surprising power of ideas that don't make sense* (WH Allen)

- [BE, OB, P]: Corporate communications genius and world-class raconteur's profoundly wise, very funny and always practical insights: how irrational thinking solves problems better than vested-interest expertise.

Syed, Matthew (2016): *Black Box Thinking* and (2020): *Rebel Ideas: The power of diverse thinking*

- [**, C, DR, P]: Hugely readable, case-based manifestos for culture change, contrasting major institutional failures and successes. How to achieve better progress: embrace and learn from failure. To better solve problems: reject preconceived notions of solutions, by inviting fresh (and different) brains to the table.

Sykes, G and Matza, D (1957): *Techniques of Neutralization: A theory of delinquency* (American Sociological Review)

- [**, P]: Another landmark; an energetic 64-year-old study. How abusive individuals try to 'reason away' their bad behaviour and its harms to other people. Has there ever been a more vital time to understand this?

Tenner, Edward (1997): *Why Things Bite Back: Technology and the revenge of unintended consequences* (Random House, New York)

- [RM]: Be careful what technologies you wish for: every innovation brings a sting in the tail.

Thaler, Richard H (2015): *Misbehaving: The making of behavioural economics* (Allen Lane)

- [BE, OB, P]: Why 'BE' came to matter. A leading exponent introduces key others – notably Kahneman, who called him 'lazy' as a compliment (why? – read this, find out).

Toft, Brian (1996): *Limits to the mathematical modelling of disasters* (in *Accident and Design: Contemporary debates in risk management*, Hood and Jones, Eds) (UCL/Routledge, London)

- [RM]: Statistics can lull you into believing your system's resilient. Don't let them; read this. Then look beyond OpRisk models and start to observe people's behaviour directly.

Tufte, Edward R (2006): *The Cognitive Style of Powerpoint* (Graphics Press)

- [DR, OB]: Fierce critique of the 'slideshow mentality' and its informational bias effects. Should we abandon slideshows altogether? Better, bias-free media are available.

Vaughan, Diane (1999): *The dark side of organizations: Mistake, misconduct and disaster* (*Annual Review of Sociology*, 25, pp 271–305)

- [DR, OB]: How misconduct 'trickles down' through management hierarchies into the workforce, undermining value and resilience, with (literally) fatal results.

Viscusi, W Kip (1992): *Fatal Tradeoffs: Public and private responsibilities for risk* (Oxford University Press)

- [OB, RM]: Why staff tend to make up their own minds about whether to follow instructions.

Weick, Karl E (1995): *Sensemaking in Organizations* (Sage, London)

- [DR, OB, P]: How control officers react to off-the-scale risk events. Crisis strikes: we receive cognitive signals that clash with what the rulebook says. What to do? Weick highlights the business value of noting front-line managers' intuition. See also Weick and colleagues' (2005) paper: *Organizing and the process of sensemaking* (*Organization Science*, 16 (4), pp 409–21).

Zimbardo, Philip (2007): *Investigating social dynamics* (chapter in *The Lucifer Effect*) (Random House, London)

- [OB, P]: How a small group of 'rule-gamers' can rapidly contaminate larger, well-behaved groups.

INDEX